The Social Net

SECOND EDITION

The Social Net
Understanding our online behavior

SECOND EDITION

Edited by

Yair Amichai-Hamburger

Director, The Research Center for Internet Psychology (CIP)
Sammy Ofer School of Communications
Interdisciplinary Center (IDC) Herzliya, Israel

OXFORD
UNIVERSITY PRESS

OXFORD

UNIVERSITY PRESS

Great Clarendon Street, Oxford, OX2 6DP,
United Kingdom

Oxford University Press is a department of the University of Oxford.
It furthers the University's objective of excellence in research, scholarship,
and education by publishing worldwide. Oxford is a registered trade mark of
Oxford University Press in the UK and in certain other countries

First Edition published in 2005
Second Edition published in 2013

Impression: 1

British Library Cataloguing in Publication Data

Data available

Library of Congress Cataloging in Publication Data

Data available

ISBN 978–0–19–963954–0

Printed and bound by
Ashford Colour Press Ltd, Gosport, Hampshire

Oxford University Press makes no representation, express or implied, that the
drug dosages in this book are correct. Readers must therefore always check
the product information and clinical procedures with the most up-to-date
published product information and data sheets provided by the manufacturers
and the most recent codes of conduct and safety regulations. The authors and
the publishers do not accept responsibility or legal liability for any errors in the
text or for the misuse or misapplication of material in this work. Except where
otherwise stated, drug dosages and recommendations are for the non-pregnant
adult who is not breast-feeding

Links to third party websites are provided by Oxford in good faith and
for information only. Oxford disclaims any responsibility for the materials
contained in any third party website referenced in this work.

My beloved father, David Hamburger,
died shortly before this book was published.
My father fled Nazi Germany at the age of seventeen
and was never able to complete his schooling.
He always encouraged me to pursue my own path,
and was delighted by my academic success.
I dedicate this book to him.

May his memory be blessed.

Dedicated to Debbie—My love, my partner, my friend.
And to our children, Michael & Shauna, Talia, Keren, and Yaron.

Preface

The Social Net was the title of my 2005 book. It was a pioneering project to bring together contributions from leading scholars on the major topics pertaining to the social aspects of the online world. The book has been a great success and has helped many, including students, academics, and lay people to attain a broad comprehensive knowledge of online social psychology. One of the leading aims of the book was to demonstrate the significant role the Internet plays in so many aspects of our social lives. Judging from the feedback we received, it appears that the book successfully fulfilled this purpose, and some people even suggested that ahead of its time, this volume predicted the colossal impact of the social networks.

Now eight years on, with around two billion people online, and countless websites covering all aspects of our existence, it is time to update our knowledge. During these years a great many articles have been published in this field, and it is important to bring this knowledge together into a more coherent whole. We have extended the book significantly and once again we have put together an A-team of leading scholars, and produced an exciting new edition of *The Social Net* which promises to be on the cutting-edge of this dynamic field of study.

The Internet is a mass medium, but also a technology that can adapt to suit the characteristics of its users. This is significant since the individual personality of a surfer is one of the leading influences governing his or her online preferences and behavior. In the first chapter Yair Amichai-Hamburger and Zack Hayat focus on the potential of the Internet as a tool to empower a range of different surfers with a variety of personality types. Their chapter opens by studying the components of the Internet, which together create a unique psychological environment. It moves on to explore the effect of the Internet on people with social inhibitions, whose personality profile makes it difficult for them to feel comfortable in social offline situations/interactions. The chapter shows how the Internet enables these people to recreate themselves and as a result become socially competent and develop an active social life online. It goes on to consider the growing evidence that increasing numbers of people appear to feel more comfortable revealing intimate layers of themselves online, rather than offline. The same psychological components that encourage such openness may lead surfers to become addicted to the Internet, and this phenomenon is explored in the section that follows. The chapter concludes with a discussion of when and how it may be possible for surfers who have become socially empowered online to transfer these skills to their offline interactions. Throughout the chapter suggestions are made for future research.

The second chapter focuses on social cognition. Yoram M. Kalman, Daphne R. Raban, and Sheizaf Rafaeli suggest that social interaction is changing, as increasingly greater portions of human creativity, conversations, and social ties are digitized and mediated by computers. The chapter examines this "netification" process, and discusses its consequences for the online presentation of the self and of the other, and also for groups online. The authors discuss the effects of the laws that govern information, on cognition and on social behavior, and review some of the major societal and personal consequences of "netification" on work and leisure, on the private and public, and on space and time. The chapter makes recommendations for multifaceted research as well as social cognition considerations in systems design.

In Chapter 3, Kathryn Y. Segovia and Jeremy N. Bailenson examine the topic of identity manipulation. They argue that the accepted norm that individuals should portray themselves to others truthfully is frequently violated in computer-mediated interactions. Even in the early days of the Internet, scholars documented crimes in cyberspace where individuals had adopted the identities of others to commit virtual crimes; and today, crime reports warn of the ease of identity disguise and the associated dangers. Do we respond differently to individuals with manipulated identities than we do to individuals who truthfully present their identities? This chapter examines that question by reviewing and synthesizing previous empirical and theoretical work on identity manipulation.

Chapter 4 focuses on online romantic relationships. In this chapter Monica Whitty considers the leading theories pertaining to traditional relationships and discusses how these may explain the initiation, development, and maintenance of relationships formed on the Internet. Whitty suggests that these traditional theories are insufficient when it comes to explaining this phenomenon, and that new hypotheses are required. These would explain, for example, why people self-disclose more in some online conditions than in others and how "hyperpersonal" relationships form online. The chapter points out that the Internet is not a homogenous space and that it is necessary to consider the different features and norms that govern the different spaces there. The chapter concludes with the claim that in the future we may no longer be taking the online/offline binary approach to relationships, but rather that the dividing line between the Internet and the physical world may actually appear seamless.

The next chapter by Brandon Van Der Heide and Erin M. Schumaker explores a variety of facets of computer-mediated persuasion and the gaining of compliance. The chapter opens with a discussion of two important theoretical frameworks that have influenced the contemporary study of persuasion and compliance gaining online: The heuristic–systematic model and Social Information Processing theory. A new sociotechnical influence model is proposed, and is used to frame the current research in the study of online persuasion and compliance gaining. Finally, several implications and new directions suggested by this model are explored including the development of interpersonal credibility impressions online, the strength of online cues, and the ways that communication in online spaces may have self-influential effects on attitudes.

Chapter 6 finds Kevin Askew and Michael D. Coovert exploring online decision-making. They suggest that as the Internet continues to enlarge its influence in people's lives, an increasing number of decisions will be taken online. With this in mind it is important to understand the components that go into online decision-making. The authors examine and summarize selective research on decision-making from the perspective of the social net. To do so, they have divided their chapter into three major sections. The first lays the foundation by discussing classical perspectives on decision-making. This allows for a more informed discussion in the second section, which focuses on decision-making through an electronic medium. In this section, they review seminal studies comparing face-to-face and computer-mediated groups on decision-making tasks, present the latest research on how people make judgments of others based on profile information, and connect decision-making on the social net to the classical research on decision-making. The third section reviews research on virtual teams—an organizational unit that is of immense importance in the digital workplace. The chapter concludes by setting out recommendations for future research.

In Chapter 7, Neil Malamuth, Daniel Linz, and René Weber consider the topic of the Internet and aggression. In this chapter, they describe research on the intersection of two domains, the Internet, its structure and function, and the social psychology of aggression. While the Internet is an environment of instant connections and opportunity, it is also an instrument of great social and personal penetration. The authors go on to define aggression, particularly as it relates to studying the Internet. Next, they focus on the social psychological processes related to aggression. There are several characteristics of the Internet world that accentuate risk of aggressive behavior.

Social Learning Theory is especially useful in understanding the elements of this environment. The authors organize their discussion of the Internet as a teaching tool organized within a framework of motivational, disinhibitory, and opportunity aspects. They go on to show that the Internet is a human communication environment with certain unique characteristics that can activate and shape various psychological mechanisms, many of these increasing the potential for aggression.

The following chapter by, Lee Sproull, Caryn A. Conley, and Jae Yun Moon, examines online prosocial behavior. This is defined as voluntary intentional actions, taking place on the Internet, to benefit others with no expectation of personal reward. Their focus is on understanding prosocial behavior in public online contexts including support group discussion forums, service projects, open collaborative work projects, and citizen science projects. The chapter discusses three main classes of variables that affect prosocial behaviors: Attributes of the online context, individual attributes and motivations, and interaction processes. The chapter describes studies of prosocial behavior in a variety of contexts that draw on diverse theories such as motivation and personality theories, Social Learning Theory, and Social Identity Theory to provide a general overview of how, why, and to what degree people engage in online prosocial behavior. Evidence of the value both to the direct providers of prosocial contributions and their beneficiaries as well as to society at large is presented. The chapter concludes with an overview of opportunities for furthering research on online prosocial behavior by extending the inquiry to include more varied contribution contexts, new technological contexts for helping, and a greater diversity in research methods.

In Chapter 9, Joseph B. Walther suggests that the potential advantages of virtual group collaborations among geographically distributed partners, using communication technology, depend on their ability to incorporate and exploit the challenges that technology offers, in order to achieve satisfactory social and instrumental outcomes. This chapter reviews several processes that have traditionally affected groups' functioning, and examines how computer-mediated communication exacerbates or alleviates the issues that groups confront. These issues include impression formation and group development, task-oriented and socioemotional communication, and trust. It also includes a discussion of the challenges groups face when seeking to incorporate the unique information that different members contribute to decision-making and problem-solving discussions. These issues are examined in traditional group settings as well as in online groups, and their implications for "flashmobs" are considered.

Crystal L. Hoyt, in Chapter 10, provides an overview of leadership within virtual contexts, with a particular focus on relevant theories and empirical research. The chapter opens with a discussion of some of the leading changes, challenges, and opportunities for leaders brought about by the proliferation of advanced information technologies. Next, classic theoretical approaches to understanding leadership in traditional face-to-face contexts are reviewed; these include the great person approach, the behavioral approach, situational contingency perspectives, relational perspectives, and transformational leadership. This is followed by a review of various theories, including those focused on advanced technologies and communication, relevant to leadership within virtual contexts. These theories include adaptive structuration theory, Zaccaro's model of leadership and virtual team processes, the social identity model of deindividuation effects, and media richness theory. Next, the extant empirical research examining leadership in virtual contexts is assessed. First, research examining the impact of leadership on group interactions and effectiveness in virtual contexts is reviewed by presenting research undertaken in the field followed by experimental investigations. Next, the ample research investigating transformational leadership in virtual contexts as well as across contexts is discussed. The review of this research ends with an overview of other approaches to leadership within virtual contexts by focusing on participative leadership, leader–member exchange theory, and emergent leadership. Finally, the chapter ends with a brief discussion of other promising theoretical approaches for future research with a focus on relational and perception-based approaches.

In Chapter 11, Kimberly Barsamian Kahn, Katherine Spencer, and Jack Glaser delve into the phenomena of prejudice and discrimination on the Internet, including an examination of the ways in which online prejudice affects offline behavior. It is hypothesized that the Internet has the potential to increase prejudice, while decreasing discrimination. The chapter begins by discussing group differences regarding who is on the Internet and what they are doing on it. The authors reveal that the "digital divide" appears to have shifted away from simple access and toward utilization. The chapter goes on to consider how the unique characteristics of the Internet, including anonymity, perceived privacy, legitimacy, and permanency, affect prejudice and discrimination. It then examines newer trends of communication on the Internet, focusing on social networking and Internet-based dating sites, and the implications of these forums for prejudice and discrimination. Finally, it concludes by detailing how scholars have utilized and can continue to harness the unique properties of the Internet to study prejudice and discrimination in innovative ways.

In Chapter 12 Béatrice S. Hasler and Yair Amichai-Hamburger examine the literature on intergroup contact as a means of reducing bias among rival groups in conflict. Their basis is the Contact Hypothesis, the leading theory in the field, which specifies the conditions for successful intergroup contact in face-to-face settings. The chapter describes how these conditions can be set out in online intergroup meetings, and goes on to discuss moderators and mediators of intergroup contact effects, and explain how these variables operate in online interactions. The chapter demonstrates how the specific characteristics of computer-mediated communication, ranging from disembodied, text-based interaction to (re)embodied, avatar-based interaction, can be used as a strategic tool to enhance intergroup contact. Based on this theoretical framework, the structure and evaluation results of organized online intergroup encounters in conflict regions are considered. The chapter concludes with an agenda for empirical studies on online intergroup contact to guide further research in this area.

In the final chapter Edward G. Sargis, Linda J. Skitka, and William McKeever tackle the topic of online research. They argue that social psychologists increasingly use the Internet to facilitate their studies and go on to examine the prevalence of Internet-based research in top-tier social psychological journals and provide an overview of the growing body of research on best practices for Internet-based research. They assess general presentation guidelines for online questionnaires, how question response formats affect scale reliability, and strategies to improve the quality of responses from online participants. They include a discussion of the considerations involved in populating online studies and general guidelines for ensuring the security of Internet-based data.

The book provides a comprehensive picture of the main areas of social psychology in the Internet arena. It shows clearly that an understanding of the net cannot be limited to the technological aspects, for without an appreciation of the human factor involved, our grasp of this medium must be incomplete.

Acknowledgments

Without the help of a number of people this book could not have come into being. First I thank the authors for their contributions. I would also like to express my gratitude to those whose comments and encouragement helped me with this project: Jeremy Bailenson, Shaul Fox, Béatrice Hasler, Tal Shani, Joseph Walther, Patrice Weiss, Yoel Yinon, and Dan Zakai. At Oxford University Press I extend my thanks to Martin Baum and Charlotte Green who helped me with this second, extended edition.

Last and not least I would like to thank my wife Debbie whose fingerprints are everywhere in my work, from the initial creative stage, down to commenting on the smallest details.

Contents

List of Abbreviations

BAR	Balance between Attractive and Real self	MAU	MultiAttribute Utility
BB	bulletin board	MMOG	Massively Multiplayer Online Game
CFO	cues-filtered-out	MMORPG	Massively Multiplayer Online Role-Playing Game
CM	Computer-Mediated	MOO	Multiuser dimensions or domains Object Oriented
CMC	Computer-Mediated Communication		
EVT	Expectancy Violation Theory	MUD	Multiple User Dungeons/MultiUser dimensions or domains
FBI	Federal Bureau of Investigation		
FtF	face-to-face	PC	personal computer
GAM	General Aggression Model	RDD	random-digit-dial
GDSS	Group Decision Support System	SCT	Social (Self-) Categorization Theory
GLM	General Learning Model	SES	social economic status
HCI	Human–Computer Interaction	SIDE	Social Identity model of Deindividuation Effects
HIT	Human Intelligence Task		
HSM	Heuristic–Systematic Model	SIP	Social Information Processing
HTTP	HyperText Transfer Protocol	SNS	Social Networking Site
HTTPS	HyperText Transfer Protocol Secure	TESS	Time-sharing Experiments in the Social Sciences
IAT	Implicit Association Test		
IMC	Instructional Manipulation Check	URT	Uncertainty Reduction Theory
IRB	Institutional Review Board	UK	United Kingdom
KN	Knowledge Networks	US	United States
LISS	Longitudinal Internet Studies for the Social Sciences	VR	Virtual Reality
		VT	Virtual Team
LMX	Leader–Member Exchange		

List of Contributors

Yair Amichai-Hamburger
The Research Center for Internet Psychology
Sammy Ofer School of Communications
The Interdisciplinary Center
Herzliya, Israel

Kevin Askew
Department of Psychology
University of South Florida
USA

Jeremy N. Bailenson
Virtual Human Interaction Lab
Department of Communication
Stanford University
USA

Caryn A. Conley
Stern School of Business
New York University
USA

Michael D. Coovert
Department of Psychology
University of South Florida
USA

Jack Glaser
Goldman School of Public Policy
University of California, Berkeley
USA

Béatrice S. Hasler
Advanced Virtuality Lab
Sammy Ofer School of Communications
Interdisciplinary Center Herzliya
Israel

Zack Hayat
Faculty of Information
University of Toronto
Canada

Crystal L. Hoyt
Jepson School of Leadership Studies
University of Richmond
USA

Kimberly Barsamian Kahn
Department of Psychology
Portland State University
USA

Yoram M. Kalman
Department of Management
and Economics,
The Open University of Israel
Israel

Daniel Linz
Department of Communication
University of California, Santa Barbara
USA

Neil Malamuth
Departments of Communication and
Psychology
University of California, Los Angeles
USA

William McKeever
Department of Psychology
University of Illinois at Chicago
USA

Jae Yun Moon
Business School
Korea University
The Republic of Korea

Daphne R. Raban
Sagy Center for Internet Research, and
Graduate School of Management,
University of Haifa
Israel

Sheizaf Rafaeli
Sagy Center for Internet Research,
and Graduate School of Management,
University of Haifa
Israel

Edward G. Sargis
Department of Psychology
University of Illinois at Chicago
USA

Erin M. Schumaker
School of Communication
The Ohio State University
USA

Kathryn Y. Segovia
Virtual Human Interaction Lab
Department of Communication
Stanford University
USA

Linda J. Skitka
Department of Psychology
University of Illinois at Chicago
USA

Katherine Spencer
Department of Psychology
University of California, Berkeley
USA

Lee Sproull
Stern School of Business
New York University
USA

Brandon Van Der Heide
School of Communication
The Ohio State University
USA

Joseph B. Walther
Department of Communication
Department of Telecommunication,
Information Studies & Media
Michigan State University
USA

René Weber
Department of Communication
University of California, Santa Barbara
USA

Monica T. Whitty
Department of Media and Communication
University of Leicester
UK

Chapter 1

Internet and Personality

Yair Amichai-Hamburger and Zack Hayat

Introduction

The Internet is a worldwide, decentralized network of hundreds of millions of computers linked to one another. However, the Internet is first and foremost not about computers, but hundreds of millions of people from all around the world who at any given moment are surfing the Internet. The Internet is an exciting and complex means of communication. In some respects, it is a mass media applying the same services across the spectrum of its users, but at the same time it enables each of its hundreds of millions of surfers to express their own individuality and create their own online profile. Our focus is the experience of the individual surfer, and in order to understand that, we have to understand what it is that the individual brings with him or her to the Internet to create their own unique surfing experience.

Personality represents "those characteristics of the person that account for his consistent pattern of behavior" (Pervin, 1993, p. 3). The key to understanding regularities in the thoughts, feelings, and overt behaviors of people is knowledge of their personality. Whereas most areas of psychology explore specific aspects of human behavior, such as perception or memory, the psychology of personality sees the individual as one integrative unit. Hamburger and Ben-Artzi (2000) argued that studies on Internet usage did not discriminate between different types of surfer. This resulted in surfers being stereotyped by being placed into one large group and the fact that surfers are uniform, but have different personalities which in turn affect their behavior on the net, was largely ignored. As Amichai-Hamburger (2002) explained, although millions of people around the world communicate with one another every day, surfing is an individual experience and, therefore, any attempt to understand behavior on the net must involve an examination of the personality of the surfer.

In this chapter we will focus on how the personality of the surfer can be utilized to promote his or her empowerment through the Internet. We will start by studying the major exceptional features of the Internet, and how they create a unique psychological environment. We will then move on to explore the effect of the Internet on people with social inhibitions which makes it difficult for them to feel comfortable socially offline, including why and how the Internet affects such people and how it extends an opportunity for them to recreate themselves. On a broader level, we discuss the growing evidence that increasing numbers of people seem able and willing to reveal intimate layers of themselves on the Internet in ways that they may not do offline. Another connection between Internet and personality is found in the area of addiction, we assess how such addiction comes about. Finally we will examine the ways in which the empowerment that many find on the Internet may be conveyed to their offline daily lives.

The Internet in its Psychological Context

The Internet has several important, interrelated psychological components that are distinguishable from those of the offline world (Amichai-Hamburger, 2005, 2008, 2012; Hamburger & Ben-Artzi,

2000; McKenna, Green, & Gleason, 2002). Among the most prominent of these is that which allows for online anonymity.

Anonymity Online

This refers to the perception of the user that he or she can surf the net without disclosing information that might lead other surfers to identify him or her. Anonymity in computer-mediated communication (CMC) research has been identified as a major factor affecting online interaction (Joinson, 1998). Disclosure in face-to-face (FtF) communication is difficult to control, because it is rich in visual cues, and social presence is fully in place. People cannot hide their race, gender, height, weight, shortcomings, or other physical characteristics. What they may attempt to control is the leakage of personal information such as political views, sexual preferences, medical conditions, and social status, but even in areas such as these, this type of information may be detected through non verbal communication. Anonymous CMC provides a higher level of control over disclosures, since it hides social cues and can potentially limit social presence. CMC is characterized by limited-channel communications—mostly text (Riordan & Kreuz, 2010)—and users can decide how much self-identifying information to disclose. Unlike other limited-channel media, where nonverbal communications are still communicated, text-based communications are extremely limited in what they disclose about an author. Since social cues are missing from CMC, a receiver's interpretations become more important (Rains, 2007). Less disclosure and greater anonymity leaves blank spaces in communications, allowing CMC receivers to fill in the blanks by attributing qualities to senders (Jiang, Bazarova, & Hancock, 2011). This attribution characteristic has been shown to increase the degree of intimacy experienced between participants. For example, Hancock & Dunham (2001), paired individuals who were asked to rate how much they liked their partner. Online singles rated their meetings higher than FtF singles, despite the fact that it was the same person in each online and FtF scenario. The authors (Hancock & Dunham, 2001) argue that the higher ratings stem from a greater ability to project or attribute qualities to the other person in CMC (see also McKenna et al., 2002; Tidwell & Walther, 2002).

Anonymity, along with the absence of social cues, often leads to disinhibition. Disinhibition means that when individuals feel anonymous, regardless of whether they really are or not, they tend to disclose more information (Joinson, 2001). Joinson (2001) found that the kind of anonymity one has in CMCs affects disclosure. For example, those who are visually anonymous tend to disclose more than those who can be seen. Additionally, feelings of social integration, or belonging to an online group tend to increase disclosure (Douglas & McGarty, 2002). In addition, anonymity might give people the courage to join online groups whose participants hold a negative social stigma. Taking part in online activities is likely to help such people to open up to each other. These disclosures may well lead participants to experience an increase in their self-esteem. This is especially likely to be the case with individuals who belong to negative marginalized groups, for example, people with non-normative sexual inclinations or non-normative political orientations. Offline, such people may be able to hide their identity, but may also suffer from being exposed to harsh comments, jokes, and criticism by others who are unaware of this part of their orientation. This type of exposure is likely to harm their self-esteem in the offline world (Bargh & McKenna, 2004; McKenna & Bargh, 1998).

Specific Internet technologies (such as web browsing, email, online chat rooms, instant messaging, social networking sites, and online games) have varying functions and degrees of anonymity that may be linked to self-expression. For instance, web browsing for information is relatively anonymous, and may not be directly related to self-expression; it does not involve giving away identifiable information or online interactions with others. On the other hand, instant messaging and email are modes of communication through which users interact with others and are identifiable in some respect (by username, posted image, available personal information, etc.); as long as these identifiable traits are not coordinated with other known traits of the person (such as name, address, etc.), users can also maintain their online anonymity (Wallace, 1999). Thus, the online interactions and the perception of anonymity allotted through these technologies may be instrumental for those looking to explore aspects of their identity and gain feedback and validation (Turkle, 1995).

Although the Internet is typically known for the anonymity it affords its users, today many surfers identify themselves and to expose different parts of themselves and their activities to others. Leading examples of this trend are blogs and social networking sites (e.g. Facebook and MySpace), which have become very popular in recent years. Many people use these technologies to express their present self, personal experience, thoughts, and feelings. There remain, however, different possibilities as to the degree of exposure. Individuals with blogs can control the availability of personally identifiable information, such as real names or pseudonyms and personal photos, and target a selected audience. In contrast, social network sites are designed as personal websites that encourage individuals to share identifiable and personal information (such as name, address, photos, interests) with a network of friends. But here too there is an expectation that the individual will choose who will see the personal details, and how limited the exposure will be. Social networking sites give people a high level of control. People can attend to most of their Internet needs through the comprehensive options available. They also give people a significant amount of control as to how much information to disclose and to whom they will reveal it. Usually people will decide to expose information based on their levels of friendship. For instance, recent studies suggest that instant messaging is positively related to the quality of adolescents' existing friendships—a tendency that is explained by the discloser of intimate information online (Valkenburg & Peter, 2009). This, however, is only true for those people who are aware of the variety of options for more or less disclosure that exist on social networks.

However, it is important to stress that despite the declared intentions of social network designers, it is clear that the rules referring to the confidentiality of information are frequently broken. Moreover, despite claims to the contrary, there appears to be a significant percentage of fake profiles on social networking sites (Bumgarner, 2007; Grimmelmann, 2009). As for the declared minimum age requirement, while Facebook maintains that surfers must be at least 13 years old to open a profile there, in reality there are many children on Facebook who are well below that age (World Internet Project, 2010).

Control of Our Physical Appearance

Related to online anonymity is the fact that surfers are able to hide or reveal their physical appearance at will. For many people this is a very important and liberating part of their Internet experience. This is due to the perception that appearance is one of the focal determinants for how we are perceived by others. Cialdini (1984) believes that in today's culture attractive people have enormous social advantages: They are better liked, more frequently helped, and seen as possessing better personality traits and intellectual capabilities. This advantage is bestowed due to what is termed the halo effect. This occurs when one positive characteristic of a person, such as attractiveness, dominates the way a person is viewed by others (Thorndike, 1920). Just as the halo effect plays in favor of the physically attractive, the reverse is true for people who are physically unappealing. The first physical impression is likely to set the course for the rest of the interaction (Dion, Berscheid,

& Walster, 1972), and will play a large part in determining the outcome of any kind of association, be it a working relationship or a romantic one (Hatfield & Sprecher, 1986). Net technologies allow surfers to display different degrees of physical exposure as they choose. The degree of exposure ranges from that of services such as chat, where the physical appearance may remain unknown, to social networking sites where people are generally expected to share photographs, thus exposing themselves physically.

However, although many surfers believe that they can control their physical exposure on social networking sites, for instance by deciding which photographs to display or even by choosing not to display their current appearance at all and by representing their presence by depicting their infant self or themselves as a dog; in fact others may well display their likeness in photographs they display on their web pages. Another way in which control is exercised on social networks is through what is known as impression management. People work hard to create the desired impression on others through the pages of their social network (Amichai-Hamburger & Vinitzky, 2010). It appears that even when most of the people on our social net are people with whom we are familiar with offline, we are still likely to invest time and energy in order to create the best impression possible. This will involve, for example, choosing carefully which photos to display. More recently with the growing use of social networking sites such as Facebook, such activity is seen as increasingly important. People consider Facebook as their identity card, which has a pivotal relevance for new encounters. Once people have our name and want to receive further information about us, one of the first places they are likely to look is our Facebook profile. This includes many employers who use Facebook profiles to screen potential candidates (Peluchette & Karl, 2010).

Physical appearance is closely linked to impression management, thus, for example, many people who are overweight will choose to display pictures where they look thinner than they actually are, and people who are very short will look for pictures where this is not emphasized. The same is true of people's efforts to look like they live charmed lives, always happy, always attractive.

As mentioned earlier, on net services where the social interaction is solely text-based such as anonymous chats or forums, the physical characteristics of the participants may remain undisclosed. This is also the case in fantasy worlds like *Second Life* where although participants do possess a physical representation, this may have no connection to their actual physical appearance (Dunn & Guadagno, 2012). This may be particularly significant for people with unsightly or unattractive physical characteristics who may well suffer from discrimination in their FtF interactions. On the Internet they have an opportunity to present themselves in any way they choose. Such individuals may hope that if and when the interaction progresses to FtF, any negative physical presence will not be relevant. However, this may remain unfulfilled as the process may actually turn out to be more complex. This may be simply because the surfer fears an FtF interaction to such an extent that he or she may limit the interaction to online only.

Greater Control

Internet surfing allows us to meet the world from our own territory, and this may well provide us with a strong sense of security which leads to feelings of confidence (Amichai-Hamburger, 2005). Moreover, many of the interactive technologies, especially the text-based ones like email, chat or Facebook messaging, are asynchronous, allowing us to see the message before it is sent and reshape it as many times as we choose, until we are satisfied with it. This too gives us a sense of control over the interaction (Riva, 2002). McKenna et al. (2002) have further shown that people have a greater sense of control in online environments, as they believe that they can stop the interaction whenever they choose.

As a result of this, when it comes to social interactions with a high degree of anxiety, for example, a romantic encounter, people are likely to feel less anxious when they interact online, rather than FtF, since they feel a high degree of control over the interaction. They feel that in the worst case they can always stop the interaction. Paradoxically, the power given by the Internet to an Internet user to sever a connection with such ease actually creates a platform for intense romantic relationships. This is because the knowledge that they have the ability to cut off the exchange and vanish at any given moment gives the user a feeling of tremendous control and so invites significant self-disclosure (Ben-Ze'ev, 2005).

The Internet allows individuals to participate in social and collaborative enterprises on an unprecedented level. This may have special meaning for individuals with physical or psychological limitations. For example, people with disabilities are able to move about freely in virtual worlds (Blair, 2006). Warr (2008) describes these virtual worlds as including role playing games (massively multiplayer online games or MMOGs), such as *World of Warcraft* as well as nongame computer mediated environments (CMEs) such as *Second Life* and *The Sims*. Individuals can use CMC to receive medical care in their homes (Nilsson, Skär, & Söderberg, 2010).

Finding Similar Others

Maslow's (1971) hierarchy of human needs includes the need to belong to a group as one of the basic human requirements. Tajfel and Turner (1986) explain that being a member of a group that shares your goals and interests is one of the major ways through which to enhance self-esteem. It is therefore extremely important for people to experience being members of a group in which they feel validated. The Internet is visited by many hundreds of millions of people, all of whom have varied interests. The ease with which it is possible to find details of the different specialized groups on the Internet, makes it exceptionally effective to discover like-minded others. The Internet is the foremost medium used by many surfers to connect to their core group members. A core group member is one to whom the surfer relates based on their main identity categorization, such as nationality or religion. Interestingly, however, the fact that on the Internet, other people with a seemingly endless variety of identities and interests may be easily found, leads the surfer to explore other, less dominant aspects of his or her identity. In this way, people are able to identify with and join groups based on mutual interests and this is likely to enrich their individual identity significantly (Amichai-Hamburger, 2012).

On the Internet, many thousands of different groups exist and it is fairly straightforward to find a group of others who are similar. This can be especially important for people who belong to marginalized or stigmatized groups. On the Internet they can find their group and join its activities without having to risk revealing their identity publicly, as a member of a stigmatized group. Visiting websites of people who are similar may make people feel that their group is much larger than they had imagined. McKenna and Bargh (1998) tested the implications of belonging to a news group (an Internet-based discussion forum about a particular topic). They concentrated their research on hidden stigmatized groups, such as those whose members had marginalized sexual interests or marginal political views and ideology. They found that people belonging to a stigmatized identity group were more likely to be involved in a news group of similar others and considered their belonging to the group as more important to their identity, compared to those who identified with a nonstigmatized interest news group. For those posting to the news group, this involvement elevated their self-esteem, self-acceptance, and reduced feelings of social loneliness. In addition, they were highly motivated to make their identity a social reality by telling their close circle of family and friends that they belonged to a stigmatized group.

High Accessibility Time and Place

The last decade has seen a major change in Internet usage patterns. This has come about through the ease with which the Internet may be accessed and the large variety of different ways with which this can be achieved. Early on, the Internet could only be accessed through a traditional, desktop computer. Today, however, people can enter cyberspace using a portable computer, or a cell phone, with the result that the Internet can accompany them wherever they are. Comprehensive surveys demonstrate that use of the Internet via mobile phone has increased dramatically (World Internet Project, 2010). This trend is encouraged by the increasingly widespread availability of WiFi. This greater accessibility to the Internet leads many people to feel that it is omnipresent.

Today, many people are online constantly, and this has led to a major change in the way they perceive the balance between their offline and online lives. If, for example, being a member of an offline group was pre-eminent in an individual's life over his or her membership in an online group, it is likely that this is no longer the case. The offline group may meet weekly or monthly, but the online group is continuously available and he or she may be available to it at all hours of the day or night. People may enrich their individual identities, exploring the less salient aspects of their personality along with their interests, by broadening the variety of groups to which they belong. As a result, such people may acquire their self-esteem from their membership of different groups, both online and offline.

Fun

The Internet is entertaining and exciting. Website designers work hard to create a significant experience for the surfer. Websites are generally interactive, visually attractive, and offer increasingly more in this regard (Kinzie, Cohn, Julian, & Knaus, 2002; Wiggins, 2007). As a result of the fierce competition between websites, the survival of the most captivating ensures the death of the more dull; assuring that the experience for the surfer will continue to be increasingly enjoyable. The field of user experience is developing commensurately, and the resulting feedback to web designers means that they can incorporate the needs of their customers more effectively into their sites (Ehmke & Wilson, 2007).

Furthermore, alongside their instrumental function as an information source and task-oriented tool, CMC is used for maintaining social networks with family and friends, as well as for making new friends, thus helping to remove limitations of geography and transportation. Moreover, many leisure activities are being offered by the web, such as photo album sharing, games, and virtual hobbies which allow far-flung family members to interact and share the type of activities that increase familial and kinship bonds (Xie, 2007). It has been argued that CMC provides a unique form of casual leisure that involves play, active entertainment, and sociable conversations (Nimrod, 2010). Online leisure activities fulfill the same functions as those considered traditional; they provide relaxation, stimulation, escape, social interaction, and the development of self-identity and lifestyle.

It seems that the new leisure technologies will lead to other changes in the contemporary experience of leisure. For example, the Internet challenges traditional conceptions of the spatial and interactional organization of leisure by blurring the boundaries between domestic, virtual, and commercial leisure spaces. The domestic use of the Internet and Internet cafés illustrate the intersection of traditional and virtual leisure spaces. The increased commercialization of the Internet and online shopping also suggest a blurring of domestic and commercial leisure spaces (Nimrod, 2010). Contemporary leisure spaces, then, may be experienced as multiple, diverse, and simultaneous.

This finding implies that we need to consider not only the new forms of leisure activities, but also the ways in which we perceive the Internet arena. We need to consider that when examining individuals who are using the Internet, we should also consider the pleasurable aspects of their online activities, and how it affects their online experiences and social interactions as well as their perception of that environment. For instance, Youn and Lee (2002) found that adult video gamers demonstrated more tolerance towards their peers in social interactions in comparison to nongamers.

Today, people expect to be able to find almost every activity online in a very entertaining form, and the "fun factor" has led many people to transfer their offline activities online.

It seems clear that the Internet creates a very unique setting which has no equivalent in the offline traditional world. This highly protected environment, which is constantly available, and in which like-minded persons on any topic in the world may be located at ease, affects people in different ways. In some cases, it releases individuals from the "normative persona mask" they wear in their FtF interactions. This may well enable them to explore who they are and experiment with different aspects of their identity (Turkle, 1995). It also creates a highly supportive net environment which might also help people to reach their deepest level of individuality, also called the true self (McKenna & Bargh, 2000). In some other cases when the group identity is very salient, it may enhance the feelings of belonging to a certain group even when the participant is anonymous. (For a fuller explanation see SIDE theory chapter 3 of this book.) Some people might direct their feelings of protection and express different forms of aggression against others on the net (Malamuth, Linz, & Yao, 2005). Others may feel that the protected environment allows them the opportunity to use the Internet as a means of helping others (Amichai-Hamburger, 2008), while still determining their limits. For others, it will speed the process of getting from the first phase of a romantic relationship to an intimacy and closeness stage (Cooper & Sportolari, 1997; McKenna & Bargh, 2000).

It is thought that personality affects how users choose and interpret different activities that are offered online (Guadagno, Okdie, & Eno, 2008). Swickert, Hittner, Harris, and Herring (2002) suggested that there are various personality factors that can explain why patterns of online consumption fluctuate. Many scholars believe that user preference is, to a large extent, influenced by personality traits (see, for example, Amichai-Hamburger, 2002; Anolli, Villani, & Riva, 2005). Researchers have singled out several personality traits that appear to act as leading components in influencing surfer behavior on the Internet. These include, for example, sensation seeking (Alonzo & Aiken, 2004; López-Bonilla & López-Bonilla, 2010; Lu, 2008); locus of control (Chak & Leung, 2004; Hoffman, Novak, & Schlosser, 2003); extroversion (Amichai-Hamburger, Wainapel, & Fox, 2002; Hamburger & Ben-Artzi, 2000); openness (Weibel, Wissmath, & Mast, 2010); neuroticism (Amichai-Hamburger et al., 2002; Hamburger & Ben-Artzi, 2000); need for closure (Amichai-Hamburger, Fine, & Goldstein, 2004; Jung, Min, & Kellaris, 2011); need for cognition (Amichai-Hamburger & Kinar, 2007; Kinar & Amichai-Hamburger, 2008) and attachment (Gerson, 2011; Lei & Wu, 2007; Weisskirch and Delevi, 2011).

In fact, though the influence of these traits has been explored in detail, it seems safe to assume that all personality theories are closely connected to surfer behavior. It is important to note that this is actually a two-way street, just as personality is relevant to Internet choices, the Internet itself may be utilized as a major tool of empowerment, and here too, the influence of the Internet will vary depending on the personality of the individual surfer. Next we explore the potential for the Internet to be exploited as a tool for empowerment for people suffering from social inhibitions. This, we believe, will serve as a good example of how the Internet can help users transform their lives.

The Poor get Richer: The Net as a Paradise for People with Social Inhibitions

Hamburger and Ben-Artzi (2000) pointed out that introverts may well be empowered by the net. The protective environment provided by the Internet enables such people to compensate themselves on a social level. On the net they can reinvent themselves and can become extroverts. In practical terms this means that the socially shy, closed, and withdrawn individuals may undergo a transformation and become highly interactive, open, social beings with a large network of online connections. Such outcomes were initially reported with regard to introverted and neurotic women (Hamburger & Ben-Artzi, 2000). The authors suggest that it is possible that these results may be due to the general higher self-awareness among women and their ability to receive social support; and that as Internet use becomes more widespread, introverted males will similarly come to realize that the Internet has the potential to respond to their social needs. This approach has been defined as "the poor get richer," in other words that those who are poor socially offline become richer socially online. These findings have been confirmed by other studies. For example, Maldonado et al. (2001) evaluated computer-mediated messages and found that actually introverted subjects send messages with an extroverted tone. Their messages contained more information than those sent by extroverted subjects. It seems that on the net, introverts do not act in accordance with their usual behavior patterns, but, due to their reaction to what they perceive as a particularly secure environment, conduct themselves in ways associated with extroverts in offline relationships.

Amichai-Hamburger et al. (2002) found that introverts perceive the online world as a preferred social environment over the offline world, and feel that their relationships on the net are more special than their relationships offline. These findings confirmed the *poor get richer theory*. However, this theory has not been without its critics, For example, Kraut et al. (2002), found that introverts who use the net reported higher levels of loneliness as compared with surfers who are extroverts. Kraut and his colleagues explained their results in terms of "the rich get richer" phenomenon. They explained that people who have better social skills and many friends offline, will exploit their highly developed social skills and make more friends on the net, whereas people who are less socially adept and have a poorer social life offline are likely to gain less from their Internet interaction. According to this idea the Internet is yet another environment in which extroverts demonstrate their dominance over introverts.

Who Actually Gets Richer?

Amichai-Hamburger, Kaplan, and Dorpatcheon (2008) considered whether *the poor get richer theory* and *the rich get richer theory* necessarily contradict one another or whether they are (at least partly) complementary theories. In their study, carried out in 2005, they examined the relationship between personality and social networking in its initial stage. They found that extroverted participants who used a social networking site made greater use of the net as a social tool (for social interaction) as compared to introverts who used the social networking site. However, introverts who did not use a social network were found to use the social services on the net more than extroverts who did not use a social networking site. This led them to suggest that when surfers' foremost behavior on the net is using social networking sites, they are basically duplicating their offline social network on the Internet. In other words, their pattern of social interaction offline is transferred to their behavior online. In this way, extroverts retain their offline social dominance when they are online. This is consistent with the rich-get-richer theory (Kraut et al., 2002).

These findings are also supported in the findings of Peter, Valkenburg, and Schouten (2005) indicating that introverts are less likely to make friends online because they communicated and self-disclosed less often than extroverts. Conversely, among people who do not use social networks, behavior on the Internet will tend to be more explorative; freed of any offline persona, such people can actually recreate themselves. They are therefore more likely to use the Internet as a compensative environment and this, in turn, may lead them to become more socially dominant on the net as compared with extroverts. This is consistent with the "poor get richer" theory (Hamburger & Ben-Artzi, 2000).

It would seem, then, that two different orientations have developed online. The first is one in which people enjoy a high degree of anonymity. Being anonymous helps them to recreate themselves. They are free to explore different aspects of their identity without the fear of others. This may be observed in fantasy games, anonymous chats, and blogs. Conversely, there is the phenomenon of people allowing themselves to be identified, often to a very high degree. Such people do not aim to recreate themselves online, but rather, to duplicate their offline identity online. This is best demonstrated by behavior on social networking sites.

Facebook, a Social Networking Site

The Facebook website reports over 800 million active users, over half of whom log on to Facebook on any given day. Each Facebook member has on average 130 friends (http://www.facebook.com/press/info.php?statistics). It is interesting to learn what kind of behavior introverts adopt on social networking sites. Given the lack of anonymity and thus lowering of perceived levels of safety found there, we may expect them to duplicate their offline behavior. This seems especially likely, given the fact that in social networking sites people tend to duplicate their FtF social networking sites and replicate them online. Even when introverts try to behave differently, their friends are likely to return them to their known position. However, the Internet is complex and has a variety of different options through which introverts may compensate themselves. In essence it was found that extroverts have more social interaction in social networks than introverts (Amichai-Hamburger & Vinitzky, 2010). It appears that introverts do in fact transfer their patterns of introverted behavior from the offline into the online world. This is reflected in the size of their social network which tends to be smaller than that of the extroverts. Interestingly though, it seems that introverts do invest more effort into building and designing their personal profile on Facebook, than is the case with extroverts. Introverts, for example, place more personal information on their Facebook profiles than extroverts. This may be explained by the fact that extroverts rely on their social skills and so feel less need to promote themselves, whereas introverts tend to feel anxious in real-life interactions and may experience exposure on Facebook as something similar. This demonstrates that even in social networking sites, introverts find ways to compensate themselves.

As discussed previously, it seems that many people with social inhibitions have found creative ways to compensate themselves even on social networking site. In addition the Internet contains many other outlets for self-expression, many of which may not seem as intrusive as social networking sites, including, for example, Wikipedia blogs, forums, and fantasy games.

Wikipedia, the Net Encyclopedia

The community of Wikipedia authors is a particularly interesting net community. Wikipedia is the well-known, web-based encyclopedia, authored by surfers. Wikipedia authors contribute a significant amount of time and effort to their endeavor, but interestingly, the public does not know who they are. They are nameless, faceless, and receive no official recognition. An examination of the difference in personality profiles between the Wikipedia members and participants who are not Wikipedia members revealed that Wikipedia members scored lower on agreeableness (Amichai-Hamburger et al., 2008). It may be that the pro-social behavior apparent in Wikipedia is primarily connected to egocentric motives, such as personal expression, raising self-confidence, and group identification-motives which are not associated with high levels of agreeableness.

Another interesting result was the significant difference found between Wikipedia members and non-Wikipedia members in the openness trait. Again, this may reflect the fact that contributing to Wikipedia serves mainly egocentric motives. The study's original hypothesis that Wikipedia members will have lower levels of extroversion was partially confirmed. A significant difference in the level of extroversion was found between Wikipedia members and non-Wikipedia members, but only for women. This may be indicative of the fact that women seem more likely to use the Internet as a compensative tool. Women who are introverted and feel a need to express themselves and find this difficult in the offline world, may be able to do so on the Internet. This is in line with the Hamburger and Ben-Artzi (2000) findings. It may indicate again that introverted women were again the first to discover the social compensative potential of the various new net opportunities. As previously discussed, the Internet with all its components has created a uniquely protected environment where a wide range of people with differing personality characteristics are able to compensate themselves for their social difficulties or their feeling of having no significant voice.

It seems that introverts may well see the Wikipedia environment as a place both to interact with others in a protective environment and also as a way of having a say in the world; things that may be challenging for them in the offline environment. In other words what is difficult for them to achieve in the offline is possible to achieve in the online. The fact that the Wikipedia authors' motivation was not extrinsic, i.e. to help others, but rather intrinsic to have a voice in the world, was supported by the findings of Yang and Lai (2010). Their aim was to examine the motivations of Wikipedia content contributors, and their results showed that internal self-concept motivation is the key motivator for knowledge sharing on Wikipedia.

Online Chat

Online chat refers to online instantaneous transmission of text messages from one sender to many receivers. Anonymous chat users have a tendency to be closed and rather introverted. They find the chat environment to be an appropriate forum to open themselves and develop personal relationships (Anolli et al., 2005). The authors point out the similarities between their findings and those of Amichai-Hamburger et al. (2002), with respect to the behavior of introverts who choose the net over offline as a preferred environment for their interactions. In this case, the chat can be seen as a forum for introverts to express themselves. Anolli et al. (2005) point out that participants in chat rooms appear to be people who need support and approval, and this forum provides this for them.

Blog

A blog is a net diary, usually personal and updated frequently. Blogs aim to build a community of people around them who comment on the posts and create a dialogue around the topic of the blog. The content of the blog is often expressive and includes links and comments regarding other web sites and blogs, news, ideas, photos, poetry, project updates, and stories (Riva, 2002). The blog technology allows a direct uploading of the text, photos and links without the reader needing a high level of technological understanding, allowing the blog to be read at any time and in any situation where there is an Internet connection. Blog owners can allow their readers to write comments after each post (Huffaker, 2004). Blogs are often written as a series of continuous comments on a specific agenda. This type of format enables a permanent and continuous information update, and provides convenient tools for use and is offered for free to everyone (Lawson-Borders & Kirk, 2005). In addition, the blogosphere allows the creation of intimate communities of communication (Ó Baoill, 2004). Herring, Scheidt, Wright, and Bonus (2005) believe that the importance of the blog as an intimate form of self-expression is underestimated. Given our previous knowledge, it may be predicted that the blog format, which allows users to maintain their anonymity, would be an ideal setting for people with social inhibitions, since their involvement in the blog would allow them to feel totally protected and so enable them to recreate themselves and express themselves freely. In fact Guadagno, Okdie, and Eno (2008) found that the personality characteristics found to be related to blogging are openness to new experiences and neuroticism, and no relationship was found between introversion and blogging. It should be pointed out however, that Guadagno et al.'s (2008) study did not actually focus on blogs where authors maintain their anonymity. Cyberspace contains many different types of blog with varying degrees of anonymity, from those where the user is totally identified, to the others where he or she is completely anonymous. Guadagno et al. (2008) report that many bloggers provide identifying information such as their name, and an identified blog is not a protective environment for the surfer with social inhibitions, and will actually produce the reverse effect. It is therefore suggested that future studies examine the relationship between introversion and blogging on unidentified blogs. We predict that such a study would find that introverts see the blog as a protective environment which helps them to express themselves freely and therefore a strong link between introversion and anonymous blogging may well exist.

The Fantasy World

In this context, a fantasy world refers to an online world containing a total environment which enables surfers to duplicate a whole range of offline activities. One prominent example is *Second Life*, where people interact with others through avatars. *Second Life* declares that it is a place to connect, to shop, to work, to love, and to explore. *Second Life* even has its own currency, the linden, which may be acquired online and used for purchasing goods and services, alternatively, surfers may also open their own business and sell to others. From a social point of view, *Second Life* allows surfers to find like-minded others, maintain friendships, and develop romantic relationships. This means that for many, *Second Life* is perceived as an attractive place in which to spend their time.

On entering *Second Life*, the surfers must choose an avatar, a graphic body, which will represent them during their stay (Bailenson & Beall, 2006). The surfer is empowered to put together the whole being, including choosing the gender, body shape, hair, and eye colors. Since *Second Life* is an anonymous environment where people not only can hide their real physical characteristics, but also create their desired physical appearance, we may predict that an introvert might try to compensate him or herself there. Introverts are known to spend more time then extroverts in building their profile on social networking sites (Amichai-Hamburger & Vinitzky, 2010), and this leads us to predict that a similar situation will arise in *Second Life*, in that introverts will devote more time to building their avatar than extroverts; and moreover, they are more likely to create an avatar that is more dissimilar and a greater improvement on their own physical body than extroverts do. This will be in line with their need to compensate themselves. When it comes to social interaction, we predict that initially introverts will be rather shy, but as they build their confidence they will increasingly start to behave as extroverts. Dunn and Guadagno (2012) studied a video game in which participants, before entering a game session, designed their avatar. They found that introverts tended to build a more attractive avatar, in comparison to extroverts. This is in accordance to our general prediction that introverts will use the game environment to compensate themselves. We suggest that future studies in this area will examine other means of compensation such as how long it takes them to build the avatar and how they interact socially with others. It would be very interesting to study this on novice introvert and extrovert players for a long period of time so that a long-term dynamic can be recorded.

Online "Real Me"

When we examine how people are empowered through the Internet, it is important to focus on where people locate their "real me." The concept of "real me" relates to people's ability to express their true selves (Rogers, 1961). When we consider empowerment through the Internet, one of the leading questions is the level of openness people experience with their friends online in comparison to offline. Rogers was the leader of the Human Potential Movement. He believed that contemporary life had led people to abandon their innate character traits and in their place develop a social persona that they believed would assure them the devotion of others. This however, would ultimately prove inadequate, for despite their pretense and their supreme efforts to gratify others, people would find that their recipients remained dissatisfied. The structure of the Rogerian personality (Rogers, 1961) contains three different selves: *The self-concept* (the phenomenological self)—the subjective perception of the self. This includes both the parts that are expressed and conscious beliefs about the self, as influenced by culture and education. *The true self*—or the organismic valuing process—represents the real self as unfulfilled for most people. *The ideal self* is what the person would like to be. This is not necessarily the same as the true self, since the person can have an ideal self that is totally at odds with that to which they should aspire. McKenna et al. (2002) offered the "real me" concept based on the true self concept of Carl Rogers. McKenna et al. (2002) believe that the secure protective environment found on the Internet is likely to have a positive effect on net relationships. They argue that the unique atmosphere created by cyberspace allows people to share self-relevant information in a way that they would be unwilling to in the offline world. McKenna and her colleagues use the concept of the "real me" to refer to a version of the self that someone believes is the truth, but that they have difficulty in expressing.

McKenna et al. (2002) differentiate between people who locate their "real me" on the Internet—that is, reveal their real self over the net—and those who locate their "real me" in FtF relationships. They suggest that the location of the "real me" defines where people will have their more significant relationships, online or offline. When a person locates their "real me" on the Internet, it is expected that they will have a more significant relationship over the net than when a person locates their "real me" in offline relationships. They found that people who found it easier to express their true self over the net reported a rapid formation of cyberspace relationships and that those relationships endured over time. They also found that people who are socially anxious and lonely can better express themselves on the Internet than in offline relationships. Social anxiety and loneliness are linked to relationship intimacy by mediation of the location of the self. There is no direct relationship between social anxiety and loneliness on one hand and intimacy and closeness on the other.

Amichai-Hamburger et al. (2002) attempted to relate the Internet "real me" concept (McKenna et al., 2002) to the Extroversion and Neuroticism personality theory (Eysenck & Eysenck, 1975). They found that among participants who were regular users of chat rooms, introverted and neurotic people locate their "real me" on the Internet, while extroverts and nonneurotic people locate their "real me" through traditional social interaction. The social services (e.g., chats, forums, communities) found on the Internet provide an excellent solution for people who experience great difficulty in forming social contacts due to their introverted neurotic personalities. The main reasons for this are the special properties of such services when they are provided on the Internet—for example, anonymity, ability to conceal appearance, ability to control the degree of information revealed in the interaction; and also the ease with which it is possible to find like-minded people. These results are reinforced by the fact that the social anxiety and loneliness variables that McKenna et al. (2002) found as relating to the location of the "real me" on the Internet are highly related to introversion and neuroticism. As Norton et al. (1997) reported, there is a positive relationship between social anxiety and neuroticism and a negative one between loneliness and extroversion.

The concept of the "real me" enables us to further understand the importance of the Internet for certain types of people; for example, those people who find that they express themselves more effectively on the Internet than through the more traditional channels of communication. This implies that for a significant number of people, such as introverts, neurotics, lonely people, and people with social anxiety, the Internet may become a very significant part of their lives and per-haps the only one in which they truly express themselves. We suggest, however, that the Rogerian (1961) concept of the "true self" be treated with caution. This concept refers to the existence of a self that is largely unknown to its host, while the phenomenon found on the Internet is for the most part related to people who feel that it is however, safe to reveal their intimate secrets to a stranger. It is possible to predict that in fact surfers may discover their true self online, should they find themselves in optimal conditions for the building of a therapeutic environment. According to Rogers this would comprise a well-protected Internet environment in which only surfers who are warm and sensitive are present.

The development of the Internet in recent years has led to a need to further adapt the "real me" concept (and questionnaire). This is particularly pertinent because of increasing the prominence of social networking sites. The questions in the "real me" questionnaire ask about anonymous net environments; for example, question 4 relates to the extent to which a respondent's family and friends would be surprised, were they to read his or her Internet email and news group postings. This is clearly applicable to a net where the surfer is unidentified, and unsuited to the social net-work environment where surfers frequently interact with people they know offline. At first sight, it would seem that the "real me" concept is not applicable to the social networking sites, since intuitively it does not make sense that people will feel more comfortable to express their intimate information in an online environment where people seem to be totally exposed. However, it seems that on social networking sites, many people do expose themselves in ways that they would not do offline. It would appear that the culture of social networking sites encourage and normalize such behavior. Thus, although they are identified, it is common to find people exposing more intimate parts of themselves and their lives on social networking sites (Mallan, 2009). What is unclear, however, is whether extroverts allow themselves more self exposure on the identified social net-working sites in comparison to introverts who are more likely to open up on the Internet, but allow themselves to do so in anonymous environments. This is a question that should be studied carefully in future research.

Addiction

The Internet enables people with social inhibitions to experience significant empowerment. However, some people become addicted to the Internet, and this may lead them to transfer most, if not all of their social and interpersonal connections to the Internet. Young (1996, 1998) explained that Internet addiction is characterized by excessive overuse of the Internet which leads to a disruption in sleep patterns, work productivity, daily routines, and social life. This dependence on Internet activities may lead such people to experience significant difficulties in their offline daily lives (see Young, 1998; also Widyanto & McMurran, 2004).

Many personality characteristics have been linked to online addiction, Shotton (1991) found that introversion and sensation seeking was related with heavy computer use, Loytsker and Aiello (1997) found massive computer use relating to a tendency to boredom, self-consciousness, loneliness, and social anxiety. Amichai-Hamburger and Ben-Artzi (2003) found that extroversion was negatively related, and neuroticism positively related, to the use of online social sites for women. Caplan (2003) found that lonely individuals may develop a preference for online social interaction which can lead to problematic Internet use. Erwin, Turk, Heimberg, Fresco, & Hantula (2004) found that socially anxious individuals spent the most time online. Chak and Leung (2004) found that shyness was related to Internet addiction—the shyer the individual, the higher his or her tendency to become addicted to the net. Such overusers and addicts of cyberspace were characterized as being more neurotic and less extroverted, more socially anxious and emotionally lonely, than nonaddicts. In addition, they gained greater support from Internet social networks than average Internet users (Hardie & Yi, 2007). Further analysis revealed that neuroticism and the individual perception of social support offered by online social networks were significant predictors of excessive Internet use (Hardie & Yi, 2007). Similarly, Anolli et al. (2005), in their investigation of personality types and Internet and chat room use, found that surfers with higher scorers of extroversion, recruited through chat rooms, tended to spend less time online, in terms of hours spent per week, and used chat significantly less than surfers with lower scores. Internet addiction is a very broad umbrella term. It may well be more useful to review specific Internet addictions, for example, addictions associated with chat, information, sex, and so on. To engage in depth with this problem and attempt to counter these behaviors, it is first necessary to gain a full understanding of the relationship between addiction to specific services and specific personality characteristics. It seems to us that the link between social inhibitions and the corresponding different personality theories, may be seen as correlated to symptoms of addiction especially in case of extreme levels of social inhibition.

Moving from Online to Offline

The Internet has been shown to be a powerful empowerment tool for people with social inhibitions. The question then arises as to whether such people transfer the skills gained from this empowerment to their offline social interactions, and whether this may lead them to transfer online relationships from the online domain to the offline arena. It seems that people who do not suffer from social inhibitions integrate the offline and online worlds and move between them smoothly, giving the matter little thought (Pew Internet & American Life Project, 2005). However, for socially inhibited people who recreate themselves in the online world and in many cases do so by utilizing the anonymity and lack of physical exposure this environment creates, the transfer from online to offline might be very challenging. Gollwitzer (1986) argued that a higher level of completeness is reached by people when their identity-relevant activities are noted by a social audience. Developing this idea, McKenna et al. (2002) suggested that people who find it easier to build online relationships will strive to move those significant relationships outside of the net, so as to make them a social reality. McKenna and her colleagues (2002) believe that the Internet psychological environment is likely to have a major impact on online relationships since: (1) the anonymity of the Internet significantly reduces the risks of self-disclosure; (2) there is a high probability that the relationship will become stable in the long run and so will be able to transfer to a successful offline relationship should the two sides decide to meet (McKenna et al., 2002). It is important to bear in mind that the process should be gradual, particularly as people with social inhibitions are likely to feel greater anxiety towards a FtF interaction than others would. Orgad (2007) discusses relationships that moved from online to offline and consequently lost their components of openness and self-disclosure. She points out that this is likely to be due to the loss of anonymity and control over the interaction. McKenna et al. (2002) suggested that the processes of moving from online to offline is possible and is common among homosexuals and people with extreme political orientations. They find their group online, and slowly through their interaction with like-minded others, build their self-confidence. This reaches a stage where they feel strong enough to face the offline world and state their tendency (McKenna et al, 2002).

We predict this process is applicable to that of most people with social inhibitions. The process may be very lengthy, but eventually it is likely to reach the stage where people with social inhibitions will find the courage to transfer an online relationship to the offline world and also to utilize the social skills developed online. However, for some people, even though they may wish to use their skills offline, this social self-efficacy, newly acquired through the net, may be confined there and they will feel unable to generalize it beyond the borders of cyberspace. This may happen particularly among people suffering from an extreme form of social anxiety, for whom the transition from an Internet connection to an offline association might be too great a leap.

Amichai-Hamburger and Furnham (2007) suggest that the Internet supplies a learning environment that may be structured to enable people to learn how to transfer their new communication skills from the net to a real-life, FtF interaction. In their paper Amichai-Hamburger and Furnham (2007) offer a model that can serve the population of extremely socially anxious individuals who are particularly prone to generalize their Internet interpersonal skills inwards; that is, to use them widely and exclusively in virtual communication. This model, advocates an exceptionally gradual process to help individuals to begin to loosen the control they feel on the Internet and so equip themselves to cope with the relative loss of control in an offline situation. Their suggested model offers four steps: (1) communicating by text only; (2) communicating by text and image; (3) communicating by video; and lastly (4) FtF interaction. Amichai-Hamburger and Furnham (2007) argue that extremely socially anxious people may be particularly helped by this model, due to the moderate ascent in the interpersonal communication richness it suggests. This process demonstrates the power of the Internet, not only as a supplier of a secure environment, but as one that provides tools to create a process of change from social anxiety to secure social relationships.

Last Word

This chapter has painted a rich and diverse picture of the Internet as a social arena. It has shown how the Internet serves as a compensatory environment for the surfer with social inhibitions mainly in anonymous environments, but also in identified ones. There is no doubt that by helping people with social inhibitions to express themselves and make friends, the Internet empowers them significantly.

It is now the time to reinforce the existing line of research into personality and Internet use by further exploring personality theories and how they interact with the different Internet possibilities and how this interaction affects their well-being. In 2002, Amichai-Hamburger (2002) suggested that designers should harness such research and start to devise an Internet that has a more positive influence on our well-being. It may take some years until our knowledge of the potential of the Internet to promote well-being will reach an optimal stage. Nevertheless when we consider the immense progress the Internet has made since its beginnings, there is no doubt that the vision of building a net that will have a better impact on our psychological well-being can become a reality.

References

Alonzo, M., & Aiken, M. (2004). Flaming in electronic communication. *Decision Support Systems, 36*(3), 205–338.

Amichai-Hamburger, Y. (2002). Internet and personality. *Computers in Human Behavior, 18*, 1–10.

Amichai-Hamburger, Y. (2005). Personality and the internet. In Y. Amichai-Hamburger (Ed.), *The social net: Human behavior in cyberspace* (pp. 27–55). New York, NY: Oxford University Press.

Amichai-Hamburger, Y. (2008). Potential and promise of online volunteering. *Computers in Human Behavior, 24*, 544–562.

Amichai-Hamburger, Y. (2012). Reducing intergroup conflict and promoting intergroup harmony in the digital age. In H. Giles (Ed.), *The handbook of intergroup communication* (pp. 181–193). New York, NY: Routledge.

Amichai-Hamburger, Y., & Ben-Artzi, E. (2003). Loneliness and internet use. *Computers in Human Behavior, 19*, 71–80.

Amichai-Hamburger, Y., Fine, A., & Goldstein, A. (2004). The impact of internet interactivity and need for closure on consumer preference. *Computers in Human Behavior, 20*, 103–117.

Amichai-Hamburger, Y., & Furnham, A. (2007). The positive net. *Computers in Human Behavior, 23*, 1033–1045.

Amichai-Hamburger, Y., Kaplan, H., & Dorpatcheon, N. (2008). Click to the past: The impact of extroversion by users of nostalgic website on the use of internet social services. *Computers in Human Behavior, 24*, 1907–1912.

Amichai-Hamburger, Y., & Kinar, O. (2007). The effects of need for cognition on internet use. *Computers in Human Behavior, 23*, 880–891.

Amichai-Hamburger, Y., & Vinitzky, G. (2010). Social network use and personality. *Computers in Human Behavior, 26*, 1289–1295.

Amichai-Hamburger, Y., Wainapel, G., & Fox, S. (2002). On the internet no one knows I'm an introvert: Extroversion, neuroticism, and Internet interaction. *CyberPsychology & Behavior, 5*, 125–128.

Anolli, L., Villani, D., & Riva, G. (2005). Personality of people using chat: An on-line research. *Cyberpsychology & Behavior, 8*, 89–95.

Bailenson, J. N., & Beall, A. C. (2006). Transformed social interaction: Exploring the digital plasticity of avatars. In R. Schroeder, & A. Axelsson (Eds.), *Avatars at work and play: Collaboration and interaction in shared virtual environments* (pp. 1–16). New York, NY: Springer-Verlag.

Bargh, J., & McKenna, K. A. (2004). The internet and social life. *Annual Review of Psychology, 55*, 573–590.

Ben-Ze'ev, A. (2005). "Detattachment": The unique nature of online romantic relationships. In Y. Amichai-Hamburger (Ed.), *The social net: Understanding human behavior in cyberspace* (pp. 115–138). New York, NY: Oxford University Press.

Blair, J. (2006). A computer and internet future: Enabling inclusion? *Learning Disability Practice, 9*(9), 32–37.

Bumgarner, B. A. (2007). You have been poked: Exploring the uses and gratifications of Facebook among emerging adults. *First Monday, 12*(11–15). Retrieved from http://firstmonday.org/htbin/cgiwrap/bin/ojs/index.php/fm/article/view/2026/1897

Caplan, S. E. (2003). Preference for online social interaction: A theory of problematic Internet use and psychosocial well-being. *Communication Research*, *30*, 625–648.

Chak, K., & Leung. L. (2004). Shyness and locus of control as predictors of internet addiction and internet use. *CyberPsychology & Behavior*, *7*(5), 559–570.

Cialdini, R. B. (1984). *Influence*. New York, NY: Quill.

Cooper, A., & Sportolari, L. (1997). Romance in cyberspace: Understanding online attraction. *Journal of Sex Education and Therapy*, *22*(1), 7–14.

Dion, K., Berscheid, E., & Walster E. (1972). What is beautiful is good. *Journal of Personality and Social Pyschology*, *24*(3), 285–290.

Douglas, K. M., & McGarty, C. (2002). Internet identifiability and beyond: A model of the effects of the identifiability on communicative behavior. *Group Dynamics*, *6*, 17–26.

Dunn, R. A., & Guadagno, R. E. (2012). My avatar and me? Gender and personality predictors of avatar-self-discrepancy. *Computers in Human Behavior*, *28*, 97–106.

Ehmke, C., and Wilson, S. (2007). Identifying web usability problems from eye-tracking data. *People and Computers XXI: HCI... but not as we know it. Proceedings of HCI 2007* (pp. 119–128). Lancaster, UK: University of Lancaster.

Erwin, B. A., Turk, C. L., Heimberg, R. G., Fresco, D. M., & Hantula, D. A. (2004). The Internet: Home to a severe population of individuals with social anxiety disorder. *Journal of Anxiety Disorders*, *18*, 629–646.

Eysenck, H. J., & Eysenck, S. E. G. (1975). *Manual: Eysenck personality inventory*. San Diego, CA: Educational and Industrial Testing Service.

Gerson, M. J. (2011). Cyberspace betrayal: Attachment in an era of virtual connection. *Journal of Family Psychotherapy*, *22*(1), 148–156.

Gollwitzer, P. M. (1986). Striving for specific identities: The social reality of self-symbolizing. In R. Baumeister (Ed.), *Public self and private self* (pp. 143–159). New York, NY: Springer-Verlag.

Grimmelmann, J. (2009). Saving Facebook. *Iowa Law Review*, *94*, 1137–1206.

Guadagno, R. E., Okdie, B. M., & Eno, C. A. (2008). Who blogs? Personality predictors of blogging. *Computers in Human Behavior*, *24*, 1993–2004.

Hamburger, Y. A., & Ben-Artzi, E. (2000). The relationship between extraversion and neuroticism and the different uses of the internet. *Computers in Human Behavior*, *16*, 441–449.

Hancock, J. T., & Dunham, P. J. (2001). Impression formation in computer-mediated communication revisited: An analysis of the breadth and intensity of impressions. *Communication Research*, *28*, 325–347.

Hardie, E., & Yi, M. (2007). Excessive internet use: The role of personality, loneliness and social support networks in internet addiction. *Australian Journal of Emerging Technologies and Society*, *5*(1), 34–47.

Hatfield, E., & Sprecher, S. (1986). *Mirror, mirror: The importance of looks in everyday life*. Albany, NY: SUNY Press.

Herring, S. C., Scheidt, L. A., Wright, E., & Bonus, S. (2005). Weblogs as a bridging genre. *Information, Technology, & People*, *18*(22), 142–171.

Hoffman, D. L., Novak, T. P., & Schlosser, A. E. (2003). Locus of control, web use, and consumer attitudes toward internet regulation. *Journal of Public Policy & Marketing*, *22*(1), 41–57.

Huffaker, D. (2004). The educated blogger: Using weblogs to promote literacy in the classroom. *First Monday*, *9*(6). Retrieved from http://firstmonday.org/htbin/cgiwrap/bin/ojs/index.php/fm/article/view/1156/1076

Jiang, L. C., Bazarova, N., & Hancock, J. T. (2011). The disclosure-intimacy link in computer-mediated communication: An attributional extension of the hyperpersonal model. *Human Communication Research*, *37*, 58–77.

Joinson, A. (1998). Causes and implications of disinhibited behavior on the internet. In J. Gackenback (Ed.), *Psychology and the internet: Intrapersonal, interpersonal, and transpersonal implications* (pp. 43–60). San Diego, CA: Academic Press.

Joinson, A. (2001). Self-disclosure in computer-mediated communication: The role of self-awareness and visual anonymity. *European Journal Social Psychology, 31*, 177–192.

Jung, J. M., Min, K. S., & Kellaris, J. (2011). The games people play: How the entertainment value of online ads helps or harms persuasion. *Psychology & Marketing, 28*(7), 661–681.

Kinar, O., & Amichai-Hamburger, Y. (2008). The effects of need for cognition on internet use revisited. *Computers in Human Behavior, 24*, 361–371.

Kinzie, M. B., Cohn, W. F., Julian, M. F., & Knaus, W. A. (2002). A user-centered model for web site design: Needs assessment, user interface design, and rapid prototyping. *Journal of the American Medical Informatics Association, 9*(4), 320–330.

Kraut, R., Keisler, S., Boneva, B., Cummings, J., Helgeson, V., & Crawford, A. (2002). Internet paradox revisited. *Journal of Social Issues, 58*, 49–74.

Lawson-Borders, G., & Kirk, R. (2005). Blogs in campaign communication. *American Behavioral Scientist, 49*(4), 548–559.

Lei, L., & Wu, Y. (2007). Adolescents' paternal attachment and internet use. *CyberPsychology & Behavior, 10*, 633–639.

López-Bonilla, J. M., & López-Bonilla, L. M. (2010). Sensation seeking and the use of the internet. *Social Science Computer Review, 28*(2), 177–193.

Loytsker, J., & Aiello, J. R. (1997). *Internet addiction and its personality correlates.* Paper presented at the annual meeting of the American Psychological Association, Chicago, IL.

Lu, H. Y. (2008). Sensation-seeking, internet dependency, and online interpersonal deception. *CyberPsychology & Behavior, 11*(2), 227–231.

Malamuth, N., Linz, D., & Yao, M. (2005). The internet and aggression: Motivation, disinhibitory and opportunity aspects. In Y. Amichai-Hamburger (Ed.), *The social net: Understanding human behavior in cyberspace* (pp. 163–190). Oxford, UK: Oxford University Press.

Maldonado, G. J., Mora, M., Garcia, S., & Edipo, P. (2001). Personality, sex and computer communication mediated through the Internet. *Anuario de Psicologia, 32*, 51–62.

Mallan, K. M. (2009). Look at me! Look at me! Self-representation and self-exposure through online networks. *Digital Culture and Education, 1*(1), 51–56.

Maslow, A. (1971). *Farther Reaches of Human Nature.* New York, NY: Viking.

McKenna, K. Y., & Bargh, J. A. (1998). Coming out in the age of the internet: Identity "demarginalization" through virtual group participation. *Journal of Personality and Social Psychology, 75*(3), 681–694.

McKenna, K. Y. A., & Bargh, J. A. (2000). Plan 9 from cyberspace: The implications of the Internet for personality and social psychology. *Personality and Social Psychology Review, 4*, 57–75.

McKenna, K. Y. A., Green, A. S., & Gleason, M. J. (2002). Relationship formation on the internet: What's the big attraction? *Journal of Social Issues, 58*, 9–32.

Nilsson, C., Skär, L., & Söderberg, S. (2010). Swedish District Nurses' experiences on the use of information and communication technology for supporting people with serious chronic illness living at home—a case study. *Scandinavian Journal of Caring Sciences. Empirical Studies, 24*, 259–265.

Nimrod, G. (2010). The fun culture in seniors' online communities. *The Gerontologist, 51*(2), 226–237.

Norton, G. R., Hewitt, P. L., McLeod, L., & Cox, B. J. (1997). Personality factors associated with generalized and circumscribed social anxiety. *Personality and Individual Differences, 21*, 655–700.

Ó Baoill, A. (2004). Weblogs and the public sphere. In L. J. Gurak, S. Antonijevic, L. Johnson, C. Ratliff, & J. Reyman (Eds.), Into the blogosphere: Rhetoric, community, and culture of weblogs. Retrieved January 4, 2012 from http://blog.lib.umn.edu/blogosphere/weblogs_and_the_public_sphere.html

Orgad, S. (2007). Interrelations between "online" and "offline": Questions, issues and implications. In: R. Mansell, C. Avgerou, D. Quah, & R. Silverstone (Eds.), *Oxford handbook of information and communication technologies* (pp. 514–537). Oxford, UK: Oxford University Press.

Peluchette, J., & Karl, K. (2010). Examining students' intended image on Facebook: "What were they thinking?!" *Journal of Education for Business*, *85*(1), 30–37.

Pervin, L. A. (1993). *Personality: Theory and research*. New York, NY: John Wiley & Sons.

Peter, J., Valkenburg, P., & Schouten, A. (2005). Developing a model of adolescent friendship formation on the internet. *CyberPsychology & Behavior*, *8*, 423–430.

Pew Internet & American Life Project. (2005). Demographics of internet users. Washington, DC: Pew Internet & American Life Project. Retrieved from http://www.pewinternet.org/Trend-Data-(Adults)/Whos-Online.aspx.

Rains, S. A. (2007). The impact of anonymity on perceptions of source credibility and influence in computer-mediated group communication; a test of two competing hypotheses. *Communication Research*, *34*(1), 100–125.

Riordan, M. A., & Kreuz, R. J. (2010). Emotion encoding and interpretation in computer-mediated communication: Reasons for use. *Computers in Human Behavior*, *26*, 1667–1673.

Riva, G. (2002). The sociocognitive psychology of computer-mediated communication: The present and future of technology-based interactions. *Cyberpsychology & Behavior*, *5*(6), 581–598.

Rogers, C. (1961). *On becoming a person*. Boston, MA: Houghton Mifflin.

Shotton, M. (1991). The costs and benefits of computer addiction. *Behaviour and Information Technology*, *10*, 219–230.

Swickert, R. J., Hittner, J. B., Harris, J. L., & Herring, J. A. (2002). Relationships among internet use, personality and social support. *Computers in Human Behavior*, *18*(4), 437–451.

Tajfel, H., & Turner, J. C. (1986). An integrative theory of intergroup conflict. In S. Orchel, & W. Austin (Eds.), *Psychology of intergroup relations* (pp. 2–24). Chicago, IL: Nelson-Hall.

The World Internet Project. (2010). *World Internet Project Report 2010*. Los Angeles, CA: USC Annenberg school center for the digital future.

Thorndike, E. L. (1920). A constant error on psychological rating. *Journal of Applied Psychology*, *IV*, 25–29.

Tidwell, L. C., & Walther, J. B. (2002). Computer-mediated communication effects on disclosure, impressions, and interpersonal evaluations: Getting to know one another a bit at a time. *Human Communication Research*, *28*, 317–348.

Turkle, S. (1995). *Life on the screen: Identity in the age of the internet*. New York, NY: Simon and Schuster.

Valkenburg, P. M., & Peter, J. (2009). The effects of instant messaging on the quality of adolescents' existing friendships: A longitudinal study. *Journal of Communication*, *59*, 79–97.

Wallace, A. (1999). *The psychology of the internet*. New York, NY: Cambridge University Press.

Warr, W. A. (2008). Social software: Fun and games, or business tools? *Journal of Information Science*, *34*(4), 591–604.

Weisskirch, R. S., & Delevi, R. (2011). "Sexting" and adult romantic attachment. *Computers in Human Behavior*, *27*, 1697–1701.

Weibel, D., Wissmath, B., & Mast, F. W. (2010). Immersion in mediated environments: The role of personality traits. *CyberPsychology Behavior & Social Networking*, *13*(3), 251–256.

Widyanto, L., & McMurran, M. (2004). The psychometric properties of the internet addiction test. *CyberPsychology & Behavior*, *7*, 443–450.

Wiggins, A. (2007). Data driven design: Using web analytics to improve information architectures. In *Proceedings of the ASIST Information Architecture Summit 2007*. Las Vegas, NV, 22–26 March, 2007.

World Internet Project. (2010). The 2010 World Internet Project report. Los Angeles, CA: USC Annenberg School Center for the Digital Future. Retrieved April 2, 2012 from http://www.digitalcenter.org/pages/site_content.asp?intGlobalId=42

Xie, B. (2007). Using the Internet for offline relationship formation. *Social Science Computer Review, 25,* 396–404.

Yang, H., & Lai, C. (2010). Motivations of Wikipedia content contributors. *Computers in Human Behavior, 26,* 1377–1383.

Youn, S., & Lee, M. (2002). Profiling adult electronic game players and buyers. In *Proceedings of the 2002 Conference of the American Academy of Advertising* (pp. 82–83). Jacksonville, Florida, 22–24 March.

Young, K. (1996). Internet addiction: The emergence of a new clinical disorder. *CyberPsychology & Behavior, 3,* 237–244.

Young, K. (1998). *Caught in the net.* New York, NY: John Wiley & Sons.

Chapter 2

Netified: Social Cognition in Crowds and Clouds

Yoram M. Kalman, Daphne R. Raban,
and Sheizaf Rafaeli

Introduction

In 2005, the same year the first version of this chapter was published (Rafaeli, Raban, & Kalman, 2005), Thomas Friedman, the New York Times columnist, published a cutting-edge bestseller titled *The World is Flat*. While the book did discuss the contribution of technology to globalization, as Mr Friedman himself is quoted: "When I wrote 'The World is Flat,' Facebook didn't exist, Twitter was a sound, 4G was a parking space, applications were what you sent to college, and Skype, for most people, was a typo" (Travers, 2011). Social technologies were absent from this award-winning book. The recent eruption of technologies that cater to our social needs is the focus of the present chapter. This upsurge followed several decades of slow and incremental changes, but the cumulative impact on cognition and on society is significant.

While the early years of the Internet were about connecting documents by hypertext or connecting web sites and information resources by links, recent years were about linking the digital representations of people in a variety of ways. This social web portrays our social ties, activities, and interests and has substantial consequences regarding social cognition. Technological systems that until recently were defined by technical layers such as the Open Systems Interconnection model (Bauer & Patrick, 2004), developed an additional, social, layer. This social component that is now integrated into the technological systems is described by Rainie and Wellman (2012) as "The new social operating system." The complex structure of this layer and its evolution, directions, and societal consequences are the topic of this chapter.

Intensive use of the Internet during the 1990s for the purpose of interacting gave way to the next level of interaction which is collaboration. Now famous collaboration technologies such as wikis and blogs demonstrated the importance of social interaction around knowledge creation and led to the rapid development of the so-called Web 2.0 applications (O'Reilly, 2007). These are platforms that host content provided by users, where technology is a host to social and intellectual activity. Online social platforms catalyzed the process of netification in which thoughts, conversations, creativity, and relationships materialize on network applications where they persist, as well as await research.

Two important concepts are becoming an integral part of netified social cognition: The crowd, and the cloud. Until recently a crowd referred to many (physical) bodies coming together. However, on the web it is redefined as networked social cognition, bringing together the minds and creativity of many people. The cloud describes large amounts of information (e.g., that crowds create) which can now be aggregated and made accessible anytime and anywhere, through a variety of devices, both mobile and stationary. Wikipedia exemplifies the crowd and the cloud as the product of many minds working together on an intangible resource stored in the cloud and accessible all over the world, and fusing cultural capital with social capital. The two concepts are interrelated, and an understanding of their relationship to netified social cognition is one goal of this paper.

Two major streams of contemporary thought, utopian and dystopian, describe the impact of notification on more and more aspects of our life, on our cognition, and our society (Fisher & Wright, 2001; Sudweeks, McLaughlin, & Rafaeli, 1998). Utopians emphasize the new opportunities afforded by technologies which expand the limits of human cognition by offering virtually unlimited memory and processing power, and by expanding the potential of human society by linking people across geographical and cultural distances, by closing socioeconomic gaps, and by making it easier than ever to seamlessly pool the cognitive abilities of enormous numbers of people and achieve societal benefits which are already beginning to unfold.

Dystopians contrast the optimistic claims about the extension of human cognition with claims that these technologies do not expand the human mind but rather act as crutches that eventually make minds lazy, less independent, and less powerful. They counter the optimistic societal predictions by suggesting that the societal benefits these technologies brought about are temporary. For example, it is suggested that the prosperity of online altruistic behavior such as open source and free software, and grand-scale volunteer-based collaborative projects such as Wikipedia, is only a temporary divergence from human nature, and that our self-interested human nature will soon reassert itself in these areas too. Dystopians warn that the same technologies that link us over time and space also isolate us from each other in everyday life, and come at the expense of fundamental relationships such as those we have with close family members and intimate friends. Table 2.1 lists a sample of books whose titles demonstrate the utopian and dystopian points of view.

Table 2.1 Book titles that demonstrate utopian and dystopian viewpoints on netification

Utopian titles	Dystopian titles
The Penguin and the Leviathan: How Cooperation Triumphs over Self-Interest (Benkler, 2011)	*The Shallows: What the Internet is Doing to Our Brains* (Carr, 2011)
Cognitive Surplus: Creativity and Generosity in a Connected Age (Shirky, 2010)	*Alone Together: Why We Expect More From Technology and Less from Each Other* (Turkle, 2011)
Here Comes Everybody: The Power of Organizing Without Organizations (Shirky, 2009)	*The Net Delusion: The Dark Side of Internet Freedom* (Morozov, 2011)
Free: The Future of a Radical Price (Anderson, 2009)	*You Are Not a Gadget: A Manifesto* (Lanier, 2011)
Crowdsourcing: Why the Power of the Crowd Is Driving the Future of Business (Howe, 2008)	*The Cult of the Amateur: How Today's Internet is Killing Our Culture* (Keen, 2007)
Everything Is Miscellaneous: The Power of the New Digital Disorder (Weinberger, 2007)	*Infotopia* (Sunstein, 2006)
The Wealth of Networks: How Social Production Transforms Markets and Freedoms (Benkler, 2006)	*Does IT Matter?* (Carr, 2004)
Wikinomics: How Mass Collaboration Changes Everything (Tapscott & Williams, 2006)	*The Internet on Earth: A Geography of Information* (Kellerman, 2002)
The Wisdom of Crowds (Surowiecki, 2004)	*Silicon Snake Oil* (Clifford, 1996)
Smart Mobs: The Next Social Revolution (Rheingold, 2003)	

The tension between utopian and dystopian approaches raises an interesting challenge: To try and understand when digital technologies help to open our minds and when they lead to the opposite. When do they aid social awareness and when do they offer false hopes? What determines whether they bring us together and enrich our lives, or whether they separate us and strengthen our dependence on the products of consumerist society?

These questions are vital when determining policies: When do we embrace the adoption of novel technologies, and when is such adoption naïve and shortsighted? This chapter attempts to move beyond the dystopia/utopia dichotomy, and explore what research has revealed so far about the relationship between these new technologies and social cognition. Social cognition is the driver of changes at the individual and group level (micro-level) which translate into large societal outcomes when viewed at the macro-level. Moreover, this chapter suggests that the netification of social cognition modified the nature of social cognition in ways that we are only beginning to understand. It is clear that the deluge of books about the promise and perils of social technologies signifies the transition our minds and our society are experiencing. Nevertheless, the books' authors do not agree on the nature of this transition, its causes, and, most importantly, its consequences. In this chapter we aim to explore various aspects of social psychology that relate to netified social cognition. We provide the readers with tools to evaluate these questions about the transition, to understand the interaction between social cognition and the rapidly evolving information and communication technologies, and to draw their own conclusions.

Following an introduction to the concept of social cognition and to the nature of the online social space, we discuss the importance of netified social cognition, and the consequences of the transition of social information into the digital realm. As growing portions of our cognitive and social activities take place online, social cognition itself seems to be altering, and extensive research efforts are made to study the nature of these alterations. We review these efforts and summarize the findings on the perception of self, on the perception of the other online, on online groups, and on the relationship between the individual and the network. We then review research findings on the influence of these changes on work and on leisure, on the division between the private and the public spheres, and on the notions of space and time. We conclude by offering some directions for future research.

Background

In the following we define social cognition and the online social space. We discuss the importance of netified social cognition, and elaborate on the link between social cognition and digital information.

Social Cognition

Social cognition describes the mutual influences between cognition and social life. Cognition is fundamentally influenced by the social environment (Levine, Resnick, & Higgins, 1993). For example, research on social facilitation (Guerin, 2009), social loafing (Forsyth, 2010), social roles, and mental representations (Kunda, 1999) has shown distinct social influences on cognitive abilities and task performance. Social cognition is also about the cognitive underpinnings of social behavior (Devine, Hamilton, & Ostrom, 1994). It studies how social structures and processes are mentally represented, and how social interaction is important for the development and practice of cognition. In short, social cognition research explores the influence of the social environment on cognition, and of cognition on social behavior.

Social cognition views individuals as being engaged most of the time in information processing. Information is encoded from a social context, is interpreted, elaborated, evaluated, inferred, and attributed. Processed information, or knowledge, is later used in judgment processes and for guiding behavior. Judgment and behavior need not be the result of a thorough mental process. Instead, judgment and behavior can be the result of short-cuts known as heuristics. Social cognition draws from both social and cognitive psychology. It deals with how people make sense of themselves and of others (Kunda, 1999). The basic social structures mentioned in the literature describe person traits or perception (Fiske, 1993), such as attitudes, beliefs, and stereotypes.

The main social processes in social cognition research have been attribution, attitude change, impression formation, social comparison, decision-making, and social construction of reality (Fulk, 1993). Social cognition is not limited to the study of individual cognition and how it is affected by the social environment. Social cognition impacts the way in which individuals and cultures perceive, define, and interpret media in general, and in our special case, the online social space. The discussion of social cognition in this chapter extends beyond the traditional boundaries of social cognition research and includes interfaces between the social and the cognitive that occur in the online social space. The Social Net is a digital space where the cognitive and social meet. This meeting is central to recent developments in this net. Consequently, our discussion of netified social cognition includes general aspects of social psychology.

The Online Social Space

The computer-mediated social space is characterized variously. For example, Slater (2002) proposes four properties which describe the online environment as a space in its own right, stressing that people do not have to reveal the offline cues used for social cognition such as age, sex, and race. This framing emphasizes that online identity can be very different than offline identity. Another analytical framework for the virtual social space claims that the interesting dimensions for Internet research include hypertextuality, synchronicity, topology, history, and interactivity (Newhagen & Rafaeli, 1996). While these constructs sound rooted in an engineering culture, they are behavioral and perceptual in nature. Despite the many differences between the various characterizations of the online social space, most frameworks imply that the online communication environment has qualities of its own. We suggest that the character of the online social space is less in the constraints it places, and perhaps more in the opportunities it raises. Rather than gauging, as is too often done, the network against an external standard set by face-to-face communication, it is more fruitful and interesting to understand the parameters of communication, perception, and thought that are specific to networked situations.

Netification of Social Cognition

Besides being an interesting and novel area for research, why is it important to study and understand social cognition in networked contexts? The answer is that the online environment defines new loci, within which new rules for social behavior may be defined. The spatial and temporal limitations on social horizons may be lifted or re-shaped. Upper limits for effective group size may be rewritten. Distance, location, and co-presence take on new meanings (Kanai, Bahrami, Roylance, & Rees, 2011). The online space affords play, frivolity, and experimentation even in serious contexts (Rafaeli, 1986). People may experiment with their own social cognition and that of others when they assume different personalities online, when they introduce themselves by chosen nicknames, perhaps forfeiting age, gender, or other cues. Essentially "first impressions" are formed over and over again for the same person, and shape that person's social behavior online. To paraphrase a famous quip, online you *do* get a second chance to make a first impression.

The overwhelmingly social nature of web services places even more weight on the importance of social cognition. The implementation of cloud computing raises new questions regarding the blurring borders between private information and collaborative spaces: How do people perceive others in the cloud? How is information perceived in the cloud?

Online social cognition is likely to be a dynamic construct subject to different game rules. Educational, managerial, regulatory, and legal systems are being crafted to deal with new realities made possible by the new online social environments. Users of social web spaces should consider the degree of privacy they wish to have, the means for verifying identities of others, and the general code of conduct as part of the tools for preserving the desired ethical behavior. Understanding netified social cognition on its own terms is crucial to the understanding of a rapidly growing segment of human and social life.

Netification describes the digitization of our thoughts, conversations, social ties, and creativity. They are all made explicit online where they also persist as digital artifacts. Netification rises every year—the exact figures vary depending on the source of data. One striking factoid is that almost a quarter of the time people spend online is devoted to social networks where social interaction is a central attraction and motivation for activity (Nielsen Wire, 2011). Over the past few years it seems that considerable development efforts were directed at enhancing social participation by trying to understand online social behavior and support social cognition through a variety of software services collectively referred to as Web 2.0. These are services that provide connectivity between people and a form of information organization. Content is then provided by people through a social process of feedback and interaction. Social processes have become so dominant in the current information landscape that the competition among companies is focused on developing applications that support these social processes. Consequently, it is tempting to present this social aspect as the eighth layer of technology, the social layer (Bauer & Patrick, 2004), on top of the traditional physical and logical layers.

Our earlier chapter on social cognition, published before the ubiquity of social networks, focused on fundamental questions relating to the way that social cognition should be studied and understood in the online space with an emphasis on avoiding technological determinism, and the risks of positing face-to-face communication as the gold standard (Rafaeli et al., 2005). In the current age of ubiquitous computing when we access networked information, peers, friends and family on an ongoing basis and become immersed in connectedness, we ask: What are the new dimensions of social cognition that should be addressed in contemporary research?

It could be argued that the longer time spent online coupled with the social influences that occur naturally in these circumstances are conducive toward information cascades, greater uniformity achieved through imitation. Yet, it seems that we are witnessing the opposite: unprecedented creativity and intensive use of social technologies for shedding light on past and current events as reported, for example, in Wikileaks or Wikipedia and in social networks by self-appointed civilian reporters in areas of unrest worldwide. While being part of an ever-increasing social network, people need to find and express their individuality and uniqueness, seeking the attention of their close circles as well as the public at large.

Social cognition is important in searching for information and organizing our knowledge. For example, it has been claimed that personalization by search algorithms confines our cognition to the limits envisioned by search software developers, a phenomenon branded "the filter bubble" (Pariser, 2011). Cynics have said that a squirrel dying in a person's front yard is more interesting to this person than larger current news events and commentary. Others suggest that communities have shifted to a "glocalized" state, where both local and global connections are important (Wellman, 2002) Some bring evidence based on academic research that our brain is changing, an actual change in cognitive abilities, due to our reliance on Google's search services (Carr, 2011; Sparrow, Liu, & Wegner, 2011). We believe this is not a zero sum game. Perhaps the poor squirrel is of interest, but who's to say that it is more interesting than other news? People may devote attention to both the small and the large picture of events. Our brain may start to exhibit a new pattern due to web surfing (Sparrow et al., 2011), but is it a reduced state of cognition? Many contemporary thinkers, such as the authors of the books in Table 2.1's left column, agree that while there are dangers and pitfalls, the overall outcome of our online presence is strongly favorable. In fact, we ask: Is it inevitable? Once the genie is out of the bottle, once information is digital and networked, is it possible to stop its rapid diffusion?

Human cognition and social interaction are the "secret sauce" that morphs the web from a network of networks governed by servers and routers to a living locale where events take place, are noticed, and disseminated, changing shape and influencing individuals, groups, and societies. The heart of online activity is not in the vastness of the infrastructure, rather, it is in the attraction it holds for people who spend more time online every year, communicating, innovating, entertaining and more.

The Social Role of Information

Information bonds people online (Seely Brown & Duguid, 2000). As stated above, social cognition views individuals as being engaged most of the time in information processing. If information is all that is needed to form a social structure, then a good library should suffice. How is the web different from a large library? Conversation, support, disagreement, and advice are all forms of information exchanged among people. They convey knowledge and emotion, the basic elements of cognition. The ubiquity and ease of use of the network make it a natural place for developing social technologies.

How does information become so contagious (Gleick, 2011), fascinating people, connecting them, and attracting them to take an active part in the global online environment? For the current discussion we shall define anything that can be digitized as information. This broad definition includes, for example, any piece of writing, photography, video, audio, data, or software. Considering the example of a piano, information related to it could be a photograph of the piano, a video of it being played, an audio recording of the music produced by the piano, software or a file that details its dimensions and technical specifications, etc. All of these could take on a digital format, be recorded on digital media such as a CD-ROM, and could be transferred over digital communication lines such as the Internet. On the other hand, the materials the piano is made from such as wood, metal, or string could not be digitized nor sent via the Internet. As an aside we will note that with the advent of nanotechnology and molecular biology, even the line that separates matter from information is blurring (N. Clark, 1998; Kearnes, 2008).

As products, various digital goods may seem visually different; however, inspecting them at the fundamental level of bits reveals a great deal of commonality. Digitization of information has several fundamental cultural, economic and social implications. Our focus is on the social implications. The following points highlight this aspect.

In the authors' view, human thought and creativity beget information; therefore, information is intriguing and it serves as cultural glue, be it via reading, listening, speaking, or reviewing. The motivation to think and to create can be extrinsic, as it often is in the workplace. More importantly, intrinsic motivation activates creativity and the need to review and refine ideas generates social interaction which is essential in the process. Engagement with information is a form of social activity, even if often it is indirect, and it feeds back into further social processes such as discussion, deliberation, and invention. Information is at the center of attention of ever increasing parts of the economy and of society.

Information is difficult to contain and protect: It can easily be copied. When we find something we like we often keep a copy for the purpose of later reuse or reference. This aids in the spread of knowledge. Realizing the value contained in such copies people often actively seek others who provide information which is useful or inspirational to them. Digital copies are identical to the digital originals, meaning there is no loss of quality in the act of sharing. In addition, ownership is not diminished by sharing. To the contrary: Often information gains value by becoming wide-spread thanks to positive externalities. People perceive this netified value in the process of acquiring and further communicating information.

Information can be reinvented. Taking the copied information, adding to it, changing it, and creating something new from it is a form of recognition of other people's information creations and at the same time it is a form of creativity. Reinvention is one of the catalysts of diffusion and acceptance of innovations, in itself a social process (Shifman & Thelwall, 2009).

Information is the raw material of more information. Standing on the shoulders of giants has long become a cliché. Thanks to this cyclical attribute people always seek information by reading, by computerized retrieval methods, and by offline or online social processes, such as following interesting or authoritative others.

Information is readily available via a wide assortment of devices. Many in the developed world have access to a multitude of devices: a desktop computer, a laptop computer, a tablet computer, a mobile telephone. Each of these devices fosters interactivity. It enables contacting others, sending them a variety of messages, and receiving responses. Device ubiquity turns the devices into an integral part of any work or leisure activity. Device interactivity has long surpassed the concept of interactivity with a database. Consumers expect interaction with friends, peers, and complete strangers via each existing or new device.

The value of information is not correlated with quantity. Value relates to time, ubiquity, and, significantly, to personal perceptions and cultural norms. Traditional economic notions of scarcity as a source of value are beginning to fade in the context of information. Information delivers a representation of one person or group which is then subjectively perceived by another. Representation can be through a crafted profile such as in social networks, or derived from conversations and from a person's writings. Impressions and perceptions are based on abundant information especially from informal sources and social networks. It would be intriguing to research how social cognition is formed from bits of information which are widely scattered. In fact, while information is abundantly available, its lack of structure and tendency to overload pose a challenge for the formation of impression, and allow for multiple impressions to be made.

Digital information is now one of the most important forms through which we interact with our surrounding. This influences our perception of self, the other, of groups and even of the computer and the network. In the next section we will review the current research on these topics.

The Netification of Individuals and Groups

This section reviews research findings on online social cognition. It begins at the level of the individual, discussing both self-presentation as well as self-perception. It then expands to the social cognition of others and of groups online. We conclude with a discussion of the implications for the study of human–computer interaction (HCI).

The Online Presentation and Perception of Self and Other

Self-perception or self-concept may seem constant. In fact, self-perception is malleable. Social cognition research has identified a variety of selves: self-concept varies in private versus public circumstances, as well as with the different roles or situations we experience. Thus, self-concept is dynamic with attention focused on the context-specific self rather than on one "global" self (Devine et al., 1994). A seminal article by Sherry Turkle (1980) provided computers' and networks' impact on perception of self with a slogan that captured the variability of self-perception, perhaps amplified, by computers and networks. In "Computers as Rorscharch" she says that users project meaning to computerized activities rather than being passive recipients. This sentiment was then echoed in HCI work on user-centered computing (Plaisant & Schneiderman, 2004), and later on user-generated content (Leung, 2009; Van Dijck, 2009) and naturally percolated into the very design of systems and networks. The projected meaning is influenced by a variety of environmental or social effects, in addition to personality of the actor.

The Internet provides numerous opportunities to affect what Goffman would call "the presentation of self" (Donath, 1999; Stone, 2001). The construction of a personal home page, the introduction one is required to make when entering an online forum, the short descriptions many provide as a rite of inclusion into various social software arenas, the constant updates one posts to social networking sites (SNSs), and the profiles one accumulates for oneself willingly or not on a variety of online systems, all have a narcissistic potential (Mehdizadeh, 2009; Ong et al., 2011; Ryan & Xenos, 2011). With the increasing prevalence of SNSs where anonymity is almost nonexistent, online deception become less prevalent than in the past (Zhao, Grasmuck, & Martin, 2008). For more on identity manipulation see Chapter 3 by Segovia and Bailenson in this book.

So far we have discussed the intimate and internal perception of self to "other" oriented cognitions. How is the other perceived online, and what are the cognitive effects of meeting others online? The perception of the "other" online and how the impression of those we interact with online is formed has been a focus of research from the first days of online communication. The initial focus was on the gap between the impressions formed online, and impressions in "real life," with an emphasis on anecdotal cases of fraud and deception. This approach follows a historical pattern of focusing on the sensational, as well as on the faults and deficiencies of a new medium in relation to traditional communication media. This is exemplified in social science research about the first days of telephone and telegraph (Pool, 1983). Much of the early work on the perception of the other online focused on the reduced social cues in comparison to face-to-face communication (Sproull & Kiesler, 1986). The reduced social cues approach highlighted the surprise and disappointment that arose when those who formed the impressions were confronted with "real life." These works concluded that online impression formation is faulty and wrought with stereotypical and prejudiced assumptions used to "fill in the blanks" (Albright, 2001) of the reduced social cues, and terms such as "fluid identities" (Turkle, 1995) were used to warn about the unsound and shifting sands of computer-mediated communication (CMC).

In retrospect it is clear that many of the early works on CMC may have failed to distinguish between the various contexts of online activities. Some popular activities such as MUDs (multiuser dungeons) were purposely structured for "play" purposes wherein impersonation and identity experimentation were the expressed purpose of these settings. Such environments flourished on university campuses among students, close to the eye and attention of researchers. This, too, may have given these contexts some increased salience. No wonder that a "reality check" in such cases reveals that the (generally) young and often experimentally minded people behind the screen names are different than imagined. More recent research approached these questions in a more nuanced manner, and showed that online self-portrayals are important, that these acts of online self-presentation actually influence the construction of self-identity, and that gaps between these portrayals and what others perceive as the truth have significant negative consequences (Boucher, Hancock, & Dunham, 2008; DeAndrea & Walther, 2011).

Research shows that senders sometimes try to optimize their self-presentation by mentioning information they perceive as impressive, while holding back information which is less so (Walther & Burgoon, 1992). This can result in disillusion when eventually a face-to-face meeting occurs, especially in cases when the receiver initially idealizes the sender, "filling in the blanks" with information that tends to be too rosy. This disenchantment received much attention in literature dealing with online dating and online relationships (Turkle, 1995), but is apparent in other online contexts too (Rouse & Haas, 2003) where inaccuracies in the perception of the personality of online "others" are mainly a result of a three important differences between Internet-mediated factors and face-to-face communication: Physical appearance has a less meaningful effect, people may behave differently online than in a face-to-face situation, and that online there is a heightened level of ambiguity due to the lack of vocal inflection and facial expression. In contrast, we wish to point out that before assertions about the inferiority of online versus offline impression formation are generalized, some more basic questions are called for. For example, is the ability to present an idealized self online similar to the ability to idealize one's physical appearance through the choice of clothing, haircut, makeup, accessories, and even plastic surgery? Are humans gradually becoming more skilled at detecting signs of such online attempts, integrating them into the emerging impression, just as they would for an attempt to conceal physical imperfections is interpreted in traditional offline interaction? Is the ambiguity of an online smiley analogous to some extent to the different interpretation a smile can have in an Eastern culture like Japan in comparison to its meaning in a Western country like England? We contend it may be too early in the evolution human online communication to simply conclude that this ability is inferior to face to face.

Research identified differences between these processes online and in traditional settings (Boucher et al., 2008), but these findings do not suggest an inferiority of the online setting. Reeves and Nass (2000, p. 70) point out in their discussion of the "perceptual bandwidth" of computer-mediated communication: "... the assumption that more is always less is misguided. An increase in the breadth and depth of media representations certainly turns up the volume knob on perceptual responses, but greater presence does not translate into greater efficacy or desirability; intensity does not equal quality." The incredible speed of adoption of social web applications suggests that not only is the online environment not inferior to face-to-face, but it fills an important social role. Online activity in general, and social networks specifically, augment more traditional social interactions by filling a variety of work and leisure needs and by maintaining and enhancing the strength of our social ties (Ellison, Steinfield, & Lampe, 2007). Online access, in fact, provides opportunities for continuous social interactions tailored to each person's needs and preferences (Carrasco, Hogan, Wellman, & Miller, 2008).

Once the issue of the superiority of face-to-face over CMC is removed, the questions that arise are questions that focus on aspects of social cognition online, and mainly questions of what influences the way users translate the special social cues of CMC, and especially text-based CMC, into impressions, and what influences these impressions.

Online impression formation is complex and multifaceted, probably not less than offline impression formation. Moreover, impression formation is a continuous process, often based on the combination of information attained over time from a variety of online and offline sources (DeAndrea & Walther, 2011). When evaluating online information, communicators constantly judge the information they receive. For example, online impression formation of members of a SNS could be influenced not only by what they post about themselves but also by what people they are linked with ("friends") say about them, and by the physical appearance of these friends (Walther, Van Der Heide, Kim, Westerman, & Tong, 2008), as well as by the number of friends they are linked to (Tong, Van Der Heide, Langwell, & Walther, 2008). As suggested by the warranting principle, information that is more difficult to manipulate, such as what others say about you, receives precedence over self-descriptions both on SNSs (Walther, Van Der Heide, Hamel, & Shulman, 2009) and on online dating sites (Gibbs, Ellison, & Lai, 2010). Online impression formation is also influenced by the nonverbal cues which are available online. These include chronemic (time related) cues, as well as a host of other CMC cues such as punctuation marks, asterisks, character repetitions, and capitalization (Kalman & Gergle, 2010; Riordan & Kreuz, 2010). For example, chronemic cues such as the time and day and delays in response have been shown to influence impression formation, and to interact with other parameters such as communicator valence and status (Kalman & Rafaeli, 2011; Sheldon, Thomas-Hunt, & Proell, 2006; Walther & Tidwell, 1995).

The findings on the importance and influence of subtle cues on online impression formation provide support for theoretical frameworks such as social information processing (SIP; Walther & Burgoon, 1992) and counter "cues filtered-out" theories (Culnan & Markus, 1987) such as media richness theory which classify various modes of communication as rich or lean in comparison to face-to-face communication (Daft & Lengel, 1986). SIP claims that "... when denied the nonverbal cues available in face to face interaction, communicators substitute the expression of impression-bearing and relational messages into the cues available through the computer-mediated communication. Thus, SIP theory posits that communicators exchange social information through the content, style, and timing of verbal messages on-line" (Walther & Parks, 2002). Despite its enduring theoretical attractiveness, little support for media richness theory was ever collected (El-Shinnawy & Markus, 1997; Kock, 1998). When revisiting media richness theory after more than a quarter century, it seems that that the interpretation of the theory was too simplistic, and that effectiveness is not linked only to the bandwidth of the medium chosen by groups, but rather also to other needs of the group. For example, the theory of media synchronicity (Dennis, Fuller, & Valacich, 2008) looks at the extent to which the medium is synchronized with the recipient's communication needs, and proposes a set of media capabilities that are important to group work.

Groups Online

All social cognitive aspects of interacting with others as well as self-perception are repeated and compounded in online groups. As in the previous sections, questions about the "reality" of online groups are the focus of researchers who place "face-to-face" groups as the benchmark. Only after this question is addressed can we look at the actual way people interact online, perceive the group as an entity, socialize, work, entertain themselves, and learn.

What are online groups and how do they compare with face-to-face groups? Many terms have been used to describe influential Internet-based interactions between several participants, including "virtual communities" (Rheingold, 1993), "virtual teams" (Lipnack & Stamps, 2000) and "virtual groups" (Wallace, 2001). These have evolved into "groups" or "circles" in commercial SNSs such as Facebook and in Google+. Interestingly, we can see how, with time, the qualifiers "online" or "virtual" are dropped, and the groups are simply treated as groups of people that share an online space. In this chapter we will use the generic term online groups.

The tools used by people to congregate online are diverse, and include email-list forums, synchronous chat systems such as Internet relay chat (IRC), asynchronous discussion forums, MUDs and MOOs (MUDs object oriented), Usenet newsgroups, virtual classrooms, web logs, groupware tools, and SNSs. Some of these are very rich, allowing real-time transmission of audio, video, and text, as well as online application sharing, while others are very rudimentary, and based only on the transmission of simple text. People participate in online groups for work, education, and leisure, acquiring, disseminating, and sharing information and knowledge, collaborating, and socializing (Haythornthwaite, 2007; McKenna, 2008; Rheingold, 1993). After discussing research on online groups, we will focus on SNSs such as Facebook, Twitter, and LinkedIn, which have emerged as the dominant form of online socializing in the first decade of the second millennium.

A central focus of research on online groups was on understanding the differences between traditional groups, and online groups. Why do people group online, how effective are online groups, and what influences this effectiveness? How does socialization happen online, and what expresses leadership in online groups? Initially, there was a lot of excitement about the possibilities opened by online groups, with the combination of a widely dispersed but closely-knit community. A good early example is The Well, established in 1985 and described in the book *The Virtual Community* (Rheingold, 1993). At about the same time, virtual communities were contrasted with "real" communities, mourning the damage inflicted by "Technopoly" (Postman, 1993). Nevertheless, it was soon realized that online groups are as "real" as any other group, and are simply different in some aspects from traditional groups. Like any group, online group too are social units in which the participants are interdependent, and behave according to explicit and implicit social norms. Online groups show, just like other groups, both examples of social compensation as well as social loafing, and even effects such as crowding and deindividuation have been documented (Spears, Postmes, Lea, & Wolbert, 2002).

How do people socialize in online groups? Socialization occurs after people join a group. They learn the norms and normative behavior. Socialization is carried out by established members who provide information about the norms of the group to newcomers. Parts of this information are communicated directly and explicitly, while other parts are implicit. In online socialization, explicit information is often communicated through established sources such as a list of frequently asked questions (FAQs), an orientation provided to newcomers, or answers to questions posted by newcomers (Ahuja & Galvin, 2003; Burnett & Bonnici, 2003). The notion of "newbies" (recent new members, and group toleration of their needs) is one of the first set of "social" notions and norms to emerge in online community dynamics (Rheingold, 1993). The need to make such norms explicit is stronger in online forums than in face-to-face communities, and these "meta-discussions" offer a window into the emerging and evolving nature of such norms. Despite the effort to document norms and make them explicit, online groups also have implicit norms, which can only be learned by newcomers through observation of the online behavior of others. Members of the group quite often debate such norms. Burnett and Bonnici (2003) extend Kemper's (1968) observation to online groups by saying that "... the process of newcomers reaching some kind of understanding of a group's implicit norms can be understood as a mechanism of socialization. As newcomers begin to enter into the discussion of a group's norms, they begin to become true participants" (p. 349). The difficulty to deduce implicit information results in newcomers proactively requesting normative information from the group, and the provision of answers to such requests is often an opportunity for established members to take on a role of a "mentor" or "liaison."

An interesting form of online group participation received the somewhat derogatory title "lurking" and was a subject of research at the turn of the millennium. Researchers were concerned with participants who spent most or all of their time observing the group's goings on, without contributing. Lurking was perceived as a problem not only in settings such as online classrooms, where active participation is perceived as essential to achieving the goals of the group. It was also construed as a problem in other communities, who perceived these noncontributing members as freeloaders. This perception gradually changed, partially as a result of research that demonstrated that participation in online groups, such as forum discussions, is not and could not be symmetric.

A small number of participants contribute. A much larger number remain receivers. The reported proportion of lurkers varied from around 90% to around 50% (Katz, 1998; Mason, 1999; Nonnecke & Preece, 2000; Soroka, Jacovi, & Ur, 2003). As research revealed that the reasons for lurking range from concerns for privacy, through respect for others' time and attention limits, to those rooted in personality (Rafaeli, Ravid, & Soroka, 2004), it was also becoming more acceptable not to contribute to every online group one is a part of. The term "lurkers" has not disappeared from the literature, but the attitude towards these members is no longer negative (e.g., Mo & Coulson, 2010), and the perception of these non-contributing members has changed from that of lurkers to that of "the audience" (Marwick & boyd, 2011; Pearson, 2009).

The question of "lurking" is a subset of a larger question about the motivations to contribute to online groups. Anecdotal evidence and informal observation suggest that such prosocial behavior occurs in online groups, perhaps at the same rate as it occurs offline. Social behavior online is, by definition, contingent on perceptions and cognition. Others are instantiated as bits, not atoms. We know that philanthropy, mobilization of social movements, altruism in the form of providing help and individual and group emotional support are all hallmarks of online networks. An interesting model suggested by Preece and Shneiderman (2009) the "reader-to-leader framework" describes how users can progress from passive observers (readers) to contributors, and then further on to collaborators and finally to leaders of online activities. The model applies Preece's concepts of usability and sociability (Preece, 2000). These terms describe two complementary aspects of online groups. Usability focuses on the aspects of the software that allow the participants to "...interact and perform their tasks intuitively and easily. Software with good usability supports rapid learning, high skill retention, low error rates and high productivity. It is consistent, controllable, and predictable, making it pleasant and effective to use" (pp. 26–7). Sociability, on the other hand, is focused on "planning and developing social policies which are understandable and acceptable to members, to support the community's purpose" (p. 26). The reader-to-leader framework details the usability and the sociability factors that might influence each of the four stages of progress from reader to leader, and touch on the many factors, both technical and social, that could influence contributions.

The reader-to-leader framework exemplifies the widening of research on online contributions from a tight focus on the motivations to contribute to online groups, to a much wider scope of questions that attempt to elucidate the mechanisms which can enhance or impair the effectiveness of online contributors. Online contributions are no longer perceived as substitutes to or alternatives for contributions in face to face situations. The success of "crowdsourced" and user-generated content projects such as Wikipedia, open source software development, You Tube, and many more, gives the impression that netified collaboration has the potential to lead to results unimaginable in traditional settings. Surowiecki's *The Wisdom of Crowds* (2004) and Rheingold's *Smart Mobs* (2003) are two of the earliest examples of books that identified the potential of netification to bring together both the minds and the ideas of large numbers of people in ways that have until recently been unimaginable. Yochai Benkler is one of the most prominent voices who suggest that netification unleashed an inborn generosity and tendency to collaborate and contribute to the general good, by dropping the cost of knowledge creation and of knowledge sharing and collaboration (Benkler, 2006, 2011). The discussion on the consequences of these changes on the nature of information and knowledge is only beginning (Carr, 2011; Gleick, 2011).

Human–Computer Interaction

One consequence of the netification of social cognition is that the discipline of HCI is now deeply involved in the challenge of interfacing not only machines to people, but also people to people.

Like any medium, computers too are not neutral media, and they influence the message as it travels from sender to recipient. Often, the inanimate computer is treated by its users as a person, and the spaces it depicts are perceived as real spaces (Reeves & Nass, 1996). This opens the door to research about HCIs as a tool to study the human mind and behavior (Nass & Yen, 2010). It also means that the design of mediated communication artifacts requires a deep understanding not only of technology and of the human senses, but also a deep understanding of social cognition and human emotion. Thus, one of the leading thinkers about HCI now advocates an approach to design that adds visceral and reflective layers to the functional layer (Norman, 2005, 2009, 2010). While empirical evidence is still scarce, the intuitive belief is that more personalized systems will be more attractive, captivating and "sticky." "Theory of Mind" and "Intuitive Psychology" are finding their way to influence a theory of computers and an intuitive or even naïve psychology of the machine. Interactivity is the foundation of this successful design of HCI. The concept of interactivity is used often, but rarely in a consistent manner. Too often it is used as a characteristic of the medium (e.g., interactive whiteboard), while in fact it is a variable that describes the communication process, whether mediated or not (McMillan, 2006; Rafaeli, 1988; Rafaeli & Ariel, 2007). It focuses on the human need for meaningful responses, and suggests that communication processes which are perceived as interactive have positive effects such as fostering engagement (Ha & James, 1998), increasing positive perceptions of brands and advertising (Macias, 2003), and heightening the sense of telepresence (Coyle & Thorson, 2001).

Life, Netified

This section discusses the implications of netification on key aspects of life. As boundaries are blurred and redrawn, fundamentals are altered in ways we are only beginning to understand. We examine three rapidly changing aspects where these effects of netification are most evident: The nature of work and leisure, of private and public, and of space and time.

Work and Leisure

A growing portion of work in the postindustrial era is taking place in the context of the knowledge economy or information society, and is performed by knowledge workers (Machlup, 1962; Porat, 1977). Human work is increasingly focused on producing knowledge goods. With the power of computer networks the focus of work shifts from the manipulation of atoms to the manipulation of bits. The netification of knowledge work in the cloud weakens the link of work to a physical place such as an office or store, and strengthens its attachment to the physical body of the knowledge worker. A similar process occurs in the context of leisure. Many forms of entertainment that in the past required a physical location are now netified. Online versions of movies, books, music, or gambling, just to name a few forms of entertainment, can now be enjoyed anytime and anywhere, using media such as the personal computer, the cellular phone, or other mobile media. Other forms of leisure are also gradually netified: Personal conversations can now be carried out over any distance as well as while each conversant moves in space; digital toys and games for children as well as for adults are ubiquitous; online shopping is becoming ever more prevalent, and the central role of SNSs in the lives of people worldwide moved the term "social networking" from the realm of sociology books and journals to the headlines of newspaper articles.

Leisure and work are undergoing a similar transformation. The blurring of the distinction between production and consumption in these two realms has consequences which are hotly debated, but data and solid research are still lacking. Work and leisure activities take place through the same physical artifacts, such as the smartphone and the computer. Thus, the traditional physical divide between "work and home" is blurring (Lewis, 2010). This is augmented by the emergence of amateurs who use digital and online tools to produce and disseminate knowledge products which compete with those produced by professionals such as reporters, analysts, photojournalists, musicians, and even the authors of encyclopedias (Allan, 2007; Allan & Thorsen, 2009; Giles, 2005).

Another consequence of the increasing ability for instant communication is the challenge of "information overload" (Eppler & Mengis, 2004), as well as of "social information overload" (Lincoln, 2011). Effects of exceeding "cognitive processing load" limits are reported in large-scale empirical measures of online behavior (Jones & Rafaeli, 1999, 2000a, 2000b; Jones, Ravid, & Rafaeli, 2001a, 2001b; Sudweeks et al., 1998). At the extreme, online information overload as a social phenomenon may amount to a new form of crowding, with all the familiar social psychological attendants of such overpopulation. More commonly, a sense of exaggerated density of neighbors, social cues, and human demands must result in acts and attitudes of increased filtering and selective availability.

Activity on SNSs demonstrates the complex change that work and leisure are undergoing. These services usually include one's friends and family, as well as past and present colleagues and other acquaintances, such as romantic partners, classmates, neighbors, etc. When one logs on to a SNS at work, is one working, or playing (DiMicco et al., 2008; Zhao & Rosson, 2009)? What are the consequences when colleagues, clients, or suppliers are exposed to personal aspects of the employee's life which are posted online? Finally, what are the ethics of using SNS data as a part of the hiring process (L. A. Clark & Roberts, 2010)? A point to consider is whether this blurring of boundaries between work and home is a new challenge, or simply the end of a relatively short period in history during which the work and the home were separated. After all, the traditional farmer family lived and worked in the same place, and even during the industrial era, the separation between work and home for women was quite tentative.

Private and Public

Netification changed the nature of the personal computer. Personal computers contain, as is suggested by their name, *personal* or private information. Once this reservoir of digitized personal information is connected to global networks such as the Internet, can this personal information still be controlled? If this personal information can now so easily be shared, searched, and viewed anywhere, is it any wonder that the chief executive officer of Sun Microsystems, Scott McNealy, said in 1999 "You have zero privacy anyway. Get over it" (Sprenger, 1999)? Should we be surprised that shortly afterwards we were told about "The end of privacy" (Sykes, 1999), and about "The death of privacy in the 21st century" (Garfinkel, 2000)? On the other hand, many activities that in the past required presence in public places can now be carried out in the apparent privacy of one's home, be it gambling, searching for medical information, or protesting against a totalitarian regime. Garfinkel points out that "To understand privacy today, we need to rethink what privacy really means today," and goes on to explain that "It's not about the man who wants to watch pornography in complete anonymity over the Internet. It's about the woman who's afraid to use the Internet to organize her community against a proposed toxic dump—afraid because the dump's investors are sure to dig through her past if she becomes too much of a nuisance" (p. 4).

There is inherent tension between the right to privacy, and the desire of others to know about us as individuals. The need to know how one is perceived by others, to try and manage this perception, and to know about others is a fundamental social cognitive need already discussed earlier in this chapter, and it encapsulates the tension between the private and the public: "Because humans are individual beings, the total elimination of privacy would eliminate human existence as we know it; because we are social beings, the elevation of privacy to absolute status would likewise render human existence impossible" (Hodges, 1994, p. 202).

The concept of privacy is context dependent and has transformed throughout history and among cultures and subcultures (Graham, 2010; Locke, 2010). For example, despite the impression that contemporary teens disregard privacy, research shows that privacy is important to teens, and that they are developing strategies for managing privacy in public spaces such as SNSs. A good example Marwick and boyd (2011) provide is steganography, the practice of hiding private information in plain sight, for example, by using codes which are meaningless to the majority of people, but meaningful to one's social circle. Additional examples for online activities which are publicly private or privately public are described by Lange's account of user behavior on YouTube. com (Lange, 2007). An interesting demonstration of the complexity of balancing the privacy needs of online users is the ongoing debate over privacy settings in SNSs (e.g., boyd, 2008; boyd & Hargittai, 2010), as well as the competition between different SNSs which offer alternative ways to categorize links between contacts, such as Facebook's unified list of "friends", versus the ability Google+ provides to assign contacts to various user-defined "circles" (Ruch & Collins, 2011).

The ongoing notification of social information and social activity enables the dissemination and sharing of private information such as photos, letters, opinions, or classified government documents, as well as to perform tasks under the protection of anonymity. The consequent disagreements over the nature of the private and public, about individual rights and societal needs, and over norms and ethical guidelines for individuals, commercial organizations, nongovernmental organizations, and government are inevitable (Miyazaki & Fernandez, 2000; Steinbrook, 2008; Tang, Hu, & Smith, 2008; Grubbs Hoy & Phelps, 2009). Nevertheless, a deep understanding of the relativity and context sensitivity of the concepts, and of the sociocognitive needs of netified individuals is a prerequisite for planning insightful research of the shifting sands of online privacy, as well as for an informed, evidence-based, approach to the development of appropriate policies (boyd, Hargittai, Schultz, & Palfrey, 2011).

Space and Time

Communication used to be limited by space and time. Letters needed to be written and delivered over water and land by couriers. With few exceptions (e.g., African drums: Gleick, 2011) until the appearance of the telegraph, communication over long distances was limited by the speed that muscles, and later engines, could provide. The telegraph followed by the telephone, radio, and later by digital communication tools, removed the constraint of physical distance and the speed of communication. Contemporary technologies enable synchronous communication between any two (or more) points on earth. In addition to the possibility of instantaneous synchronous communication, the emergence of digital asynchronous communication tools such as email and SMS (short message service, or texting) allow users to receive and to respond to messages at their convenience and to multitask. Moreover, location-based services constantly record and transmit time-stamped information about the location of users of mobile devices. What are the implications of these changes on our perception of space and of time?

Research suggests that although communication technologies opened new possibilities that significantly influenced concepts such as work and leisure, the fundamentals of human cognition remain relatively stable. The Internet has not killed distance, and although email and telephony are extensively used to bridge distances, these technologies are also used as a convenient tool to communicate with people who are nearby. Moreover, a contemporary study shows that the frequencies of both face-to-face and phone contacts still drop significantly over distance in a manner that has not changed since the 1970s, well before the emergence of the Internet (Mok, Wellman, & Carrasco, 2010). Geography also influences economic relationships among organizations (Morgan, 2004; Rodríguez-Pose & Crescenzi, 2008). For example, netification catalyzes the rapid globalization of corporations.

One possible explanation for the variable influence of digital technologies on distance is that the sense of closeness or propinquity when communicating online is complex and interacts with various contextual factors such as the availability of alternative communication channels, bandwidth, information complexity, and the communication skills of the users (Walther & Bazarova, 2008). A similar complex relationship is found between CMC and time. Despite expectations that asynchronous communication tools will increase the degrees of freedom of users, we see that users of asynchronous media such as email are expected to respond swiftly, and that failure to meet these expectations is interpreted similarly to the manner these chronemic expectancy violations are interpreted in face-to-face communication (Kalman & Rafaeli, 2011; Sheldon et al., 2006).

The added spatial and temporal flexibility afforded by the netification of communication facilitates multitasking. Activities such as work, entertainment, learning, and interpersonal communication are no longer tied to a place and time meaning that these activities can and do occur anytime and anywhere. Data show that simultaneous use of more than one communication medium is now the norm (Foehr & Henry J. Kaiser Family Foundation, 2006; Rafaeli, 2011; Rideout, Foehr, & Roberts, 2010), and multitasking has been suggested as both the cause of and the solution to challenges such as information overload. With young American adults exchanging, on average, more than 100 text messages per day (median 50 messages) (Smith, 2011), with the ubiquity of mobile phones and other mobile devices as well as of Internet access, and with the expectations for high responsiveness, it is not surprising that online communication activities such as texting and emailing overlap offline activities such as participating in face-to-face meetings at work and home, driving, and TV viewing. The consequences of this multitasking are not yet fully understood (Jenness et al., 2010) and the jury is still out on whether multitasking is an effective way to get more done in less time (Tractinsky & Shinar, 2008), is alienating our society (Turkle, 2011), is changing the brains of the young generation (Bennett, Maton, & Kervin, 2008), or is simply a mistaken belief (Ophir, Nass, & Wagner, 2009).

It is possible to conclude that the influence of netification on the social cognitive perception of time and space is often discussed but still poorly understood. The research that has accumulated suggests, on the one hand, an impressive ability to adapt to the new technologies and use them to overcome the barriers of space and time, and on the other hand little evidence for neurologically hardwired change of biological attributes of the human brain (Sparrow et al., 2011).

Implications for Research

The research of social cognition in the context of its ongoing netification is important and challenging. The first challenge is disciplinary. As is evidenced by the work referenced in this chapter, many insights on social cognition require combining findings from several disciplines—behavioral sciences, communication, sociology, and computer science/information systems. This is in addition to disciplines such as political science, education, or marketing, where the findings on online social cognition are applied to disciplinary research questions. Online social cognition research requires both interdisciplinary and multidisciplinary approaches. This disciplinary challenge is exacerbated by the rapid changes in the field: The artifacts constantly change, technologies that were virtually unknown only a few years ago enter the mainstream, and technologies that were hyped are replaced and disappear. In this multidisciplinary and constantly shifting innovation environment, the challenge of researchers is to develop theory, clearly identify its assumptions and boundaries, and to effectively operationalize the critical variables under examination (Walther, 2009, 2010).

The notification of social cognition changes the nature of scientific research itself. Large datasets that record almost any type of human activity are constantly created by digital artifacts such as computers, cellular phones, and cameras. Using these "big data" datasets for research in the social sciences is promising, but new research methods need to be developed to analyze these datasets, the nature of social science theory needs to be reconsidered, policies to remove institutional barriers need to be developed, and issues relating to privacy and access policy need to be tackled and resolved (Anderson, 2008; Lazer et al., 2009). In addition, notification opens up new tools to social science researchers: The emergence of citizen science (Jonathan, 2009), and the ongoing improvement of technologies that allow spatially-dispersed scientific collaboration (Olson, 2009) as well as the efficient dissemination of scientific findings (Evans & Reimer, 2009) should all be leveraged to improve the quality of research, and to speed up and to improve the quality of social policy decisions.

Conclusion

This chapter explored the netification of social cognition. It analyzed the consequences of the expansion of social cognition from the physical world of atoms, hormones, neurons, and the close interaction of physical bodies, into a world of electronic bits. If in the past, cognition and social behavior were mainly influenced by the laws of physics and chemistry, netification now added to these influences the unique and sometimes surprising laws that govern information. Consequently, some of the parameters and perimeters of social cognition are being altered, and it is necessary to adapt old frameworks, as well as to develop new frameworks, to the study of these alterations. This chapter attempts to assist in this task. It outlines the ongoing research on netification of individuals and groups, striving not to encompass the extensive work already carried out, but rather to point out some of the false starts and fallacies encountered in over 30 years of research, as well as by emphasizing directions that seem promising. It then outlines three aspects of everyday life in which the effects of netification are evident. Here too the goal was not to provide a comprehensive review of the literature, but rather to balance two apparently incompatible viewpoints: The first is that netification changes all the rules and that everything we learned so far about individuals and societies can be discarded; and, the second viewpoint that nothing is new under the sun, and that the same norms, laws, and ethical principles that served our society before the dawn of the digital age can be applied to the present and the future.

We propose to closely study the changes as well as the permanence of the parameters and perimeters of social cognition. The current findings seem to indicate that the fundamental cognitive aspects of humans remain unaltered: The processing power of brains and the fundamental needs and desires of humans seem to be stable and relatively immutable. On the other hand, netification seems to alter the capabilities of humans to fulfill these hardwired needs and desires: To have access to more and more knowledge, and particularly to socially valuable knowledge; to meaningfully connect with others; to control the knowledge others have of oneself; to earn a living; to enjoy leisure; to reach personal fulfillment.

We recognize the need to closely examine the potential and the dangers of netification, but suggest shying away from policy deliberations that fall into the utopia/dystopia trap. Instead, applied research and public policy efforts should inform the design of systems to optimize usability and sociability, designing technological and social mechanisms (Maskin, 2008; Nisan & Ronen,

1999) that achieve the desired goals. A nuanced and evidence-based approach to technological innovation will not prevent the inevitable trial and error associated with any form of human progress. It will, though, make this process less daunting, and improve our ability to use these innovations to affect positive social change.

References

Ahuja, M. K., & Galvin, J. E. (2003). Socialization in virtual groups. *Journal of Management, 29*(2), 161–185.

Albright, J. M. (2001). *Impression formation and attraction in computer mediated communication.* Los Angeles, CA: University of Southern California.

Allan, S. (2007). Citizen journalism and the rise of "Mass self-communication": Reporting the London bombings. *Global Media Journal, 1*(1), 1–20.

Allan, S., & Thorsen, E. (2009). *Citizen journalism.* New York, NY: Peter Lang Publishing.

Anderson, C. (2008). The end of theory: The data deluge makes the scientific method obsolete. *Wired Magazine, 16*(07). Retrieved from http://www.wired.com/science/discoveries/magazine/16-07/pb_theory/

Anderson, C. (2009). *Free! Why $0.00 is the future of business.* New York, NY: Hyperion.

Bauer, B., & Patrick, A. S. (2004). A human factors extension to the seven-layer OSI reference model. Retrieved March 20, 2011 www.andrewpatrick.ca/OSI/10layer.html

Benkler, Y. (2006). *The wealth of networks: How social production transforms markets and freedom.* New Haven, CT: Yale University Press.

Benkler, Y. (2011). *The penguin and the leviathan: How cooperation triumphs over self-interest.* New York, NY: Random House, Inc.

Bennett, S., Maton, K., & Kervin, L. (2008). The "digital natives" debate: A critical review of the evidence. *British Journal of Educational Technology, 39*(5), 775–786.

Boucher, E. M., Hancock, J. T., & Dunham, P. J. (2008). Interpersonal sensitivity in computer-mediated and face-to-face conversations. *Media Psychology, 11*(2), 235–258.

boyd, d. (2008). Facebook's privacy trainwreck: Exposure, invasion, and social convergence. *Convergence: The International Journal of Research into New Media Technologies, 14*(1), 13–20.

boyd, d., & Hargittai, E. (2010). Facebook privacy settings: Who cares? *First Monday, 15*(8).

boyd, d., Hargittai, E., Schultz, J., & Palfrey, J. (2011). Why parents help their children lie to Facebook about age: Unintended consequences of the "children's online privacy protection act." *First Monday, 16*(11).

Burnett, G., & Bonnici, L. (2003). Beyond the FAQ: Explicit and implicit norms in Usenet newsgroups. *Library & Information Science Research, 25*(3), 333–351.

Carr, N. (2011). *The shallows: What the internet is doing to our brains.* New York, NY: WW Norton & Co.

Carr, N. G. (2004). *Does IT matter?: Information technology and the corrosion of competitive advantage.* Cambridge, MA: Harvard Business Press.

Carrasco, J. A., Hogan, B., Wellman, B., & Miller, E. J. (2008). Agency in social activity interactions: The role of social networks in time and space. *Tijdschrift Voor Economische En Sociale Geografie, 99*(5), 562–583.

Clark, L. A., & Roberts, S. J. (2010). Employer's use of social networking sites: A socially irresponsible practice. *Journal of Business Ethics, 95*(4), 507–525.

Clark, N. (1998). Materializing informatics: From data processing to molecular engineering. *Information Communication & Society, 1*(1), 70–90.

Clifford, S. (1996). *Silicon snake oil: Second thoughts on the information highway anchor.* New York (NY): Anchor Books.

Coyle, J. R., & Thorson, E. (2001). The effects of progressive levels of interactivity and vividness in web marketing sites. *Journal of Advertising, 30*(3), 65–77.

Culnan, M. J., & Markus, M. L. (1987). Information technologies. In F. M. Jablin, L. Putnam, K. H. Roberts, & L. W. Porter (Eds.), *Handbook of organizational communication: An interdisciplinary perspective* (pp. 420–443): Thousand Oaks, CA: Sage.

Daft, R. L., & Lengel, R. H. (1986). Organizational information requirements, media richness and structural design. *Management Science, 32*(5), 554–571.

DeAndrea, D. C., & Walther, J. B. (2011). Attributions for inconsistencies between online and offline self-presentations. *Communication Research, 38*(6), 805–825.

Dennis, A. R., Fuller, R. M., & Valacich, J. S. (2008). Media, tasks, and communication processes: A theory of media synchronicity. *MIS Quarterly, 32*(3), 575–600.

Devine, P. G., Hamilton, D. L., & Ostrom, T. M. (1994). *Social cognition: Impact on social psychology*: San Diego, CA: Academic Press.

DiMicco, J., Millen, D. R., Geyer, W., Dugan, C., Brownholtz, B., & Muller, M. (2008). Motivations for social networking at work. In *Proceedings of the 21st ACM Conference on Computer Supported Cooperative Work* (pp. 711–720). New York, NY: ACM Press.

Donath, J. S. (1999). Identity and deception in the virtual community. In M. A. Smith & P. Kollock (Eds.), *Communities in cyberspace* (pp. 25–59). London, UK: Routledge.

Ellison, N. B., Steinfield, C., & Lampe, C. (2007). The benefits of Facebook "friends": social capital and college students' use of online social network sites. *Journal of Computer-Mediated Communication, 12*(4), 1143–1168.

El-Shinnawy, M., & Markus, M.L. (1997). The poverty of media richness theory: explaining people's choice of electronic mail vs. voice mail. *International Journal of Human-computer Studies, 46*(4), 443–467.

Eppler, M. J., & Mengis, J. (2004). The concept of information overload: A review of literature from organization science, accounting, marketing, MIS, and related disciplines. *The Information Society, 20*, 325–344.

Evans, J. A., & Reimer, J. (2009). Open access and global participation in science. *Science, 323*(5917), 1025.

Fisher, D. R., & Wright, L. M. (2001). On utopias and dystopias: Toward an understanding of the discourse surrounding the internet. *Journal of Computer-Mediated Communication, 6*(2).

Fiske, S. T. (1993). Controlling other people: The impact of power on stereotyping. *American Psychologist, 48*(6), 621–628.

Foehr, U. G., & Henry J. Kaiser Family Foundation. (2006). *Media multitasking among American youth: Prevalence, predictors and pairings.* Manlo Park, CA: Henry J. Kaiser Family Foundation.

Forsyth, D. R. (2010). *Group dynamics.* Belmont, CA: Wadsworth Cengage Learning.

Fulk, J. (1993). Social construction of communication technology. *Academy of Management Journal, 36*(5), 921–950.

Garfinkel, S. (2000). *Database nation: The death of privacy in the 21st century.* Sebastopol, CA: O'Reilly Media.

Gibbs, J. L., Ellison, N. B., & Lai, C. (2010). First comes love, then comes Google: An investigation of uncertainty reduction strategies and self-disclosure in online dating. *Communication Research, 38*, 70–100.

Giles, J. (2005). Internet encyclopaedias go head to head. *Nature, 438*, 900–901.

Gleick, J. (2011). *The information: A history, a theory, a flood.* New York, NY: Pantheon.

Graham, P. (2010). Public space, common goods, and private interests: Emergent definitions in globally mediated humanity. In R. Wodak, & V. Koller (Eds.), *Handbook of communication in the public sphere* (pp. 45–66). Berlin, Germany: Mounton de Gruyter.

Grubbs Hoy, M., & Phelps, J. (2009). Online privacy and security practices of the 100 largest US nonprofit organizations. *International Journal of Nonprofit and Voluntary Sector Marketing, 14*, 71–82.

Guerin, B. (2009). *Social facilitation.* Cambridge, UK: Cambridge University Press.

Ha, L., & James, E. L. (1998). Interactivity reexamined: A baseline analysis of early business web sites. *Journal of Broadcasting & Electronic Media, 42*(4), 457–474.

Haythornthwaite, C. (2007). Social networks and online community. In A. N. Joinson, K. McKenna, & T. Postmes (Eds.), *The Oxford Handbook of Internet Psychology* (pp. 121–137). Oxford, UK: Oxford University Press.

Hodges, L. (1994). The journalist and privacy. *Journal of Mass Media Ethics, 9*(4), 197–212.

Howe, J. (2008). *Crowdsourcing: Why the power of the crowd is driving the future of business.* New York, NY: Crown Publishing.

Jenness, J. W., Prada, L. R., Lerner, N. D., Nass, C. I., McGehee, D. V., & Lee, J. D. (2010). Safe driving in the multi-tasking generation. *Proceedings of the Human Factors and Ergonomics Society Annual Meeting, 54*(24), 2048–2051.

Jonathan, S. (2009). A new dawn for citizen science. *Trends in Ecology & Evolution, 24*(9), 467–471.

Jones, Q., Ravid, G., & Rafaeli, S. (2001a). *Empirical evidence for information overload in mass interaction.* Paper presented at the ACM Digital Library and CHI (Computers and Human Interaction) Conference, Seattle, WA.

Jones, Q., Ravid, G., & Rafaeli, S. (2001b). *Information overload and virtual public discourse boundaries.* Paper presented at the eighth IFIP Conference on Human-Computer Interaction, Tokyo, Japan.

Jones, Q., & Rafaeli, S. (1999). User population and user contributions to virtual publics: A systems model. In: *The ACM International Conference on Supporting Group Work (Group99)* (pp. 239–248). New York, NY: ACM Press.

Jones, Q., & Rafaeli, S. (2000a). What do virtual tells tell? Placing cybersociety research into a hierarchy of social explanation. In *Proceedings of the 33rd Annual Hawaii International Conference on System Sciences.* Maui, HI: IEEE Press.

Jones, Q., & Rafaeli, S. (2000b). Time to split, virtually: "Discourse Architecture" and "Community Building" as means to creating vibrant virtual publics. *Electronic Markets: The International Journal of Electronic Commerce and Business Media, 10*(4), 214–223.

Kalman, Y. M., & Gergle, D. (2010). *CMC cues enrich lean online communication: The case of letter and punctuation mark repetitions.* Paper presented at the 5th Mediterranean Conference on Information Systems, September 12–14, Tel-Aviv, Israel.

Kalman, Y. M., & Rafaeli, S. (2011). Online pauses and silence: Chronemic expectancy violations in written computer-mediated communication. *Communication Research, 38*(1), 54–69.

Kanai, R., Bahrami, B., Roylance, R., & Rees, G. (2011). Online social network size is reflected in human brain structure. *Proceedings of the Royal Society B: Biological Sciences, 279*(1732), 1327–1334.

Katz, J. (1998). Luring the lurkers. Retrieved March 20, 2011, from http://news.slashdot.org/ story/98/12/28/1745252/luring-the-lurkers.

Kearnes, M. (2008). Informationalising matter: Systems understandings of the nanoscale. *Spontaneous Generations: A Journal for the History and Philosophy of Science, 2*(1), 99–111.

Keen, A. (2007). *The cult of the amateur: How today's internet is killing our culture broadway business.* New York, NY: Broadway Business.

Kellerman, A. (2002). *The internet on earth: A geography of information.* Chichester, UK: Wiley.

Kemper, T. D. (1968). Reference groups, socialization and achievement. *American Sociological Review, 33*, 31–45.

Kock, N. (1998). Can communication medium limitations foster better group outcomes? An action research study. *Information & Management, 34*(5), 295–305.

Kunda, Z. (1999). *Social cognition: Making sense of people.* Cambridge, MA: MIT Press.

Lange, P. G. (2007). Publicly private and privately public: Social networking on YouTube. *Journal of Computer-Mediated Communication, 13*(1), 361–380.

Lanier, J. (2011). *You are not a gadget: A manifesto vintage.* New York, NY: Vintage Books.

Lazer, D., Pentland, A., Adamic, L., Aral, S., Barabási, A., Brewer, D., ... Van Alstyne, M. (2009). Computational social science. *Science, 323*(5915), 721–723.

Leung, L. (2009). User-generated content on the internet: An examination of gratifications, civic engagement and psychological empowerment. *New Media & Society, 11*(8), 1327.

Levine, J. M., Resnick, L. B., & Higgins, E. T. (1993). Social foundations of cognition. *Annual Review of Psychology*, *44*(1), 585–612.

Lewis, S. (2010). The integration of paid work and the rest of life. Is post-industrial work the new leisure? *Leisure Studies*, *22*(4), 343–345.

Lincoln, A. (2011). FYI: TMI: Toward a holistic social theory of information overload. *First Monday*, *16*(3).

Lipnack, J., & Stamps, J. (2000). *Virtual teams: People working across boundaries with technology* (2nd ed.). New York, NY: John Wiley & Sons.

Locke, J. L. (2010). *Eavesdropping: An intimate history*. Oxford, UK: Oxford University Press.

Machlup, F. (1962). *The production and distribution of knowledge in the United States*. Princeton, NJ: Princeton University Press.

Macias, W. (2003). A preliminary structural equation model of comprehension and persuasion of interactive advertising brand web sites. *Journal of Interactive Advertising*, *3*(2), 36–48.

Marwick, A. E., & boyd, D. (2011). I tweet honestly, I tweet passionately: Twitter users, context collapse, and the imagined audience. *New Media & Society*, *13*(1), 114–133.

Maskin, E. S. (2008). Mechanism design: How to implement social goals. *American Economic Review*, *98*(3), 567–576.

Mason, B. (1999). Issues in virtual ethnography. In K. Buckner (Ed.), *Ethnographic Studies in Real and Virtual Environments Inhabited Information Spaces and Connected Communities* (pp. 61–69). Edinburgh, UK: Queen Margaret College.

McKenna, K. (2008). Influences on the nature and functioning of online groups. In A. Barak (Ed.), *Psychological Aspects of Cyberspace: Theory, Research, Applications* (pp. 228–242). Cambridge, UK: Cambridge University Press.

McMillan, S. J. (2006). Exploring models of interactivity from multiple research traditions: Users, documents and systems. In L. L. Lievrouw & S. Livingstone (Eds.), *Handbook of new media: Social shaping and consequences of ICTs* (pp. 205–229). London, UK: Sage.

Mehdizadeh, S. (2009). Self-presentation 2.0: Narcissism and self-esteem on Facebook. *Cyberpsychology, Behavior, and Social Networking*, *13*(4), 357–364.

Miyazaki, A. D., & Fernandez, A. (2000). Internet privacy and security: An examination of online retailer disclosures. *Journal of Public Policy & Marketing*, *19*, 54–61.

Mo, P. K. H., & Coulson, N. S. (2010). Empowering processes in online support groups among people living with HIV/AIDS: A comparative analysis of "lurkers" and "posters." *Computers in Human Behavior*, *26*(5), 1183–1193.

Mok, D., Wellman, B., & Carrasco, J. (2010). Does distance matter in the age of the internet? *Urban Studies*, *47*(13), 2747.

Morgan, K. (2004). The exaggerated death of geography: Learning, proximity and territorial innovation systems. *Journal of Economic Geography*, *4*, 3–21.

Morozov, E. (2011). *The net delusion: The dark side of internet freedom public affairs*. New York, NY: Public Affairs.

Nass, C. I., & Yen, C. (2010). *The man who lied to his laptop: What machines teach us about human relationships current hardcover*. New York, NY: Penguin.

Newhagen, J. E., & Rafaeli, S. (1996). Why communication researchers should study the internet: A dialogue. *Journal of Communication*, *46*(1), 4–13.

Nielsen Wire. (2011). Social media report: Spending time, money and going mobile. Retrieved March 20, 2011 http://blog.nielsen.com/nielsenwire/online_mobile/social-media-report-spending-time-moneyand-going-mobile/

Nisan, N., & Ronen, A. (1999). Algorithmic mechanism design. In *Proceedings of the Thirty-First Annual ACM Symposium on Theory of Computing* (pp. 129–140). New York, NY: ACM Press.

Nonnecke, B., & Preece, J. (2000). Lurker demographics: Counting the silent. In *Proceedings of the SIGCHI Conference on Human Factors in Computing Systems* (pp. 73–80). New York, NY: ACM Press.

Norman, D. (2005). *Emotional design: Why we love (or hate) everyday things.* New York, NY: Basic Books.

Norman, D. (2009). *The design of future things.* New York, NY: Basic Books.

Norman, D. (2010). *Living with complexity.* Boston, MA: MIT Press.

Olson, G. M. (2009). The next generation of science collaboratories. In *2009 International Symposium on Collaborative Technologies and Systems (CTS 2009)* (pp. xv–xvi). Washington, DC: IEEE Computer Society,

Ong, E. Y. L., Ang, R. P., Ho, J. C. M., Lim, J. C. Y., Goh, D. H., Lee, C. S., & Chua, A. Y. K. (2011). Narcissism, extraversion and adolescents' self-presentation on Facebook. *Personality and Individual Differences, 50*(2), 180–185.

Ophir, E., Nass, C., & Wagner, A. D. (2009). Cognitive control in media multitaskers. *Proceedings of the National Academy of Sciences, 106*(37), 15583–15587.

O'Reilly, T. (2007). What is web 2.0: Design patterns and business models for the next generation of software. *Communications & Strategies, 1,* 17.

Pariser, E. (2011). *The filter bubble: What the internet is hiding from you.* New York, NY: Penguin.

Pearson, E. (2009). All the world wide web's a stage: The performance of identity in online social networks. *First Monday, 14*(3).

Plaisant, C., & Schneiderman, B. (2004). *Designing the user interface: Strategies for effective human-computer interaction.* Boston, MA: Pearson Higher Education.

Pool, I. S. (1983). *Forecasting the telephone: A retrospective technology assessment.* Norwood, NJ: Ablex.

Porat, M. U. (1977). *The information economy: Definition and measurement.* Washington, DC: Office of Telecommunications.

Postman, N. (1993). *Technopoly: The surrender of culture to technology.* New York, NY: Vintage.

Preece, J. (2000). *Online communities: Designing usability and supporting socialbilty.* New York, NY: John Wiley & Sons, Inc.

Preece, J., & Shneiderman, B. (2009). The reader-to-leader framework: Motivating technology-mediated social participation. *AIS Transactions on Human-Computer Interaction, 1*(1), 13–32.

Rafaeli, S. (1986). The electronic bulletin board: A computer driven mass medium. *Computers and the Social Sciences, 2*(3), 123–136.

Rafaeli, S. (1988). Interactivity: From new media to communication. In R. P. Hawkins, J. M. Wiemann, & S. Pingree (Eds.), *Sage annual review of communication research: Advancing communication science* (pp. 110–134). Beverly Hills, CA: Sage.

Rafaeli, S. (2011). Multitasking. *Odyssea, 10,* 64–73.

Rafaeli, S., & Ariel, Y. (2007). Assessing interactivity in computer-mediated research. In A. N. Joinson, K. McKenna, & T. Postmes (Eds.), *The Oxford Handbook of Internet Psychology* (pp. 71–88). Oxford University Press.

Rafaeli, S., Raban, D. R., & Kalman, Y. M. (2005). Social cognition online. In Y. Amichai-Hamburger (Ed.), *The social net: The social psychology of the internet.* Oxford, UK: Oxford University Press.

Rafaeli, S., Ravid, G., & Soroka, V. (2004). *De-lurking in virtual communities: A social communication network approach to measuring the effects of social and cultural capital.* Paper presented at the 37th Annual HICSS Conference (Hawaii International Conference on System Sciences), Hawaii, USA.

Rainie, L., & Wellman, B. (2012). *Networked: The new social operating system.* Boston, MA: MIT Press.

Reeves, B., & Nass, C. (1996). *The media equation: How people treat computers, television, and new media like real people and places.* Chicago, IL: University of Chicago Press.

Reeves, B., & Nass, C. (2000). Perceptual user interfaces: Perceptual bandwidth. *Communications of the ACM, 43*(3), 65–70.

Rheingold, H. (1993). *The virtual community: Homesteading on the electronic frontier.* Reading, MA: Addison-Wesley.

Rheingold, H. (2003). *Smart mobs: The Next Social Revolution.* Cambridge, MA: Basic Books.

Rideout, V. J., Foehr, U. G., & Roberts, D. F. (2010). *Generation M2: Media in the lives of 8-to 18-year-olds.* Menlo Park, CA: Henry J. Kaiser Family Foundation.

Riordan, M. A., & Kreuz, R. J. (2010). Cues in computer-mediated communication: A corpus analysis. *Computers in Human Behavior*, *26*(6), 1806–1817.

Rodríguez-Pose, A., & Crescenzi, R. (2008). Mountains in a flat world: Why proximity still matters for the location of economic activity. *Cambridge Journal of Regions, Economy and Society*, *1*(3), 371–388.

Rouse, S. V., & Haas, H. A. (2003). Exploring the accuracies and inaccuracies of personality perception following internet-mediated communication. *Journal of Research in Personality*, *37*(5), 446–467.

Ruch, A., & Collins, S. (2011). Zoning laws: Facebook and Google. *M/C Journal*, *14*(5).

Ryan, T., & Xenos, S. (2011). Who uses Facebook? an investigation into the relationship between the big five, shyness, narcissism, loneliness, and Facebook usage. *Computers in Human Behavior*, *27*(5), 1658–1664.

Seely Brown, J., & Duguid, P. (2000). *The social life of information.* Boston, MA: Harvard Business School Press.

Sheldon, O. J., Thomas-Hunt, M. C., & Proell, C. A. (2006). When timeliness matters: The effect of status on reactions to perceived time delay within distributed collaboration. *Journal of Applied Psychology*, *91*, 1385–1395.

Shifman, L., & Thelwall, M. (2009). Assessing global diffusion with web memetics: The spread and evolution of a popular joke. *Journal of the American Society for Information Science and Technology*, *60*(12), 2567–2576.

Shirky, C. (2009). *Here comes everybody: The power of organizing without organizations.* New York, NY: Penguin Group USA.

Shirky, C. (2010). *Cognitive surplus: Creativity and generosity in a connected age.* New York, NY: Penguin.

Slater, D. (2002). Social relationships and identity online and offline. In L. A. Lievrouw, & S. Livingstone (Eds.), *The handbook of new media* (pp. 533–546). London, UK: Sage Publications.

Smith, A. (2011). *Americans and text messaging.* Washington, DC: Pew Internet & American Life project.

Soroka, V., Jacovi, M., & Ur, S. (2003). We can see you: A study of communities' invisible people through Reachout. In M. Huysman, E. Wenger, & V. Wulf (Eds.), *Proceedings of International Conference on Communities and Technologies* (pp. 65–79). Amsterdam, the Netherlands: Kluwer Academic Publishers.

Sparrow, B., Liu, J., & Wegner, D. M. (2011). Google effects on memory: Cognitive consequences of having information at our fingertips. *Science*, *333*, 776–778.

Spears, R., Postmes, T., Lea, M., & Wolbert, A. (2002). When are net effects gross products? communication. *Journal of Social Issues*, *58*(1), 91–107.

Sprenger, P. (1999, January 26). Sun on privacy: "Get over it." *Wired News*. Retrieved from http://www.wired.com/politics/law/news/1999/01/17538

Sproull, L., & Kiesler, S. (1986). Reducing social context cues: Electronic mail in organizational communications. *Management Science*, *32*(11), 1492–1512.

Steinbrook, R. (2008). Personally controlled online health data—the next big thing in medical care? *New England Journal of Medicine*, *358*(16), 1653–1656.

Stone, A. R. (2001). Will the real body please stand up?: Boundary stories about virtual cultures. In Trend D. (Ed.), *Reading Digital Culture* (pp. 185–198). Oxford, UK: Blackwell.

Sudweeks, F., McLaughlin, M. L., & Rafaeli, S. (Eds.). (1998). *Network and NetPlay: Virtual groups on the internet.* Cambridge, MA: AAAI MIT Press.

Sunstein, C. R. (2006). *Infotopia: How many minds produce knowledge.* New York, NY: Oxford University Press.

Surowiecki, J. (2004). *The wisdom of crowds: Why the many are smarter than the few and how collective wisdom shapes business, economies, societies, and nations.* New York, NY: Doubleday.

Sykes, C. J. (1999). *The end of privacy: The attack on personal rights at home, at work, on-line, and in court.* New York, NY: St. Martin's Press.

Tang, Z., Hu, Y. J., & Smith, M. D. (2008). Gaining trust through online privacy protection: Self-regulation, mandatory standards, or caveat emptor. *Journal of Management Information Systems*, *24*(4), 153–173.

Tapscott, D., & Williams, A. (2006). *Wikinomics: How mass collaboration changes everything*: New York, NY: Portfolio Hardcover.

Tong, S. T., Van Der Heide, B., Langwell, L., & Walther, J. B. (2008). Too much of a good thing? the relationship between number of friends and interpersonal impressions on Facebook. *Journal of Computer-Mediated Communication, 13*(3), 531–549.

Tractinsky, N., & Shinar, D. (2008). Do we bump into things more while speaking on a cell phone? In *CHI EA '08 CHI '08 extended abstracts on Human Factors in Computing Systems* (pp. 2433–2442). New York, NY: ACM Press.

Travers, A. (2011, July 1). Friedman: World still flat and America still sinking. *Aspen Daily News*. Retrieved from http://www.aspendailynews.com/print/147687

Turkle, S. (1980). Computer as Rorschach. *Society, 17*(2), 15–24.

Turkle, S. (1995). *Life on the screen: Identity in the age of the internet*. New York, NY: Simon & Schuster.

Turkle, S. (2011). *Alone together: Why we expect more from technology and less from each other*. New York, NY: Basic Books.

Van Dijck, J. (2009). Users like you? theorizing agency in user-generated content. *Media, Culture & Society, 31*(1), 41–58.

Wallace, P. M. (2001). *The psychology of the internet*. Cambridge, UK: Cambridge University Press.

Walther, J. B. (2009). Theories, boundaries, and all of the above. *Journal of Computer-Mediated Communication, 14*(3), 748–752.

Walther, J. B. (2010). Computer-mediated communication. In C. R. Berger, M. E. Roloff & D. R. Roskos-Ewoldsen (Eds.), *Handbook of communication science* (2nd ed.), (pp. 489–505). Los Angeles, CA: Sage.

Walther, J. B., & Bazarova, N. N. (2008). Validation and application of electronic propinquity theory to computer-mediated communication in groups. *Communication Research, 35*(5), 622–645.

Walther, J. B., & Burgoon, J. K. (1992). Relational communication in computer-mediated interaction. *Human Communication Research, 19*, 50–88.

Walther, J. B., & Parks, M. R. (2002). Cues filtered out, cues filtered in. In M. L. Knapp & J. A. Daly (Eds.), *Handbook of interpersonal communication* (pp. 529–563). Thousand Oaks, CA: Sage.

Walther, J. B., & Tidwell, L. C. (1995). Nonverbal cues in computer-mediated communication, and the effect of chronemics on relational communication. *Journal of Organizational Computing and Electronic Commerce, 5*(4), 355–378.

Walther, J. B., Van Der Heide, B., Hamel, L. M., & Shulman, H. C. (2009). Self-generated versus other-generated statements and impressions in computer-mediated communication: A test of warranting theory using Facebook. *Communication Research, 36*(2), 229–253.

Walther, J. B., Van Der Heide, B., Kim, S., Westerman, D., & Tong, S. T. (2008). The role of friends? Appearance and behavior on evaluations of individuals on Facebook: Are we known by the company we keep? *Human Communication Research, 34*(1), 28–49.

Weinberger, D. (2007). *Everything is miscellaneous: The power of the new digital disorder*. New York, NY: Macmillan.

Wellman, B. (2002). Little boxes, glocalization, and networked individualism. In M. Tanabe, P. van den Besselaar, & T. Ishida (Eds.), *Digital cities II: Computational and sociological approaches* (Vol. 2362, pp. 337–343). Berlin, Germany: Springer.

Zhao, D., & Rosson, M. B. (2009). How and why people twitter: The role that micro-blogging plays in informal communication at work. *Proceedings of the ACM 2009 International Conference on Supporting Group Work* (pp. 243–252). New York, NY: ACM Press.

Zhao, S., Grasmuck, S., & Martin, J. (2008). Identity construction on Facebook: Digital empowerment in anchored relationships. *Computers in Human Behavior, 24*(5), 1816–1836.

Chapter 3

Identity Manipulation—What Happens When Identity Presentation is Not Truthful

Kathryn Y. Segovia and Jeremy N. Bailenson

Introduction

Imagine a world where another person could choose to look like you—exactly like you. Effortlessly donning your clothes, hairstyle, skin tone, even the subtleties of your facial characteristics, this individual could parade as you in countless interactions with others. Cyberspace, through avatar-based interactions, makes this phenomenon possible. Many scholars describe avatars and virtual worlds as opportunities for individuals to safely and constructively explore their identities. But what happens when identity exploration goes wrong? In a famous example from a very early iteration of the Internet, Julian Dibbell (1994) describes a true story about a rape in cyberspace; one individual took on the identities of others in a very early virtual world to commit virtual crimes. While the acts of rape elicited outrage on their own, the way in which the rapist manipulated his identity to complete the acts made the crime even more offensive and provides an interesting case study to begin this chapter.

The crime occurred in a virtual community called LambdaMOO where users from across the world were chatting in the intimate and communal context of LambdaMOO's text-based living room. Mr Bungle used a Voodoo doll program to control other avatars' actions and force them to service him sexually while others in LambdaMOO watched. Quickly, he became more violent, forcing other users to engage in disgusting and humiliating sexual behavior. Users whose avatars were abused and virtually raped claimed that even though it did not affect them physically, they suffered much emotional trauma.

Eventually, Mr Bungle was removed from LambdaMOO; he had falsely taken on the identities of other users and behaved in criminal ways—he could no longer be trusted in this virtual community. Still, many LambdaMOO users remember and are bothered by the ease with which Mr Bungle could become any person or any thing he wanted—a next-door neighbor, a nice landlord, or even a friend—without any sign to others about who he really was. It is said that, not too long after Mr Bungle was removed from LambdaMOO, a new user emerged: Mr Jest. It was unknown for sure if Mr Jest was friend or foe, but many say that Mr Bungle reemerged as another character and began lurking again.

The Mr Bungle story took place in the early days of the Internet, but the theme of identity manipulation continues to be reiterated in accounts of today's computer-mediated interactions. Several examples of identity replacement in digital contexts have recently garnered media attention. In the documentary *Catfish* (Joost & Schulman, 2010), Nev, a college boy in New York, meets Megan, a young artist from Michigan, over Facebook. Through chatting, emails, and eventually phone calls, the two fall in love. After a long relationship via the computer and phone, Nev drives up to Michigan to surprise Megan—for their first face-to-face meeting. However, when Nev arrives in Michigan he discovers that the Megan he knows does not exist. The person behind Megan's digitally-mediated personae has a husband and life completely different from the life she constructed using fake photographs and more.

In another recent case, Lori Drew from Missouri created a fake MySpace account posing as a cute teenage boy. Lori said her goal was to draw in Megan Meier, a former friend of her daughter, to learn about her and rumors she may have been spreading. Megan Meier was severely humiliated by some of the interactions and committed suicide (Steinhauer, 2008). These examples highlight the ease, prevalence, and implications of such identity replacement acts and make this a worthy area for further study.

Chapter Overview

The freedom offered by computer-mediated communication, and more specifically avatar-based communication, to manipulate how one presents him- or herself can induce both liberating and potentially destructive consequences, not just for the individual actor but for other social interactants as well. The purpose of this chapter is to review the theory and research on manipulated identity presentation, via face-to-face, text-based, and avatar-based communications especially within the context of antisocial behavior. We cover research on social influence, examining how identity manipulation can cause changes in both behavior and attitude. We review empirical work that has examined face-to-face identity manipulation to provide a foundation for experimental research on text-based and avatar-based identity manipulation. It is important to note that few studies compare the effects of face-to-face and computer-mediated identity manipulation. Although there are significant differences in how identity manipulation is implemented in these two contexts, there are various similarities, some of which are pointed out throughout the chapter, that make this an interesting comparison for further investigation.

First, we define some key terms to categorize different types of identity manipulation. Next, we briefly review the relevant theoretical work that has guided research in this field. In addition, we provide an overview of the empirical research that has been conducted by examining various types of identity manipulation. We will conclude with limitations of this empirical research and a discussion of the implications and future directions of this research.

Key Terms

In this first section we define some key terms. First, the word avatar is adapted from the Sanskrit word for "descent," used to describe a Hindu god emerging from the heavens and bodily manifesting itself in order to intervene in human affairs (Bailenson & Blascovich, 2004). Generically, the term avatar can refer to any representation of a human. Names, online profiles, and dolls can all be considered types of avatars by this broad definition (Bailenson, Yee, Blascovich, & Guadagno, 2008). Neal Stephenson (1992), in his science fiction novel *Snow Crash*, popularized the use of the word as it is commonly understood today, to describe a digital representation in a virtual environment.

In addition, we wish to define some terms that will help categorize different types of identity manipulation: Anonymity, misrepresentation, and identity replacement. While terminology in the current literature on identity manipulation is very diverse, we attempt to outline a few categories that will organize this chapter and perhaps provide an introductory framework for discussing and studying these various types of identity manipulation.

Anonymity

Anonymity is defined as "the degree to which a communicator perceives [an individual] as unknown or unspecified" (Anonymous, 1998, p. 100). This definition is important because it classifies anonymity as a continuous construct. That is to say, an individual's identity can range from completely concealed (or anonymous) to partially concealed (e.g., revealing one's name but not one's physical appearance) to completely revealed (for a review of different identity concealment dimensions see Marx, 1999 or Rains & Scott, 2007).

In addition to anonymity being a continuous construct, Marx points out that the construct of anonymity is "fundamentally social" (1999, p. 100). More specifically this means that an individual cannot be anonymous in and of herself nor can a medium, technology, or given social context completely determine one's anonymity—it requires an interpersonal context and awareness. For example, Anonymous, the secretive group of hackers portrayed in many current news headlines, is not inherently anonymous; rather, the group's anonymity can only be defined with reference to specific perceivers (individuals or groups of individuals). Hackers from the group may be completely identified to each other yet remain somewhat anonymous to various government officials and corporate officers.

Previous interactions with an actor may also affect how anonymous he is to others. For example, in a study by Hayne, Pollard, and Rice (2003), participants who had previously interacted in face-to-face contexts brainstormed in anonymous computer-mediated sessions with one another. Immediately after each session, participants were asked to attribute authorship to a sample of the session's anonymous comments (authorship was known by the researchers). The study's participants made attributions that were significantly more accurate than chance guessing. This study revealed that regardless of the participants' technical anonymity, co-participants did not perceive each other to be completely anonymous. Other research points to similar findings as well (Hayne & Rice, 1997).

Identity Misrepresentation

Misrepresentation has been defined by previous scholars as the creation of false and misleading impressions (Cornwell & Lundgren, 2001), and specifically in this context, about one's identity. For example, Cornwell and Lundgren (2001) and Hancock, Toma, and Ellison (2007) have studied various types of misrepresentation in romantic relationships and dating profiles including misrepresentation of an individual's interests, hobbies, religious orientation, age, occupation, education, hair color, weight, or height. As Tooke and Camire (1991) note, such an act may be engaged to make oneself appear more desirable than one really is.

Identity Replacement

The next identity manipulation term and category, identity replacement, moves beyond misrepresenting portions of one's identity to completely misrepresenting oneself as another individual. We define identity replacement as the act of substituting another identity for one's own. In our conceptualization of identity replacement, the newly assumed identity can be one of another real person, as it was in the case of Mr Bungle and LambdaMOO, or the newly assumed identity can be a completely fictitious identity as it was in the MySpace and Facebook examples already described. Identity replacement is different from and largely more difficult to implement than just anonymity. An anonymous individual conveys to others that he is anonymous via the lack of a name, a physical identity, or other identifying characteristics; but, an identity-replaced individual does not always reveal that his real identity has been replaced. Furthermore, identity replacement requires that one not only masks or conceals her true identity, as in the case of anonymous interactions, but also convincingly replaces her identity with a new identity. Identity replacement may require adapting a new physical appearance, new nonverbal behavior, a new name, a new accent, or a new way of speaking, among many other changes. However, avatar-based social interactions have made human identity replacement easier and more prevalent. The next section reviews examples of identity manipulation in various contexts.

Identity Manipulation in Computer-Mediated Contexts

The pioneering scholars of computer-mediated interactions predicted that identity manipulation would be a prevalent phenomenon in computer-mediated interaction contexts (Donath, 1999; Turkle, 1997) and subsequent empirical work has confirmed this prediction (Cornwell & Lundgren, 2001; Riva, 2002; Whitty, 2002). In addition to identity replacement in text-based chat rooms and profiles as described earlier, the widespread use of avatars has opened up another opportunity to study identity replacement.

In avatar-based environments, users have the option to create avatars that look similar to them but can also design avatars that are dissimilar to them on a variety of facets including gender, body-build, hair color, and more. Regarding the prevalence of identity concealment, Savicki, Kelley, and Oesterreich (1999) posited that anonymity in computer-mediated interactions was so high in the 1990s that many users had difficulty determining the gender of the person with whom they were communicating. Noonan (1998) points out that the anonymity of cyberspace interaction can be pushed to the point where individuals' physical and social characteristics are not only omitted but "exaggerated" or "falsified" (p. 64). In effect, chat rooms and other computer-mediated communication contexts make it easy for one to pretend to be someone he or she isn't.

In the vein of identity manipulation and replacement, Kendall (1998, p. 130) notes that "accounts in both the academic and popular press [...] frequently emphasize the potential for portraying identities online that differ from offline identities." Research reveals that this potential has become a reality; for example, a significant number of male users parade as virtual-females in *Second Life* (Ducheneaut, Wen, Yee, & Wadley, 2009). In contrast to face-to-face interactions, humans need not bear any certain degree of resemblance to the avatars they control (Nowak & Rauh, 2005; Yee & Bailenson, 2007). Individuals may choose to replace their physical world identities with virtual, avatar-based identities that do not look like them, an act that Suler and Phillips describe as "impostering" (1998, p. 285).

Identity manipulation in face-to-face, real-world environments is much more difficult and less prevalent than identity manipulation in computer-mediated interactions. For example, in some cases, identity replacement may involve gender switching, and as Utz reaffirms "pretending to be male as a female or vice versa, is very difficult in face-to-face interactions" (2005, p. 50). In one example, Conrad Zdzierak, a Caucasian male, used a lifelike mask to change his apparent identity to that of a generic African American man before robbing a bank. An African American male was actually arrested for the crime before Zdzierak's identity replacement attempts were discovered (Dwyer, 2010). This criminal, along with many others who have been identified throughout history (Wade, 1976), went to great lengths to replace their true identities with new identities.

Text-based and avatar-based identity manipulations can be as easy as the click of a button or the movement of slider bar. Furthermore, avatars as media specifically do not guarantee that the controller has truthfully and realistically revealed his or her identity in his or her avatar. However, just as there are expectations that individuals truthfully reveal their identities in face-to-face interactions (Goffman, 1959), there may be consequences, both positive and negative, when individuals attempt to manipulate their real identities with digital identities.

Relevant Theoretical Work

The next section of this chapter addresses several theoretical frameworks that can be applied to better understand (1) how individuals with manipulated identities in computer-mediated contexts may behave differently than those individuals without manipulated identities and (2) how individuals with manipulated identities in computer-mediated contexts may be perceived differently than individuals whose identities are not manipulated.

Why Individuals with Manipulated Identities May Behave Differently

Self-Perception Theory

Self-Perception Theory posits that people infer their own attitudes from observing themselves as if from a third-person perspective (Bem, 1972). Some of the older and classic experiments in this vein of work demonstrate how one's perceived identity, not necessarily one's true identity (much like when someone misrepresents or replaces his identity), can change how an individual perceives of himself and behaves. Valins (1966) conducted a study where participants were made to believe that their own heartbeat increased while viewing certain photographs. Participants who believed their heart rate had increased inferred that it must have been due to heightened arousal and their perception of the people in the photographs as attractive. This observation of their own behavior led the participants to rate the people in those photographs as being more attractive. Further research has revealed that this type of self-perception can be gleaned from one's physical representation in the real world (Frank & Gilovich, 1988), and even from one's digital representation in the virtual world (Peña, Hancock, & Merola, 2009).

Nick Yee has conducted a series of studies on what he termed the Proteus Effect (Yee & Bailenson, 2007). He has examined how avatars that vary according to specific characteristics such as height, attractiveness, or gender, change their controller's behavior both inside and outside of computer-mediated interactions. In one of his most recent studies, Yee (Yee, Ducheneaut, Yao, & Nelson, 2011) found that players' virtual sexes in *World of Warcraft* had significant effects on players' in-game behaviors. More specifically, while players' physical world sexes did not have a significant effect on how often players chose to engage in healing behaviors in the game environment, players' avatar sexes did have a significant effect on how often players chose to engage in healing behaviors. Female avatars, regardless of the sex of the player controlling the avatar, were more likely to engage in healing behaviors than male avatars. This research shows that individuals with manipulated identities, especially misrepresented or replaced identities, may come to behave in ways that are consistent with the characteristics of their manipulated identities. This effect may be further demonstrated in situations where users select to represent themselves in ways that are different from their physical selves as compared to when users are merely assigned or given a dissimilar identity to control.

Deindividuation

Deindividuation theory argues that when individuals lose their sense of individual identity, whether that be via membership in a group (Spears & Lea, 1994) or, as is specifically relevant to this chapter, via disguise of their own identity (Zimbardo, 1969), they are less likely to abide by social norms. In Zimbardo's explanation, anonymity, along with other variables, produces a state of deindividuation that in turn produces a general disinhibition of previous inhibited behavior. The behaviors that will be disinhibited by anonymity depend upon which behaviors have previously been inhibited. Examples of such inhibited behaviors that have been shown by research to become disinhibited include making negative comments about parents, college women's use of obscene words, and subjecting others to pain (Johnson & Downing, 1979).

Social Identity Model of Deindividuation

In the last few decades, scholars have challenged deindividuation theory with the more specific predictions of the Social Identity Model of Deindividuation (SIDE; Reicher, Spears, & Postmes, 1995). Reicher, Spears, and Postmes point out that the deindividuation model does not consider how one's response to deindividuation may be affected by how one's identity is viewed in a social context. In contrast to deindividuation theory, SIDE theory posits that the self should be defined at various different levels including the categorical self (considering those with whom the individual associates in a social context) as well as the personal self. Empirical evidence shows that the effects of deindividuation manipulations may be better explained when an individual's social identity is taken into account.

For example, in an experiment by Johnson and Downing (1979), some participants' identities were manipulated through the donning of costumes. Some participants were given costumes that resembled the clothing of Ku Klux Klan members. Participants whose true identities were disguised by these costumes behaved more aggressively during the experimental session than participants whose identities were not disguised. These results are consistent with deindividuation theory predictions. However, in the same study, other participants' identities were manipulated via another type of costume—a nurse's uniform. While deindividuation theory would predict that individuals with disguised identities, regardless of the type of social category activated by the disguise, would be more likely to be aggressive or act in an antinormative way, SIDE predicts that identity disguise changes the relative salience of one's social identity and thus usually leads the individual to behave in ways that conform to the norms of his or her social identity. For example, individuals disguised as nurses would be more likely to change their behavior in ways that would conform to a nurse's behavior while those individuals disguised as Ku Klux Klan members would be more likely to change their behavior in ways that would conform to a Ku Klux Klan member's behavior. And, indeed, that is exactly what the study revealed. Individuals who were disguised as nurses behaved less aggressively than those who were not disguised, while those who were disguised as Ku Klux Klan members behaved more aggressively than those who were not disguised.

While the previously discussed bodies of literature offer explanations for why identity manipulated individuals may behave differently than individuals whose identities have not been manipulated, the following theoretical frameworks help address the question of why individuals with manipulated identities may be perceived differently than individuals whose identities are truthfully revealed.

Why Individuals with Manipulated Identities May Be Perceived Differently

Rains and Scott (2007) can be credited with developing the first theoretical model aimed at better understanding and more clearly conceptualizing perceivers' (as opposed to actors') responses to anonymity. Their model focuses on understanding the factors that may influence a receiver's attempts at identifying an anonymous other (more specifically an anonymous communicator or message source); these factors include the context of the communication, the degree to which the source is perceived to be anonymous, the receiver's desire to identify the source, and the receiver's potential ability to determine the source's identity. Rains and Scott not only predict that these factors will affect the receiver's desire to identify the communicator but also that these factors will affect the way in which the message and source are perceived. In addition to Rains and Scott's model, however, other bodies of social psychology research also speak more generally to why individuals with manipulated identities may be perceived differently than those with nonmanipulated identities.

Expectancy Violation Theory

Social interaction is founded on a presumption of truth (Goffman, 1959). As humans, we expect that individuals will dress, behave, speak, and generally convey information that corresponds with their true identity. Identity manipulation, at least in the physical world, violates perceivers' expectations. When such expectations are violated, dramatic effects can result (Burgoon & Walther, 1990). Violations of normative behavior demand an explanation (Feldman & Chesley, 1984), and this cognitive appraisal may prompt perceivers to differentially analyze motivations for subsequent behavior (Bond et al., 1992; Kraut, 1978). According to Expectancy Violation Theory, perceivers accept at face value nonverbal behaviors that are expected and scrutinize unexpected behaviors. This additional scrutiny can lead to more positively or negatively valenced assessments based on how the perceiver assesses the violator and the violation (Burgoon & Hale, 1988; Walther & Burgoon, 1992). While actors in avatar-based interactions may hold fewer identity-based expectations about other interactants than actors in face-to-face interactions, recent research suggests that specific avatar characteristics elicit their own unique expectations.

Nowak and Rauh (2008) suggest that different types of avatars may elicit different expectations about the users that control them. In one study (Nowak & Rauh, 2008), participants rated individuals who were represented by more anthropomorphic, or human-like, avatars as more credible than individuals represented by less anthropomorphic avatars. In another study (McGloin, Nowak, Stiffano, & Flynn, 2009), scholars replicated this finding showing that both increased avatar anthropomorphism and realism led to greater attributions of user credibility. Participants in this study who perceived the reviewer's avatar to be more anthropomorphic and more realistic also found the reviewer to be more trustworthy and the accompanying review to be more credible than participants who perceived the reviewer's avatar to be less anthropomorphic.

While all avatar-based interactions may not elicit the same expectations, when users interact via realistic and anthropomorphic avatars they will generally be expected to be trustworthy and credible. Thus, a user that uses a realistic looking avatar to replace his or her physical world identity may be perceived to be a trustworthy or credible individual even though this identity replacement may be a type of deceit. For example, an older male who has represented himself digitally as a young female using a highly anthropomorphic avatar may be perceived to be a trustworthy and credible individual based on his digital representation, but if or when his true identity is revealed this expectation will be violated. Just like expectancy violations in the physical world, expectancy violations in the virtual world may lead to differential analysis of subsequent behavior.

Uncertainty Reduction Theory

The fundamental assumption of Uncertainty Reduction Theory (URT) is that uncertainty can be unpleasant and, as a result, individuals may seek to reduce it. "Anonymity represents a special type of uncertainty facing message receivers, concerning information about the source's identity" (Rains & Scott, 2007, p. 64). When Berger and Calabrese (1975) introduced URT they outlined seven axioms to help further explicate the effects of uncertainty. Axiom seven states: "Increases in uncertainty level produce decreases in liking; decreases in uncertainty level produce increases in liking" (p. 107). Using this specific axiom and URT at large, we might predict that in comparison to actors who reveal their identity, anonymous actors might incite more uncertainty in those they interact with and thus induce decreased levels of liking.

Recently other scholars have utilized some of the core ideas in URT to further conceptualize how uncertainty may influence information-seeking behavior (Ramirez, Walther, Burgoon, & Sunnafrank, 2002) and a desire to identify (Rains & Scott, 2007). For example, Rains and Scott predict that certain factors increase an individual's desire to identify the identity manipulated source (or reduce the uncertainty). These factors include an increased need to hold the actor accountable, an increased need to evaluate the actor's message or behavior, and a decreased perceived appropriateness of the anonymity.

Interestingly, and in apparent contradiction to URT, a series of studies by Wilson and others (Wilson, Centerbar, Kermer, & Gilbert, 2005) revealed that uncertainty in pleasurable contexts can actually prolong positive responses to stimuli. For example, participants in three different experimental settings received an unexpected gift of a dollar coin with a short message from a passerby. When it was difficult for participants to ascertain who gave them the gift and why, participants' positive moods lasted longer than when it was relatively easy for participants to rationalize who gave them the gift and why. These findings together with URT may suggest that uncertainty (or actor anonymity) may simply serve to amplify or prolong the perceiver's natural response, such that actor anonymity in negative or painful contexts induces even greater negative feelings while uncertainty in pleasurable contexts leads to even more positive feelings.

Perceived Accountability

Suler states that "[w]hen people have the opportunity to separate their actions online from their in-person [...] identity, they feel less vulnerable about [...] acting out. Whatever they say or do can't be directly linked to the rest of their lives" (2004, p. 322). Thus, perceivers may believe that identity manipulated individuals, in comparison to identity revealed individuals, feel relieved of their inhibitions and less accountable for their actions. This difference in appraisal of the identity manipulated actors' motivations may lead others to sanction antisocial actors with replaced identities more heavily.

Previous Research on Identity Manipulation

This section reviews a variety of previous studies on identity manipulation starting with the early studies that focused on face-to-face interactions. The studies focus on various types of identity manipulation (anonymity, misrepresentation, and replacement) and are organized by whether the research is conducted from the perspective of the actor who manipulates his or her identity or the individual who perceives the identity manipulated actor. A large majority of research has focused on the former category (i.e., why do individuals with manipulated identities behave differently than individuals whose identities are not manipulated?), but slowly scholars have directed more focus on the latter.

Research on anonymity and identity manipulation was less common in the 1970s and early 1980s, but with the advent of the Internet and the huge surge of digital media that has become available in the last 25 years, scholars have found tremendous importance in studying how the veil of a manipulated identity changes human interaction. The phenomenon of identity manipulation, from anonymity to misrepresentation and identity replacement, is one that strikes a chord in many academic arenas including, but not limited to, journalism (Rosenberry, 2010), research methods (Joinson, 1999; O'Malley, Johnston, Bachman, & Schulenberg, 2000), group decision-making (Postmes & Lea, 2000), interpersonal communication (Ekstrand, 2003; Joinson, 2001), organizational communication (Scott & Rains, 2005), law (O'Brien, 2001), and social psychology (Kurzban, DeScioli, & O'Brien, 2007).

In this review of research on the effects of identity manipulation, we present research that was conducted in face-to-face contexts as well as research that focuses on computer-mediated contexts. Furthermore, we organize the research first by whether the studied effects of identity manipulation pertain to the actor or the perceiver and, secondly, by the identity manipulation category the research addresses: Anonymity, identity misrepresentation, or identity replacement.

Effects of Identity Manipulation on Actors

The research in this section focuses on how individuals with manipulated identities may think, feel, and behave differently than individuals whose identities have not been manipulated. We will begin with research on anonymity and move into research on identity misrepresentation followed by research on identity replacement.

Anonymity

Zimbardo (1969) was one of the first scholars to explore the effects of anonymity on individuals instructed to engage in antisocial behavior and a lot of his work went to inform the deindividuation theory described earlier. In one of his studies, participants were asked to wear either identifying name tags or lab coats and hoods to conceal their identity. All participants were then given a sanctioned opportunity to administer electrical shocks to another individual. The subjects wearing lab coats and hoods administered longer shocks than the subjects wearing name tags. Zimbardo hypothesized that deindividuation—a state of decreased self-evaluation due to anonymity—led to increased antisocial and antinormative behaviors.

In two other lab-based studies, Donnerstein and others (Donnerstein, Donnerstein, Simon, & Ditrichs, 1972) manipulated whether participants thought they were anonymous or identifiable to other participants in the study. White male subjects were given an opportunity to aggress against targets who were black or white using electric shocks of differential intensities. Each subject was either introduced to his target in a face-to-face scenario before the experimental session began (identifiable) or viewed his target over a purportedly one-way closed-circuit television system (anonymous). Results show that subjects aggressing against black males administered more intense shocks when they were led to believe that they were aggressing anonymously than when they believed they were identifiable.

Furthermore, researchers have examined the relation between anonymity and antisocial behavior in several real-world contexts. Rehm, Steinleitner, and Lilli (1987) conducted a field experiment where elementary school children were randomly divided into teams and played games of handball wearing their own gym shirts (of various colors, sizes, and designs) or orange team T-shirts. The solid colored shirts were reasoned to induce a level of anonymity for the students who wore them. Results show that students uniformed in orange shirts committed more aggressive acts during the game than participants who wore their own personal T-shirts.

More recently, Silke (2003) conducted an analysis on the violent interpersonal assaults that occurred in Northern Ireland. Of the 500 attacks studied, 206 were perpetrated by offenders who wore masks, hoods, or other clothing to cover or obscure their faces. Results from this study revealed a significant positive relationship between anonymity and several measures of violence. Anonymous offenders, in comparison to offenders who revealed their identities, inflicted more serious physical injuries, engaged in more acts of vandalism, attacked more people at the scene, and were more likely to threaten victims after the attacks. While this study does not provide evidence about the direction of the causal relationship between anonymity and increased levels of violence, it does show that a relationship between the two factors exists outside of the laboratory.

In addition, actor anonymity has been shown to affect actors in computer-mediated contexts as well. For example, Joinson (2001) conducted an experiment in which participants engaged in short discussions about a moral dilemma prompt. Half of the participants engaged in face-to-face discussions, while half of the participants engaged in computer-mediated discussions via a chat program. The participants who engaged in computer-mediated, chat-based discussions revealed more about themselves during the discussion than participants who interacted face-to-face. Joinson predicted that visual anonymity (which was high in the computer-mediated, chat-based interactions and low in the face-to-face interactions) was the mechanism at work. But in order to further understand this finding Joinson conducted a follow-up study. In this study, participants engaged in the same moral dilemma discussion; however, participants were either assigned to a visually nonanonymous chat-based interaction (where a video image of the user was displayed in the chat window) or a visually anonymous chat-based interaction (where no image of the user appeared). Results revealed that visually anonymous participants disclosed significantly more information about themselves than nonvisually anonymous participants.

Identity Misrepresentation

In addition, scholars have shown that identity misrepresentation in computer-mediated interactions with others can impact how individuals behave and perceive of themselves. In a study by Gonzales and Hancock (2008), participants were asked to present themselves with one of two traits, extroversion or introversion, in public or private computer-mediated communication. Public presentations were online, whereas private presentations took place in a text document. As such, participants engaged in varying degrees of identity misrepresentation depending on their personalities. Some participants who would not normally identify themselves as extroverts presented themselves as extroverts, and some participants who would not normally identify themselves as introverts presented themselves as introverts. Only participants who publicly presented their manipulated identities came to behave more like the representation of their identity—that is, more extroverted or more introverted, depending on assignment to condition—suggesting that an identity shift took place in the public context. Such research suggests that individuals who misrepresent their identities in computer-mediated contexts as compared to those who veridically represent their identities may come to adopt characteristics of their misrepresented identity.

Identity Replacement

Scholars have also shown that when individuals are allowed to replace their physical identities with virtual identities, changes in their behavior and self-perceptions may arise. Galanxhi and Nah (2007) conducted an experiment where participants interacted in dyads via text-based chat environments where their names were not revealed. Half of the participants saw a simple chat window with no avatar representation of themselves, while the other half of the participants saw the same simple chat window with an image of an avatar to represent themselves in the corner of the window. The avatars for these participants, however, were not designed to physically resemble the participants. Thus the participants' physical world identities were replaced with dissimilar virtual identities or avatars. The study revealed that among participants who experienced the chat environment without an avatar, participants who were instructed to deceive their partners experienced higher anxiety levels than those who were instructed to be truthful to their partners; however, the same phenomenon was not observed in the avatar-supported chat environment. This study suggests that "wearing a mask" in computer-mediated interactions may reduce the actor's anxiety in deceiving others.

Effects of Identity Manipulation on Perceivers

While the research described in the section "Effects of Identity Manipulation on Actors" focused on how identity manipulated individuals may behave differently than identified actors and message senders, considerably less research has focused on how others perceive anonymous actors and sources. The rest of this chapter will focus precisely on this side of the two-way interaction.

Identity manipulation creates both challenges and opportunities for perceivers. In interactions with anonymous individuals or individuals who are otherwise known to have manipulated identities, perceivers are not constrained by many of the cues, such as the status markers or indicators of competence that typically impact perceptions of others. However, at the same time, perceivers cannot rely on these cues when they attempt to interpret the behavior of and messages from anonymous individuals. This context may elicit perceptions of anonymous actors that are different than those of identified actors.

Anonymity

One of the older bodies of research in which scholars have explored questions about perceptions of anonymous actors and message senders is in the context of news and information sources (e.g., Adams, 1962; Riffe, 1980; Wilson, Babcock, & Pribek, 1997; Wulfemeyer, 1985). Some studies report that anonymous sources (referring to an individual such as "a political leader" or an institution like "the government") are rated as credible as identified sources in news stories (Adams, 1962; Riffe, 1980), while others report that anonymous sources are perceived as less credible.

In a recent study by Rains (2007) participants were charged with rating group members' hypothetical contributions to a case study on an ethical dilemma scenario. Some participants believed that the contributions came from group members who were identified by their first names, and some participants believed that the contributions came from group members who were anonymous. The contributions were actually written by the experimenters. Results revealed that when participants' perceptions of confederate anonymity were controlled for, anonymity undermined perceptions of group members. The supposedly anonymous contributors were less trustworthy, less persuasive, and had less goodwill toward the group.

In a field experiment about the effects of anonymity in upward (subordinate-to-manager) feedback systems, Antonioni (1994) found that managers who received feedback from identified subordinates viewed the appraisal process more positively than did managers who received feedback from anonymous subordinates. In addition, Antonioni also reported that subordinates felt more comfortable giving anonymous responses.

Identity Misrepresentation

While insects and birds are not directly comparable to humans, studies on their punitive responses to identity misrepresentation have implications for similar research with humans. In this research, experimenters altered aspects of the birds' or insects' physical appearances to study how other members of the species would respond to the identity misrepresentation. The social status of female paper wasps can be gauged based on the design of their yellow and black facial patterns. Larger dominant wasps tend to have facial patterns that appear more "broken"—like the tiles of a mosaic. Tibbetts and Dale (2004) conducted a study where they experimentally manipulated and misrepresented the natural facial patterns of the female wasps; some of the subordinate wasps were painted with the facial patterns of dominant wasps while others were left with their natural facial patterns. In this case the wasps did not intentionally manipulate their own identities, but instead research assistants manipulated the wasps' identities and set out to measure how other wasps would respond to the identity manipulation. The wasps were then placed in staged conflicts with other unfamiliar wasps, and punitive response was measured as the amount of physical violence wasps showed toward each other.

Subordinate wasps who were experimentally manipulated to look like dominant wasps received considerably more aggression from dominant wasps than those wasps whose subordinate identities were not manipulated. These results indicate that identity misrepresentation, even among insects, can impose social costs. Rohwer (1977) conducted a similar study with Harris Sparrows. These sparrows signal their social dominance status by variation in the amount of black feathering on their crowns and throats. In the experiment, researchers dyed the feathers of the subordinate birds to mimic the darker feathering of more dominant birds. When released to interact with other birds, these birds with misrepresented identities were persecuted by the legitimately dominant birds more than they had been attacked and persecuted before the feather dying and identity misrepresentation took place. This research strongly suggests that identity misrepresentation, when detected, is a punishable offense in social settings.

Identity Replacement

In the Galanxhi and Nah (2007) study described earlier, the scholars also assessed how perceivers may differentially respond to identity replaced actors. Their results revealed that the general use of avatars (regardless of their similarity to their users) in a computer-mediated chat environment did not have an impact on one's perceived trustworthiness. To be clear, participants who replaced their physical world identities with dissimilar virtual identities or avatars were not perceived to be any less trustworthy than those individuals who did not use avatars to represent themselves.

Proulx and Heine (2008) conducted a study where they found that perceived identity replacement can lead to punitive acts toward unrelated others. Participants in their study evaluated a hypothetical case in which a prostitute was arrested. In the control condition, participants were exposed to the same experimenter for the length of the study. But, half of the participants were assigned to the "changing-experimenter" condition. In this condition, while participants answered the short questionnaire, the female research assistant conducting the experiment was surreptitiously replaced with another, identically dressed female experimenter. The first experimenter went to a filing cabinet to retrieve the next questionnaire and after opening the filing cabinet, she stepped back and was replaced by the second experimenter, who shut the cabinet and continued the experiment. Only five percent of participants explicitly noticed the change in experimenters. After reading the report about the arrest of a prostitute, the participants were asked to set a bond for the prostitute as if they were a judge reviewing the case. Participants in the changing-experimenter condition set larger more punitive bonds than did participants in the control condition. Proulx and Heine (2008) reasoned that participants' attitudes toward a lawbreaker became more punitive following a surreptitious experimenter switch which suggests that the visual anomaly was (implicitly) noticed and provoked fluid punitive responses toward someone other than the identity manipulated actor (the prostitute).

Participants in a study by Segovia and Bailenson (2012) were ostracized by other virtual humans who didn't throw them the ball in a ball tossing game. Identity replacement was implemented in the study by modeling the ostracizing avatars to be either physically similar to the people who controlled them (revealing the controller's identity) or dissimilar (replacing the controller's identity with a dissimilar avatar). After the virtual ball tossing game, participants began a second experiment about taste preferences that was supposedly unrelated to the first experiment. In this experiment, participants, the perceivers of the identity manipulated or un-manipulated actors, were given the chance to aggress against the ostracizer from the ball tossing game by allotting a sample of food that the participant learned was strongly disliked by the ostracizer—red hot sauce. The participant could allocate as much as he wished, and he was informed the ostracizer would be required to consume the whole sample. The sample was weighed in grams and recorded as a way of measuring the participant's aggression toward the ostracizer. Participants more severely punished ostracizers who had acted under a replaced identity than ostracizers who had acted under a revealed identity. These results could likely be explained by the perceived accountability theory described earlier in addition to Johnson and Downing's argument that aggression toward identity manipulation "in many instances, could reflect a simple reduction in perceived negative sanctions" (1979, p. 1537).

In a follow-up study, Segovia and Bailenson (2012) examined whether the perceived volition of the actor in his or her identity manipulated state would affect to what degree participants (or perceivers) punished the ostracizer. In this study, all of the participants were ostracized by avatars that were physically dissimilar to the individuals who controlled the avatars, but half the participants were told that the ostracizers had merely been assigned dissimilar looking avatars while the other half of the participants were told that the ostracizers had chosen to replace their physical world identities with dissimilar avatars. Results revealed that participants punished ostracizers more severely if the ostracizer had chosen to replace his or her identity via an avatar than if the ostracizer had been merely assigned a dissimilar looking avatar.

Limitations and Future Directions

The final section of this chapter identifies both limitations and suggestions for future work in the context of identity manipulation. First, as can be noted in the way we structured the review of previous research in this chapter, most past research in this area focuses on identity manipulation in either a computer-mediated or face-to-face context. While there are significant differences in how identity manipulation is implemented in these two different contexts (as described in earlier sections), there are various similarities that make this an interesting comparison for further investigation.

If we think of identity manipulation as a continuum, levels of low and high identity manipulation can be achieved in both contexts. For example, one's name could be concealed in a face-to-face context (by actively withholding one's name or opting out of wearing a name tag) or a computer-mediated context (by replacing one's real name with a generic user name like "user1"). Higher levels of identity manipulation can also be achieved in both contexts. For example, a male in the physical world may choose to undergo transgender surgery, effectively replacing his male identity with a new female identity. Similarly, although more easily, male users in *Second Life* may choose to replace their male identities in the physical world with female identities or avatars in the virtual world. Each level of identity manipulation in the computer-mediated context (anonymity, misrepresentation, and replacement) has a largely similar and corresponding manipulation in the face-to-face context. In future work on this topic, scholars should further work to explicate identity manipulation irrespective of the context in which it is implemented.

Next, the research reviewed in this chapter comes from very diverse research programs and contexts. Because of this, the field is lacking a unified set of terms to describe and study the new types and levels of identity manipulation that are possible in computer-mediated interactions. Additionally, the field also lacks a theoretical model that addresses various categories of identity manipulation and explains both the prosocial and antisocial effects of such manipulations. Rains and Scott (2007) have initiated such a theoretical model but only with respect to anonymous communication, and we believe this model could be expanded to include other types of identity manipulations as well.

Finally, with the increasing growth of the Internet and the amount of personal information that many individuals knowingly and unknowingly store or share on the Internet, it is likely that the act of identity replacement will become more prevalent. Aside from websites like Facebook, Twitter, and others where personal data is obviously presented and shared, there are other more subtle ways in which online activity leaves data trails and cues that can point to users' identities. In their recent book, Blascovich and Bailenson (2011) describe how an individual's digital footprint, including such small details as his word choices and how he navigates digital spaces, may allow others to predict with reasonable accuracy aspects of his identity such as gender and more thus reducing one's ability to completely disguise his or her identity in computer-mediated interactions.

Conclusion

With the ever-increasing usage of digital media in our world today, identity manipulated actors will likely continue to be a more prevalent part of our daily lives. This reality poses interesting questions for scholars to address and unique ways of manipulating anonymity via digital media. It is our duty as social scientists to embrace this phenomenon in a way that makes our research relevant to the questions and concerns identity manipulation raises in our societies.

Acknowledgements

We would like to thank Karena Chicas for her help in conducting a literature review for this book chapter. Additionally, we would like to thank Jakki Oni Bailey, Mailyn Fidler, Cody Karutz, and Andrea Stevenson Won for their help in editing drafts of this chapter.

References

Adams, J. B. (1962). The relative credibility of 20 unnamed news sources. *Journalism Quarterly*, *39*, 79–82.

Anonymous. (1998). To reveal or not to reveal: A theoretical model of anonymous communication. *Communication Theory*, *8*(4), 381–407.

Antonioni, D. (1994). The effects of feedback accountability on upward appraisal ratings. *Personnel Psychology*, *47*(2), 349–356.

Bailenson, J. N., & Blascovich, J. (2004). Avatars. In W. S. Bainbridge (Ed.), *Encyclopedia of Human-Computer Interaction* (pp. 64–68). Great Barrington, MA: Berkshire Publishing Group.

Bailenson, J. N., Yee, N., Blascovich, J., & Guadagno, R. E. (2008). Transformed social interaction in mediated interpersonal communication. In E. Konijn, S. Utz, M. Tanis, & S. B. Barnes (Eds.), *Mediated Interpersonal Communication* (pp. 77–99). New York, NY: Routledge.

Bem, D. J. (1972). Self-perception theory. *Advances in Experimental Social Psychology*, *6*, 1–62.

Berger, C. R., & Calabrese, R. J. (1975). Some explorations in initial interaction and beyond: Toward a developmental theory of interpersonal communication. *Human Communication Research*, *1*(2), 99–112.

Blascovich, J., & Bailenson, J. (2011). *Infinite Reality: Avatars, Eternal Life, New Worlds, and the Dawn of the Virtual Revolution*. New York, NY: HarperCollins.

Bond, C. F., Omar, A., Pitre, U., Lashley, B. R., Skaggs, L. M., & Kirk, C. T. (1992). Fishy-looking liars: Deception judgment from expectancy violation. *Journal of Personality and Social Psychology*, *63*(6), 969–977.

Burgoon, J. K., & Hale, J. L. (1988). Nonverbal expectancy violations: Model elaboration and application to immediacy behaviors. *Communication Monographs*, *55*(1), 58–79.

Burgoon, J. K., & Walther, J. B. (1990). Nonverbal expectancies and the evaluative consequences of violations. *Human Communication Research*, *17*(2), 232–265.

Cornwell, B., & Lundgren, D. C. (2001). Love on the Internet: Involvement and misrepresentation in romantic relationships in cyberspace vs. realspace. *Computers in Human Behavior, 17*(2), 197–211.

Dibbell, J. (1994). A rape in cyberspace or how an evil clown, a Haitian trickster spirit, two wizards, and a cast of dozens turned a database into a society. *Annual Survey of American Law, 3*, 471–489.

Donath, J. S. (1999). Identity and deception in the virtual community. In M. A. Smith & P. Kollock (Eds.), *Communities in Cyberspace* (pp. 29–59). London, UK: Routledge.

Donnerstein, E., Donnerstein, M., Simon, S., & Ditrichs, R. (1972). Variables in interracial aggression: Anonymity, expected retaliation, and a riot. *Journal of Personality and Social Psychology, 22*(2), 236–245.

Ducheneaut, N., Wen, M. H., Yee, N., & Wadley, G. (2009). Body and mind: a study of avatar personalization in three virtual worlds. In *Proceedings of the 27th international conference on Human factors in computing systems (CHI2009)* (pp. 1151–1160). New York, NY: ACM Press.

Dwyer, D. (2010, December 2). White man used lifelike black mask to evade arrest in robberies. *ABC News*. Retrieved from http://abcnews.go.com/US/white-man-lifelike-black-mask-evade-arrest-robberies/story?id=12288529

Ekstrand, V. S. (2003). Unmasking Jane and John Doe: Online anonymity and the First Amendment. *Communication Law and Policy, 8*(4), 405–427.

Feldman, R. S., & Chesley, R. B. (1984). Who is lying, who is not: An attributional analysis of the effects of nonverbal behavior on judgements of defendant believability. *Behavioral Sciences and the Law, 2*(4), 451–461.

Frank, M. G., & Gilovich, T. (1988). The dark side of self-and social perception: Black uniforms and aggression in professional sports. *Journal of Personality and Social Psychology, 54*(1), 74–85.

Galanxhi, H., & Nah, F. H. (2007). Deception in cyberspace: A comparison of text-only vs. avatar-supported medium. International Journal of Human-Computer Studies, 65(9), 770–783.

Goffman, E. (1959). *The Presentation of Self in Everyday Life*. Oxford, UK: Doubleday.

Gonzales, A. L., & Hancock, J. T. (2008). Identity shift in computer-mediated environments. *Media Psychology, 11*(2), 167–185.

Hancock, J. T., Toma, C., & Ellison, N. (2007). The truth about lying in online dating profiles. In *Proceedings of the 25th international conference on Human factors in computing systems (CHI2007)* (pp. 449–452). New York, NY: ACM Press.

Hayne, S. C., & Rice, R. E. (1997). Attribution accuracy when using anonymity in group support systems. *International Journal of Human-Computer Studies, 47*(3), 429–452.

Hayne, S. C., Pollard, C. E., & Rice, R. E. (2003). Identification of comment authorship in anonymous group support systems. *Journal of Management Information Systems, 20*(1), 301–329.

Johnson, R. D., & Downing, L. L. (1979). Deindividuation and valence of cues: Effects on prosocial and antisocial behavior. *Journal of Personality and Social Psychology, 37*(9), 1532–1538.

Joinson, A. (1999). Social desirability, anonymity, and Internet-based questionnaires. *Behavior Research Methods, 31*(3), 433–438.

Joinson, A. N. (2001). Self-disclosure in computer-mediated communication: The role of self-awareness and visual anonymity. *European Journal of Social Psychology, 31*(2), 177–192.

Joost, H., & Schulman, A. (Directors). (2010). *Catfish* [Motion picture]. United States: Universal Pictures.

Kendall, L. (1998). Meaning and identity in "cyberspace": The performance of gender, class, and race online. *Symbolic Interaction, 21*(2), 129–153.

Kraut, R. E. (1978). Verbal and nonverbal cues in the perception of lying. *Journal of Personality and Social Psychology, 36*(4), 380–391.

Kurzban, R., DeScioli, P., & O'Brien, E. (2007). Audience effects on moralistic punishment. *Evolution and Human Behavior, 28*(2), 75–84.

Marx, G. T. (1999). What's in a name? Some reflections on the sociology of anonymity. *The Information Society, 15*(2), 99–112.

McGloin, R., Nowak, K. L., Stiffano, S. C., & Flynn, G. M. (2009). The effect of avatar perception on attributions of source and text credibility. In the Proceedings of the International Society for Presence Research. Los Angeles, CA. Retrieved from http://ispr.info/presence-conferences/previous-conferences/presence-2009/.

Noonan, R. J. (1998). The psychology of sex: A mirror from the Internet. In J. Gackenbach (Ed.), *Psychology and the Internet: Intrapersonal, Interpersonal, and Transpersonal Implications* (pp. 143–168). San Diego, CA: Academic Press.

Nowak, K. L., & Rauh, C. (2005). The influence of the avatar on online perceptions of anthropomorphism, androgyny, credibility, homophily, and attraction. *Journal of Computer-Mediated Communication, 11*(1), 153–178.

Nowak, K. L., & Rauh, C. (2008). Choose your buddy icon carefully: The influence of avatar androgyny, anthropomorphism and credibility in online interactions. *Computers in Human Behavior, 24*(4), 1473–1493.

O'Brien, J. (2001). Putting a face to a (screen) name: The first amendment implications of compelling ISPs to reveal the identities of anonymous Internet speakers in online defamation cases. *Fordham Law Review, 70,* 2745.

O'Malley, P. M., Johnston, L. D., Bachman, J. G., & Schulenberg, J. (2000). A comparison of confidential versus anonymous survey procedures: Effects on reporting of drug use and related attitudes and beliefs in a national study of students. *Journal of Drug Issues, 30*(1), 35–54.

Peña, J., Hancock, J. T., & Merola, N. A. (2009). The priming effects of avatars in virtual settings. *Communication Research, 36*(6), 838–856.

Postmes, T., & Lea, M. (2000). Social processes and group decision making: Anonymity in group decision support systems. *Ergonomics, 43*(8), 1252–1274.

Proulx, T., & Heine, S. J. (2008). The case of the transmogrifying experimenter. *Psychological Science, 19*(12), 1294.

Rains, S. A. (2007). The anonymity effect: The influence of anonymity on perceptions of sources and information on health websites. *Journal of Applied Communication Research, 35*(2), 197–214.

Rains, S. A., & Scott, C. R. (2007). To identify or not to identify: A theoretical model of receiver responses to anonymous communication. *Communication Theory, 17*(1), 61–91.

Ramirez Jr, A., Walther, J. B., Burgoon, J. K., & Sunnafrank, M. (2002). Information-seeking strategies, uncertainty, and computer-mediated communication. *Human Communication Research, 28*(2), 213–228.

Rehm, J., Steinleitner, M., & Lilli, W. (1987). Wearing uniforms and aggression – A field experiment. *European Journal of Social Psychology, 17*(3), 357–360.

Reicher, S. D., Spears, R., & Postmes, T. (1995). A social identity model of deindividuation phenomena. *European Review of Social Psychology, 6,* 161–198.

Riffe, D. (1980). Relative credibility revisited: How 18 unnamed sources are rated. *Journalism Quarterly, 57*(4), 618–23.

Riva, G. (2002). The sociocognitive psychology of computer-mediated communication: The present and future of technology-based interactions. *CyberPsychology & Behavior, 5*(6), 581–598.

Rohwer, S. (1977). Status signaling in Harris Sparrows: some experiments in deception. *Behaviour, 61*(1), 107–129.

Rosenberry, J. (2010). What's in a (missing) name? Newspaper online forum participants sound off about civility and anonymity. Paper presented at the annual meeting of the Association for Education in Journalism and Mass Communication, The Denver Sheraton, Denver, CO.

Savicki, V., Kelley, M., & Oesterreich, E. (1999). Judgments of gender in computer-mediated communication. *Computers in Human Behavior, 15*(2), 185–194.

Scott, C. R., & Rains, S. A. (2005). Anonymous communication in organizations. *Management Communication Quarterly, 19*(2), 157–197.

Segovia, K. Y., & Bailenson, J. N. (2012). Virtual imposters: Responses to avatars that do not look like their controllers. *Social Influence, 7*(4), 285–303.

Silke, A. (2003). Deindividuation, anonymity, and violence: findings from Northern Ireland. *The Journal of Social Psychology*, *143*(4), 493–499.

Spears, R., & Lea, M. (1994). Panacea or panopticon? *Communication Research*, *21*(4), 427.

Steinhauer, J. (2008, November 21). Woman who posed as boy testifies in case that ended in suicide of 13-year-old. *The New York Times*. Retrieved from http://www.nytimes.com/

Stephenson, N. (1992). *Snow Crash*. New York: Bantam Books.

Suler, J. (2004). The online disinhibition effect. *CyberPsychology & Behavior*, *7*(3), 321–326.

Suler, J. R., & Phillips, W. L. (1998). The bad boys of cyberspace: Deviant behavior in a multimedia chat community. *CyberPsychology & Behavior*, *1*(3), 275–294.

Tibbetts, E. A., & Dale, J. (2004). A socially enforced signal of quality in a paper wasp. *Nature*, *432*(7014), 218–222.

Tooke, W., & Camire, L. (1991). Patterns of deception in intersexual and intrasexual mating strategies. *Ethology and Sociobiology*, *12*(5), 345–364.

Turkle, S. (1997). *Life on the Screen: Identity in the Age of the Internet*. New York, NY: Touchstone Books.

Utz, S. (2005). Types of deception and underlying motivation. *Social Science Computer Review*, *23*(1), 49–56.

Valins, S. (1966). Cognitive effects of false heart-rate feedback. *Journal of Personality and Social Psychology*, *4*(4), 400–408.

Wade, C. (1976). *Great Hoaxes and Famous Impostors*. Middle Village, NY: Jonathan David Publishers.

Walther, J. B., & Burgoon, J. K. (1992). Relational communication in computer-mediated interaction. *Human communication research*, *19*(1), 50–88.

Whitty, M. (2002). Liar, liar! An examination of how open, supportive and honest people are in chat rooms. *Computers in Human Behavior*, *18*(4), 343–352.

Wilson, S. L., Babcock, W. A., & Pribek, J. (1997). Newspaper ombudsmen's reactions to use of anonymous sources. *Newspaper Research Journal*, *18*(3-4), 109–118.

Wilson, T. D., Centerbar, D. B., Kermer, D. A., & Gilbert, D. T. (2005). The pleasures of uncertainty: Prolonging positive moods in ways people do not anticipate. *Journal of Personality and Social Psychology*, *88*(1), 5–21.

Wulfemeyer, K. T. (1985). How and why anonymous attribution is used by Time and Newsweek. *Journalism Quarterly*, *62*(1), 81–86.

Yee, N., & Bailenson, J. N. (2007). The Proteus effect: The effect of transformed self-representation on behavior. *Human Communication Research*, *33*(3), 271–290.

Yee, N., Ducheneaut, N., Yao, M., & Nelson, L. (2011). *Do men heal more when in drag? Conflicting identity cues between user and avatar. In Proceedings of the 2011 annual conference on Human factors in computing systems* (pp. 773–776). New York, NY: ACM Press.

Zimbardo, P. G. (1969). The human choice: Individuation, reason, and order versus deindividuation, impulse, and chaos. In W. J. Arnold & D. Levine (Eds.), *Nebraska Symposium on Motivation* (*Vol. 17*) (pp. 237–307). Lincoln, NE: University of Nebraska Press.

Chapter 4

Online Romantic Relationships

Monica T. Whitty

Introduction

Ever since the early days of the Internet people have been finding ways to engage in online romantic and sexual activities—some of these healthy activities, others not so. Despite some theorists' early claims that relating online could cause harm to one's psychological health, we soon learnt that the Internet is a very interpersonal space—a space where potentially very healthy relationships are formed and maintained. Although, we also learnt that these relationships are not all the same as their offline counterparts and sometimes these relationships remain online.

This chapter begins with a brief overview on how relationships formed before there was an Internet and highlights some of the important theories on relationship initiation and development. These theories on traditional relationships, I argue, are still important to consider with regards to explaining the initiation, development, and maintenance of relationships formed on the Internet. However, as researchers soon learnt, new theories also needed to be developed as scholars started to observe differences in the ways people relate online compared to more traditional spaces. For example, we learnt that in some online conditions people self-disclose more intimate aspects about themselves, leading to "hyperpersonal relationships." The chapter also makes the case that the Internet is not a homogenous space and so there is no real place for a "one theory fits all" approach. Instead we need to understand the "features" and the norms that govern the space where people are relating. In order to make this point clear I describe how the Internet looked like in its early days and the types of relationships that formed in these spaces. As this chapter points out, in its infancy, online relating was mostly text-based. The chapter then moves to consider how the spaces online changed and with these changes how online relationships changed. The future of online relating is also considered in this chapter. I make the argument that in the future we may no longer be taking the online/offline binary approach to relationships. Instead, as seems to be panning out in current times, individuals use multiforms of media as well as face-to-face (FtF) to develop and maintain their relationships.

Traditional Relationships: Offline World

Brief History of Offline Relationships

As Whitty and Carr (2006) explain, in detail, the initiation and maintenance of relationships offline have changed over the years, and cultural differences should also be acknowledged. Romantic attraction was not always the main motivator for people to marry. In early nineteenth-century Europe, marriages were arranged (Murstein, 1974; Rice, 1996). As Rice explains: "arranged marriages sought to merge the property and good name of the families to ensure economic well-being and the perpetuation of family status and prestige" (p. 96).

Cate and Lloyd (1992) and Murstein (1974) have explained that at the same time in America, due to social (e.g., the need to populate) and economic conditions (e.g., women could not afford not to work), young people had more autonomy in their choice of a partner. The choice of a partner was based more on reason than love or affection. Individuals met in social settings, such as church, and parents would give the young couple privacy.

In the mid nineteenth century, men's and women's social roles in America had changed. Women were back in the home and valued for their domestic abilities (Cate & Lloyd, 1992). Women were seen as the more virtuous sex (Coontz, 1988; Murstein, 1974). Courtship became more formalized. According to Cate and Lloyd (1992), it was at this time that the formal wedding ceremony emerged, together with the white wedding dress to symbolize the purity of the bride. This was also a time when romantic love began to flourish.

Towards the end of the nineteenth century and the beginning of the twentieth century courtship in America became increasingly more formalized. Courtship at this time initiated in the home. Potential young couples needed to be formally introduced to another before they were allowed to speak. After this formal introduction, the women's mother would ask the young man to call upon her daughter. After their first meeting, the young lady was permitted to do the asking (Cate & Lloyd, 1992).

In the early twentieth century courtship moved again to outside the home. This time the surveillance of the couple was mostly informal through community control (Cate & Lloyd, 1992; Koller, 1951). However, towards the mid twentieth century, dating became more informal, and the peer group established the rules of dating. With this change in how individuals developed their relationships, there was a change in who traditionally made the first move (Mongeau, Hale, Johnson, & Hillis, 1993). Since the turn of the twentieth century, men began to initiate the courtship, generally because they had to pay for the date and arrange transportation. Cate and Lloyd (1992) made the claim that, at this time in history, courting was more about competition than love.

From the mid twentieth century to the 1960s love was still the main reason for marriage (Cate & Lloyd, 1992). However, in this post-war era women moved back to the home, and according to Cate and Lloyd (1992), became more passive in the courting process. Of course the sexual revolution in the 1960s again changed courting for both men and women. The end goal was not necessarily marriage, and cohabitation began to become a popular choice. Concern over HIV arose in the 1980s and consequently monogamous sexual relationships were once again more valued. In the twenty-first century there have been further changes—one of the most obvious changes is the use of new media to initiate, develop and maintain romantic relationships.

Of course, Whitty and Carr's (2006) history of relationships, by their own admission, is a more Westernized story. However, their description of the twists and turns in how relationships form is relevant here given it sheds light on the fact that the Internet is just another way of forming relationships. Even when we consider offline relationship formation, there is not one single model. Arranged marriages are still common in many cultures, and these cultures now utilize the Internet to assist in these arrangements.

Although online relating is a fairly new form of relating in the history of the development of romantic relationships, this does not mean that previously developed theories on romantic relationships are not relevant or helpful to consider when attempting to understand these new forms of relationships. This chapter next turns to consider theories formed about relationships before there was an Internet and considers their utility when it comes to explaining Internet relationships.

Theories on Romantic Relationships

Poets, philosophers, theologians, psychologists, and many others have tried to define romantic love. There is no agreed upon definition and to provide a summary of all the theories of love is beyond the scope of this chapter. However, there are a few psychological theories on relationship initiation and development that have been developed to explain relationship formation from the late 1960s to current times that are worthwhile mentioning—social evolutionary theory, social penetration theory, exchange, and equity theory. These theories have also been considered with regards to online relationships.

Social evolutionary theory, in brief, explains that through natural selection the human species has inherited certain traits and emotional reactions. Humans have evolved to value certain qualities in the opposite sex. When it comes to forming romantic relationships, the more an individual possesses certain characteristics the more likely they are to attract others of the opposite sex (Buss, 1987). According to this theory, women are more attracted to men who can provide for their offspring. Men, in contrast, are attracted to women who are fertile and reproductively valuable. Numerous studies on attraction have found support for this theory, finding that men seek out women who are physically attractive and women are more romantically interested in men who have high social economic status (see, for example, Buss & Barnes, 1986; Greenless & McGrew, 1994; Kenrick, Sadalla, Groth, & Trost, 1990; Townsend & Wasserman, 1997).

Social penetration theory is one such theory which was initially proposed by Altman and Taylor (1973), and modified by others (e.g., Morton, Alexander, & Altman, 1976). According to this theory, relationships move from less intimate to more intimate involvement over time. The process has been described using the "onion analogy," arguing that people self-disclose deeper and deeper aspects about themselves as the relationship progresses. This theory discusses the depth and breadth of relationship formation. Depth represents dimensions starting from the surface and moving to the central core aspects of personality. Breadth refers to information about a broad range of topics, such as one's family, career, and so forth. According to social penetration theory, in the early phases of relationship development one moves with caution, discussing less intimate topics and checking in the conversations for signs of reciprocity. Gradually one feels safer to admit to other aspects of themselves.

Exchange theory and equity theory have also been drawn upon to examine the types of choices individuals make when selecting a romantic partner. Exchange theories explain relationships in terms of rewards and costs. Thibaut and Kelley (1959) developed the first of these theories and argued that whatever our feelings are for someone (no matter how pure and admirable our motives might seem) individuals pursue relationships with others only so long as they are satisfying in terms of the overall rewards and costs. Exchange theory contends that individuals try to maximize their profits; that is, rewards should outweigh the costs. These theorists also argued that in order to predict how satisfied an individual is likely to be with a given relationship it is necessary to take their expectations into account. For instance, individuals develop expectations about relationships based on their past relationships and observations of relationship outcomes with other people similar to themselves.

Therefore, to be satisfied with a relationship the outcomes must match or exceed one's comparison levels. Like exchange theory, equity theory argues that individuals in personal relationships are trying to maximize their outcomes. It argues that when individuals find themselves in inequitable relationships they experience distress, and the degree of distress increases in proportion to the perceived inequity. When individuals experience such distress they will attempt to restore equity.

In contrast to Thibaut and Kelley's (1959) theory, which says that information for generating comparison levels comes from one's past experiences and/or from observations of similar others, equity theory focuses on the relative contributions and outcomes of the partners. Therefore, the relevant information for deciding what is fair in the relationship comes from within the relationship. Those who make more of a contribution should expect to get more out of it; those who put in less should expect less from the relationship. There is also a fair amount of research to support these theories. For example, Harrison and Saeed (1977) performed a content analysis on 800 heterosexual personal ads. They found complementary but gendered differences between what individuals offered of themselves and what they hoped for in a potential partner. In other words, they found that individuals seek out others of about equal attractiveness as themselves and if they sought out someone more attractive they typically offered some other quality in return (e.g., social status and wealth) to balance out the difference.

Applying Old Theories to Online Relationships

New theories have been developed to explain how people initiate, develop, and maintain relationships in cyberspace and how they progress to offline spaces. However, before outlining these new theories this chapter considers some of the theories on traditional relationships just outlined.

Social Evolutionary Theory

Researchers have found the traditional gender differences in online attraction that this theory would predict. Dawson and McIntosh (2006), for example, found that in online personal advertisements men were more likely to emphasize wealth, while women were more likely to place emphasis on physical attributes. With respect to online dating, researchers have found that women are more likely to go to efforts to have an attractive photograph representing themselves on their profile (Whitty, 2008; Whitty & Carr, 2006). Moreover, women, more than men, lie about their looks or used outdated photographs, while men more than women exaggerated or lied about their social status. Whitty and Buchanan (2010) in their study on online dating screen names found that men more than women, were attracted to screen names that indicated physical attractiveness, and women, more than men were attracted to screen names that indicated intelligence or were neutral. Similarly, men, more than women, were motivated to contact screen names which indicated physical attractiveness and women, more than men, were more motivated to contact screen names which indicated intellectual characteristics.

Social Penetration Theory

Researchers have found that when individuals are online they are more likely to self disclose depth and breath aspects about themselves more quickly than they might FtF (e.g., Joinson, 2001). Given that self-disclosure can be different online to traditional settings new theories have been developed to explain this type of relating (see "Disinhibition Effect" and "Hyperpersonal communication" sections later in this chapter). However, it is important to understand, as this chapter demonstrates, that one theory cannot be applied to explain the whole of online communications. Whitty (2008, p. 1721) has argued that social penetration theory cannot be applied to explain relationship initiation and development via an online dating site.

> On an Internet dating site the profiles are set-up in such a way to reveal both depth and breadth. For instance, within the profiles, individuals typically have to provide information about surface levels aspects of themselves, such as, eye color, drinking and smoking habits, relationship status, number and types of pets, and occupation. In addition, they are given space to write more in-depth about themselves, where they are asked to describe their personality, interests (what they read, music they listen to and so forth), their ideal date, their political persuasion. They are encouraged on these sites to open up about all aspects of themselves online – so that they will attract the most appropriate person . . .

Therefore, online dating is arguably even more removed from what people are used to when it comes to developing a relationship. There is not any real opportunity to test the waters gradually and check for reciprocity, instead, reciprocity is determined prior to communication with the individual.

Exchange Theory and Equity Theory

Researchers have described the characteristics online daters looked for in others as an exhaustive shopping list (Whitty, 2008b; Whitty & Carr, 2006). These researchers argue that profiles can be understood as commodities that individuals are looking to buy into, and sometimes people do not get the product they were hoping to purchase. Some of these characteristics include looks (typically through a photo), interests and activities, personality, humor, occupation, intelligence, uniqueness, and hopes and dreams (see Whitty & Carr, 2006, for an exhaustive list and percentages). Whitty (2008b) has also found that online daters presented long lists of positive characteristics rather than a just a few. As explained earlier in this chapter, exchange theory posits that individuals look to maximize rewards when it comes to deciding upon an appropriate relationship. Hence, it would seem a sensible strategy to outline as many positive characteristics as possible to appear a highly rewarding option. Moreover, one has to appear a more rewarding choice than the many other available profiles.

New Theories to Explain Online Relating

How people interact and relate online can sometimes be very different to more traditional spaces. Given this difference in relating, new theories have been devised to explain some of the unique interactions that take place in some online spaces.

Disinhibition Effect

Researchers have found that individuals, in some online spaces, are more likely to open up about aspects about themselves in cyberspace and act out behaviors they might not otherwise in traditional FtF settings (Joinson, 2001). This is known as the "disinhibition effect" (Suler, 2004). Suler (2004) describes this as a double-edged sword as some people reveal secret emotions, fears, and wishes or show unusual acts of kindness and generosity, which he refers to as "benign disinhibition." Barak, Boniel-Nissim, and Suler (2008) found that because of the online disinhibition effect individuals are able to open up more in online support groups. This, they argue, fosters personal empowerment, control, self-confidence, and improved feelings. In contrast, there are times when people are ruder, harsh critics, show anger, hatred, or even threats than they typically would be FtF. This Suler calls "toxic disinhibition." Cyber-bullying is an example of this type of toxic disinhibition, for example, when young people write cruel messages on social networking sites. Kowalski and Limber (2007) found that 11% of their sample of middle-school students had been bullied at least once in the last couple of months.

Social Presence Theory

Social presence theory was one of the first theories to be applied to online communication. It is worthwhile noting that this theory was devised when individuals were communicating online mostly exclusively via textual exchanges. The theory contends that social presence is the feeling that one has that other individuals are involved in a communication exchange. Since online communication involved fewer nonverbal cues (such as facial expression, posture, dress, and so forth) and auditory cues in comparison to FtF communication, it was said to be extremely low in social presence (Hiltz, Johnson, & Turoff, 1986). According to this theory, as social presence declines communication becomes more impersonal. In contrast, when more information is available about how one physically looks this leads to greater positive regard. Hence, given that there is less social presence online compared to other media online, communication was said to be less personal and intimate. The problem with this theory, with regards to online relationships, was that real relationships were forming online (as this chapter illustrates). Given the evidence contradicted what this theory predicted other theories emerged to explain how real relationships were being formed via text with strangers in online environments.

Social Information Processing Theory

Walther (1995) criticized the early theories, such as social presence theory. While he still subscribed to the reduced social cues view, he believed that many of these studies did not account adequately for time. Given the shortcomings of previous research, Walther and his colleagues sought to develop a more thorough understanding of the exchanges that take place in online environments. In doing so, Walther came up with the "social information processing (SIP) theory."

The SIP theory "refers to the way by which communicators process social identity and relational cues (i.e., social information) using different media" (Walther, 1995, p. 190). This theory proposes that the main difference between FtF communication and computer-mediated communication (CMC) is the pace that relationships develop in each space rather than capability to develop relationships. Walther argued that although CMC may be more aggressive at first, with time this dissipates. Walther (1992, 1995, 1996) stressed in this theory that many of the differences between online relationships and FtF relationships diminish over time, and although restricted bandwidth may limit the rate of information exchange, this problem can be alleviated by allowing longer and/ or more frequent communication.

Hyperpersonal Communication

Walther extended his SIP theory to develop a hyperpersonal communication framework. This theory posits that "CMC users sometimes experience intimacy, affection, and interpersonal assessments of their partners that exceed those occurring in parallel FTF activities or alternative CMC contexts" (Walther, Slovacek, & Tidwell, 2001, p. 109). This theory posits that people use the technical capacities of the Internet to assist in impression development (Walther, 1996). According to Walther (2007, p. 2539), the model "specifies several concurrent dynamics in sender, receiver, channel, and feedback systems that are affected by CMC attributes, which promote the development and potential exaggeration of impressions and relationships online…" According to this theory, receivers idealize partners because of the messages they receive, which they believe demonstrate the similarity in their online partner as well as a highly desirable character. In contrast, senders exploit the technology to selectively self-present aspects about themselves that the other would deem socially desirable. The CMC features allow one to be strategic in their presentation of self and the CMC environment creates a space where the outside world is filtered out and cognitive resources are instead employed to focus on the online communications. As Walther (2007) explains: "The CMC channel facilitates editing, discretion, and convenience, and the ability to tune out environmental distractions and re-allocate cognitive resources in order to further enhance one's message composition" (p. 2539). Once this cycle of communication has begun Walther argues that "CMC may create dynamic feedback loops wherein the exaggerated expectancies are confirmed and reciprocated through mutual interaction via the bias-prone communication processes" (p. 2539).

Researchers have found support for this theory in both dyads and groups. For example, in a study by Hancock and Dunham (2001) participants were assigned to either a text-based conversation condition or an FtF dyadic interaction. In this study 80 participants rated their partners' personality profile on breadth and intensity. They found, just as the hyperpersonal theory would predict, that impressions formed in the CMC environment were less detailed but more intense than those formed FtF. In more recent research, Jiang, Bazarova, and Hancock (2012) found that partners' initial self-disclosures via text-based CMC were more intimate than disclosures in FtF. The communications that followed via CMC continued to be higher in intimacy.

"Real Me"

Over 10 years ago researchers proposed that the Internet was the ideal space to present what Rogers termed the "real self" (e.g., Bargh, McKenna, & Fitzsimons, 2002; McKenna & Bargh, 2000; McKenna, Green & Gleason, 2002). Although they replaced the term with the "real me" they understand this term to be equivalent to Roger's (1951/2003, 1961/2004) real self. They use the term "real me" to mean the traits or characteristics that an individual possesses and would like to but is typically unable to express to most people. It is a construct that refers to the aspects of a person's inner core (or who they "really are"). They argued that this is because cyberspace was anonymous and that it is easier to express oneself to individuals unknown to someone where the traditional gating features evident in FtF interactions are absent. Although it can be argued that Roger's real self and McKenna and Bargh's "real me" are quite dissimilar, empirical evidence has found support for their understanding of the "real me."

McKenna et al. (2002) developed the "real me" scale to measure the real self. The "real me" scale consists of four questions. The first two require a yes/no response. First, participants are asked whether they reveal more about themselves to people they know from the Internet to people they know in real life (non-Net friends). Second, they are asked if there were aspects that their Internet friend knew about them that they felt they could not share in "real life" with "non-Net" friends. The following two questions ask participants to rate on a 7-point scale the extent to which their family and friends would be surprised if they were to read their Internet email and newsgroup postings. This study provided clear evidence for their theory.

In addition to the measure mentioned, these researchers employed a different method to measure the "real me". Bargh et al. (2002) measured the "real me" by asking participants to list a maximum of ten traits or other characteristics that they possessed, and would like to express, but typically feel unable to. In this study they found that those who were better able to express their true selves online rather than FtF were more likely to form close relationships with people they met on the Internet, (see more on the "real me" in Chapter 1).

The BAR Theory

An argument made throughout this chapter is that the Internet is not a homogenous space. Therefore, theories are needed to account for the different features of the online space and the rules that govern each space. Whitty (2007) developed the BAR theory to explain how successful presentations of self on online dating sites can lead to successful relationships. She found that online daters are acutely aware that the best strategy for developing a "successful" profile (i.e., one that will attract a desirable potential partner) is to create a balance between an "attractive" and a "real" self (BAR). She also found that participants did not feel too comfortable revealing too much of their inner core on their profiles, given that online daters typically met fairly quickly after initial contact on the site. This is a little different to what theorists, such as Bargh et al. (2002) and McKenna et al. (2002) contend (as highlighted previously). However, these theorists were considering relationship development in newsgroups. In the spaces they investigated individuals were not necessarily or at least obviously seeking out a romantic partner, nor do they typically display photographs or videos of themselves. This is very different to a profile on an online dating site, which contains all the information an individual needs to make a decision about FtF contact.

Brief History of Online Relating

As I write this chapter, I'm fully aware that the Internet will continue to evolve and new online fads will emerge. The Internet, as it exists, allows individuals to communicate with each other across the world at lightning speeds. Some countries have made restrictions on these communications (e.g., China) and some laws have emerged in some countries to restrict certain types of online activities (e.g., virtual pedophilia is illegal in the United States). Different online spaces have set out rules for how people are permitted to behave in that space. However, in the main, cyberspace is still a fairly liberal space. Social networking sites continue to be popular and online dating sites are increasing as a popular means to find a partner. Ample bandwidth allows for online activities that were either impossible or time-consuming less than 15 years ago (e.g., downloading of video, web cams, playing music, sharing photographs, etc.).

It is almost impossible to imagine that less than 15 years ago most online romantic activities, in the main, involved "pure" textual exchanges. New ways needed to be found to overcome the lack of nonverbal cues in online interactions (e.g., in the form of emoticons). Those who formed friendships and romantic relationships online were frequently stigmatized. Moreover, there was no opportunity to be immediately sexually satisfied via erotic talk—individuals needed to be patient. In this next section I outline some of the online spaces that emerged where online relationships began to initiate and form.

Bulletin Board Systems: Line by Line Relationships

Bulletin board (BB) systems were an especially popular space in the early days of the Internet and many of these BB systems were quite sexual in nature. BBs were a precursor to the World Wide Web; however, they looked very different from spaces currently available on the Internet. BBs were typically single-line systems, which meant that only one user could be online at a time. Individuals could only communicate using text. Even in the early days, BBs were social spaces where people met, had discussions, published articles, downloaded software, and even managed to play games. A system's operator would sometimes censor the messages on these sites, but in the main they were fairly liberal.

Users could leave both public and private messages. Some BBs were especially designed for people to meet others who shared their sexual interests and to live out their sexual desires online or offline. Social scientists have examined the sites and the people who use them (e.g., Wysocki, 1998; Wysocki & Thalken, 2007). Wysocki (1998), for instance, was interested in seeing whether online sex was a replacement for FtF relationships or whether instead it enhanced them. She interviewed participants using a BB called the "Pleasure Pit." In this study, she identified five main reasons for using sexually explicitly BBs, including anonymity, time constraints in one's personal life, the ability to share sexual fantasies with other people, the desire to participate in online sexual activity, and to find people with similar sexual interests to meet FtF.

MUDs/MOOs: A Place for Real Relationship Formation

MUDs (multiple-user dungeons, more commonly understood these days to mean multiuser dimensions or domains) and MOOs (MUD, object oriented) were text-based online virtual systems in which multiple users were connected at one time. These were spaces where interactive role-playing games could be played, very similar to *Dungeons and Dragons*. MUDs and MOOs were a form of synchronous communication. Participants took on a chosen character and communicated with other characters online.

In the early days researchers were divided over whether real friendships and romantic relationships could actually form in these spaces. The empirical work suggested that they did and sometimes moved successfully from these spaces to the offline world. Parks and Roberts (1998), for instance, examined relationships developed in MOOs and found that most of the participants they surveyed (93.6%) formed at least one ongoing personal relationship during their time on MOOs. A variety of kinds of relationships was identified, including, close friendships (40.6%), friendships (26.3%), or romantic relationships (26.3%). They concluded that "the formation of personal relationships on MOOs can be seen as the norm rather than the exception" (p. 529) Interestingly, the majority of the online relationships were with members of the opposite sex. This finding was consistent across ages and relationship status. As Parks and Roberts point out, this result is quite different to real life where same-sex friendships are far more common than cross-sex friendships. Parks and Roberts explained this result saying "that MOOs break down the structural and normative constraints on cross-sex friendships off line" (p. 531). The structural constraints they refer to include the lack of opportunities for men and women to interact on an ongoing basis as well as the status differences that exist between men and women, especially in the workplace. These theorists concluded that "MOOs provide users with the perception of a safe environment for social interaction in which individuals can explore all types of relationships without fear of repercussions in their physical lives" (Parks & Roberts, 1998, p. 531).

Utz (2000) examined the interactions that take place in MUDs. In her study she found that 76.7% of her respondents reported forming a relationship online that developed offline, of which, 24.5% stated this was a romantic relationship. In addition, she found that with time people do learn how to "verbalize nonverbal cues." The MUDers she surveyed typically utilized emoticons to denote feelings and emotions. Interestingly, Utz also found that not all those who spend a great deal of time playing MUDs necessarily formed friendships. Utz argued that this might be because not everyone playing MUDs believed that they were going to form friendships in this space, nor do all MUDers play in order to develop friendships. Turkle (1995) wrote about Netsex stating:

> Many people who engage in netsex say that they are constantly surprised by how emotionally and physically powerful it can be. They insist that it demonstrates that truth of the adage that ninety percent of sex takes place in the mind. This is certainly not a new idea, but netsex has made it commonplace among teenage boys, a social group not usually known for its sophistication about such matters. A seventeen-year-old high school student tells me that he tries to make his erotic communications on the net "exciting and thrilling and sort of imaginative" (p. 21).

Sexual encounters in this space were not always titillating. The infamous rape in cyberspace, known as the "Mr Bungle affair" caused much controversy when it took place in 1992 in *Lambda* MOO (see Turkle, 1995). In cyberspace a player masqueraded as another player's character by using a MUD programming technique often referred to as a voodoo doll. The Mr Bungle character used the voodoo doll to force another character to perform sexual acts on him.

Chat Rooms: Less Means More

Chat rooms involve synchronous communication or according to Whitty, Buchanan, Joinson, and Meredith (2012) "near synchronous" communication. Most chat rooms have a particular theme, although this is not necessary. When one enters a chat room a user can type a message that will be visible to all other individuals. Hundreds of people can be in the same virtual room at the same time typing messages to the group. They are similar to instant messenger except with more than two people. Sometimes these rooms are moderated. Chat rooms were very popular in the early days of the Internet and were text only. In more recent times, individuals often represent themselves as an avatar. Moreover, individuals file share photographs and videos and use webcams.

Researchers have found that romantic relationships and friendships also initiated and were formed in chat rooms. Whitty and Gavin (2001), for instance, found in their study where they interviewed 60 Internet users, that ideals that are important in traditional relationships, such as trust, honesty, and commitment were just as important in relationships formed in these spaces. Rather than finding evidence of less "real" or less satisfying relationships online, some of the participants in their study reported that their relationships seemed to work better solely on the Internet. As this 18-year-old women reports:

> It [the relationship] developed through an interesting chat on IRC and a series of about 500 e-mails. The attraction was merely someone who cared and listened. He was very sensitive and caring, and his picture was hot! {laughs} . . . we exchanged addresses and he sent me presents on Valentines Day and Easter. We would write a two page e-mail every day, send sounds to each other, and eventually after six months we talked on the phone. Our phone conversation was very weak so we decided to stick to e-mail . . . We met after eight months of exchanging e-mails. He was a great guy, and it would have worked but he lived in email. It was a good experience though and he was exactly like his photo (Whitty & Gavin, 2001, p. 628).

In their study, they also found that chat room users reported feeling less self-consciousness and less aware of being socially evaluated, which in turn allowed these individuals to reveal intimate details about themselves while maintaining distance and personal space. Ironically, many of the male participants in this study believed that by disguising their identity they could be more emotionally honest and open.

In more recent research chat rooms have been found to be a place where adolescences feel able to explore sexuality. Subrahmanyam, Smahel, and Greenfield (2006) examined a large sample of conversations in both monitored and unmonitored teen chat rooms. In their study, they found that 5% of the conversations in these places were sexual. Participants who claimed to be female produced more implicit sexual communication and participants who identified as male produced more explicit sexual communication.

Discussion Groups/Usenet Newsgroups: A Place for the "Real Me"

A discussion group or Usenet newsgroup is a continuous public discussion about a particular topic. This is a form of asynchronous communication. Sometimes these groups are moderated. These were very popular in the early days of the Internet. These groups still exist today and are still often in text-based form only, although pictures and video can also be posted up on the sites. With regards to personal relationships, Parks and Floyd (1996) found in their research on newsgroups that almost two-thirds of their sample (60.7%) admitted to forming a personal relationship with someone they had met for the first time in a newsgroup. Of these, 7.9% stated that this was a romantic relationship. They found that women were more likely than men to have formed a personal relationship online. It is also noteworthy that those who participated in more newsgroups were more likely to have developed personal relationships. Parks and Floyd also found that many of the relationships that began online also moved to interactions in other channels, including, for some, FtF.

As explained earlier in this chapter, McKenna et al. (2002) were interested in what they refer to as the "real me," which they define as traits or characteristics that individuals posses and would like to express, but are usually unable to demonstrate to others. In this study they were interested in learning whether individuals who are better able to disclose their "real me" online than offline were more equipped to form close relationships online and then take these relationships offline successfully. They randomly selected 20 Usenet newsgroups to include in their study. Over a 3-week period questionnaires were emailed to every fifth poster in each of the newsgroups (excluding spam). Their first study found that when people convey their "real me" online they developed strong Internet relationships and took these relationships offline. Two years after this initial study 354 of the 568 participants were emailed a follow-up survey (the remainder of the sample had email addresses that were no longer valid). In line with these researchers' prediction, these relationships remained relatively stable and durable over the 2-year period. McKenna et al. (2002) concluded from this research that:

> rather than turning to the Internet as a way of hiding from real life and from forming real relationships, individuals use it as a means not only of maintaining ties with existing family and friends but also of forming close and meaningful new relationships in a relatively nonthreatening environment. The Internet may also be helpful for those who have difficulty forging relationships in face-to-face situations because of shyness, social anxiety, or a lack of social skills (p. 30).

Contemporary Online Spaces

The online sites previously discussed, as already pointed out, were mainly text-based exchanges. However, another feature worthwhile noting is that a norm for these places was to meet strangers; that is, to meet others that the individual had never met FtF. In current times, some of these spaces are still in existence. Some of these, such as discussion groups, still exist as textual exchanges, although most include pictures, sound, and video. Researchers are also finding that individuals are no longer using online spaces as much to meet strangers. Subrahmanyam and Greenfield (2008), for example, have found that adolescents use electronic communication, such as instant messaging, email, text messaging, blogs, and social networking sites to reinforce existing relationships, both with friends and romantic partners. Moreover, they contend that adolescents are increasingly integrating these tools into their offline worlds. For example, using social networking sites to garner information about new people they meet in their offline world. This section next turns to consider more contemporary online spaces and the ways relationships are developed within these spaces.

MMORPGs: Still a Very Social Space

Earlier in this chapter I wrote about MUDs and MOOs. These days massively multiplayer online role-playing games (MMORPGs) have taken over from these. In MMORGPs, players take on the role of a fictional character, typically in a fantasy world, and have agency over many of their character's actions. MMORPGs differ from MUDS and MOOS in that they are not text-based only, but instead have sophisticated graphics. In addition to playing the game, individuals can still write text to one another and be social in these spaces. The worlds created in these games continue to evolve even when the player is absent from the game—examples include *EverQuest*, *World of Warcraft*, *Final Fantasy XI*, and, more recently, *Warhammer*. The popularity of these games continues to grow. More recently, the nature of this interaction with some MMORPGs has become more "adult"-based. *Age of Conan*, *Warhammer*, *2 Moons*, and *Requiem: Bloodymare*, for example, provide increased opportunities for extreme violence and more graphic depictions of violent outcomes.

Researchers have found that players are still drawn to these games, in part, for their social element. Yee (2006), for instance, has identified five motivations for why individuals play MMORPGs, including achievement, relationship, immersion, escapism, and manipulation. In his work he found that male players are more likely to be driven by the achievement and motivation factors, while female players are more likely to be driven by the relationship factor. He also found that players developed meaningful relationships with others they met in MMORPGs. Interestingly, Yee (2001) found that 60% of male players and 75% of female players believed that some of their *EverQuest* friendships were comparable with or better than their offline friendships. He also found that 3% of male players and 15% of female players formed offline relationships (i.e., married, dating, or engaged to) someone they first met in *Norrath*.

Second Life is an example of a MMORPG. It is an online virtual world developed by Linden Lab and was launched in 2003. *Second Life* users, known as residents, interact with each other through avatars. Unlike other MMORPGs there is no game objective. Instead, residents meet other residents and explore and help create the virtual environment. Participants can socialize, participate in individual and group activities, and create and trade virtual property. Romantic relationships and friendships have been known to initiate and develop in *Second Life*. Gilbert, Murphy, and Avalos (2011) surveyed 199 participants who had been involved in an intimate relationships in *Second Life*. They found that the majority of participants viewed their *Second Life* relationships as real rather than as a form of game-playing. However, not all their findings presented these relationships in glowing terms. A portion of their participants believed that their virtual relationship was deemed a threat to their real-life relationship with the potential for "detrimental effects rising as the couple progressively adds nonimmersive digital and physical channels of communication to the original 3D relationship" (p. 2039).

Social Networking Sites: FtF and virtual friends

Boyd and Ellison (2007) define social networking sites (SNSs) "as web-based services that allow individuals to (1) construct a public or semipublic profile within a bounded system, (2) articulate a list of other users with whom they share a connection, and (3) view and traverse their list of connections and those made by others within the system. The nature and nomenclature of these connections may vary from site to site." Friendster, which emerged in 2002, was one of the first mainstream social networking sites. This was followed by MySpace and LinkedIn. Facebook was launched in 2004 and is currently the largest social networking site in the world.

Research into SNSs has found that adolescents and young adults use these sites to strengthen different aspects of their offline connections (Pempek, Yermolayeva, & Calvert, 2009; Subrahmanyam, Reich, Waechter, & Espinoza, 2008). However, researchers have found that SNSs are being used to find new friends (Raacke & Bonds-Raacke, 2008). Interestingly, Pempek et al. (2009) found that Facebook users spent more time observing content than posting content.

Not all experiences on SNSs are positive. Muise, Christofides, and Desmarais (2009) found that increased Facebook use significantly predicted Facebook-related jealousy. Utz and Beukeboom (2011) examined SNS jealousy and SNS relationship happiness and the consequences of SNS use for romantic relationships. Overall, they found that participants experienced more happiness than jealousy in reaction to their partner's activities on social networking sites. However, individuals low in self-esteem where more SNS jealous than those high in self-esteem. Self-esteem also moderated the effects of SNS use and the need for popularity on SNS jealousy and SNS relationship happiness.

Online Dating Sites: Shopping for Love

No chapter on online relationships would be complete without considering online dating sites. Online dating sites, in a fairly primitive form to the way we know them today, started appearing in the 1980s. In the early days online dating was stigmatized and researchers were finding that more shy people were gravitating to these sites to find a mate (Scharlott & Christ, 1995). In the 1980s these sites were largely text-based with limited space for individuals to create a dating profile in the hope to attract others. Currently, many online dating sites attempt to effectively match users of the service. These dating sites are continuing to work on refining tools to match the most suitable people together. Online daters are often expected to complete personality tests, as well as surveys on their interests and what aspects they are looking for in a partner. From there matches are often given compatibility ratings. Other sites allow clients to find their own matches—where they need to work through a sea of profiles to make their choices. In addition to the generic online dating sites that exist, such as, e-Harmony, True.com, and Match.com, there are also more specialized online dating sites, which gather like-minded individuals together. For example, there are sites designed specifically for Christians, Jews, Vegans, Goths, or Spiritual people. Sites like these are similar to social groups which one might join in the hope to find another that shares the same values or interests (Whitty, 2008a). Moreover, they potentially cut out some of the work involved with the search for the perfect other (Whitty, 2007).

Researchers have found that some individuals use online dating sites exclusively to find a partner, while others use this as one tool out of many (Whitty & Buchanan, 2009). Whitty and Buchanan (2009) found this varies with age, with older people more likely to use online dating exclusively. Albright (2007) believed that people use online dating sites because of the appeal of a large pool of availables in an environment, which enhances romantic projections. Others have found in their research that individuals choose to use online dating sites—as an alternative to the pubs and clubs scene; because they were shy or reserved; they felt they had no other options; it was convenient; and because of the privacy it affords (Whitty, 2008b; Whitty & Carr, 2006).

Decisions about how to present oneself on an online dating site can be difficult. Researchers in the past have described online dating profiles as a commodity that clients are shopping for (Whitty, 2008b). Online daters have described the writing of profiles as a process of "selling themselves." For example, one online dater described his experience as the following:

> The other thing for me personally is I'm great at writing trade manuals for someone, but when it comes to writing about yourself and trying to sell yourself it's a very different story. I don't know whether that's more of a male trait than a female trait. It depends how good you want to try selling yourself too isn't it? (Wayne) (Whitty, 2008b; p. 1714).

Online daters admit to sometimes "overselling" themselves in order to attract potential mates to their profiles. Interestingly, they are unforgiving of anyone who lies on their own profiles, but when they misrepresent themselves they perceive this more as an exaggeration than a blatant lie (see Whitty, 2008; Whitty & Carr, 2006). Whitty (2008, p. 1715) provides some examples:

> Suszi: Actually, it's quite funny that there is, you can pick, there is a thing for body type and you can pick 'slim, average, athletic, a bit overweight'. Do you know any chick that is going to tell you that they are a bit overweight?
>
> Interviewer: Wouldn't know, I guess not?
>
> Suszi: That is right, so I just say average.
>
> Interviewer: It's like the idea of perception of what is 'average', and average is you know probably a bit overweight anyway.
>
> Matthew: Well it's all perception of reality isn't it. Everyone's view of the world is different, my view of myself may be very different to what someone else thinks it is. But you know, my view is that you had to sell yourself without being. I mean the last thing you want is reality shock, when people get there and go 'that is not what he said he was about', so you have got to make the most of what you have got

without exaggerating it so much that they never see you again. So, I would say it was probably 90% accurate with a few little embellishments you know.

Interviewer: Tell us about the embellishments.

Matthew: Oh gosh . . . you know things like portraying things in the most positive light. You know things like interests. I don't think I really have definite music interests or anything, but I just said, 'I am on a first name basis with people at HMV' but I am not really but it doesn't matter. You know that sort of thing.

Future Development in the Field

As already acknowledged in this chapter, the Internet will continue to grow and new fads will arise and so it is difficult to confidently predict what psychologists will be researching with regards to relationships in the future. No doubt the Internet will become quicker and there will be even more bandwidth available.

In their theorizing about the Internet, I urge scholars to consider the Internet as containing a variety of different types of spaces, governed by different rules. Hancock, Thom-Santelli, and Ritchie's (2004) feature-based model provides guidance here, where they consider media features such as whether the media are synchronous, recordable, and distributed. Whitty et al. (2012) have argued that some media, such as instant messenger are "near synchronous." Moreover, Whitty and her colleagues have argued that the leanness of the media might also need to be taken into account when predicting online behavior and communication.

Most scholars, to date, have considered the differences between online spaces and offline spaces when it comes to initiating, developing, and maintaining relationships. However, the reality is that individuals use a variety of media together with traditional communication. When getting to know someone in the early days of a relationship, no longer is it typically the case that they get to know them in one space online, and media switch until they finally meet FtF. Instead individuals incorporate different media together. New research about relationships needs to take these changes in media usage into account. In fact, the term online relationship may well become obsolete.

Conclusions

The world has changed very quickly in the last 20 years with the evolution of the Internet. However, as this chapter has pointed out not everything we do when it comes to forming relationships is all that different. New theories have been developed to explain online relating; however, many of the theories developed to explain traditional forms of dating and relationship development still provide a useful lens. In the future we might not be taking the binary view of online/offline relationships that many scholars currently take. Moreover, in our considerations of relationship development, I would recommend that scholars consider the features of each space and the unique rules govern that space.

References

Albright, J. M. (2007). How do I love thee and thee and thee: Self-presentation, deception, and multiple relationships online. In M. T. Whitty, A. J. Baker, J. A. Inman (Eds.), *Online matchmaking*. (pp. 81–93). London, UK: Palgrave Macmillan.

Altman, I., & Taylor, D. A. (1973). *Social penetration: The development of interpersonal relationships.* New York, NY: Holt, Rinehart & Winston.

Barak, A., Boniel-Nissim, M., & Suler, J. (2008). Fostering empowerment in online support groups. *Computers in Human Behavior, 24,* 1867–1883.

Bargh, J. A., McKenna, K. Y. A., & Fitzsimons, G. M. (2002). Can you see the real me? Activation and expression of the "true self" on the internet. *Journal of Social Issues, 58*, 33–48.

boyd, d. m., & Ellison, N. B. (2007). Social network sites: Definition, history, and scholarship. *Journal of Computer-Mediated Communication, 13*(1), article 11. Retrieved August 8, 2011 from http://jcmc.indiana.edu/vol13/issue1/boyd.ellison.html

Buss, D. M. (1987). Sex differences in human mate selection criteria: An evolutionary perspective. In C. Crawford, M. Smith, and D. Krebs (Eds.), *Sociobiology and Psychology: Ideas, issues and perspectives* (pp. 335–352). London, UK: Lawrence Erlbaum.

Buss, D. M., & Barnes, M. (1986). Preferences in human mate selection. *Journal of Personality and Social Psychology, 50*, 559–570.

Cate. R., & Lloyd, S. (1992). *Courtship.* Newbury Park, CA: Sage.

Coontz, S. (1988). *The social origins of private life: A history of American families 1600-1900.* New York, NY: Verso.

Dawson, B. L., & McIntosh, W. D. (2006). Sexual strategies theory and Internet personal advertisements. *CyberPsychology & Behavior, 9*(5), 614–617.

Gilbert, R. L., Murphy, N. A., & Avalos, M. C. (2011). Realism, idealization, and potential negative impact of 3D virtual relationships. *Computers in Human Behavior, 27*(5), 2039–2046.

Greenless, I. A., & McGrew, W. C. (1994). Sex and age differences in preferences and tactics of mate attraction: Analysis of published advertisements. *Ethology and Sociobiology, 15*, 59–72.

Hancock, J., Thom-Santelli, J., & Ritchie, T. (2004). Deception and design: The impact of communication technologies on lying behavior. *Proceedings, Conference on Computer Human Interaction, New York, 6*(1), 130–136.

Hancock, J. T., & Dunham, P. J. (2001). Impression formation in computer-mediated communication revisited: An Analysis of the Breadth and Intensity of Impressions. *Communication Research, 28*, 325–347.

Harrison, A., & Saeed, L. (1977). Let's make a deal: An analysis of revelations and stipulations in lonely hearts advertisements. *Journal of Personality and Social Psychology, 35*, 257–264.

Hiltz, S., Johnson, M., & Turoff, M. (1986). Experiments in group decision making: Communication process and outcome in face-to-face versus computerized conferences. *Human Communication Research, 13*, 225–252.

Jiang, L. C., Bazarova, N. N., & Hancock, J. T. (in press). From perception to behaviour: Disclosure reciprocity and the intensification of intimacy in computer-mediated communication. *Communication Research*

Joinson, A. N. (2001). Self-disclosure in computer-mediated communication: The role of self-awareness and visual anonymity. *European Journal of Social Psychology, 31*, 177–192.

Kenrick, D. T., Sadalla, E. K., Groth, G., & Trost, M. R. (1990). Evolution, traits, and the stages of human courtship: Qualifying the parental investment model. *Journal of Personality, 58*, 97–116.

Koller, M. R. (1951). Some changes in courtship behavior in three generations of Ohio women. *American Sociological Review, 16*, 266–370.

Kowalski, R. M., & Limber, S. P. (2007). Electronic bullying among middle school students. *Journal of Adolescent Health, 41*, S22–S30.

McKenna, K. Y. A., & Bargh, J. A. (2000). Plan 9 from cyberspace: The implications of the internet for personality and social psychology. *Journal of Personality and Social Psychology, 4*, 57–75.

McKenna, K. Y. A., Green, A. S., & Gleason, M. E. J. (2002). Relationship formation on the Internet: What's the big attraction? *Journal of Social Issues, 58*, 9–31.

Mongeau, P. A., Hale, J. L., Johnson, K. L., & Hillis, J. D. (1993). Who's wooing whom? An Investigation of female initiated dating. In P. J. Kabfleisch (Ed.), *Interpersonal communication: Evolving interpersonal relationships* (pp. 51–68). Hillsdale, NJ: Lawrence Erlbaum Associates, Inc.

Morton, L., Alexander, J., & Altman, I. (1976). Communication and relationship definition. In G. R. Miller (Ed.), *Explorations in interpersonal communication* (pp. 105–125). Beverly Hills, CA: Sage.

Muise, A., Christofides, E., & Desmarais, S. (2009). More information that you ever wanted: Does Facebook bring out the green-eyed monster of jealousy? *CyberPsychology & Behavior, 12*(4), 441–444.

Murstein, B. (1974). *Love, sex and marriage through the ages.* New York, NY: Springer.

Parks, M. R., & Floyd, K. (1996). Making friends in cyberspace. *Journal of Communication, 46,* 80–97.

Parks, M. R., & Roberts, L. D. (1998). "Making MOOsic": The development of personal relationships online and a comparison to their off-line counterparts. *Journal of Social and Personal Relationships, 15,* 517–537.

Pempek, T. A., Yermolayeva, Y. A., & Calvert, S. L. (2009). College students' social networking experiences on Facebook. *Journal of Applied Developmental Psychology, 30*(3), 227–238.

Raacke, J., & Bonds-Raacke, J. (2008). MySpace and Facebook: Applying the uses and gratifications theory to exploring friend-networking sites. *CyberPsychology & Behavior, 11*(2), 169–174.

Rice, F. P. (1996). *Intimate relationships, marriages, and families.* Mountain View, CA: Mayfield Publishing.

Rogers, C. (2003). *Client-centered therapy.* London, UK: Constable & Robinson Ltd. (Original work published 1951.)

Rogers, C. (2004). *On becoming a person: A therapist's view of psychotherapy.* London: Constable & Robinson Ltd. (Original work published 1961.)

Scharlott, B. W., & Christ, W. G. (1995). Overcoming relationship-initiation barriers: The impact of a computer-dating system on sex role, shyness, and appearance inhibitions. *Computers in Human Behavior, 11*(2), 191–204.

Subrahmanyam, K., & Greenfield, P. (2008). The future of children. *Online Communication and Adolescent Relationships, 18*(1), 119–146.

Subrahmanyam, K., Reich, S. M., Waechter, N., & Espinoza, G. (2008). Online and offline social networks: Use of social networking sites by emerging adults. *Journal of Applied Developmental Psychology, 29*(6), 420–433.

Subrahmanyam, K., Smahel, D., & Greenfield, P. (2006). Connecting developmental constructions to the internet: Identity presentation and sexual exploration in online teen chat rooms. *Developmental Psychology, 42*(3), 395–406.

Suler, J. (2004a). The online disinhibition effect. *CyberPsychology & Behavior, 7,* 321–326.

Thibaut, J. W., & Kelley, H. H. (1959). *The social psychology of groups.* New York, NY: Wiley.

Townsend, J., & Wasserman, T. (1997). The perception of sexual attractiveness: Sex differences in variability. *Archives of Sexual Behavior, 26,* 243–268.

Turkle, S. (1995). *Life on the screen: Identity in the age of the Internet.* London, UK: Weidenfeld & Nicolson.

Utz, S. (2000). Social information processing in MUDs: The development of friendships in virtual worlds. *Journal of Online Behavior, 1*(1). Retrieved February 7, 2005 from http://www.behavior.net/JOB/v1n1/utz.html

Utz, S., & Beukeboom, C. J. (2011). The role of social network sites in romantic relationships: Effects on jealousy and relationship happiness. *Journal of Computer-mediated Communication, 16*(4), 511–527.

Walther, J. B. (1992). Interpersonal effects in computer-mediated interaction: A relational perspective. *Communication Research, 19,* 52–90.

Walther, J. B. (1995). Relational aspects of computer-mediated communication: Experimental observations over time. *Organizational Science, 6,* 186–203.

Walther, J. B. (1996). Computer-mediated communication: Impersonal, interpersonal and hyperpersonal interaction. *Communication Research, 23,* 3–43.

Walther, J. B. (2007). Selective self-presentation in computer-mediated communication: Hyperpersonal dimensions of technology, language, and cognition. *Computers in Human Behavior, 23,* 2538–2557.

Walther, J. B., Slovacek, C., & Tidwell, L. (2001). Is a picture worth a thousand words? Photographic images in long-term and short-term computer-mediated communication. *Communication Research, 28,* 105–134.

Whitty, M. T. (2007). The art of selling one's self on an online dating site: The BAR Approach. In M. T. Whitty, A. J. Baker, & J. A. Inman (Eds.), *Online matchmaking* (pp. 57–69). Houndmills, UK: Palgrave Macmillan.

Whitty, M. T. (2008a). The joys of online dating. In E. Konjin, T. Martin., S. Utz, & A. Linden (Eds.), *Mediated Interpersonal Communication: How Technology Affects Human Interaction* (pp. 234–251). New York, NY: Taylor & Francis Group/ Routledge.

Whitty, M.T. (2008b). Revealing the "real" me, searching for the "actual" you: Presentations of self on an internet dating site. *Computers in Human Behavior, 24,* 1707–1723.

Whitty, M.T., & Buchanan, T. (2009). Looking for Love in so many Places: Characteristics of Online Daters and Speed Daters. *Interpersona: An International Journal on Personal Relationships, 3*(2), 63–86.

Whitty, M.T. & Buchanan, T. (2010). "What's in a 'screen name'?" Attractiveness of different types of screen names used by online daters, *International Journal of Internet Science, 5*(1), 5–19.

Whitty, M. T., Buchanan, T., Joinson, A.N., & Meredith, A. (2012). Not all lies are spontaneous: An examination of deception across different modes of communication. *Journal of the American Society for Information Science and Technology, 63*(1), 208–216.

Whitty, M. T. & Carr, A. N. (2006). *Cyberspace romance: The psychology of online relationships.* Basingstoke, UK: Palgrave Macmillan.

Whitty, M. & Gavin, J. (2001). Age/Sex/Location: Uncovering the social cues in the development of online relationships. *CyberPsychology and Behaviour, 4*(5), 623–630.

Wysocki, D. K. (1998). Let your fingers to do the talking: Sex on an adult chat-line. *Sexualities, 1,* 425–452.

Wysocki, D. K., & Thalken, J. (2007). Whips and chains? Fact or fiction? Content analysis of sadomasochism in Internet personal advertisements. In M. T. Whitty, A. J. Baker, & J. A. Inman (Eds.), *Online matchmaking* (pp. 178–196). Basingstoke, UK: Palgrave Macmillan.

Yee, N. (2001). The Norrathian Scrolls. Retrieved October 15, 2008 from http://www.nickyee.com/EQt/home.html

Yee, N. (2006). The Demographics, Motivations and Derived Experiences of Users of Massively-Multiuser Online Graphical Environments. *PRESENCE: Teleoperators and Virtual Environments, 15,* 309–329.

Chapter 5

Computer-Mediated Persuasion and Compliance: Social Influence on the Internet and Beyond

Brandon Van Der Heide and Erin M. Schumaker

Introduction

The idea that a message may influence a person not only on the basis of the structural components of message contents but also on the basis of the perceptions a recipient has of the speaker's character, charisma, and credibility is not a new one. Indeed, Aristotle suggests: "the orator must not only try to make the argument of his (sic.) speech demonstrative and worthy of belief; he must also make his character look right, and put his hearers, who are to decide, into the right frame of mind" (Aristotle, trans. 1924). Who we are, or more precisely, who our audience perceives us to be, can have a profound effect on the success of a persuasive attempt.

This provides an interesting backdrop to the story of persuasion and compliance gaining in online environments. On the Internet, where one relies primarily on text to make a persuasive case, where one does not know if a message sender is wearing a three-piece-suit or rags, is tall or short, or is black or white, how do people make sense of the messages they hear? Does the Internet truly equalize persuasion—that is, does it provide an environment wherein all potential persuaders are given equal footing regardless of socioeconomic status, dress, organizational position, and the like? Or, do users of text-based technologies adapt to the medium, both encoding and extracting information about a message sender's credibility in new ways? Further, if a message recipient cannot see, hear, taste, touch, or smell a message sender, is it not also true that the normal channels by which one would judge a message sender to be untrustworthy are obscured? What tools do message recipients use to make sense of this? These questions and others have captivated social scientists exploring computer-mediated persuasion.

Chapter Overview

This chapter explores the ways that messages exchanged—primarily via the Internet's text-based channels—exert influence on attitudes and behavior. Specifically, the chapter utilizes a dual-process approach to attitude change on the Internet. The dual-process approach suggests that message receivers can be persuaded through a careful reflection on a message's arguments, structure, and quality; however, sometimes message receivers may be less engaged in the persuasion process, and in those times a message receiver might revert to using simple decision rules, or heuristics, to formulate an attitude (see Booth-Butterfield & Welbourne, 2002; Todorov, Chaiken, & Henderson, 2002). This chapter discusses these dual-process models (i. e., the elaboration likelihood model and the heuristic–systematic model; Petty & Cacioppo, 1981, 1986; Chaiken, 1980; 1987, respectively) and additionally explores one theory of online relating, Social Information

Processing (SIP) theory (Walther, 1992). SIP theory suggests that, although information about other people accumulates more slowly in text-based environments, given enough time and motivation, people can form impressions of other message senders (e.g., credibility impressions) online using the verbal cues present in text-based messages.

Through these theoretical lenses, the chapter derives some basic propositions about the nature of online persuasion and explores how these propositions might provide a guide for understanding previous empirical work in computer-mediated persuasion and compliance gaining as well as provides a framework for future research. Finally, the chapter considers the impact of these propositions in terms of how they may be practically and theoretically applied and extended to a variety of new media applications.

Cueless Persuasive Influence

Early computer-mediated communication (CMC) researchers argued that because nonverbal cues were filtered out of CMC, and because impression formation relies on nonverbal cues, impressions could not form via CMC. Indeed, Dubrovsky, Kiesler, and Sethna (1991) suggest that interpersonal impression formation is difficult for those interacting via computers. If interpersonal heuristic cues cannot be readily transmitted via text, the personal characteristics of an influencer (e.g., credibility, attractiveness, status) should have no effect on the persuasiveness of an influence attempt. While it is theoretically plausible that CMC may present an environment where the quality of one's message structure is all that matters in determining the persuasiveness of a message, this chapter also proposes an alternative theoretical perspective wherein in certain settings source credibility, expertise, and status may factor into our judgments of persuasive messages online.

Some specific types of interpersonal impressions have potent effects on persuasive outcomes both online and off. Specifically, information about an individual's hierarchical status is one heuristic cue that, when received and processed in conjunction with a persuasive message, can affect the attitudes one has following the reception of that persuasive message (Chaiken, 1980, 1987). One perspective on CMC, commonly called the cues-filtered-out (CFO) perspective (Culnan & Markus, 1987) proposes that CMC filters information about the hierarchical status or organizational position of individuals out of dialogue. As Kiesler et al. (1984) argue: "electronic communication is blind with respect to the vertical hierarchy in social relationships and organizations" (p. 1125). Kiesler et al. reasoned that, because contextual cues (i.e., one's dress or seating at the head of the table) and dynamic behavioral cues (i.e., gaze, touch, and other paralinguistic cues) are filtered out of CMC, in CMC high status people should (1) have less influence on other group members and (2) participate at equal levels as other group members. Consistent with this proposition, Dubrovsky et al. (1991) found that in face-to-face groups a member with high status dominated group discussion; however, in computer-mediated groups, individuals participated more equally despite status differences.

Dual-process models of persuasive message processing (Chaiken, 1980, 1987; Petty & Cacioppo, 1981, 1986) have offered an answer to the question of how individuals judge the messages they receive. These models suggest that individuals rely on central message cues such as message strength or argument quality and peripheral message cues such as the status, expertise, or credibility of the message sender as they process persuasive messages. This judgment predicts the degree of influence a persuasive message will have on a message recipient. In line with early perspectives on CMC (Kiesler, Siegel, & McGuire, 1984; Sproull & Kiesler, 1986), which suggested that CMC was devoid of social context cues, other research on CMC (Guadagno & Cialdini, 2002, 2007) has suggested that users of CMC systems might instead process persuasive messages differently than do individuals processing messages in face-to-face communication environments. Such research suggests that CMC users do not rely on the heuristic processing of interpersonal characteristics.

If social information cues are filtered out of CMC, one should expect to find specific persuasive effects according to dual-process models of persuasion (Chaiken, 1980, 1987; Petty & Cacioppo, 1981, 1986). Specifically, one should expect that any interpersonal information that might have been conveyed with a message (e.g., that the message source is an expert on the message topic or that the message originates from a trustworthy source) should be filtered out of a computer-mediated message. Consequently, any observed persuasive outcome of such a message should arise because of other specific message features such as argument quality. Because of the centrality of dual-process persuasive models to understanding the way computer-mediated persuasion and compliance gaining works, this chapter will introduce the basic tenets of one popular dual-process model of persuasive influence: the heuristic–systematic model (HSM).

The Heuristic–Systematic Model

Dual-process models posit two distinct paths to persuasion. First, according to Chaiken, Liberman, and Eagly (1989) people process persuasive messages systematically—carefully and thoroughly scrutinizing messages they receive. They are more likely to be persuaded by a well-reasoned, logically consistent message than a poorly-formed, logically inconsistent message.

Another manner by which persuasive messages affect perceivers is through heuristic message processing, wherein individuals focus on information allowing them to "use simple decision rules or cognitive heuristics to formulate their judgments and decisions" (Eagly & Chaiken, 1993, p. 327). For example, if an individual processes a message heuristically, a message originating from an expert would be more persuasive than the same message from a layperson. Research has examined a number of possible alternative heuristically valuable message cues and source characteristics that may influence how people evaluate influential messages: the number of persuasive messages and the likeability of a source (Chaiken, 1980; Chaiken & Eagly, 1983), as well as the reliability of a source (Chaiken & Maheswaran, 1994) can trigger persuasive effects.

A central assumption of Chaiken (1980, 1987; Chaiken et al., 1989) and colleagues' model is that the two processing modes can occur concurrently. That is, an individual could simultaneously process a persuasive message both systematically and heuristically (Chaiken & Maheswaran, 1994; Maheswaran & Chaiken, 1991; Maheswaran, Mackie, & Chaiken, 1992; Todorov et al., 2002; Trope & Gaunt, 1999). Because both heuristic and systematic message processing can occur at the same time according to the HSM, a message receiver can carefully scrutinize the quality of an argument while at the same time attending to social cues indicating that a message sender is a trustworthy expert. However, the CFO perspective argues that interpersonal impression cues about a message sender's identity are not available to a message recipient in CMC. Therefore, in CMC, persuasive messages may be processed without the benefit of this information.

Dual-Processing in Mediated Contexts

The dual-process approach has been used to understand how people process mediated messages. Early research found that individuals who received a written message displayed less opinion change as a result of a written message compared with the same message delivered via video or audiotape (Chaiken & Eagly, 1983). When Chaiken and Eagly manipulated communicator likeability (a heuristic cue) by praising or derogating the location, faculty, and students of the university where the research was conducted, message recipients were influenced to a much greater degree in the audio and videotape conditions than they were in the written message condition. The authors proposed that this effect occurred because cues to the likeability of the communicator were filtered out of the written messages. Consequently, messages were most persuasive when they originated from a likeable communicator and were delivered via media that could convey the heuristic cues associated with likeability.

More recent research has sought to extend Chaiken and Eagly's (1983) findings to CMC. Guadagno and Cialdini (2002, 2007) compared CMC with face-to-face interaction in order to understand the role of CMC in persuasion. Consistent with the CFO perspective and Chaiken's dual-process model, Guadagno and Cialdini conceptualized CMC to be socially constrained. They stated: "To date, CMC has been highly socially constrained, restricted for the most part to text-based, impersonal forms" (2002, p. 39). Guadagno and Cialdini predicted that CMC would not allow for heuristic cues to be transmitted, and that persuasiveness would vary on the basis of message strength alone. In order to test these claims, Guadagno and Cialdini conducted a series of studies wherein college students engaged in an interview with a confederate about the possibility of implementing senior comprehensive exams as a requirement for graduation. Participants were instructed to ask their partners a list of questions, and confederates supplied a prepared response either via email or face-to-face. In the CMC condition, these responses consisted of a written transcription of the scripted answer to each interview question. In the face-to-face condition these syntactically identical scripted responses were recited to participants. After the interview portion of the experiment, participants completed attitude measures and engaged in a thought-listing exercise to measure systematic and heuristic processing. Consistent with their predictions, Guadagno and Cialdini (2002, study 1) found that women were persuaded more by face-to-face messages than computer-mediated messages and that CMC caused participants to recall fewer communicator-related thoughts—a measure of heuristic processing—than did face-to-face interaction. Both Chaiken and Eagly's (1983) finding that written messages elicit less heuristic processing than audio or video taped messages and Guadagno and Cialdini's (2002) finding that there were significantly more communicator thoughts in the face-to-face condition than in the CMC condition seem consistent with CFO predictions that text-based communication modalities are unable to convey interpersonal information that could be of heuristic value to a message recipient.

It is important that any theoretical model of computer-mediated persuasion adequately account for these data. Thus, as Walther (1994) suggests, a rote dismissal of the CFO perspective as "a dead horse no longer to be beaten" (p. 476) is ill-founded. Although this chapter critiques the assumption that interpersonal information is filtered out of CMC and is not useful to message recipients, it is, nonetheless, important for theory to account for the conditions that make the reception of heuristically valuable interpersonal information difficult and determine conditions which make the reception of this information possible. This chapter proceeds by introducing a perspective on Internet communication suggesting that Internet users draw on a variety of cues in order to form impressions of website credibility, and extends this logic to explain how interpersonal source credibility impressions may develop in CMC. Then, it presents a theoretical framework, which synthesizes two empirically supported perspectives on CMC and persuasive message processing, in order to explain and predict when heuristically valuable interpersonal credibility cues matter in CMC and when they do not.

A Social Information Processing Perspective on Persuasion

While some research suggests that CMC is not capable of transmitting heuristically valuable information, other perspectives suggest that source credibility may affect online influence processes

(Metzger, Flanagin, Eyal, Lemus, & McCann, 2003). Metzger et al. argued that source, message, and channel credibility can affect how influential a message is on the Internet. Further, they argue that the distinct properties of communication on the Internet should be taken into account when investigating credibility on the Internet.

Many current approaches to understanding the effects of technology on source credibility approach credibility as a feature of a website. For example, Sundar (2008) suggested that the source credibility judgments people attribute to websites arise from simple decision rules based in the modality, agency, interactivity, and navigability of a website. In this work, Sundar offers a typology of heuristics that might be activated while people use the Internet by summarizing a variety of heuristic mechanisms that users may utilize. For instance, Sundar describes one modality decision rule, the novelty heuristic as, "young people who are not particularly involved in the subject matter transmitted by a digital device… may be so enamored by the novelty of the technology (i.e., using podcasts in blogs) that they ascribe higher credibility to the content in that podcast than if they had received the same content through a non-novel delivery mechanism such as a radio broadcast" (p. 82). Similarly, Metzger et al. (2003) discussed source credibility primarily in terms of organizations as sources. They argued that the credibility of an organization that owns a website could be judged on the basis of the content present on that organization's website. They suggest several features that can have beneficial and detrimental effects on the perceived organizational credibility of a website. For instance, perceived expertise can be communicated through websites that contain more complete coverage of a topic (Alexander & Tate, 1999), or display a photograph of the author (Fogg et al., 2001a). Alternatively, Fogg et al. (2001a) also found that the presence of a non-reputable web-advertisement banner reduces the perceived expertise of an article posted on the web. Alexander and Tate (1999) also found that judgments of greater trustworthiness were caused by third-party endorsements. Fogg and colleagues (2001b) found that while broken hyperlinks or excessive advertising can reduce perceived trustworthiness, perceived trustworthiness of a website increases when an organization's website lists the organization's real-world location. These findings suggest that people are able to make judgments of organizations' credibility on the basis of information contained on the Internet. Specifically, people scour these organizational web pages to find cues that inform them about whether an organization should be judged to be credible or not on the basis of the cues present on their website.

Because of the emergence of public, interpersonal communication at various Internet venues, it is important not only to understand the organizational credibility of a website, but also these issues of credibility should be discussed concerning the judgments of others' expertise and trustworthiness that people make online. Following Metzger and colleagues' (2003) logic that people make organizational source credibility judgments based on certain factors, it seems possible that people might also make interpersonal source credibility judgments based on features present in Internet interactions. Resnick, Zeckhauser, Friedman, and Kuwabara (2000) suggested that reputation systems, systems on websites that aggregate and distribute individuals' positive or negative ratings of another individual, can influence how trustworthy others are judged to be. Resnick and Zeckhauser (2002) found that these reputation systems can influence Internet users' purchasing behavior. A controlled field experiment of purchasing behavior on eBay.com found that users with a strong reputation were able to sell products for a higher price than did users without an established reputation (Resnick, Zeckhauser, Swanson, & Lockwood, 2006).

It seems reasonable to extend Metzger and colleagues' argument to interpersonal source credibility judgments on the Internet: Under some conditions, interpersonal judgments of trust and credibility do form in CMC. Knowing that CMC is capable of sustaining interaction that allows for these sorts of interpersonal judgments to be made is important, but it is also important to develop a theoretical understanding of the conditions that allow these judgments to be made. In order to better understand this process, this chapter turns to a discussion on SIP theory (Walther, 1992), which explains how interpersonal impressions of an individual's source credibility can accrue in CMC.

SIP theory (Walther, 1992) argues that interpersonal information can accumulate when people interact using text-based communication media such as CMC. In contrast to the CFO perspective, SIP theory assumes that relational information is transmitted via "nonverbal or verbal, linguistic, and textual manipulations" (p. 69). SIP theory also contends that this information accumulates over the course of several interactions; although this accumulation is slower than in face-to-face interactions because messages take longer to process in CMC. Subsequent tests of SIP theory have confirmed SIP theory's predictions about the development of relational communication over time (Ramirez, 2007). Further, Walther (1993) found that individuals were able to form progressively stronger impressions of one another over time. As is specified in SIP theory, individuals must have adequate time for interaction, and/or there must be some expectation of future interaction for people to form impressions via CMC (Walther, 1994; Walther & Parks, 2002).

Walther's initial statement (1992) of SIP theory notes several factors that are likely to restrict the amount of interpersonal information that CMC can convey. First, SIP theory suggests that the amount of time individuals spend communicating with each other via CMC should impact relational outcomes. Specifically, when the amount of time people interact via CMC is limited, people process smaller amounts of expressive textual communication. Thus, CMC can appear to restrict the transmission of interpersonal information when the true limiting factor is the amount of time individuals had to interact.

A second factor that may have appeared to restrict the amount of social information conveyed by CMC in previous research is the use of written transcripts of oral communication as a proxy for naturally occurring computer-mediated interaction. According to Walther (1992), early CMC research examining verbal-only data assumed that a lack of intimacy and relational development was due to the fact that nonverbal cues were filtered out of CMC. However, this research did not observe nonverbal cues in face-to-face groups. Walther argued that while these nonverbal cues from face-to-face groups may convey greater intimacy, they could be just as likely to convey non-immediacy and other negative socioemotional information. Therefore, concluding that CMC was more formal and less immediate than face-to-face interaction on the basis of verbal-only data was premature.

This second issue can be extended somewhat. When experimental methodologies constrain text-based messages to be the written transcript of speech (thereby eliminating all original nonverbal affect, as in Guadagno & Cialdini, 2002, 2007), these messages do not represent naturally occurring CMC fairly. For example, when people communicate using CMC they tend to encode more social information into their verbal messages than they would have otherwise done. Research has suggested, for example that when people seek to express disliking for a partner in CMC they express disagreement with their partner, while people who seek to express affinity toward their partner verbally agree with that partner more readily (Walther, Van Der Heide, Tong, Carr, & Atkin, 2010). However, research exploring the expression of affect in face-to-face communication suggests that these expressions are enacted primarily nonverbally (Burgoon & Hale, 1987). Therefore, procedures that substitute verbal transcriptions of face-to-face communication as a proxy for CMC impose artificial restrictions on the ability of text-based interaction to convey social information. In short, verbal transcripts of speech filter out nonverbal cues of affect that people using natural CMC convey in other linguistic ways (see Walther, Loh, & Granka, 2005; Walther et al., 2010). These cues may convey intimacy, credibility, or other forms of social information.

Taken together with SIP theory's assumptions about text-based interaction, these limiting factors help to interpret some of the findings previously reviewed. Namely, both Chaiken and Eagly (1983) and Guadagno and Cialdini (2002) found that people processed messages less heuristically when exposed to text-based messages than when people were exposed to face-to-face, video taped, or audio taped messages. However, both of these studies were methodologically constrained in that neither study systematically varied the degree to which participants were exposed to text-based, heuristically valuable information. Allowing for variance in exposure to these cues may allow individuals to form heuristically valuable impressions of a message sender's credibility. Thus, the present work proceeds by deriving a number of theoretical propositions from the assumptions of the HSM and SIP theory.

A Sociotechnical Influence Model

To this point, much of the empirical work in interpersonal persuasion in CMC has been conceptualized to occur on the basis of systematic processing alone because heuristically valuable interpersonal information was expected to be filtered out of text-only messages. The present model challenges this assumption and instead, formally extends SIP theory to help explain and predict the conditions under which heuristically valuable information may affect the persuasive impact of text-only messages. By synthesizing SIP theory and the HSM, this model offers insight into how people process persuasive messages.

Chaiken and colleagues' (1980, 1987; Chaiken et al., 1989) HSM of persuasive message processing assumes that message recipients process both systematically (attending carefully to the content and argument quality of a message) and heuristically (using simple rules—e.g., experts should be trusted) to evaluate a persuasive message. SIP theory assumes that interpersonal impressions develop in CMC because of social information transmitted via textual/verbal cues and that messages take longer to process in CMC than in face-to-face interaction, which causes interpersonal impressions to develop over time because increased interaction with others in CMC allows for greater exposure to social information (Walther, 1992).

From both SIP theory and the HSM, one may derive the following basic assumptions about the way the influence process is carried out online. First, individuals decode social information from verbal, linguistic, and textual manipulations, and they use this information to inform heuristic judgments of a message sender's source credibility in CMC. Next, individuals are persuaded by messages in CMC on the basis of available heuristic and systematic cues. Finally, heuristically valuable interpersonal impressions accrue over the course of repeated exposure to social information in CMC.

SIP theory argues that interpersonal impressions can form when individuals have enough time to interact and anticipate future interaction with their communication partner (Ramirez, 2007; Walther, 1992, 1994). When people have ample time for interaction or anticipate future interaction with their partner, text-based communication media will be sufficient to allow heuristically useful information about a discussion partner to accrue. In this case, persuasion will occur on the basis of both systematic and heuristic message features. However, when people do not anticipate some degree of future interaction, or interaction is constrained, heuristically useful impressions of a message sender are not allowed to accrue. Because heuristically valuable impressions of a message sender cannot form in these conditions, individuals using CMC will find messages most persuasive when those messages are comprised by strong arguments compared to weak arguments because research has indicated that people tend to be persuaded by systematic cues alone when heuristic cues are absent (Chaiken & Eagly, 1983).

It is possible to synthesize SIP theory and the HSM to generate a theoretical hybrid of these two models by combining SIP theory's predictions about the conditions under which heuristically useful impressions form in CMC and HSM's arguments about the manner by which persuasive messages are processed. The synthesis posits the following set of propositions.

Proposition 1

In CMC when (1) heuristically valuable impressions of a persuasive message sender are not allowed to accrue and (2) an argument is strong, persuasive effects are realized on the basis of systematic processing.

The first proposition states that when heuristically useful impressions are not allowed to accumulate in CMC, the persuasive effects of that message should be realized on the basis of message strength alone. This proposition is similar to the CFO perspective's predictions about persuasive effects in CMC. However, where this research parts with CFO is in its statement of conditions that bound the CFO predictions. Namely, this model argues that heuristically valuable impressions of a persuasive message sender can form when time available for interaction is adequate or participants anticipate some degree of future interaction with one another.

To date there are several studies which support the first proposition. In addition to the previously mentioned work consistent with this proposition (Chaiken & Eagly, 1983; Guadagno & Cialdini, 2002, 2007) more recent work has established that when given a limited amount of time for impressions of others' credibility to accrue (and allowing the strength of influential messages to vary freely) several researchers have concluded that face-to-face communication more effectively allows for attitude change than CMC (Di Blasio & Milani, 2008; Schlosser, 2009). Other work exploring compliance gaining in CMC has generated similar results. Guéguen and Jacob (2001) found that the use of specific message inductions (use of the foot-in-the-door strategy) significantly affected donation rates to a cause promoted on a website. Other research suggests that compliance to an email request to fill out a survey is boosted significantly by the use of the foot-in-the-door strategy (Guéguen, 2001). Consistent with the first proposition, in these studies, it appears that the lack of a formed credibility impression, which was impeded by a short interaction time in CMC, may have led to a greater focus on actual message strength and other message characteristics rather than any credibility judgments.

Proposition 2

In CMC when (1) heuristically valuable impressions of a persuasive message sender are allowed to accrue, (2) an argument is strong, and (3) the heuristic cues that accompany that argument are positive, persuasive effects are realized on the basis of both heuristic and systematic processing.

The second proposition states that when heuristically valuable impressions of a message sender have accrued in CMC, persuasive effects will be realized on the basis of both systematic and heuristic information processing. For example, when a strong argument is delivered by an expert source, persuasive effects will be realized on the basis of both heuristic and systematic processing. These heuristically valuable impressions may have either a positive or negative valence. For instance, if an individual were processing a message according to an "experts can be trusted" heuristic (Todorov et al., 2002), cues that indicated high levels of expertise or low levels of expertise would be heuristically valuable. This discussion will refer to a positive heuristic cue as a cue that, for reasons other than the strength of a persuasive argument, inclines one to look favorably upon a message sender. A negative heuristic cue shall be referred to as a cue that, for reasons other than the strength of a persuasive argument, inclines one to look unfavorably upon a message sender.

The first proposition is consistent with the CFO and SIP theory perspectives on persuasion, while this second one is consistent with the SIP theory perspective alone.

S. -H. Lee's (2009) work suggests support for the proposed model. This work examined the effects of consumer-generated online reviews' argument quality (a systematic cue) and argument quantity (a heuristic cue) on participants' intentions to make online purchases. Lee found both a significant main effect of argument quality and quantity on intentions to make purchases online. The presence of these main effects suggests support for the critical assumption of the second proposition. Heuristic cues can effectively be transmitted and affect attitudinal and behavioral outcomes in CMC even in the presence of strong arguments.

Other research (E.J. Lee, 2008) seems generally supportive of this proposition, as well. Lee conducted a study that examined the effect of anonymity (i.e., individuated participants vs. group identified participants) and message strength on attitudes. This research found that when participants were individuated and met with a strong argument their perceptions of argument quality were greatest for the strong argument and least for the weak argument. Moreover, in terms of conformity to a presented position, individuated participants (who, ostensibly, could form some credibility impression of his or her partner) conformed most to strong arguments, as one would expect if both heuristic and systematic processes were at work. However, both deindividuated participants and individuated participants exposed to a weak message showed less conformity as predicted by the model proposed here.

E. J. Lee's (2008) work also raises another interesting question: How do users of CMC navigate the attitude change process when exposed to weak arguments, but heuristic cues that, when processed, indicate that a message sender is credible? Specifically, Lee found no differences among participants who were deindividuated (i.e., group identified). In other words, when participants were group identified, they may have attended to a group identification heuristic to assess argument quality whereas when they were identified as being an individual they did not have that heuristic with which to make credibility judgments. Thus, in some situations (i.e., when individuals are deindividuated), the effects of argument strength on persuasive efficacy may be suppressed in CMC, giving way to a *purely heuristic* mode of message processing. This foreshadows our third proposition.

Proposition 3

In CMC when (1) heuristically valuable impressions of a persuasive message sender are allowed to accrue, and (2) an argument is weak, but (3) the heuristic cues that accompany a message are positive, persuasive effects are realized on the basis of heuristic processing.

As noted earlier, in some situations it is conceivable that a weak argument could be paired with positive heuristic cues which, when processed, should lead one to be more likely to believe a message. For instance, an expert source may attempt to influence another person with a weak argument delivered via email. According to this synthetic framework, one would expect different results depending on whether heuristically valuable impressions had formed. If heuristically valuable impressions had not formed, the influence attempt should be relatively unsuccessful, as the recipient will process the weak influential message systematically (in the framework posited here there are no formal predictions of null propositions stated). Thus, any attitude change that occurs on the basis of a weak argument before heuristically useful impressions of a message sender have formed should not occur on the basis of either systematic or heuristic processing. However, after heuristically valuable impressions of a message sender have formed, this model proposes that an influential attempt will be based on the positive, heuristically useful impressions.

Van Der Heide and Walther (2009) have found general support for this proposition. In a study that looked at the impact of advice provided on an online discussion forum participants were asked to form opinions of the main attitude object (in this case attitudes toward two apartment complexes near a college campus) referred to in the advice-giver's message. The study experimentally varied the amount of heuristically valuable social information that an individual provided in an online message (which portrayed a consistently weak argument), and heuristically valuable social information was shown to affect credibility judgments of the message sender, and, in turn, the credibility of the sender was related to participants' ratings of the apartment complex. This finding is consistent with the proposition that in some conditions the heuristic processing of social information can lead users of computer-mediated interaction to utilize a variety of tools to form credibility impressions that impact attitudes.

Derivations, Extensions, and Applications

Despite the model's brevity, these three propositions suggest many fruitful lines of research. Additionally, it may be possible to apply some of the formal extensions of the HSM into the present model. For example, the additivity hypothesis of the HSM (Maheswaran et al., 1992; Todorov et al., 2002) may be applied to this framework. The additivity hypothesis argues that when participants are motivated to process a message through both heuristic and systematic processing, the result of this concurrent processing can have additive effects on persuasion. For instance, if a message is both strong and originates from an expert source, it should be more persuasive than a strong argument processed systematically but not heuristically. According to the first proposition, in some situations heuristically valuable information is not allowed to accrue in CMC. In these situations, there may be limited information available upon which to heuristically process messages. However, when heuristic information is strong and is allowed to accrue in CMC, and a persuasive argument is strong, there should be greater persuasive effects realized than when heuristically valuable impressions are not allowed to accrue. Thus, one extension of the model would suggest that in CMC when (1) arguments are strong and (2) heuristic cues are positive, persuasive attempts are more effective after heuristically valuable impressions are allowed to accrue. Additional derivations along this same line are possible, and future work should seek to explore these and other theoretical derivations.

Secondly, recent research concerning the effects of online product reviews on the intention to purchase products highlights the importance of involvement as a moderating factor. S.-H. Lee (2009) found that in a mock online review system participants who were highly involved in seeking information about a product tended to process information more centrally, focusing most directly on argument quality, than did participants who were less involved in the product search process. These less involved participants, instead, focused on heuristically valuable information about a message sender. In addition to highlighting the importance of involvement level, Lee's research also suggests support for the notion that heuristic judgments can play an important role in the influence process as it occurs online.

One of the extensions this model suggests is that future research should seek to explore several types of cues that may carry heuristically valuable information about message senders. Although only a partial list is presented here (see Sundar, 2008 for a more exhaustive review of heuristics which may be activated in mediated environments), this work presents several classes of cues with potential heuristic value that should be examined in future research. System-generated cues (cues that are generated by computing systems themselves), aggregated feedback systems (such as reputation systems; Resnick, et al., 2000), and self-disclosure behaviors are three different classes of cues that may impact heuristic judgments of computer-mediated message senders.

System-generated cues are pieces of information that are present in online environments that have not been generated directly by a computer user, but have been collected (and displayed) by the computer system itself. For example, one system-generated cue in the popular online social networking website Facebook is the number of friends an individual has. The number of friends one has is calculated by the system and is not directly provided by a user. In this example, system-generated cues arise from actual user behavior and thus may be useful in making attributions about users on the basis of the system-generated cues associated with them. Indeed previous research has indicated that individuals do form impressions of people's social attractiveness and general positivity on Facebook according to the number of friends they have (Kleck, Reese, Behnken, & Sundar, 2007; Tong, Van Der Heide, Langwell, & Walther, 2008). System-generated cues are most likely to provide heuristically valuable information to computer-mediated message recipients when that information provides some information about a user or that user's behavior. Other examples of system-generated cues that may inform interpersonal judgments include information such as the date a user last logged on to a website or online discussion forum or cues that indicate the amount of a user's participation in an online community (i.e., the number of posts in an online forum). Such system-generated cues may provide heuristically valuable cues which message recipients may use to make judgments of others online.

Resnick et al. (2000) suggest that aggregated feedback systems such as reputation systems can help technology users to establish trust with one another. As previously mentioned, other work by Resnick and colleagues (2006) has established that on the popular eBay online auction site (http://www.eBay.com), favorable feedback aggregated from other online auction users can generate greater market rewards for users with stronger aggregated reputations. Findings such as these suggest that in online venues people may find that such aggregated feedback can provide a user with heuristically valuable information about a target individual's credibility in an online community.

Self-disclosure behaviors are another type of information that may be of heuristic value to computer-mediated message recipients. Research has demonstrated that, in comparison to face-to-face interaction, in CMC people tend to use a greater proportion of self-disclosures to reduce uncertainty about one another (Tidwell & Walther, 2002). If self-disclosures are one method CMC users employ to overcome the lack of nonverbal cues in CMC, it is possible that self-disclosures of expertise or trustworthiness may serve as heuristically valuable cues that guide the processing of persuasive messages in CMC. Donath (1999) suggests that several types of self-disclosures offer clues to the identity of a computer-mediated message sender. In addition to the direct self-disclosures found to reduce uncertainty, Donath suggests that signature files (files attached to the end of email messages that often contain contact information as well as information about place of employment) and self-generated credentials are other user-generated information that may carry clues about a user's identity. Such clues may have heuristic value.

Unlike system-generated cues and aggregated feedback systems that provide information about a single user from the reports generated by a large community of users (e.g., the eBay reputation system), self-disclosures can more easily be manipulated by an individual. For example, a person may say that they are an expert even if they are not actually so (Donath, 1999; Stone, 1995; Walther & Parks, 2002). Donath argues that some signals are easy to falsify and may be treated (by a message recipient) with a modicum of suspicion. On one hand, this may lead one to the conclusion that self-disclosures indicating high credibility are not trusted online. Alternatively, it is possible that because self-disclosures are an efficient, direct, and visible method of communicating one's qualifications that these disclosures may be particularly effective cues to credibility.

Although system-generated cues and aggregated feedback systems may be difficult to "fake", they may not necessarily be reliable. For instance, if one wanted advice about how to change the oil in his or her car from an Internet discussion forum, it is possible that one might interpret a message from a user with the system-generated email domain "harvard.edu" as less credible than a similar message from a user with the email domain of "jiffylube.com". What the message recipient may not know is that the message originating from the "harvard.edu" address is from the physical plant employee whose full-time job it is to change the oil in the Harvard University maintenance vehicles, but the writer of the message from "jiffylube.com" is actually an executive who has never actually changed the oil in his or her own vehicle. Future research should seek to understand when self-disclosures are effective cues to credibility especially in comparison to less manipulable system-generated cues and aggregated user feedback.

Cue Potency

Some cues may be especially informative about a message source's credibility. These "sticky" cues may allow individuals to quickly form a well-developed impression of another individual's personal characteristics because these cues have great informational value. Kiesler, Sproull, and Waters (1996) suggest that because of a scarcity of social information in CMC—at least at a point in an interaction before much social information has accrued—each piece of social information that is transmitted may have a significant impact on a receiver. For example, research shows that when an individual receives an email containing a compliance request from a person with the same first (Guéguen, 2003) or last (Guéguen, Pichot, & Le Dreff, 2005) name, recipients are substantially more likely to comply than when the request ostensibly comes from a person with a different first or last name. In this example, similarity between a given surname provides a potent cue that causes an individual to be more likely to comply with a received request. Other recent research examining impression formation on the popular social networking website http://www.Facebook.com, has found that people are more likely to base their judgments of a target's attractiveness on what their friends say about them rather than what they say about themselves (Walther, Van Der Heide, Hamel, & Shulman, 2009). Thus, in some cases it seems that these third-person testimonials are more potent cues than are the first-person accounts about a person's attractiveness. Future work should attempt to understand what dynamics predict whether or not a cue is potent.

Walther and colleagues (2009; Walther & Parks, 2002) suggest that the warranting value of a cue may be one factor that predicts whether some cues are potent or not in the process of impression formation. They argued that online cues that are more difficult to falsify, because they are not easily manipulable by the person to which they refer, are more trusted by observers as observers can be more certain that the information refers to a person's actual offline characteristics. For instance, it is quite simple for an online dating website user to self-disclose that he or she is wealthy. However, because one can say whatever they wish online, this cue is rather easily manipulable, and accordingly relatively low in warranting value. On the other hand, if the person, rather than simply verbally self-disclosing his or her wealth, posted a hyperlink to an online news story that he or she had recently made a sizeable donation to a charity, such a cue would indicate wealth—and because it would be difficult to "fake" such a news report, this type of information should have greater warranting value. Walther and colleagues' (2009) research suggested that for interpersonal qualities which may be socially desirable to present oneself in a particular way (e.g. it is likely to be more socially desirable to be perceived to be physically attractive than unattractive), information about a person that emanates from a third-party provides more potent predictors of interpersonal judgments than first-person disclosures do.

Cue distinctiveness may also make some cues more informative than others. A distinctive cue does not easily lend itself to multiple interpretations. For instance, an email from Bill is a distinctive cue that the originator of the message was male (Bill is a name rarely applied to women), while an email from Mary is a distinctive cue that the originator of the message was female (Mary is a name rarely applied to men). When a cue is highly distinctive, it should also be perceived to have high informational value to a person seeking to make an impression judgment.

Cue relevance may also play a role in determining the informational value of a cue. A cue is relevant when it provides information about some dynamic of interest. For example, if an individual was deciding whether to bid on an item at an online auction website, that individual might find aggregated feedback from other users about the reliability of the seller of that item to be highly relevant in establishing an impression of the seller's trustworthiness. Meanwhile, the individual might find the seller's self-disclosure that she is an organized person to be relatively irrelevant to his judgment of the seller's trustworthiness. Research should examine these and other possible dynamics that may influence the stickiness of a particular cue.

The variables that make some cues more influential than other cues are of theoretical interest because they may limit the situations in which heuristically valuable impressions are unable to form in CMC. That is, if particularly potent cues that provide heuristically valuable information about a message source's credibility are present in a message, less exposure to other cues of heuristic value may be necessary in order to form a heuristically valuable impression of a message source. In short, if heuristically valuable information is positive and present, heuristic message processing may play an even greater role in the processing of influential messages in CMC than many might expect.

Interpersonal Credibility Online

Various Internet locales afford users flexibility in the degree to which their online moniker reflects their offline identity. On social network websites such as Facebook or LinkedIn, individuals tend to display their actual name on their personal profiles and are frequently linked to other individuals—often other members of offline social networks of either a professional or personal nature. Other Internet environments provide for anonymous communication. In these settings (e.g., *Second Life*, 4Chan) communication can occur where one's offline identity is obscured from the people with whom one interacts. Much of the research that explores differences in opinion shift that arises from variations of identifiably has explored the differences between anonymity in both CMC and face-to-face groups (e.g., Dubrovski et al., 1991; Sassenberg & Postmes, 2002; Weisband, 1994). It is difficult from this type of research to infer how differences in anonymity vary from differences in medium as much of this research confounds anonymity with CMC and identifiability with face-to-face interactions. While little research sheds light on questions of the effects of anonymity and identifiability in computer-mediated environments separate from the effects of mediated and non-mediated interaction, the model forwarded in this chapter does suggest several possible effects relative to the effects of anonymity in online persuasive attempts.

The proposed model suggests that technology changes the way people form interpersonal judgments of a message sender's credibility. Specifically, because information of heuristic value is proposed to accrue over the course of increased exposure, the temporal dynamics of credibility may be fundamentally different than they have been conceptualized in traditional face-to-face interpersonal interaction. For instance, one perspective on source credibility argues that credibility develops over the course of an interaction (Burgoon & Ruffner, 1978). Initial credibility may be conveyed through system-generated cues such as email domain or some display of the amount of participation in an online community in an online discussion forum. The credibility judgments that arise through interaction with another individual (transactional credibility) may be conveyed through self-disclosures in a mediated message. Finally, terminal credibility—a message receiver's perception of the source at the end of an encounter—may be aggregated and displayed for future message recipients through aggregated feedback systems. The interesting dynamic here that deserves future research is that for traditional face-to-face interaction these types of temporally sensitive credibility judgments occur over the course of some period of time. However, communication technologies have essentially allowed for these stages of credibility judgments to be collapsed. Because of this, it is possible to receive initial, transactional, and terminal credibility cues simultaneously in a mediated message. Future research should examine the effects of this temporal collapse in terms of how it facilitates credibility judgments as well as message processing.

On one hand, the temporal dimensions of credibility judgments in some technological applications may be collapsed as previously stated; however, other dimensions of credibility may show the opposite effect. Although different labels may apply to these dimensions, researchers have traditionally conceptualized credibility to be comprised of several main dimensions including trustworthiness, expertise, and goodwill (for review see O'Keefe, 1990). In face-to-face communication, people form impressions concerning these credibility dimensions according to both verbal and nonverbal information. In CMC, where nonverbal information is occluded, people only form impressions based on smaller packets of verbal/textual information. Because of this, it is possible that, in CMC, the dimensions of credibility are established one at a time, or message recipients may attend to the one most important dimension of credibility to inform their credibility judgments and attitudes. If this is the case, it is possible that heuristically valuable information about an individual's trustworthiness, for example, may be less important to that individual's credibility than is heuristically valuable information about that individual's expertise. In face-to-face interaction these impressions of these dimensions may form unilaterally. However, CMC may allow impressions of these dimensions to form sequentially. Future research should address these various possibilities.

Because the Internet holds a wide range of information and provides relatively easy access to many services, it is often used as a resource for many important contexts, thus the credibility and influence people attribute to messages in these contexts is important. For instance, medical doctors may send patients to a website that contains information about a diagnosed illness, or provide information about online support groups for others suffering with similar illnesses. The proposed model suggests that it may be possible to predict which individuals in an online social support community send the most influential messages by examining the heuristically valuable information contained in those messages. Future research should seek to understand which bits of heuristically valuable information in these contexts are the most effective at conveying judgments of credibility to a message recipient. Specifically, it would be useful to conduct research that systematically addresses system-generated cues, aggregated feedback cues, and self-disclosures as well as message strength variables so that it is possible to determine which cues are the most potent predictors of credibility and topical attitude judgments in online health communities and if different types of heuristically valuable information may interact with the strength of a persuasive message.

Beyond predicting which messages are influential, it may be possible to select those individuals identified as highly influential in an online community on the basis of system-generated cues (such as high frequency of community participation, or a reputable email domain). Once selected, these individuals may be targeted with communication campaigns that spread accurate and beneficial information. This could effectively limit the spread of misinformation even in the absence of a gatekeeper in these communities.

Self-Influential Aspects of Mediated Influence

Several recent studies have suggested that a computer-mediated environment may impact the way individuals' own behavior and self-perceptions assist the formation of attitudes and behavior online. For instance, Walther et al. (2010) conducted a study that evaluated the way that participants' interpersonal goals impact their behavior and how that behavior, in turn, may affect their own attitudes. Walther and colleagues conducted an experiment that experimentally manipulated whether one member of a dyad had a relational goal of being explicitly nice or mean toward a conversational partner. Their research then evaluated the way participants sought to achieve their relational goals (to be either kind or unkind) in the context of a conversation about participants' preferences toward an attitude object. They found that when participants had affiliative relational goals (i.e., they were instructed to be nice), participants made more positive statements of agreement about their partners' likes and dislikes, and when participants had disaffiliative relational goals (i.e., they were instructed to be mean) they made more negative statements about their partners' preferences. In turn, the expression of these positive or negative statements of disagreement relative to their partners' likes and dislikes was related to significantly different convergence toward or divergence away from participants' partners' attitude preferences relative to an initial attitude measure.

Walther and colleagues' (2010) research points to an interesting new direction for studying social influence in the context of a computer-mediated environment. Specifically, these findings suggest that in CMC peoples' relational goals may influence them to conduct themselves in such a way that they attitudinally position themselves in a manner such that they can achieve their relational goals using the "verbal-only" tools they have available. While communicating with a person in a face-to-face setting people use nonverbal means to achieve relational affinity or disafffinity (Burgoon & Hale, 1987). However, in CMC, if people like their partners, they may verbally communicate in a way that is consistent with their partner's attitudes; however, if people dislike others they may communicate in a way that is inconsistent with their attitudes. This change may, in and of itself, cause individuals' attitudes to be more eligible for shift simply because individuals observe their own attitudinal positioning and seek to maintain consistency with the attitudes that they have previously espoused, which is an observation consistent with self-perception theory (Bem, 1972). For example, if Bob likes Jenny and wants Jenny to like him too, Bob may communicate in such a way that he verbally states his agreement with Jenny's opinions. Consequently, even though Bob knows that he was only agreeing with Jenny to try to get her to like him, he may inadvertently influence his own attitudes in the process.

Other research has explored the effect of self-perception in CMC in an immersive virtual environment. Yee and Bailenson's (2007) work on the Proteus effect, also premised in Bem's (1972) self-perception theory, has illustrated that when people inhabit a virtual representation of themselves, they alter their behavior to be consistent with that virtual representation. For example, Yee, Bailenson, and Duchenaut (2009) found that in the popular massively-multiplayer role-playing game *World of Warcraft*, individuals who inhabited a taller and more attractive avatars (i.e., digital self-representations) also obtained generally greater success in the game environment, and that in an immersive virtual environment, individuals assigned to a taller avatar negotiated more aggressively than did individuals assigned a shorter avatar. Additionally, Fox, Bailenson, and Binney (2009) found that when an avatar was visually responsive to participant's online behavior, women were more likely to adjust their eating behavior to be more healthy when their avatar became more overweight after they made unhealthy (virtual) eating choices (i.e., eating candy instead of carrots). Moreover, in another study, Fox and Bailenson (2009) found that participants in immersive virtual environments who were exposed to a computerized self-representation that either gained or lost weight in response to unhealthy or healthy (respectively) eating behaviors were more likely to voluntarily exercise after an experiment than those participants who saw no virtual representation of themselves. Also, participants who viewed themselves running on a treadmill were more likely to exercise than those who viewed others running on a treadmill.

Taken together these findings suggest that in some cases observing one's own behavior may lead to attitude and behavior change. For Walther and colleagues (2010) the observed behavior was the generation of arguments that either reinforced or contradicted one's partner's attitudes, while for Fox, Yee, and colleagues (Fox & Bailenson, 2009; Fox et al., 2009; Yee & Bailenson, 2007; Yee et al., 2009) self-observation of the outcome of behavior in a virtual environment was shown to affect participants' behaviors both in virtual environments and persisted after a participant had left that virtual environment. These findings suggest that perceiving one's own behaviors in CMC (whether via immersive embodiment in virtual reality or in simple text-based exchanges) may lead to attitude and behavior change.

Future research should seek to explore why these effects occur. For example, mediation may allow people to observe their own behavior more easily. In a face-to-face environment the arguments one makes in a discussion are ephemeral; most often once one's stated arguments have been spoken there is no official written record to hold a person accountable. Moreover, as mentioned, the task of achieving the relational goals that accompany these conversations in a face-to-face setting may be carried out primarily nonverbally (Burgoon & Hale, 1987). Online, however, the persistence of written arguments (Herring, 2001) may cause individuals to be more likely to maintain consistency with those arguments, regardless of whether the stated attitude in question was generated out of a desire to maintain social relationships or was an authentic statement of an actual, well-formed attitude. Similarly, because either textual mediation or mediation in an immersive virtual environment likely makes one's own behaviors more salient to users, self-perceptive processes have a significant impact on the formation of one's own attitudes and behaviors. That is, because one sees oneself making an argument or because one sees the positive effects of healthy behavioral choices on a virtual self-representation's figure, a person's attitude and behavior may shift. Another possibility is that because a restriction of nonverbal cue systems in CMC forces people to encode affect verbally, sometimes through agreement or disagreement with attitudes they may not have initially espoused, simply enacting these verbal behaviors may cause attitude change. In short, future research should address whether it is seeing oneself do something (advocating for a particular attitude, for example), or actually enacting a behavior, regardless of whether a user actively observes their behavior, that actively influences behavior and attitudes in CMC.

Conclusion

How do people make judgments about what sources they find credible and what messages they find influential? The model presented here along with the research supporting it suggests that message strength and systematic message processing is not the only route to persuasion in CMC. Instead, this chapter suggests that under the right conditions, people are able to make determinations about not only the strength of a persuasive message, but also the credibility of the sender of that message in CMC. To date, the research in this area is relatively underdeveloped. Moving forward researchers should focus their energies on exploring the ways that heuristic cues affect attitude change in online communication.

Additionally, future research should address how people wade through the multitude of cues available in the contemporary Internet environment in order to find the specific types of information that help them to form impressions of others' credibility. To date, while researchers have developed a solid understanding of the types of information that contribute to organizational credibility online, less work has focused on the types of cues that confer an individual expertise and trustworthiness in online environments. One of the hallmarks of the modern Internet is the creation of spaces wherein individual users generate content for websites. This extends from product evaluations to movie reviews to individuals recording their experiences with businesses. As users turn to these consumer reviews, understanding the cues and types of evidence (e.g., Hong & Park, 2012) that people use to make judgments about the credibility of these user-generated content providers and form attitudes toward specific products will become increasingly important.

Finally, as research on computer-mediated communication and influence moves forward researchers should attend to the ways that the visibility of one's online behavior affects one's own attitudes. As we have discussed, seeing one's own behavior and verbal communication may have a self-influential effect. Future research energies should also be directed toward understanding exactly how, why, and when online communication most strongly affects our own attitudes and behaviors.

Acknowledgments

The authors are grateful to Dr Joe Walther for helpful comments made in the composition of this manuscript.

References

Alexander, J. E., & Tate, M. A. (1999). *Web wisdom: How to evaluate and create information quality on the Web*. Hillsdale, NJ: Erlbaum.

Aristotle. (1924). *Rhetoric*. (W. R. Roberts, Trans.). Mineola, NY: Dover Publications. (Original work published n.d.).

Bem, D. (1972). Self-perception theory. In L. Berkowitz (Ed.), *Advances in experimental social psychology* (Vol. 6, pp. 1–62). New York, NY: Academic Press.

Booth-Butterfield, S., & Welbourne, J. (2002). The elaboration likelihood model: Its impact on persuasion theory and research. In J. Dillard & M. Pfau (Eds.), *The persuasion handbook: Developments in theory and practice* (pp. 155–173). London, UK: Sage.

Burgoon, J. K., & Hale, J. L. (1987). Validation and measurement of the fundamental themes of relational communication. *Communication Monographs, 54*, 19–41.

Burgoon, M., & Ruffner, M. (1978). *Human communication*. New York, NY: Holt, Rinehart, and Winston.

Chaiken, S. (1980). Heuristic versus systematic information processing and the use of source versus message cues in persuasion. *Journal of Personality and Social Psychology, 39*, 752–766.

Chaiken, S. (1987). The heuristic model of persuasion. In M. P. Zanna, J. M. Olson, & C. P. Herman (Eds.), *Social influence: The Ontario Symposium* (Vol. 5, pp. 3–39). Hillsdale, NJ: Lawrence Erlbaum.

Chaiken, S., & Eagly, A. H. (1983). Communication modality as a determinant of persuasion: The role of communicator salience. *Journal of Personality and Social Psychology, 45*, 241–265.

Chaiken, S., Liberman, A., & Eagly, A. H. (1989). Heuristic and systematic information processing within and beyond the persuasion context. In J. S. Uleman & J. A. Bargh (Eds.), *Unintended thought* (pp. 212–252). New York, NY: Guilford Press.

Chaiken, S., & Maheswaran, D. (1994). Heuristic processing can bias systematic processing: Effects of source credibility, argument ambiguity, and task importance on attitude judgment. *Journal of Personality and Social Psychology, 66*, 460–473.

Chen, S., & Chaiken, S. (1999). The heuristic-systematic model in its broader context. In S. Chaiken & Y. Trope (Eds.), *Dual-process theories in social psychology* (pp. 73–96). New York, NY: Guilford.

Culnan, M. J., & Markus, M. L. (1987). Information technologies. In F. M. Jablin, L. L. Putnam, K. H. Roberts, & L. W. Porter (Eds.), *Handbook of organizational communication: An interdisciplinary perspective* (pp. 420–443). Newbury Park, CA: Sage.

Di Blasio, P., & Milani, L. (2008). Computer-mediated communication and persuasion: Peripheral vs. central route to opinion shift. *Computers in Human Behavior, 24*, 798–815.

Donath, J. (1999). Identity and deception in the virtual community. In M. A. Smith & P. Kollock (Eds.), *Communities in cyberspace* (pp. 29–59). New York, NY: Routledge.

Dubrovsky, V. J., Kiesler, S., & Sethna, B. N. (1991). The equalization phenomenon: Status effects in computer-mediated and face-to-face decision-making groups. *Human Computer Interaction, 6*, 119–146.

Eagly, A. H., & Chaiken, S. (1993). *The psychology of attitudes.* Belmont, CA: Wadsworth.

Fogg, B. J., Marshall, J., Kameda, T., Solomon, J., Rangnekar, A., Boyd, J., & Brown, B. (2001a). Web credibility research: A method for online experiments and early study results. In *CHI 2001: ACM Conference on Human Factors and Computing Systems, Short Talks* (pp. 295–296). Seattle, WA: ACM.

Fogg, B. J., Marshall, J., Laraki, O., Osipovich, A., Varma, C., Fang, N.,… Treinen, M. (2001b). What makes web sites credible? A report on a large quantitative study. CHI 2001: ACM Conference on Human factors and Computing Systems, *CHI Letters*, 61–68.

Fox, J., & Bailenson, J. (2009). Virtual self-modeling: The effects of vicarious reinforcement and identification on exercise behaviors. *Media Psychology, 12*, 1–25.

Fox, J., Bailenson, J., & Binney, J. (2009). Virtual experiences, physical behaviors: The effect of presence on imitation of an eating avatar. *Presence: Teleoperators and Virtual Environments, 18*, 294–303.

Fox, S. (2006). Online health search 2006. Pew Internet and American Life Project. Retrieved February 8, 2008 from http://www.pewinternet.org/pdfs/PIP_Online_Health_2006.pdf.

Gigerenzer, G., & Goldstein, D. (1996). Reasoning the fast and frugal way: Models of bounded rationality. *Psychological Review, 103*, 650–669.

Guéguen, N. (2001). Foot-in-the-door technique and computer-mediated communication. *Computers in Human Behavior, 18*, 11–15.

Guéguen, N. (2003). Help on the web: The effect of the same first name between the sender and receptor in a request made by email. *The Psychological Record, 53*, 459–466.

Guéguen, N., & Jacob, C. (2001). Fund-raising on the web: The effect of an electronic foot-in-the-door on donation. *Cyberpsychology and Behavior, 4*, 705–709.

Guéguen, N., Pichot, N., & Le Dreff, G. (2005). Similarity and helping behavior on the web: The impact of the convergence of surnames between a solicitor and a subject in a request made by e-mail. *Journal of Applied Social Psychology, 35*, 423–429.

Guadagno, R. E., & Cialdini, R. B. (2002). Online persuasion: an examination of gender differences in computer-mediated interpersonal influence. *Group Dynamics: Theory Research and Practice, 6*, 38–51.

Guadagno, R. E., & Cialdini, R. B. (2007). Persuade him by email, but see her in person: Online persuasion revisited. *Computers in Human Behavior, 23*, 999–1015.

Herring, S. C. (2001). Computer-mediated discourse. In Schiffrin, D., D. Tannen, & H. Hamilton (Eds.), *The Handbook of Discourse Analysis* (pp. 612–634). Oxford, UK: Blackwell Publishers.

Hong, S., & Park, H. S. (2012). Computer-mediated persuasion in online reviews: Statistical versus narrative evidence. *Computers in Human Behavior*, *28*, 906–919.

Kiesler, S., Siegel, J. & McGuire, T.W. (1984). Social psychological aspects of computer-mediated communication. *American Psychologist*, *39*, 1123–1134.

Kiesler, S., Sproull, L., & Waters, L. (1996). A prisoner's dilemma experiment on cooperation with people and human-like computers. *Journal of Personality and Social Psychology*, *70*, 47–65.

Kleck, C. A., Reese, C. A., Behnken, D. Z., & Sundar, S. S. (2007, May). *The company you keep and the image you project: Putting your best face forward in online social networks*. Paper presented at the annual meeting of the International Communication Association, San Francisco, CA.

Lee, E. J. (2008). When are strong arguments stronger than weak arguments? Deindividuation effects on message elaboration in computer-mediated communication. *Communication Research*, *35*, 646–665.

Lee, S. -H. (2009). How do online reviews affect purchasing intention? *African Journal of Business Management*, *3*(10), 576–581.

Maheswaran, D., & Chaiken, S. (1991). Promoting systematic processing in low-motivation settings: Effect of incongruent information on processing and judgment. *Journal of Personality and Social Psychology*, *61*, 13–25.

Maheswaran, D., Mackie, D. M., & Chaiken, S. (1992). Brand name as a heuristic cue: The effects of task importance and expectancy confirmation on consumer judgments. *Journal of Consumer Psychology*, *1*, 317–336.

Metzger, M. J., Flanagin, A. J., Eyal, K., Lemus, D. R., & McCann, R. M. (2003). Credibility for the 21st century: Integrating perspectives on source, message, and media credibility in the contemporary media environment (pp. 293–335). In P. J. Kalbfleisch (Ed.), *Communication Yearbook*, *27*. New York, NY: Routledge.

O'Keefe, D. J. (1990). *Persuasion: Theory and research*. Newbury Park, CA: Sage.

Oskamp, S., & Schultz, P. W. (2005). *Attitudes and opinions* (3rd ed.). Mahwah, NJ: Lawrence Erlbaum Associates.

Petty, R. E., & Cacioppo, J. T. (1981). *Attitudes and persuasion: Classic and contemporary approaches*. Dubuque, IA: Wm. C. Brown.

Petty, R. E., & Cacioppo, J. T. (1986). *Communication and persuasion: Central and peripheral routes to attitude change*. New York, NY: Springer-Verlag.

Ramirez, Jr., A. (2007). The effect of anticipated future interaction and initial impression valence on relational communication in computer-mediated interaction. *Communication Studies*, *58*, 53–70.

Resnick, P., & Zeckhauser, R. (2002). Trust among strangers in Internet transactions: Empirical analysis of eBay's reputation system (pp. 127–157). In M. R. Baye (Ed.), *The economics of the Internet and e-commerce*. Amsterdam, the Netherlands: Elsevier Science.

Resnick, P., Zeckhauser, R., Friedman, E., & Kuwabara, K. (2000). Reputation systems. *Communications of the ACM*, *43*(12), 45–48.

Resnick, P., Zeckhauser, R., Swanson, J., & Lockwood, K. (2006). The value of reputation on eBay: A controlled experiment. *Experimental Economics*, *9*, 79–101.

Sassenberg, K., & Postmes, T. (2002). Cognitive and strategic processes in small groups: Effects of anonymity of the self and anonymity of the group on social influence. *British Journal of Social Psychology*, *41*, 463–480.

Schlosser, A. E. (2009). The effect of computer-mediated communication on conformity vs. nonconformity: An impression management perspective. *Journal of Consumer Psychology*, *19*, 374–388.

Sproull, L., & Kiesler, S. (1986). Reducing social context cues: Electronic mail in organizational communication. *Management Science*, *32*, 1492–1512.

Stone, A. R. (1995). *The war of desire and technology at the close of the mechanical age*. Cambridge, MA: MIT.

Sundar, S. S. (2008). The MAIN model: A heuristic approach to understanding technology effects on credibility (pp. 73–100). In M. J. Metzger & A. J. Flanagin (Eds.), *Digital media, youth, and credibility.* Cambridge, MA: The MIT Press.

Tidwell, L. C., & Walther, J. B. (2002). Computer-mediated communication effects on disclosure, impressions, and interpersonal evaluations: Getting to know one another a bit at a time. *Human Communication Research, 28,* 317–348.

Todorov, A., Chaiken, S., & Henderson, M. D. (2002). The heuristic-systematic model of social information processing. In J. P. Dillard & M. Pfau (Eds.), *The persuasion handbook: Developments in theory and practice* (pp. 195–212). London, UK: Sage.

Tong, S. T., Van Der Heide, B., Langwell, L., & Walther, J. B. (2008). Too much of a good thing? The relationship between number of friends and interpersonal impressions on Facebook. *Journal of Computer-Mediated Communication, 13,* 531–549.

Trope, Y., & Gaunt, R. (1999). A dual-process model of overconfident attribution inferences. In S. Chaiken & Y. Trope (Eds.), *Dual-process theories in social psychology* (pp. 161–178). New York, NY: Guilford.

Van Der Heide, B., & Walther, J. B. (2009, May). *Computer-mediated communication and persuasion: Testing a social information processing/heuristic-systematic synthesis.* Paper presented at the annual meeting of the International Communication Association in Chicago, IL.

Walther, J. B. (1992). Interpersonal effects in computer-mediated interaction: A relational perspective. *Communication Research, 19,* 52–90.

Walther, J. B. (1993). Impression development in computer-mediated interaction. *Western Journal of Communication, 57,* 381–398.

Walther, J. B. (1994). Anticipated ongoing interaction versus channel effects on relational communication in computer-mediated interaction. *Human Communication Research, 20,* 473–501.

Walther, J. B. (1996). Computer-mediated communication: Impersonal, interpersonal, and hyperpersonal interaction. *Communication Research, 23,* 3–43.

Walther, J. B. (2007). Selective self-presentation in computer-mediated communication: Hyperpersonal dimensions of technology, language, and cognition. *Computers in Human Behavior, 23,* 2538–2557.

Walther, J. B., Loh, T., & Granka, L. (2005). Let me count the ways: The interchange of verbal and nonverbal cues in computer-mediated and face-to-face affinity. *Journal of Language and Social Psychology, 24,* 36–65.

Walther, J. B., & Parks, M. R. (2002). Cues filtered out, cues filtered in: Computer-mediated communication and relationships. In M. L. Knapp & J. A. Daly (Eds.), *Handbook of interpersonal communication* (3rd ed., pp. 529–563). Thousand Oaks, CA: Sage.

Walther, J. B., Van Der Heide, B., Hamel, L., & Shulman, H. C. (2009). Self-generated versus other-generated statements and impressions in computer-mediated communication: A facebook test of warranting theory. *Communication Research, 36,* 229–253.

Walther, J. B., Van Der Heide, B., Tong, S. T., Carr, C. T., & Atkin, C. K. (2010). Effects of interpersonal goals on inadvertent intrapersonal influence in computer-mediated communication. *Human Communication Research, 36,* 323–347.

Wang, Z., Walther, J. B., & Hancock, J. T. (2009). Social identification and interpersonal communication in computer-mediated communication: What you do versus who you are in virtual groups. *Human Communication Research, 35,* 59–85.

Weisband, S. (1994). Overcoming social awareness in computer-supported groups: Does anonymity really help? *Computer Supported Cooperative Work, 2,* 285–297

Yee, N., & Bailenson, J. (2007). The proteus effect: the effect of transformed self-representation on behavior. *Human Communication Research, 33,* 271–290.

Yee, N., Bailenson, J., & Ducheneaut, N. (2009). The proteus effect. Implications of transformed digital self-representation on online and offline behavior. *Communication Research, 36*(2), 285–312.

Chapter 6

Online Decision-Making

Kevin Askew and Michael D. Coovert

Introduction

The Internet has changed the world in which we live. It has changed not only our social lives through enabling new channels of communication and the way individuals connect, but it has changed the business world as well. E-commerce drives a respectable portion of the world's economy and the way businesses and individuals exchange information, goods, and products. Organizations must strive to sustain a competitive advantage in the world market place. Businesses following a business-to-business (B-to-B) model can directly exchange supplies and products with one another. Similarly, individuals can purchase items directly from a company via online shopping or from one another through direct sales and auctions. These changes in both connectedness and the ability to directly exchange goods and services with businesses and individuals are two of the forces impacting the way we must consider constructs fundamental to organizations and individuals. This connected world of ours has demonstrated that never before has an understanding of decision-making—a process central to both individual and organizational effectiveness—been more important.

Our chapter examines decision-making from the perspective of the social net. Having stated that, it is important to recognize that research on decision-making fills volumes. Our goal here is to provide an overview of the research on decision-making, relate it to the social net, and connect it to people's everyday experiences. To do this, we must first lay a foundation by discussing classical or seminal perspectives on decision-making. Having done that, we can then present new research and perspectives on decision-making as it occurs online, and in the process relate classical perspectives to the new research and current events—such as the rise of social networks. After discussing decision-making as it occurs online, we will discuss online decision-making in a context that dominates a significant portion of most people's lives—the work context. This will culminate with a set of recommendations for future research.

Classical Research on Decision-Making: The Foundation

With our roadmap clearly laid out, we now move to our first major section of the chapter, classical perspectives on decision-making. Here, we introduce select classical decision-making models, categories of "heuristics," and social processes related to decision-making. Our overview of the traditional, non-Internet centered literature will allow for a smoother, more informed discussion of the Internet-centered decision-making literature in the next section. We start with perspectives on how individuals make decisions, before moving on to the more complex topic of decision-making in groups.

Bayes' Theorem

Bayes' theorem is our first classical model of decision-making. In a decision-making context, Bayes theorem is used to model the probability of a decision (or behavior) given some prior event or situation. Bayes theorem is straightforward in the sense that if one has a belief about an event, and the event has a probability distribution (Prior; P(E)), and additional information with known reliability (Likelihoods; P(I | E)) is available (or attainable), then the initial belief can be revised (Posterior; P(E | I)) according to the new information. Following this notion of conditional probability, Bayes' theorem is stated as: P(A | B) = P(A ∩ B)/P(B), where P(A | B) is the probability of Event A, given that Event B has occurred; P(A ∩ B) is the probability of both Events A and B occurring together; and P(B) is the probability of Event B.

Computerized help systems often rely on Bayes' theorem to try and predict a user's intention and/or behavior. As an example, consider a person working with a browser on the Internet and event E is the probability the person will click the "help" button at the company website. The indicator event, I, is a pop-up window (additional information) explaining how to navigate the site. The pop-up window may or may not be helpful given nothing is known about the users who enter the site, and if the provided information fits their mental model for site navigation.

The prior probability of E is P(E), and 0 ≤ P(E) ≤ 1. We are trying to determine the probability of someone clicking the help button given that a pop-up window explaining site navigation has already been provided to the user. Mathematically this is stated as P (E | I) = P(E ∩ I)/P(I). Through rearranging terms we have, P(E ∩ I) = P(E | I) * P(I). Bayes deduced that through symmetry the following also had to be true: P(E ∩ I) = P(I | E) * P(E). Through further manipulations, Bayes' theorem is given as:

$$P(E \mid I) = \frac{P(I \mid E) * P(E)}{P(I \mid E) * P(E) + P(I \mid E') * P(E')}$$

Where E' is the complement of E.

We couldn't do Bayes' theorem justice without presenting the math. But if you didn't follow the math, just keep in mind the big picture: Bayes' theorem can be used to calculate the probability of a behavior given that some other event has already occurred. It can be incredibly useful for decision support systems where predicting future behavior (given a current situation) is the goal.

Multiattribute Utility

Our second classical perspective on decision-making is multiattribute theory (Edwards & Fasolo, 2001). Multiattribute utility (MAU) can be a description of how people make decisions (assuming people are behaving rationally) or its tools can be used to mathematically to compare alternatives and help a decision-maker chose the best alternative. To apply the MAU strategy, all the alternatives are identified as well as the attributes that will be used to compare them. As an example, consider an individual deciding which of three cell-phones to buy: A, B, or C. Each cell-phone (alternative) has certain attributes (e.g., operating system, keyboard type, battery life, screen size). Weights are assigned to each attribute according to its importance to the decision (e.g., 1, 2, 3, 4; or alternately spreading 100 points over the alternatives). The separate decision alternatives are scored on each attribute using a scale (e.g., 1–10). Multiplying the importance weight by the attribute weight, and summing those determine the utility of each alternative. Table 6.1 presents an example.

Table 6.1 Example of MAU for a cell-phone purchase decision.

Alternative	Attributes			Utility	
	Screen size 20	Keyboard type 25	Battery life 15	Operating system 40	Sum
Cell-phone A	1 * 20	2 * 25	3 * 15	1 * 40	155
Cell-phone B	2 * 20	3 * 25	1 * 15	3 * 40	250
Cell-phone C	3 * 20	1 * 25	2 * 15	2 * 40	195

Given the attributes, their values, and the ranking of each alternative on those attributes MAU makes it easy to determine which alternative should be chosen. Having an explicit model can be very useful in group decision-making since everyone can see how an alternative is chosen. In our example, cell-phone B has the greatest total points, so it is the chosen alternative. With MAU it is also easy to change the attribute value weights to determine the impact of such shifts of importance on the decision outcome.

Prospect Theory

Whereas MAU is mainly used to help people arrive at a decision, Prospect Theory is focused on *describing* how people make decisions (given multiple alternatives with known probabilities). Before Prospect Theory, a common view was that people choose the option with the highest subjective expected utility—that is, people choose the option that would result in the highest value (on average) given the probability of success, the objective payout, and the individual's personal preferences. One of Prospect Theory's key insights is that people make decisions based on the value of *gains and losses* rather than the absolute value of the outcomes. And what is considered a gain and a loss is based on a subjective reference point set by the decision-maker. In other words, the value of an outcome is a function of *change* from a reference point rather than the objective amount. Two other key insights from Prospect Theory are that people underweight outcomes that are probable compared to outcomes that are certain, and that people make decisions in stages— the first stage involves setting a reference point and ranking the desirability of outcomes, and the second stage involves computing values for each alternative and choosing the alternative with the highest utility. Prospect Theory is an incredibly interesting and well-validated model, and we encourage those interested to read Kahneman and Tversky's (1979) original paper for more detail.

Heuristics

It is interesting that many models of the individual as a decision-maker assume that one is always attempting to maximize the decision and/or arrive at the "correct" decision. More and more research is demonstrating that individuals often violate predictions of this rational choice (maximization) model. Effects that can bias or lead to non-optimal decisions include framing effects, response modes, stimulus contexts, and the environment (Payne, Bettman, & Johnson, 1992).

Moving away from the maximization perspective is a theory that views the decision-maker as a "rule follower" (March, 1994). Following rules, or "heuristics," minimizes effort and allows individuals to avoid difficult tradeoffs (Mellers, Schwartz, & Cooke, 1998). Traditionally, the heuristics decision-making strategy has been viewed as inferior to classical approaches such as Bayes. Heuristics, by their very nature, ignore information for simplicity's sake. When all information is known—as has been the case in most experimental settings—heuristics only approximate or equal the best solution obtained by classical approaches. Knowing all information includes knowing all alternative options, probabilities, and outcomes.

However, these perfect "small worlds" where everything is certain are extremely rare outside of experimental and gambling settings. In the world where these models are applied, alternative options, probabilities, and possible outcomes are estimated from sample information or are simply unknown. Thus, the real world violates the assumptions made by rational decision-making theory, which is why heuristics sometimes lead to better outcomes—the so-called "less-is-more effect."

In the online context, we believe the heuristic perspective is particularly useful in understanding how people make decisions. When decision-making occurs in a context involving the Internet, the decision is almost always being made in a "large world." There is no way for someone to evaluate all possible options when buying something on the Internet, for example. With the Internet, one needs to manage information overload, and heuristics are an efficient way to do this since they allow one to ignore extraneous information. To give you a flavor of the different types of heuristics, we now describe four broad categories of heuristics (Gigerenzer & Gaissmaier, 2011). These categories are not exhaustive, but they will serve as a framework for our purposes.

Recognition-Based Heuristics

Recognition-based heuristics are rules of thumb centered on how easily recognizable or familiar an option is. According to the heuristic, the more familiar a choice, the more likely the choice will lead to a favorable outcome. For example, suppose one is trying to figure out what website to use to collect survey data. How does one decide which survey website is best out of the multitude of sites that exist. According to the *recognition* heuristic, the survey website that is the most recognizable is most likely the best website. For some people, this might be SurveyMonkey's (http://www. SurveyMonkey.com). There are various kinds of recognition-based heuristics, such as the *fluency* heuristic (choose the alternative that is recognized fastest) and the *take-the-first* heuristic (choose the alternative that first comes to mind). Various studies have shown that people do rely on the *recognition* heuristic (Pohl, 2006), particularly in situations where it is appropriate to do so (Pachur, Todd, Gigerenzer, Schooler, & Goldstein, 2011).

One-Reason Heuristics

Whereas recognition-based heuristics rely on familiarity, the *one-reason* heuristics rely on identifying one critical cue. This one "clever" piece of information is used to make the decision; all other cues are ignored. To illustrate, consider a manager trying to hire an employee for a job by looking through resumes on an employment site such as http://www.Monster.com. The manager compares the candidates' years of experience and hires the candidate with the most experience, ignoring all other information about the candidates such as letters of recommendation, skills, and so forth. Other types of *one-reason* heuristics include the *hiatus* heuristic for classifying customers as active or inactive (if the customer has not purchased anything within a given number of months, classify as inactive; otherwise, classify as active) and the *circle* heuristic used to predict the area a serial killer lives (the most likely location of the serial killer's home is near the center of a circle drawn from the two most distant crime sites). One-reason heuristics are simple, but they can outperform much more complex statistical methods in certain circumstances (Snook, Zito, Bennell, & Taylor, 2005; Wübben & Wangenheim, 2008).

Trade-Off Heuristics

In contrast to *recognition* or *recall* (i.e., one-reason) heuristics, *trade-off* heuristics are based on a compensatory strategy. That is, all cues or alternatives are given equal weight. The *tally* heuristic, for example, entails searching for a set number of cues, and choosing the alternative that is favored by the greatest number. Consider again the example of a manager trying to identify an employee to hire from http://www.Monster.com. A manager using the *tallying* heuristic would look at a number of cues relevant to job performance, count the number of cues that favor each applicant (alternative), and hire the applicant with the highest number.

There are other examples of *trade-off* heuristics as well, such as the 1/N Rule used to allocate resources among a number of different alternatives. The 1/N Rule states one simply distribute the resources equally to the N alternatives. So if a business has a $50,000 budget and five departments, a manager following the 1/N Rule would provide $10,000 to each of the five departments. *Trade-off* heuristics have been shown to be useful in such diverse areas as detecting strokes (Kattah, Talkad, Wang, Hsieh, & Newman-Toker, 2009) and avoiding avalanche accidents (McCammon & Hageli, 2007). However, their effectiveness relative to other competing heuristics and rational decision-making strategies has not been extensively examined, and the extent to which people use trade-off heuristics in daily life is unknown.

Social Heuristics

The majority of us spend a large part of the day navigating the social world, whether it is at work, school, or home. As social animals, humans gain a lot of knowledge directly from other people. Not surprisingly, a number of heuristics exist that are decidedly social in focus. For example, the *imitate-the-successful* heuristic involves modeling an individual who is receiving a desired outcome. It has been shown to be a particularly useful strategy in helping novices because it quickly speeds-up the learning of effective cue order (Garcia-Retamero, Takezawa, Gigerenzer, 2009). Other social heuristics include *tit-for-tat*, and averaging the judgments of others (Hertwig & Herzog, 2009). Fiske (1992) argues that social decisions can be covered by the application of only four rules: communal sharing, authority ranking, equality matching, and market pricing. Preliminary research provides some support for these rules.

Process Loss in Groups

Our focus thus far has been on decision-making that occurs by individuals. But decisions are not made in a social vacuum. Nor are group decisions simply the sum of individual choices. Individuals influence others. The mere presence of someone else can be enough to change performance (Zajonc, 1966). Now that we have a foundation of decision-making at the individual level, we expand our focus and discuss how people arrive at decisions in groups.

The idea that groups of people make better decisions than individuals is deceptively intuitive. Groups should be able to generate more ideas (via brainstorming), should have more collective expertise, and should be able to better spot flaws in logic than any one individual. After all, the more heads the better, right? Interestingly, decades of research has shown that this is not always the case. Furthermore, only a handful of studies (e.g., Laughlin, Bonner, & Miner, 2002; Tindale & Sheffey, 2002) have reported the elusive "process gain"—group performance that is better than the most capable group member and better than the sum of all members. So interestingly, groups often do not perform as well or make as good of decisions as the best individual in the group (Kerr & Tindale, 2004).

What can account for this drop in effectiveness? There are a number of group processes that may be at work. First, groups often fail to reach their full potential because of a phenomenon called social loafing (Latane, Williams, & Harkins, 1979)—the tendency for individual members to slack off when in a group. Social loafing is more likely to occur in groups that are large and where individual contributions are not transparent (Latane et al., 1979). Second, groups tend to focus on shared information and so the full collective knowledge of the group is rarely made available to all group members (Stasser & Titus, 1985). Groups sometimes also fail to recognize the most capable members because they rely on inappropriate cues, such as talkativeness, confidence, or dominance to infer expertise (Littlepage & Mueller, 1997; Littlepage, Schmidt, Whisler, & Frost, 1995). Situations that increase the groups' recognition of capable members include having the members train together (Liang, Moreland, & Argote, 1995), providing regular performance feedback (Henry, Strickland, Yorges, & Ladd, 1996), and giving explicit instructions to share unique information or identify the most capable group member for each task (Henry, 1995).

Improving Group Decisions

Instead of asking how to get groups to surpass their optimal performance level (the collective sum of their members), a potentially more fruitful approach is simply to identify situations and processes that lead to better group performance or decisions. One consistent finding is the importance of trust and cohesiveness for group performance (Beal, Cohen, Burke, & McLendon, 2003); groups high on these variables have higher collective efficacy, and in turn higher performance (Gully, Incalcaterra, Joshi, & Beaubian, 2002). Trust also appears to affect team performance through higher levels of communication among team members (Marks, 1999). Goal-setting has been shown to increase team performance, but only when the goals are specific, difficult, and time-bound; as opposed to vague "do-your-best" goals (although these effects have not been as consistent or as large as those observed at the individual level; Locke, Alavi, & Wagner, 1997). Also important is the prevention of conflict among group members that can result through the forming of strong subgroups (Gibson & Vermeulen, 2003) and setting up situations that facilitate the identification of the most capable group members.

An important caveat to this discussion on the improvement of team performance is needed: Group decision-making and performance is a complex, dynamic process. A condition that facilitates performance in one situation might very well hurt performance in another. For example, high team cohesion increases performance in most situations, but if the norms of the group are low performance, high team cohesion actually decreases performance (Hackman, 1987). Other important moderators are the amount of time the group has worked together and the type of task that the group is performing (Martin, Gilson, & Maynard, 2004). It appears that the simple act of working in a group may lead the members to undervalue the input of information coming from outside the group (Minson & Meuller, 2012). So when groups are charged with making a decision, it is important we carefully evaluate what is gained and what is lost by this format.

Groupthink

Groupthink is a phenomenon in which social processes cause a group to make a poor decision. The phenomenon is characterized by group resistance to differences of opinion and a blind adherence towards the group's preferred plan or strategy. Groupthink usually occurs when there is a time pressure to make a decision, when the leader of the group is dominant and directive, and when the group is isolated from outside influence. Although some of the historical illustrations are compelling, the evidence supporting the theory of groupthink have been mixed. Groups sometimes make disastrous decisions in the absence of groupthink conditions (Tindale et al., 1996), and groups sometimes make good decisions when groupthink conditions are present (e.g., high cohesion, Mullen & Cooper, 1994; directive leaders, Peterson, 1997). Regardless of the robustness of the groupthink phenomenon, techniques such as the stepladder method have been demonstrated to prevent it (Rogelberg, Barnes-Farrell, & Lowe, 1992). In situations where groupthink could potentially occur, the use of the stepladder technique (described later) is appropriate.

Summary

The goal of this chapter is to provide an overview of the research on decision-making, relate it to the social net, and provide some general guidelines that follow from the literature. In this first section, we laid a foundation for our discussion of decision-making on the Internet by reviewing classical perspectives on decision-making, as well as some relevant social phenomenon. Specifically we described some "maximization" perspectives, which view decision-making as an individual choosing an alternative that maximizes some criterion, and the heuristic perspective, which views human decisions as a rule-following process. We also reviewed two social phenomenon—process loss and groupthink—and presented research on how to reduce process loss. Having laid the foundation, we now move to discuss decision-making as it occurs through an electronic medium. As you will see, these researchers that have studied computer-mediated decision-making have, for the most part, not approached the topic from the classical perspectives.

Decision-Making on the Internet

In this section, we review the literature on decision-making when technology is used as a medium. This includes situations where groups are working together via an intranet (a local Internet) and situations where individual decision-making is done using the Internet as a tool. We start our review with seminal studies that look at how the decision-making process changes as one moves from a physical environment to a computer-mediated one. Here, we discuss how face-to-face groups differ from computer-mediated groups, as well as the effects of anonymity. Next, we review the latest research on social networking as it relates to decision-making, addressing the question of how people make judgments of other people online. Finally, we conclude the section with a discussion on how this research can be viewed from a heuristics perspective.

Computer-Mediated Communication

There are many themes of research examining the outcome of taking a process such as decision-making and moving it to a computerized environment to examine the impact on a process or outcome. A couple of main streams of research have focused on comparing face-to-face (FtF) versus computer-mediated (CM) decision-making. It is interesting to note that for the most part, these studies have not followed the classic models of decision-making (e.g., Bayes' theorem, MAU), but rather have merely compared the results of a decision-making task when conducted FtF versus CM.

For example, Jonassen and Kwon (2001) examined communication patterns in FtF versus CM groups and found that CM groups more closely followed the classic general problem solving process (problem definition, orientation, and solution development) while the FtF groups tended to follow a linear sequence of interactions. Interestingly, the participants in the CM groups also reported higher satisfaction with the process and also believed their proposed solutions were of higher quality.

Maznevski and Chudoba (2000) studied virtual teams in globally dispersed organizations. They found that the most effective teams tailored communication patterns to the task and used a combination of FtF communications supplemented by computer-mediated communication (CMC). It also appears that the order of the FtF and CM discussions are important. Dietz-Uhler and Bishop-Clark (2001) compared FtF groups versus synchronous and asynchronous CM groups that needed to discuss topics. They report FtF discussions that are preceded by CM discussions (either synchronous or asynchronous) are perceived to be more enjoyable by the participants and include a greater diversity of ideas than are FtF discussions not preceded by CM exchanges.

Thompson and Coovert (2002) explored FtF versus CM decision-making decision-making for groups using the stepladder decision-making strategy. The stepladder approach (Rogelberg et al.,1992) is thought to improve decision-making by staggering members entry into a discussion. Thompson and Coovert compared both traditional decision-making groups and stepladder groups in both FtF and CM conditions. They found that FtF participants felt more influential and satisfied than did the CM groups regardless of which decision-making technique (traditional or step ladder) was used.

Exploring the notion that the type of task might moderate some findings in the FtF and CM literature, Murthy and Kerr (2003) focused on a communication process task that required either the conveyance of information (idea generation), or convergence to a best solution (problem solving). They found an interaction between communication mode and communication process goals. When the individual's goal was merely to convey information, the FtF and CM teams performed equally well. When the goal was to converge on a best solution, however, the FtF communication resulted in better performance.

Anonymity

A special topic in the CMC literature is anonymity. Traditional decision-making research has held that if the identity of individuals in a group is not known, the group can make better decisions. There are many reasons for this, such as low-status individuals who have helpful information but are not wanting to express their views in front of high-status individuals; individuals making incorrect attributions about another's expertise and incorrectly deferring to them; high-power individuals commanding too much discussion time; and conformity to the group. (These are some of the reasons the stepladder technique mentioned earlier was developed.) In CMCs, anonymity can be easily manipulated and a few studies have examined its impact on decision-making performance of the group. One study (Sia, Tan, & Wei, 2002) focused on the effects of anonymity on group polarization. Polarized groups do not always make the best decisions, as the *groupthink* literature has effectively demonstrated. Sia and colleagues conducted two experiments and found in both that anonymity increased group polarization by causing individuals to generate more novel arguments and also engage in more one-upmanship behaviors. They also report that CM conditions where individuals are identified result in less polarization while anonymous CM groups led to stronger polarization.

Postmes and Lea (2000) conducted a series of meta-analyses to carefully evaluate the studies published on anonymity and group decision support systems. They focused on a variety of performance indicators to see if anonymity always led to better group decisions. Their conclusion was that the only reliable effect of anonymity was to lead to more contributions to the group, especially critical contributions. The authors further developed a model in which social norms and the social context of the decision must be considered for anonymity to lead to better group decisions.

Finally, a study conducted by Hayne, Pollard, and Rice (2003) examined the issue of whether anonymous comments entered by group participants are truly anonymous. They looked at the influence of comment length, evaluative tone, prior group membership, and prior communication among group members on attributions made about the identity of the authors' comments. The question they were asking is really as simple as: Can group members who have a history with other group members look at an anonymous comment and determine who it came from? Examining data from 32 groups on a brain storming task, it turns out the study's participants made attributions that were significantly more accurate than guessing. Factors that positively influenced the accuracy of the attributions were the evaluative tone (especially the use of humor), and the amount of prior communication among the group members. Even though the attributions were significantly better than chance, most of the attributions were, however, incorrect.

Critical Thinking

A special type of decision-making is required when individuals need to think critically about a problem or issue. This is especially important when individuals work in a group or team and need to collaborate and think critically about a situation. Work in this area is extremely important for both organizations and institutions dealing with defense issues (Alberts, 2001). Research has begun to address the nature of decision-making when groups must collaborate and think critically (Freeman et al., 2003). In addition to the work by Freeman and colleagues, others are conducting research that has implications for collaborative critical thinking and decision-making. We now review a couple studies to provide the reader a flavor for the area.

Focusing on comparing FtF and CM groups for a judgmental decision-making task, Cornelius and Boos (2003) sought to augment CM chats with training to see if performance could equal that obtained by FtF groups. Their premise was that individuals who engage in CM chats rarely understand the mechanisms whereby effective communication occurs, as it does in FtF encounters, and that technology might actually get in the way. Their view is that effective performance is competency based, both in terms of communication and use of the technology. These authors developed a competency-based training program that focused on both communication and media competency. Experimental tests of the training revealed it increased mutual understanding and satisfaction within the CM groups. Furthermore their performance approximated that achieved in FtF conditions.

Whitworth, Gallupe, and McQueen (2001) examined agreement when the groups must work in a CM environment. Agreement is an important social outcome of group processes. The authors were examining a proposed cognitive model in which agreement does not depend on the exchange of rich information, but can be obtained through the exchange of "lean" text data. In an experimental context, groups of five individuals exchanged a few characters of text information while solving three rounds of choice problems. Results indicated that agreement can be achieved in asynchronous anonymous CM groups while exchanging only a few characters of information about their respective positions. Conclusions indicate the key software design criteria for obtaining agreement is not richness, but dynamic many-to-many linkages between the group members.

Impression Formation on Social Networking Sites

The last 10 years have seen a major shift in the way people use the Internet, with Internet users becoming content creators as well as consumers. Social networking sites (e.g., Facebook) are now immensely popular and constitute a major way that time is spent on the Internet. CMC researchers have responded accordingly, and a lot of exciting new research is coming out on how people use these networks to communicate. Here we review the latest research on how people make judgments (i.e., form impressions) of other people based on their social networking profile.

The most popular social network is Facebook, and appropriately most research in this area has used the Facebook platform. Your Facebook friends are able to write on your "wall"—a personal digital bulletin board that people can post to. This wall is a part of your profile, and it appears below the information you entered about yourself when you signed up for the site (e.g., hobbies, quotes, about me).

Walther and his colleagues (2008) were interested in how cues deposited by friends on a profile wall affect an observer's impression of the profile owner. Walther et al. hypothesized that having attractive friends post on an owner's wall would increase an observer's perception of the profile owner's physical attractiveness, an assimilation effect found in offline studies. Moreover, the authors hypothesized that having attractive people post on one's wall would increase people's judgments of social attractiveness as well, a transfer effect based on the idea of "what is beautiful is good."

To test their hypotheses, the researchers sent participants a single URL address that would randomly forward them to one of the stimulus conditions. In each of the conditions, participants viewed a profile created for the study and rated the profile owner on physical attractiveness, social attractiveness, and competence. The profiles for the study varied by the valence of the comments (positive or negative) and attractiveness of the commenting friend's picture (unattractive or attractive). The results were consistent with Walther and colleagues' predictions: People were rated as being more physically and socially attractive if their friends are physically attractive. They also found that positive friends' statements on a profile owner's site raised the perceived attractiveness of the profile owner. These findings are especially impressive considering that a profile picture of the profile owner was also present (and prominent) on the wall.

Walther and his colleagues (2008) concluded that people use cues left by friends on social networking walls to make inferences about the attractiveness of profiler owner in the absence of better information (e.g., actual interactions with the person). However an important question remained: How do people decide what cues to use when making inferences? Facebook profiles can contain a lot of information. Which cues do people use and *why*?

The warranting principle (Walther & Parks, 2002) states that observers give greater credence to cues that are harder to fake for the person being judged. The warranting principle is based on the assumptions that people try to present themselves in the best possible way and that observers know this and take it into account by weighting the information based on the difficulty of being manipulated by the target. A competing perspective is the negativity effect, which states that people give more credence to negative information (as opposed to positive information), and is supported by much research in social psychology (Baumeister, Bratslavsky, Finkenauer, & Vohs, 2001).

Walther and his team (2009) conducted a follow-up study to test these two theories. They used a similar procedure to their earlier study, except the study was conducted in the lab and the participants were under the impression that they would actually meet the person in the profile picture (to increase participants motivation to pay attention, allowing for a more sensitive test). In the procedure, participants were shown the Facebook profile with a neutrally attractive photo, and then asked to rate the profile owner on a number of dimensions, including physical attractiveness. The experimenters manipulated the profile so that it included either self-statements implying physical attractiveness ("Just hanging out... getting better looking every day.") or self-statements implying physical unattractiveness ("I like to hang out online, and I'm trying my best to lose a few pounds."). They also manipulated the implied attractiveness of friend's comments. For example, an attractive comment was "Hey gorgeous, you looked great last night, you're bringing sexy back," and an unattractive comment was "Hey, Chris, much better picture of you... the last one wasn't all that flattering." The negativity hypothesis would predict that negative comments would carry the most weight; the warranting hypothesis would predict that friend's comments (good or bad) would carry the most weight because friend's comments are impervious to manipulation by the profile owner (and thus contain more "warranting value"). The pattern of means clearly supported the warranting hypothesis: People's ratings of the attractiveness of the profile user were most strongly related to one's friend's opinion, suggesting that a major way that people make judgments of people online is by using cues that are harder to manipulate by the person being judged.

It is important to keep in mind that the profile picture was held constant across conditions in the Walther et al. (2009) study. This was intentional as the purpose of their study was to test two competing hypotheses of impression formation. However, pictures certainly can influence the impression formation process and understanding their influence is key to understanding how impression formation occurs in the real world. Recently, Van Der Heide and his colleagues (2012) have begun examining this topic. A study by the group, investigated the relative importance of verbal versus photographic cues with both cues presented in isolation and presented together in judgments of extraversion. What they found is when the two types of stimuli were presented separately, a textual primacy effect was observed, but when the two stimuli were presented together, a visual primacy effect occurred. Interestingly, the researchers also found some support for the negativity hypothesis: Textual disclosures were only influential when the self-statement was introverted in nature (evidence suggests that extraversion is associated with positivity). The authors conclude that strongest approach to understanding impression formation in a real-world context lies in combing the visual primacy and negativity perspectives.

Impression formation in the online environment is burgeoning and exciting area of research. The different perspectives on how people form impressions online all have their empirical support, and it will be interesting to see what the boundary conditions are for each perspective. It will also be interesting to see how these boundaries change as technology changes. We are sure many readers have noticed that the described studies were conducted using Facebook walls, which have now been replaced with the timeline format. Although we expect that much of the research will carry over, it is an open question on how such formats can change the general findings or shift boundary conditions.

The Social Net and Heuristics

In academic settings, things are divided into neat categories. There are colleges for broad areas such as "Arts & Sciences" and "Humanities." These colleges are broken down into smaller departments for areas like "Psychology," which as a field is broken into clinical, social, and industrial/organizational psychologies, and these subdisciplines are broken down even further into individual topics. The distinctions imply that these areas deal with separate, nonoverlapping domains. But nature is not academia; many areas deal with overlapping phenomenon. When different areas of study approach the same topic, they often develop different terminology for similar concepts. Or, their focus and perspective is somewhat different.

The research on impression formation on social networking sites is focused on understanding why and how people make judgments of others based on the available information, and the field has adopted terminology that is best suited for this goal. Viewed from a slightly different perspective, however, the topic is one of heuristics. The research question addressed by these studies is essentially: "What heuristics do people use to make judgments of others when using social networking sites?" The Walther et al. (2008, 2009) studies found that people use information that cannot be easily manipulated by the target to make decisions—the warranting principle. This finding could be reinterpreted as people following the heuristic "Identify information that cannot be manipulated; weight each piece of information accordingly; arrive at a decision." This would be a tradeoff heuristic because it involves looking at multiple cues and weighting them appropriately.

Heuristics can be used to interpret other types of online behavior. Many shopping websites allow people to rate and review the products they are selling. These ratings appear alongside the product and can help others in deciding what specific product to buy. When people choose the product that has the highest rating in its category, they are using the "choose the best" heuristic, a type of one-reason heuristic. Many people make decisions based on the popularity (or unpopularity) of the product among their friends—the "what is popular is good" heuristic, a type of social heuristic. And the recognition heuristic is used frequently by Internet users to decide what site to visit or what online service to use. One obstacle that Microsoft has been trying to overcome with their new search engine Bing is that the fact that Google has such good recognition as a search engine.

Our point is that heuristics are used online and that much research has a heuristic component even though it may not be explicitly stated as such. In fact, when we consider what heuristics are— rules of thumb that help people arrive at a decision efficiently by ignoring information—it's hard to see how it could be any other way. The Internet is full of information, and even relatively short tasks like forming an impression of someone using profile information, require ignoring certain pieces of information (most people on Facebook have so much content related to them that looking through it all would take hours). For these reasons, we believe heuristics are a useful perspective for understanding online behavior.

Summary

In this section, we reviewed the literature on decision-making when an electronic medium such as the Internet is involved. We presented summaries of seminal studies in CMC, many of which focused on how decision-making in groups differs from decision-making in FtF groups. Next we presented a few of the latest studies on how people make judgments of others in an online context. There is one important area of research we left out, however: The research on decision-making in virtual teams. Our omission is intentional. The research on virtual teams is quite large and, in our opinion, quite important; work constitutes a major aspects of many people's lives and increasingly more work is being done in online teams. For these reasons, we gave decision-making in virtual teams its section. We now turn to our last major section of the chapter to present snippets of perspective on this complex and interesting topic.

Decision-Making in Virtual Teams

The interplay between all the possible factors that can affect decision-making quality makes understanding the decision-making process itself a complex task. Adding to the complexity, decision-making in organizations is more multifaceted than it is in laboratory settings. In the real world, groups make decisions in a dynamic business environment under financial, regulatory, and other logistic constraints.

In this section, we review the literature comparing CM and FtF groups in actual organizations. We will refer to CM groups in organizations as virtual teams (VTs) and FtF groups in organizations as "traditional teams." The switch to the word "team" is also useful because it emphasizes the interdependence that is usually present between members. To help with presentation, our review is structured around the Input–Process–Output model (the I–P–O model) shown in Fig. 6.1 (Hackman & Morris, 1975). This model states that team and environment qualities (inputs) affect team outcomes (outputs) through various team processes.

A couple of caveats are in order. First, the purpose of this section is to place decision-making in a wider context of the organization. Research in this area rarely examines decision quality alone as an outcome. Rather, decision-making is either combined with team effectiveness or is examined in conjunction with other outcome variables such as number of ideas generated. We will discuss other outcome variables such as team effectiveness (which is often intertwined with decision quality since making decisions is what many teams do) but our primary focus will remain with decision-making. Second, most researchers now view VTs and traditional teams as opposite ends on

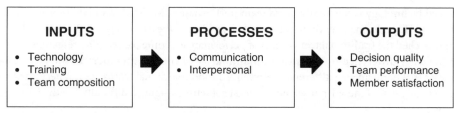

Fig. 6.1 An Input–Process–Output model of virtual teams.

the "virtualness" continuum. We agree with the spirit of this perspective but still employ the terms "virtual team" and "traditional team" when beneficial for clarity. With those caveats in mind, let's consider the literature looking at "inputs" to virtual teams.

Inputs

Inputs are the initial conditions and qualities of the VT and environment. VT researchers have identified a number of important factors that influence decision-making. For our discussion, we group these inputs into the three broad categories: Technology, training, and team composition.

Technology

No communication technology is inherently superior (Ebrahim, Ahmed, & Taha, 2009). The best technology for a specific situation depends on the qualities of task and the communication technology. To illustrate, consider five product managers located in different countries who need to reach an agreement on a business strategy. The managers are in a competitive industry and need to make a (good) decision fast on how to proceed with their business. The managers could use email to discuss their business strategy, but the asynchronous nature of email and the fact that a lot of back-and-forth conversation is necessary would make it difficult to make the decision quickly. Furthermore, the leanness of email might lead to a loss of important nonverbal information. In this situation, video chat would be preferable since it would allow members to quickly exchange information and would allow members to more easily incorporate important nonverbal information. However, in other situations, email would be a more appropriate technology. Imagine if your boss scheduled a video chat just to inform everyone of the company picnic details!

A couple of findings are relevant to choosing a communication medium. First, VTs take longer to make decisions (e.g., Cramton, 2001; Hollingshead, 1996) and team members are less able to accurately assess other members' knowledge (Ebrahim, Ahmed, & Zahari, 2009). There is evidence that these difficulties are due to reductions in nonverbal cues present in most CMC (Martins, Gilson, & Maynard, 2004). Second, these difficulties can be partially mitigated by using more rich communication mediums (e.g., video chat). Studies have found that the use of rich communication technologies can improve decision quality (Baker, 2002), and increase general team performance (Baker, 2002; Carlson & Zmud, 1999, May & Carter, 2001). Furthermore, the use of rich communication technologies can promote trust (Pauleen & Yoong, 2001) and team commitment in certain circumstances (Workman, Kahnweiler, & Bommer, 2003).

Training

Having the best technology does not ensure that the team will perform well or make good decisions. VT members need to be proficient in utilized technology or the benefits of the technology will not be realized. In fact, if VT members are not proficient with technology, the use of the advanced technology can actually harm team performance. McGrath and Hollingshead (1994) found that VTs perform lower than traditional teams during the early stages of the team's life cycle, but approached the traditional teams' level of performance as time passed. The researchers attributed the early difference to the initial unfamiliarity of the VT members to the technology. It appears that performance difference between VTs and traditional teams are not necessarily due to the "virtualness" of the VT per se, but—at least sometimes—due to difficulties with learning the technology.

Because of McGrath and Hollingshead and other similar findings, an interest has developed in using training to increase VT members' proficiency with technology. Studies examining the effects of training have found mostly favorable results: Training has been shown to increase decision-making quality and team performance (Kaiser, Tullar, & McKowen, 2000) as well as foster team members' feelings of cohesiveness, trust, and commitment to team goals (Beranek, 2000). An alternative training approach—mentoring programs—have also been found to be effective (Suchan & Hayzak, 2001). For a more extensive discussion of training virtual teams, see Hertel, Geister, and Konradt (2005).

Team Composition

When VTs are used, geography and time (i.e., time zones) are no longer limiting factors in choosing members for a team—the best person can be selected regardless of physical location. This advantage, however, comes at a price. Research has shown that teams with culturally diverse group members tend to have more difficulty both communicating and coordinating (Van Ryssen & Godar, 2000). In fact, even team members from different regions of the same country may have difficulty coordinating with each other (Robey, Khoo, & Powers, 2000). Fortunately, having VT members make an attempt to understand and accept these differences can mitigate the negative effects (Robey et al., 2000), as can developing clear protocols and project roles (Malhotra & Majchrzak, 2004).

Team size is another important input variable. Research in decision-making has shown that large groups do not necessarily make better decisions than small ones (Kerr & Tindale, 2004). This is due to negative effects like production blocking and process loss. Interestingly, there is evidence that production blocking is sometimes less problematic in VTs than traditional teams—particularly on tasks such as idea generation (Valacich, Dennis, & Nunamaker, 1992). The most likely explanation for this is that certain technologies used in CMC allow for multiple members of the group to speak at once, in contrast to FtF communication which typically allows only one member to speak at a time (Leenders, van Engelen & Kratzer, 2003).

Processes

Processes are the meat of the I–P–O model: They explain how inputs are turned into outputs. Simply put, processes explain *how* teams achieve their goals. There are two broad categories of processes that have received particular attention from researchers: Communication and interpersonal. Each is now considered.

Communication

Team members are dependent on one another by definition. This dependence makes communication critical relative to how well the team performs. To illustrate the importance of communication and how poor communication can result in substantial process loss, consider a VT that is responsible for bringing a cell-phone to market. The team consists of three subgroups, one responsible for design, one for manufacturing, and one for marketing. After reviewing some new market research, the design team decides to replace the planned five-megapixel camera for one with a 12-megapixel capability. However, the design team does not immediately inform the manufacturing or the marketing research subgroups due to confusion as to which member of the design team are responsible for communicating the changes to the other subgroups. As a result, the manufacturing and marketing subgroups develop the product based on the premise that a five-megapixel camera will be used. When the error is eventually discovered, the manufacturing and marketing groups have to modify or redo some of the work. The error is particularly problematic for the manufacturing subgroup, who now must find a new supplier for the cell-phone camera as well as include a larger imagine sensor. As a result of the change, the phone is late to market and does not sell as well as it could have. As this simple example illustrates, minor breakdowns in communication can lead to substantial amounts of wasted time and effort.

Unfortunately, research suggests that VTs typically do not communicate as well as their traditional counterparts (Bhappu, Griffith, & Northcraft, 1997; Ebrahim et al., 2009; Hollingshead, 1996). The observed difference is often attributed to reduced nonverbal information in CM discussions (Sproull & Kiesler, 1986) and difficulty with the CM technologies themselves. Furthermore, another difficulty arises with the use of asynchronous forms of electronic communication: How does one interpret a nonresponse? Does a nonresponse mean the person has not seen the message? Or does it mean that the person agrees/disagrees with the statement? While nonresponses are usually readily interpreted in FtF discussions, their meaning can be quite ambiguous in the CM context.

CMC, however, has its benefits as well. First, communicating over an electronic medium has been found to have an equalizing effect in regards to social status (e.g., Bikson & Eveland, 1990; Straus, 1996). That is, people lower in status are more likely to contribute when the communication in done through an electronic medium. In decision-making contexts, using electronic communication mediums can be useful in encouraging low-status individuals to share critical information. Second, certain communication technologies keep a digital record of the dialogue, which can be useful for referencing decisions made during the meeting. Finally, certain types of groupware can increase team effectiveness by reducing the occurrence of harmful group phenomenon. For example, Shepards and colleagues (1996) found that social comparisons enabled by these technologies were effective at reducing social loafing in electronic brainstorming groups.

Interpersonal Processes

A second stream of research has focused on the interpersonal processes related to VTs and performance. One interpersonal procedure that has received considerable attention is the formation of trust. Interestingly, the factors that contribute to the formation of trust seem to depend on the history of the team and the phase of team's life cycle. When the team is just forming, trust is primarily determined by members' initial propensity to trust and the members' perceptions of their teammates' integrity and competence (Aubert & Kelsey, 2003). Later on, trust is less influenced by perceptions of others' competence, while the importance of perceived integrity and one's propensity to trust remain the same.

Conflict has also received considerable attention in the literature. One general finding is that conflict is more common in VTs than in traditional teams (Hinds & Mortensen, 2005). Early research on VT found that people are more likely to swear, insult, or name-call in CMC (Siegel, Dubrovsky, Kiesler, & McGuire, 1986). This led researchers to conclude that the increase in conflict was due to inhibition caused by the medium. Although it is true that people generally are less inhibited in virtual environments, recent research has suggested that conflict in actual VT in organizational settings is primarily due to miscommunications

(Hertel, Geister, & Konradt, 2005). Furthermore, disagreements are not necessarily a bad thing—as long as they are carried out in a professional manner. Disagreements cause groups to question assumptions, generate and consider more alternatives, and have been shown in many cases to result in better decisions (Jehn & Mannix, 2001).

Outputs

In the I–P–O framework, decision quality is a result of a complex interplay between initial inputs (e.g., technology, training), and processes (e.g., communication processes). In our discussion of inputs and processes, we have already touched upon the factors that lead to good decisions (e.g., good technology-fit, communication). We have also highlighted some differences between the workings of VTs and traditional FtF teams. But do VTs make better decisions than traditional ones? The evidence is mixed. Some researchers have reported instances where VTs have outperformed their traditional counterparts (e.g., Chidambaram & Jones, 1993), but the majority of studies resulted in either no difference between VTs and traditional teams in terms of decision quality (e.g., Archer, 1990) or number of ideas generated (e.g., Lind, 1999). Perhaps the only consistent finding in regards to online decision-making is that online teams take longer than non-virtual teams (e.g., Cappel & Windsor, 2000; Graetz, Boyle, Kimble, Thompson, & Garlock, 1998).

Summary

In the previous section, we followed up our consideration of online decision-making with a discussion of decision-making in a broader context—decision-making in VTs. To help us organize our review, we used the well-worn I–P–O framework. We hope by now the reader is convinced that online decision-making in organizations is a complex and dynamic phenomenon. Many of the effects are context dependent, and so it may be quite a while before we truly understand the intricacies. Nonetheless, significant progress has been made, and we have arrived at the point where summaries like this can be useful for people working in VTs.

Future Directions

Online decision-making is such a complex process that it will be quite some time before we tease apart all the intricacies. We do, however, think there are a couple of areas that are particularly relevant to the immediate future. First, we believe the area of technology-fit is of particular importance. Other researchers do as well, as evidenced by the continued interest in the area. Technology-fit will likely continue to be a fruitful area of research for two reasons: (1) Technology can substantially influence decision quality, and (2) new technologies are being introduced frequently. Furthermore, older technologies are being improved and the population itself is becoming more tech-savvy. Identifying the "best" technology for a particular situation is therefore like hitting a moving target; how best is defined keeps changing. For example, video chat is beneficial in many more settings today than it was in 1995 because the technology itself has advanced, making it easier to set-up and use.

The second area of research that we find particularly promising is focused on how the diversity of groups affects decision outcomes. The spread of inexpensive, communication technology has led to more globalization and consequently more diverse teams. However, much of the research on diversity has focused on either gender or cultural values (Martin et al., 2004). Other forms of diversity—such as race, age, or organizational tenure—and how these influence decision-making have not been extensively studied. A clearer understanding of these other types of diversity will allow researchers to better comprehend the types of groups that make decisions in the modern, globalized world.

Finally, we find it interesting that the focus of decision-making on the Internet, or CM decision-making for that matter, is not following a classic paradigm (e.g., Bayes). Rather, the focus tends to be on how the medium might be impacting a decision outcome—that is, do individuals (groups) who use a computer to arrive at a decision achieve the same outcome as individuals (groups) who do not use the computer. The focus is on how the technology is changing the decision-making process, as opposed to understanding the core cognitive strategies involved with human decision-making. This implies either (1) we know all we need to know about fundamental human decision-making and need to move on; or, (2) the medium (computer, Internet) has changed decision-making so drastically that we first need to identify if it is different or not when using the new medium before we move to modeling it as part of the system of human–computer (Internet) decision-making. It will be interesting to see how researchers define the criterion space for future research in the area.

Conclusion

Our chapter is an overview of decision-making on the Internet. Our presentation began with classic paradigms in the area (Bayes' theorem, multiattribute utility theory, and maximized subjective expected utilities) and common categories of heuristics. We then expanded our scope and discussed social influences on decision-making. With a solid foundation of the traditional literature, we moved to discuss decision-making on the Internet. This consisted of a literature review of the effects of CMC in simple contexts and the decision-making process in actual organizations. An Input–Process–Output model was used to organize our presentation of this vast area of research. Our review of the online literature culminated with recommendations for future directions that stem from gaps in the literature.

Based on the literature review, we came to a number of conclusions. First, decision-making is a complex process that becomes even more so as one considers the effects of other individuals and/or mediums. Second, decision-making has been approached in different ways: In the traditional literature, the focus has been on the basic human processes related to how a person makes a decision; in the online decision-making literature, the focus has been on how the medium affects decision-making outcomes. Finally, although much progress has been made, there is still much to learn. Promising areas of future research include examining technology-fit, various types of diversity, and how these constructs affect decision quality in virtual teams.

Finally, we conclude by confirming that the Internet is bringing both great promise and challenges to the area of decision-making. The future is an exciting one for individuals and teams that occupy decision-making roles in organizations.

References

Alberts, D.S., Gartska, J.J., Hayes, R.E. & Signori, D.A. (2001). *Understanding Information Age Warfare.* Washington, DC: CCRP Publication Series.

Archer, N. P. (1990). A comparison of computer conferences with face-to-face meetings for small group business decisions. *Behaviour & Information Technology, 9,* 307–317.

Aubert, B. A., & Kelsey, B. L. (2003). Further understanding of trust and performance in virtual teams. *Small Group Research, 34*(5), 575.

Baker (2002). The effects of synchronous collaborative technologies on decision making: A study of virtual teams. *Information Resources Management Journal*, *15*, 79–93.

Baumeister, R. F., Bratslavsky, E., Finkenauer, C., & Vohs, K. D. (2001). Bad is stronger than good. *Review of General Psychology*, *5*, 323–370.

Beal, D. J., Cohen, R. R., Burke, M. J., & McLendon, C. L. (2003). Cohesion and performance in groups: a meta-analytic clarification of construct relations. *Journal of Applied Psychology*, *88*(6), 989.

Beranek, P. M. (2000). The impacts of relational and trust development training on virtual teams: An exploratory investigation. In *Proceedings of the 33rd Hawaii International Conference on Systems Sciences*. Los Alamitos, CA: IEEE Computer Society Press.

Bhappu, A. D., Griffith, T. L., & Northcraft, G. B. (1997). Media effects and communication bias in diverse groups. *Organizational Behavior and Human Decision Processes*, *70*(3), 199–205.

Bikson, T. K., & Eveland, J. D. (1990). *The Interplay of Work Group Structures and Computer Support*. Lawrence Erlbaum Associates, Inc., Mahwah, NJ.

Cappel, J. J., & Windsor, J. C. (2000). Ethical decision making: A comparison of computer-supported and face-to-face group. *Journal of Business Ethics*, *28*(2), 95–107.

Carlson, J. R., & Zmud, R. W. (1999). Channel expansion theory and the experiential nature of media richness perceptions. *The Academy of Management Journal*, *42*(2), 153–170.

Chidambaram, L. & Jones, B. (1993). Impact of communication medium and computer support on group perceptions and performance: A comparison of face-to-face and dispersed meetings. *MIS Quarterly*, *17*, 465–491.

Cornelius, C. & Boos, M. (2003). Enhancing mutual understanding in synchronous computer-mediated communication by training trade-offs in judgment tasks. *Communication Research*, *30*, 147–177.

Cramton, C. D. (2001). The mutual knowledge problem and its consequences for dispersed collaboration. *Organization science*, *45*, 346–371.

Dietz-Uhler, B., & Bishop-Clark, C. (2001). The use of computer-mediated communication to enhance subsequent face-to-face discussions. *Computers in Human Behavior*, *17*(3), 269–283.

Ebrahim, N. A., Ahmed, S., & Taha, Z. (2009). Virtual teams: a literature review. *Australian Journal of Basic and Applied Sciences*, *3*(3), 2653–2669.

Edwards, W., & Fasolo, B. (2001). Decision technology. *Annual Review of Psychology*, *52*(1), 581–606.

Fiske, A. P. (1992). The four elementary forms of sociality: Framework for a unified theory of social relations. *Psychological Review*, *99*(4), 689.

Freeman, J., Hess, K. P., Spitz, G., Garrity, M. J., Lintern, G., Coovert, M. D.,... King, V. T. S. (2003). Collaborative critical thinking. In *Proceedings of the 8th International Command and Control Research and Technology Symposium*. Washington, DC: CCRP Press.

Garcia-Retamero, R., Takezawa, M. & Gigerenzer, G. (2009). Does imitation benefit cue order learning? *Experimental Psychology*, *56*, 307–320.

Gibson, C., & Vermeulen, F. (2003). A healthy divide: Subgroups as a stimulus for team learning behavior. *Administrative Science Quarterly*, *48*(2), 202–239.

Gigerenzer, G. & Gaissmaier, G. (2011). Heuristic decision making in individuals and organizations. *Annual Review of Psychology*, *62*(1), 451–482.

Graetz, K. A., Boyle, E. S., Kimble, C. E., Thompson, P., & Garloch, J. L. (1998). Information sharing in face-to-face, teleconferencing, and electronic chat groups. *Small Group Research*, *29*(6), 714.

Gully, S. M., Incalcaterra, K. A., Joshi, A., & Beaubien, J. M. (2002). A meta-analysis of team-efficacy, potency, and performance: Interdependence and level of analysis as moderators of observed relationships. *Journal of Applied Psychology*, *87*(5), 819–832.

Hackman, J. R. (1987). *The Design of Work Teams: Handbook of Organizational Behavior*. Englewood Cliffs, NJ: Prentice Hall.

Hackman, J. R., & Morris, C. G. (1975). Group tasks, group interaction process, and group performance effectiveness: A review and proposed integration. *Advances in Experimental Social Psychology*, *8*, 45–99.

Hayne, S. C., Pollard, C. E., & Rice, R. E. (2003). Identification of comment authorship in anonymous group support systems. *Journal of Management Information Systems, 20*(1), 301–329.

Henry, R. A. (1995). Improving group judgment accuracy: Information sharing and determining the best member. *Organizational Behavior and Human Decision Processes, 62*(2), 190–197.

Henry, R. A., Strickland, O. J., Yorges, S. L., & Ladd, D. (1996). Helping groups determine their most accurate member: The role of outcome feedback. *Journal of Applied Social Psychology, 26*(13), 1153–1170.

Hertel, G., Geister, S., & Konradt, U. (2005). Managing virtual teams: A review of current empirical research. *Human Resource Management Review, 15*(1), 69–95.

Herzog, S. M., & Hertwig, R. (2009). The wisdom of many in one mind. *Psychological Science, 20*(2), 231.

Hinds, P. J., & Mortensen, M. (2005). Understanding conflict in geographically distributed teams: The moderating effects of shared identity, shared context, and spontaneous communication. *Organization Science, 16*(3), 290–307.

Hollingshead, A. B. (1996). Information suppression and status persistence in group decision making the effects of communication media. *Human Communication Research, 23*(2), 193–219.

Jehn, K. A., & Mannix, E. A. (2001). The dynamic nature of conflict: A longitudinal study of intragroup conflict and group performance. *The Academy of Management Journal, 44*(2), 238–251.

Jonassen, D. H., & Kwon, H. (2001). Communication patterns in computer mediated versus face-to-face group problem solving. *Educational Technology Research and Development, 49*(1), 35–51.

Kahneman D. & Tversky, A. (1979). Prospect theory: An analysis of decision under risk. *Econometrica, 47,* 263–292.

Kaiser, P., Tullar, W., & McKowen, D. (2000). Student team projects by Internet. *Business Communication Quarterly, 63,* 75–82.

Kattah, J. C., Talkad, A. V., Wang, D. Z., Hsieh, Y. H., & Newman-Toker, D. E. (2009). Hints to diagnose stroke in the acute vestibular syndrome: Three-step bedside oculomotor examination more sensitive than early MRI diffusion-weighted imaging. *Stroke, 40*(11), 3504–3510.

Kerr, N. L., & Tindale, R. S. (2004). Group performance and decision making. *Annual Review of Psychology, 55,* 623–655.

Latane, B., Williams, K., & Harkins, S. (1979). Many hands make light the work: The causes and consequences of social loafing. *Journal of Personality and Social Psychology, 37*(6), 822–832.

Laughlin, P. R., Bonner, B. L., & Miner, A. G. (2002). Groups perform better than the best individuals on Letters-to-Numbers problems. *Organizational Behavior and Human Decision Processes, 88*(2), 605–620.

Leenders, R. T. A. J., van Engelen, J. M. L., & Kratzer, J. (2003). Virtuality, communication, and new product team creativity: a social network perspective. *Journal of Engineering and Technology Management, 20*(1-2), 69–92.

Liang, D. W., Moreland, R., & Argote, L. (1995). Group versus individual training and group performance: The mediating role of transactive memory. *Personality and Social Psychology Bulletin, 21*(4), 384–393.

Lind, M. (1999). The gender impact of temporary virtual work groups. *IEEE Transactions on Professional Communication, 42,* 276–285.

Littlepage, G. E., & Mueller, A. L. (1997). Recognition and utilization of expertise in problem-solving groups: Expert characteristics and behavior. *Group Dynamics: Theory, Research,* and Practice, *1*(4), 324–328.

Littlepage, G. E., Schmidt, G. W., Whisler, E. W., & Frost, A. G. (1995). An input-process-output analysis of influence and performance in problem-solving groups. *Journal of Personality and Social Psychology, 69*(5), 877–889.

Locke, E. A., Alavi, M., & Wagner, J. (1997). Participation in decision-making: An information exchange perspective. In G. Ferris (Ed.), *Research in personnel and human resources management* (Vol. 15, pp. 293–331). Greenwich, CT: JAI Press.

Malhotra, A., & Majchrzak, A. (2004). Enabling knowledge creation in far-flung teams: Best practices for IT support and knowledge sharing. *Journal of Knowledge Management, 8,* 75–88.

March, J. G. (1994). *A primer of decision making*. New York: Free Press.

Marks, M. A. (1999). A test of the impact of collective efficacy in routine and novel performance environments. *Human Performance, 12*(3), 295–309.

Martins, L. L., Gilson, L. L., & Maynard, M. T. (2004). Virtual teams: What do we know and where do we go from here? *Journal of management, 30*(6), 805–835.

May, A., & Carter, C. (2001). A case study of virtual team working in the European automotive industry. *International Journal of Industrial Ergonomics, 27*(3), 171–186.

Maznevski, M. L., & Chudoba, K. M. (2000). Bridging space over time: Global virtual team dynamics and effectiveness. *Organization Science, 45*, 473–492.

McCammon, I., & Hageli, P. (2007). An evaluation of rule-based decision tools for travel in avalanche terrain. *Cold Regions Science and Technology, 47*(1–2), 193–206.

McGrath, J. E. & Hollingshead, A. B. (1994). *Groups interacting with technology: Ideas, evidence, issues,* and an agenda. London, UK: Sage.

Mellers, B. A., Schwartz, A., & Cooke, A. D. J. (1998). Judgment and decision making. *Annual Review of Psychology, 49*, 100–150.

Minson, J. A. & Mueller, J. S. (2012). The cost of collaboration: Why joint decision making exacerbates rejection of outside information. *Psychological Science, 23*(3), 219–224.

Mullen, B. & Cooper, C. (1994). The relation between group cohesiveness and performance: An integration. *Psychological Bulletin, 115*, 210–227.

Murthy, U. S., & Kerr, D. S. (2003). Decision making performance of interacting groups: an experimental investigation of the effects of task type and communication mode. *Information & Management, 40*(5), 351–360.

Pachur, T., Todd, P. M., Gigerenzer, G., Schooler, L. J., & Goldstein, D. G. (2011). When is the recognition heuristic an adaptive tool. *Ecological Rationality: Intelligence in the World, 40*, 202–241.

Payne, J. W., Bettman, J. R., & Johnson, E. J. (1992). Behavioral decision research: A constructive processing perspective. *Annual Review of Psychology, 43*, 87–131.

Pauleen, D. J., & Yoong, P. (2001). Relationship building and the use of ICT in boundary-crossing virtual teams: a facilitator's perspective. *Journal of Information Technology, 16*(4), 205–220.

Peterson, R. S. (1997). A directive leadership style in group decision making can be both virtue and vice: Evidence from elite and experimental groups. *Journal of Personality and Social Psychology, 72*(5), 1107.

Pohl, R. F. (2006). Empirical tests of the recognition heuristic. *Journal of Behavioral Decision Making, 19*(3), 251–271.

Postmes, T., & Lea, M. (2000). Social processes and group decision making: Anonymity in group decision support systems. *Ergonomics, 43*(8), 1252–1274.

Ramesh, V., & Dennis, A. R. (2002). The object-oriented team: Lessons for virtual teams from global software development. *Proceedings of the Thirty-Fifth Annual Hawaii International Conference on System Sciences*, Hawaii.

Rogelberg, S. G., Barnes-Farrell, J. L., & Lowe, C. A. (1992). The stepladder technique: An alternative group structure facilitating effective group decision making. *Journal of Applied Psychology, 77*(5), 730–737.

Shepard, M. M., Briggs, R. O., Reinig, B. A., Yen, J., & Nunamaker, J. (1996). Invoking social comparison to improve electronic brainstorming: Beyond anonymity. *Journal of Management Information Systems, 12*, 155–170.

Sia, C. L., Tan, B. C. Y., & Wei, K. K. (2002). Group polarization and computer-mediated communication: Effects of communication cues, social presence, and anonymity. *Information Systems Research, 13*(1), 70–90.

Siegel, J., Dubrovsky, V., Kiesler, S., & McGuire, T. W. (1986). Group processes in computer-mediated communication. *Organizational Behavior and Human Decision Processes, 37*(2), 157–187.

Snook, B., Zito, M., Bennell, C., & Taylor, P. J. (2005). On the complexity and accuracy of geographic profiling strategies. *Journal of Quantitative Criminology*, *21*(1), 1–26.

Sproull, L., & Kiesler, S. (1986). Reducing social context cues: Electronic mail in organizational communications. *Management science*, *32*(11), 1492–1512.

Stasser, G., & Titus, W. (1985). Pooling of unshared information in group decision making: Biased information sampling during discussion. *Journal of Personality and Social Psychology*, *48*(6), 1467–1478.

Straus, S. G. (1996). Getting a clue. *Small Group Research*, *27*(1), 115–142.

Suchan, J. & Hayzak, G. (2001). The communication characteristics of virtual teams: A case study. *IEEE Transactions on Professional Communication*, *44*, 174–186.

Thompson, L. F., & Coovert, M. D. (2002). Stepping up to the challenge: A critical examination of face-to-face and computer-mediated team decision making. *Group Dynamics: Theory, Research*, and Practice, *6*(1), 52–64.

Tindale, R. Scott, C. S., Thomas, L., Filkins, J., & Sheffey, S. (1996). Shared representations and asymmetric social influence processes in small groups. In E. Witte and J. Davis (Eds.), *Understanding Group Behavior: Consensual Action by Small Groups* (pp. 81–103). Mahwah, NJ: Lawrence Erlbaum Associates.

Tindale, R. S., & Sheffey, S. (2002). Shared information, cognitive load, and group memory. *Group Processes & Intergroup Relations*, *5*(1), 5–18.

Valacich, J. S., Dennis, A. R., & Nunamaker, J. F. (1992). Group size and anonymity effects on computer-mediated idea generation. *Small Group Research*, *23*(1), 49–73.

Van Der Heide, B., D'Angelo, J. D., & Schumaker, E. M. (2012). The effects of verbal versus photographic self-presentation on impression formation in Facebook. *Journal of Communication*, *62*(1), 98–116.

Van Ryssen, S., & Godar, S. H. (2000). Going international without going international: multinational virtual teams. *Journal of International Management*, *6*(1), 49–60.

Walther, J. B. & Parks, M. R. (2002). Cues filtered out, cues filtered in: Computer-mediated communication and relationships. In M. L. Knapp & J. A. Daly (Eds.), *Handbook of interpersonal communication* (3rd ed., pp. 529–563). Thousand Oaks, CA: Sage.

Walther, J. B., Van Der Heide, B., Hamel, L. M., & Shulman, H. C. (2009). Self-generated versus other-generated statements and impressions in computer-mediated communication: A test of warranting theory using Facebook. *Communications Research*, *36*, 229–253.

Walther, J. B., Van Der Heide, B., Kim, S., Westerman, D. & Tong, S. T. (2008). The role of friends' appearance on evaluations of individuals on Facebook: Are we known by the company we keep? *Human Communications Research*, *34*, 28–49.

Whitworth, B., Gallupe, B., & McQueen, R. (2001). Generating agreement in computer-mediated groups. *Small Group Research*, *32*(5), 625–665.

Workman, M., Kahnweiler, W., & Bommer, W. (2003). The effects of cognitive style and media richness on commitment to telework and virtual teams. *Journal of Vocational Behavior*, *63*(2), 199–219.

Wübben, M., & Wangenheim, F. (2008). Instant customer base analysis: Managerial heuristics often "get it right". *Journal of Marketing*, *72*(3), 82–93.

Zajonc, R. B., & Sales, S. M. (1966). Social facilitation of dominant and subordinate responses. *Journal of Experimental Social Psychology*, *2*(2), 160–168.

Chapter 7

The Internet and Aggression: Motivation, Disinhibitory, and Opportunity Aspects

Neil Malamuth, Daniel Linz, and René Weber

Introduction

In this chapter we describe research on the intersection of two domains, the Internet, its structure and function, and the social psychology of aggression. The Internet is an environment of instant connections and opportunity. It is also an instrument of great social and personal penetration. We then define aggression especially as it relates to studying the Internet. Next we focus on the social psychological processes related to aggression. There are several characteristics of the Internet world that accentuate aggression risk and Social Learning Theory is especially useful in understanding the elements of this environment and make the Internet an excellent teaching tool for aggression. Our discussion of the Internet as a teaching tool is organized within a framework of motivational, disinhibitory, and opportunity aspects. The Internet is a human communication environment with certain unique characteristics that can activate and shape various psychological mechanisms, many of these increasing the potential for aggression.

The Internet: Instant Connections, Opportunity, and Depth

We begin by making a series of observations that guide our conceptualization of the characteristics of the Internet and its intersection with the social psychology of aggression. First, we recognize the important interrelationship between the medium and the message. Every communication medium has certain unique features that shape the characteristics of the messages conveyed through it: In other words, features that enhance the effectiveness of certain types of messages and correspondingly limit the effectiveness of other types of messages. In that sense, the introduction and growth of the Internet—much like television some 50 years earlier, and radio before that, and the telephone even before—affected the types of communications transmitted.

Connections and Opportunity

Unlike older mediums, the Internet has transformed the world into a network of trillions of instant connections between people and ideas. This has resulted in a tremendous multiplication of *opportunities* for aggression, opportunities simply not available before the widespread use of this communication technology (Castells, 2009).

   Consider the implications for a form of devastating aggression—terrorism. Israel's intelligence chief Yuval Diskin, chief of Israel's internal security agency Shin Bet has warned (Rueters, 2010): "The terrorist threat... has become more complex. The world has turned into a 'global village' and everything is available to everyone." "Technology has made the world smaller and flatter," (the) "technology that has revolutionized economy and communications has also given rise to many global terror opportunities." Computer applications such as Google Earth and other Internet applications can be downloaded to Apple's iPhone and are available for terrorists to use and obtain intelligence that they could not receive before.

Although we often associate terrorism with certain areas of the world, such as the Middle East, the Anti-Defamation League has noted many other areas of the world where use of the Internet for terrorist activities is common. Latin American guerrilla movements are among the most electronically sophisticated extremist groups, according to a study in the *Wall Street Journal*. Mexico's Zapatista guerrillas have been rallying support online since their 1994 uprising. The Revolutionary Armed Forces of Colombia (FARC) fields press inquiries through electronic mail. The Web site of Peru's primary terrorist organization, Shining Path, contains scrolls of Marxist-Leninist propaganda.

Terrorism is an extreme example, but the point is that these instant connections vastly increase the opportunity for exposure to aggression for all participants. The Internet results in people being more likely than with other media to be exposed to aggressive material they deliberately seek or material that they did not necessarily seek out. For young people TV still heads the ranking but the Internet has become the major source of information and entertainment and as others have noted (e.g., von Feilitzen, 2009), it is perhaps the one medium where children may come across nonintentionally content that is less available in traditional media. We have, for example, heard of the child of a colleague who was attempting to gather information on the Internet for a book report and typed the phrase "Little Women." She was connected to various pornography sites. Other seemingly innocuous entries such as "whitehouse" could include exposure to severe violence, violent pornography, child pornography, and hate groups.

Depth

But, there is also a kind of paradox with the Internet. While there is a broadening of connections and opportunity there is also the possibility of deeper, more narrow penetration both into content areas and into the private psychological spaces of users. While the user is led to ever more detailed levels of information the Internet also penetrates the home, the individual computer, the mailbox or the private space of people who use it. The degree of penetration into the private spaces of individual users for the production of psychological effects may not be seen with other technologies. Again, thinking about terrorism consider the following quote from the Internet site of the Hezbollah organization (quoted in *Yediot Aharonot*, December 16, 1998, p. 7) (Tsfati & Weimann, 2002): "By means of the Internet Hezbollah has succeeded in entering the homes of Israelis, creating an important psychological breakthrough—Ibrahim Nasser al–Din, Hezbollah military leader." The "breakthrough" by terrorist organizations could not be achieved in media such as television. Terrorists could probably achieve an equally powerful "shock" impact on a larger number of people just by the widespread broadcast of their threatening acts on traditional media outlets—a primary goal of the terrorists. With the Internet, on the other hand, the terrorists may be better able to target specific segments of the population with a more subtle and tailored "informational" strategy.

Research confirms the use of this narrow targeting by terrorist groups. Tsfati and Weimann (2002) conducted content analyses of various terrorist Internet sites. Indeed, terrorists are using the Internet to target specific segments of the population with more subtle and detailed information. In their study they focused on the way terrorists communicate through this medium as compared to more traditional means of communication. While some similarities with conventional types of communication were found, the researchers described three key differences. First, on the Internet the terrorist groups played down their violence and were much more "pacifistic" in their rhetoric than in other media outlets. The researchers suggested that their intent here was to attract web surfers sympathetic to issues of human rights and free speech.

A second difference is that the web pages contained a great deal of detailed information, not possible on mass media channels that operate with more limited space constraints and where some journalists may be loathe to allow certain information favorable to terrorists to be widely disseminated. Blunt (2003) has used the term "e-jihad" to describe Islamist organizations which use the Internet to propagate a message of religious violence. He claims that since 9/11 jihadists have been very successful in leveraging the Internet to amplify or broadcast their message by creating videos which they then post online. The use of beheading videos which were once simply broadcast as the primary form of communication are now only a small part of a larger, sophisticated media campaign which has grown and evolved in a complex way. Early videos included "last will and testament" films of suicide bombers, recording their motivations and enshrining them as martyrs. The videos were played after the attack to claim credit and recruit more martyrs. One beheading video included footage of the surveillance and actual kidnapping of the victim, followed by his confinement, questioning, and murder, and thus served as a "how to" or documentary film.

A third difference is that the sites offered visitors ample and varied possibilities to take action such as soliciting donations, protesting, disseminating messages, but advocating violence was rarely one of the approaches (at least directly; violence was indirectly advocated through calls for Jihad on Islamic sites). Messages designed to elicit sympathy among certain segments of the population might be much more effectively communicated via the Internet.

It is difficult to disentangle the effects of the Internet per se since its use is typically embedded within the context of various other media uses and other experiences. And, we certainly do not assume that the Internet *always* makes the potential for aggression worse. We do, though, focus in this chapter on the possibility that aggression can become more widespread and easier to accomplish. Dempsey, Sulkowski, Dempsey, and Storch (2011), for instance, have shown that the Internet provides new tools for young aggressors who already engage in aggressive behaviors in the physical world to victimize a larger group of peers in cyberspace. Of course, we also recognize that it holds the promise of making some situations involving aggression arguably better.

In summary, there are a number of distinctive features of this technology that invoke specific social psychological processes related to aggression. And, while earlier communication technologies may have revolutionized the way and, at times, even the content of what was communicated, they did not offer the same capacity for invoking as many fundamental social psychological processes that may be related to aggression as does the Internet.

Defining Aggression for Studying the Internet

Although the concept may not be easy to define precisely, most social psychologists have agreed to define aggression as a behavior directed toward the goal of harming or injuring another living being, who is motivated to avoid that harm (e.g., Baron & Richardson,1994). This definition includes several key elements, wherein:

◆ aggression is a behavior, not an attitude, motive, or emotion

◆ an intention exists to cause harm to the victim

◆ some type of aversive consequences occur

- the victim is a living being
- the victim is motivated to avoid the harm (Berkowitz, 1993).

Social psychologists are fascinated by the fact that a vast range of people, depending on the situation, can participate in various forms of aggression (see Malamuth & Addison, 2001, for further elaboration), on a continuum of behavior ranging from verbal assaults to extreme forms of physical violence.

A widely used distinction in the social psychological literature is between *hostile* and *instrumental* aggression (Geen, 2001). Definitions of *instrumental* aggression emphasize that any harm is primarily a tactical means of attaining other goals, such as social status or money (e.g., Berkowitz, 1993). Typically, the definition of *hostile* aggression emphasizes that harm or injury to the target is the primary goal of the behavior. Berkowitz (1993) links hostile aggression with anger in response to frustration. His model is based on the network theory of emotion which states that emotions, cognitions, and even action tendencies are connected in memory through association. The activation of one element (e.g., anger) can spread to other "nodes" in the associative network, such as aggression.

Rather than considering hostile and instrumental aggression as distinct entities, some researchers have argued that both types of aggression actually share some common underlying mechanisms. For instance, Huesmann (1998) suggests that a key distinguishing element is the degree to which emotional anger underlies the aggressive response. He proposes that a continuum is the most suitable conceptualization, with instrumental and hostile aggression being at opposite ends of this emotional anger continuum.

These definitions and distinctions are especially important when thinking about aggression and the Internet. Certain characteristics of the Internet result in some forms of aggression being rare and other forms much more common. A discussion of aggression and the Internet cannot be limited to a consideration of only extreme forms of violence such as homicide with guns, or terrorism with explosives, committed directly against a victim.

Aggression as a social psychological phenomenon as accomplished through the communication medium of the Internet is often both more subtle and more encompassing. What we recognize as aggression on the Internet often has little to do with directly hitting, stabbing, or shooting. For example, aggression from senders whose identities are shielded may take the form of written or audio-verbal messages designed to hurt or humiliate. Indirect aggression (Lagerspetz et al., 1988), which may take such forms as telling lies or stealing in the form of destructive messages, codes, "viruses," or "worms" designed to hinder or destroy others' work or computer software, also occurs. Hate words designed to incite other people, unseen by and usually unknown to the message composer, are used to urge others to engage in violent behavior. Attempts are now routinely made to steal the "identities" and credit information from victims who are never seen. In all of these cases, the broad definition of aggression would still apply because of the intention to harm the victim.

Social Psychological Processes Related to Aggression

The general theoretical perspective on media effects that we subscribe to recognizes the need to study media exposure within the context of other factors, i.e., media exposure is considered one of many risk factors and not a unique cause of aggressive behavior. Moreover, it is important to consider bidirectional interactive influences (Malamuth, Addison, & Koss, 2000; Slater, Henry, Swaim, & Anderson, 2003), i.e., individuals with certain predispositions (e.g., relatively more aggressive tendencies) are likely to seek out media that are consistent with those pre-existing predispositions, which are then likely to strengthen those predispositions.

Different types of people seek out and respond to media content differently in accordance with their individual predispositions and their ongoing social relationships, and media exposure in turn may reinforce certain tendencies. Research seeking to identify the effects of Internet experiences per se may attempt to systematically focus on these while controlling for other factors, but it may often prove more realistic to analyze such exposure as part of a larger set of media and other experiences within which Internet experiences are often largely embedded.

One way to organize ideas about the social psychology of aggression is by reference to the General Learning Model (GLM). The original incarnation of this model (the General Aggression Model, aka GAM) dealt exclusively with the effects of violent content on aggression (Anderson & Bushman 2002). However, it was argued recently (Buckley & Anderson, 2006) that the model is "general" enough to be applied to all types of media content, including that presented through the Internet.

The GAM is a dynamic, social-cognitive, developmental model that provides an integrative framework for domain-specific aggression theories. It includes situational, personological, and biological variables. GAM draws heavily on social-cognitive and social learning theories that have been developed over the past 40 years by social, personality, cognitive, and developmental psychologists (e.g., Bandura, 1977; Berkowitz, 1989, 1993; Dodge, 1980, 1986). This model begins with the assumption that social situations represent an opportunity for learning. The learning that takes place is influenced by the interaction of person (e.g., attitudes, goals, emotions, traits) and situation variables such as the use of the Internet. These learning encounters influence both the subsequent internal state of the person (their arousal, emotions and cognitions) and also their appraisal of the environment and thus subsequent decisions and behavior (Murphy, 2007).

This model was developed in an attempt to merge elements from several existing theoretical perspectives within the social cognition frame. The key theoretical perspectives in the GLM include the cognitive-neoassociation model (Anderson and Bower, 1973), the social cognitive information processing theory (Huesmann, 1998), and social cognitive theory (Bandura, 2002; see Buckley and Anderson, 2006, for a complete review).

Empirical research has found consistent support for the idea that the activation of one thought may spread to other related thoughts and feelings (Berkowitz, 1993; Graham and Hudley, 1994). There has been some empirical support for the cognitive-neoassociation model and the GLM in the area of video game violence. For example, a recent meta-analysis (Anderson et al., 2004a) found that increases in video game violence could be linked with increases in aggressive cognition, affect, arousal, and behavior. (However, there is debate about these effects, see Bushman, Rothstein, & Anderson, 2010; Ferguson, 2007; Ferguson & Kilburn, 2009).

Internet Characteristics, Aggression Risk, and Social Learning Theory

The features of the Internet that may facilitate aggression may be organized within a general framework suggested by social learning theorists focusing on the causes of aggressive behaviors (e.g., Bandura, 1973, 1977). They emphasize that it is essential to consider the role of interactive multiple factors, such as those creating the motivation to commit aggression, those reducing internal and external inhibitions that might prevent acting out of the desire to aggress, and those factors providing the opportunity for the act to occur. These headings serve as broad categories that are useful for discussing various relevant features of the Internet and, therefore, our following discussion will be organized by such a framework consisting of motivational, disinhibitory, and opportunity aspects.

Motivational Aspects

As we mentioned earlier, a critical social feature of the Internet is the instant connection with people, messages, and ideas. As a social communication device the Internet is always "on." This increases the possibility of extensive exposure to cognitive scripts and emotions potentially priming and thereby *motivating* aggression. Moreover, the images and ideas are often accessed with little if any discernible cost. The Internet's ubiquitous availability creates the potential for high levels of exposure to violence that may be highly graphic.

The Internet is a network of connected information, and because the ideas and information are connected through hypertext links, people can follow one node to another. A user can rapidly build exposure to violent information. The same images can be viewed repeatedly, and similar content can be pursued with greater and greater depth and specialization.

The social cognitive approach to aggression is the most applicable to this set of features. The cognitive or information-processing approach to aggression subsumed by the GLM is one of the most fully explicated social psychological approaches and is based on the assumption that memory can be represented as a complex associative network of nodes representing cognitive concepts and emotions. Research has shown that the processes by which hostile schemas or aggressive "scripts"— indeed, all types of knowledge structures—are activated is cognitive, but with practice may become "automatic" and operate without awareness (Schneider & Shiffrin, 1977; Todorov & Bargh, 2002).

Many Can Access

The Internet is available to virtually anyone. Unlike older technologies, there is no "family viewing" time, or "daytime programming" wherein there is a guarantee that certain ideas and images that are potentially harmful or offensive to certain audiences are restricted. The Internet provides widespread access to images and ideas not normally present in many people's social environment—especially children's. They may use the Internet to download games, watch video clips, and generally have access to information around the clock which would often be restricted to them were it not for this medium. Valkenburg and Soeters (2001) conducted a survey among 194 Dutch children (aged 8–13 years) who had home access to the Internet. Children's spontaneous descriptions of their positive experiences with the Internet most frequently included playing or downloading computer games (17%), watching video clips and songs (13%), visiting kids' entertainment sites (12%), and seeking information about animals (7%). As a negative experience, children most frequently reported a virus or computer crash (10%), violence (4%), and pornography (4%).

To the Extent the User Engages Interactively with the Internet it is an Excellent Teaching Tool

Unlike older forms of mass media, the Internet is interactive and may therefore be an especially potent source of social psychological factors that may increase the risk for aggression. This may be illustrated by focusing on video games, since the Internet has become an important arena for such interactions. A study by Polman, De Castro, and Van Aken (2008) shows that active participation of actually playing a violent video game versus watching a passive, recorded game, leads to increased aggressive behavior after exposure. Other studies, however, found no significant interaction between interactivity and aggressive outcomes. In an experimental study by Weber, Bates, and Behr (2011), for instance, game interactivity did not interact with violent game content, but showed a main effect on aggressive behavior in low-skilled players. Apparently, high levels of interactivity, which requires more cognitive resources from players, combined with low skills, was experienced as overwhelming and frustrating which in turn increased aggressive behaviors after exposure.

Who plays games online? According to an Entertainment Software Association 2009 report 23% of most frequent gamers pay to play online games. This is an increase from 22% in 2008 and a marked increase from 8% in 2004. Further, 57% of online game players are male while 43% of online game players are female. And, 37% of heads of households report they play games on wireless devices such as a cell-phone or PDA (personal digital assistant), up from 20% in 2002.

PlayStation, Xbox, and Wii all have online services. Even the United States (US) Army has jumped into the game scene to capitalize on people's increased interest in the Internet and America's military prowess. They have created freely available army experience video games on the Army's Website (http://www.americasarmy.com) that are now downloaded millions of times.

Although not the majority of the content, considerable video game content portrays violence (for an overview, see Smith, 2006). Some video game violence has particularly alarmed parents and legislators. For example, *Grand Theft Auto: Vice City*, popular several years ago, featured the rape and mutilation of female prostitutes and the assault of police officers (see the *Seattle Post-Intelligencer*, Friday, March 21, 2003). In their report *About the Computer and Videogame Industry 2009: Sales, demographic and usage data essential facts* the Entertainment Software Association (2009) reports that in 2008 among the most popular included: fifth place *Grand Theft Auto IV*, sixth place *Call of Duty: World at War*, and seventh place *Gears of War 2*.

Slater et al. (2003) found support for the assertion that more alienated individuals seek out violent website content which may include violent gaming sites. Moreover, they found evidence that visiting violence-oriented Internet sites contributes to youths' aggressiveness above and beyond the effects due to other factors, including other media experiences.

As an example of this alienation effect, consider the terrorist attack in Oslo, Norway in the summer of 2011 that killed 77 and injured 151 people. This attack has been linked to video games by the killer himself. In a "manifesto" concerning his anger at what he felt was the take over of Europe by Muslims the terror suspect wrote extensively about his use of Activision's *Call of Duty: Modern Warfare 2* game and Blizzard Entertainment's *World of Warcraft* game to help him in his preparations for the killings. "I just bought *Modern Warfare 2*, the game. It is probably the best military simulator out there and it's one of the hottest games this year.... I see MW2 more as a part of my training- simulation than anything else. I've still learned to love it though and especially the multiplayer part is amazing. You can more or less completely simulate actual operations."

Over the years, violent video games have been associated with violent attacks on others. The Columbine High School massacre in Colorado in 1999 involved two teenage killers, Eric Harris and Dylan Klebold, said to have had extensively played the violent games *Doom* and *Quake*.

Most recently, violent video games have been the subject of legislation limiting their availability to children. In a decision and an opinion by the Supreme Court of the United States regarding the constitutionality of such limitations the Court specifically addressed this issue of interactivity—the majority opinion in the California case Brown, Governor of California, et al. v. Entertainment Merchants Association et al. Decided June 27, 2011.

Associate Justice Breyer dissented from this opinion. From his perspective he felt there was considerable evidence that California's statute significantly furthers this compelling interest in reducing harm to children. Justice Breyer based his opinion on his reading of the research on video games and his conclusion from that work that video games are excellent teaching tools. He noted that video games can help develop habits, accustom the player to performance of the task, and reward the player for performing that task well. Most importantly for our purposes here, Justice Breyer in his opinion takes seriously the differences in the medium with which violence is experienced and compares the effects of playing video games to the more passive media such as TV viewing—one of the central organizing themes of this chapter. He notes that researchers have investigated the ways that violent video games, including those experienced on the Internet, differ from violent TV programs and films. He concludes that video games possibly cause more harm than can typically passive media, such as books or films or television programs.

Taking note of the important trends in investigating video game violence Justice Breyer listed the four important differences between passive exposure to media violence and interactive video game play presented by social psychologists to the Court, all of which have been found to increase the risk for aggressive tendencies (for reviews see Anderson & Bushman, 2001; Anderson & Dill, 2000; Anderson et al., 2003; Bushman & Anderson, 2002).

The first difference relates to the *involvement level of individuals and identification with violent characters*. TV viewing is a relatively passive activity video game playing is highly active. While viewers of violent TV programs and films watch other characters behave aggressively; players of violent video games "become" the aggressive characters—they are the ones who pull the trigger and throw the punches. Viewers of violent films might identify with the characters they see. Such role taking is covert. However, players of some violent video games are required to take on the identity of a violent game character. This form of role-taking is overt. In first-person games, the player controls the actions of the violent game character and sees the game environment from the character's visual perspective. In third-person games, the player can "become" one of an array of characters that differ in gender, appearance, and special fighting skills. In some games, the player can apply scanned images to characters in the game (called "skins").

The second difference is to do with *reinforcement of violent acts*. In the mass media, aggression often pays (e.g., the fighter is rewarded by getting what he or she wants). When people watch a TV program or film, this reinforcing effect is indirect and vicarious. In contrast, the violent video game player is directly reinforced for aggressing by seeing visual effects, hearing sound effects (e.g., groans of pain from the enemy), hearing verbal praise (e.g., when an enemy is killed the computer says "nice shot" or "impressive"), receiving points, and advancing to the next highest level of the game.

The *frequency of violent scenes* is another important difference. Compared to violent TV programs and films, the violence shown in violent video games is almost continuous. The player must constantly be on the alert for hostile enemies, must constantly choose and enact aggressive behaviors, and is reinforced for doing so. In addition, the violent video game player is exposed to constant gory scenes filled with blood, screams of pain, and suffering. All of this takes place in a context in which emotions, incompatible with normal empathic feelings, are at the fore. Instead, the scenes of gory death evoke emotions such as excitement and exhilaration. Thus, desensitization is likely to proceed at a faster and more effective pace for the violent video game player than for the violent TV/film viewer.

The final important difference lies in the *perceived realism*. Video games are becoming increasingly more realistic. In fact, CBS's "60 Minutes" program (broadcast August 6, 2003) reported that the richest man in the world, Bill Gates (Chairman of Microsoft), has decided to seriously invest in video games and to help create technology which makes the games so realistic that "people forget they are playing a game."

Justice Breyer also noted that "cutting-edge neuroscience" has shown that "virtual violence in video game playing results in those neural patterns that are considered characteristic for aggressive cognition and behavior" (Weber, Ritterfeld, & Mathiak, 2006). In Weber et al.'s study, 13 experienced, male video game players were observed playing a latest-generation violent video game for one hour while brain images were taken via functional magnetic resonance imaging. The players' virtual interactions were content coded as either "passive/dead, no interactions"; "active/safe, no imminent danger/no violent interactions"; "active/potential danger occurs, violent interactions expected"; "active/under attack, some violent interactions"; and "active/fighting and killing, many violent interactions." Based on previous neuroscientific studies on aggressive cognitions and behaviors, Weber et al. hypothesized that virtual aggressive interactions engage the same neural mechanisms as real-world aggressive interactions. Comparing playing episodes with many versus no violent interactions in a within-subject design, the authors found indeed that virtual violence is able to activate the same brain patterns when people have aggressive thoughts or a pronounced tendency to act aggressively and thus, playing violent video games can not be considered as playing "just a game." For example, on a neurophysiological level, virtual violent interactions lead to an active suppression of affective processing such as empathy with rather large effect size up to d = 0.92 (Cohen's d; Cohen, 1988). However, Weber et al. also note that even if the neural patterns in the physical and virtual world are identical, the corresponding subjective experiences may not be. For example, it is clearly a difference to be mugged at gunpoint in the physical or in the virtual world for instance. Therefore, with the current state-of-the-art in the neurosciences, virtual experiences may look the same as non-virtual experiences on a neurophysiological level, but feel different from them. Nevertheless, Weber et al.'s study specified what it means when the earlier mentioned GAM (Anderson & Bushman, 2002) posits a causal relationship between learning encounters and a subsequent internal state of the person characterized by arousal, emotions, and cognitions.

In summary, social psychologists have identified four elements that may be expected to make violent video games more harmful than violent TV programs and films: Involvement level of individuals and identification with violent characters, reinforcement of violent acts, frequency of violent scenes, and perceived realism. Each of these contributes to make the Internet an excellent teaching tool for aggression.

Disinhibitory Aspects

Content is Unregulated

The Internet was designed as a highly decentralized system. This decentralization defies regulation. Unlike television and radio in the past, it is a decentralized, distributed network. This decentralization poses a challenge to would-be inhibitors or censors who wish to impose normative limitations. The decentralization and associated lack of normative limitations is important for aggression. Violent material previously inaccessible is now available; there are no external inhibitors. Broadcast television was the primary source of media depictions of violence and censorship was imposed upon this medium, although it has come to be far less restricted recently. The Federal Communications Commission has not yet attempted to regulate the Internet, as it has the older communication technologies of radio and television.

Because of this lack of regulation the content found on the Internet may be much more extreme than that found on other media. Baron and Kimmel (2000) conducted a content analysis of the degree of sexual violence in various types of popular media. They found that sexual violent content was the highest on the Internet. They concluded that the relatively "democratic" unregulated characteristics of the Internet enabled content that would otherwise be strongly discouraged (e.g., by pressures from women's groups) to be more widely distributed.

Participation is Often Private and Anonymous

Rubin (1994) describes certain characteristics of electronic technologies that increase the propensity for acts that transgress moral boundaries. One element of the cyber world is that it is possible for users to simultaneously maintain both privacy and public contact. Using the Internet is often a solitary activity and inhibitors normally present in face-to-face interaction with others are absent.

It has been suggested that there are really two broad categories of anonymity: Technical anonymity and social anonymity (Hayne & Rice, 1997). Technical anonymity refers to the removal of all meaningful identifying information about others in the exchange of material. This can include the removal of one's name or other identifying information from Internet communications. Social anonymity refers to the perception of others and/or one's self as unidentifiable because of a lack of cues to use to attribute an identity to that individual. In other words, it may not be the case that one is truly anonymous in a social context, but the individual perceives him or herself to be anonymous to others. Both categories of anonymity have traditionally been investigated by social science researchers and both categories have been investigated in computer mediated environments.

Although many researchers suggest that it is overly deterministic to view the computer-mediated environment as an inherently impersonal medium that always fosters antisocial behavior (e.g., Lea et al., 1992; Spears & Lea, 1994; Walther, 1992, 1994, 1996; Walther et al., 1994), they generally believe that a computer-mediated environment decreases or eliminates cues and sources of information that have been identified as important in the development of polite, friendly, courteous interpersonal interactions (Daft & Lengel, 1984; Kiesler, Siegel, & McGuire, 1984; Rice, 1993). Communication via a network of computers "seems to comprise some of the same conditions that are important for deindividuation—anonymity, reduced self-regulation, and reduced self-awareness" (Kiesler, et al., 1984, p. 1126). More specifically, the reduction of social cues in a computer-mediated environment is believed to decrease users' overall self-awareness, leading to a state of deindividuation.

Participation is Unmonitored by Others

Unlike other media experiences, viewing and interacting on the Internet can be free of the social costs associated with viewing socially unapproved deviant material. There are no embarrassing or social mores to inhibit the user. This may be particularly important for children and their access to the Internet, which is predominantly unmonitored by parents. The Kaiser-Family Generation M2 report states that 60% of parents do not impose rules when using the computer. For a brief overview check: http://www.slideshare.net/AlHaqqNetwork/kaiser-family-foundation-generation-m2. There has been considerable discussion concerning parental controls, an issue that will not be discussed here.

Contact with Similar Others Provides Social Support

Even without actually interacting with anyone else, the Internet can give the impression to the user that many others share his/her interests. One can access links to droves of images and ideas similar to the content at hand almost no matter how obscure, specialized, or even deviant the images may be. Thus, the impression is fostered of great social support and potentially disinhibiting effects on exposure to the images, ideas, and/or messages in which the user is interested.

Because it is possible to seek out others and make contact with those who share your interests in message-sharing centers, through personal addresses, or on websites devoted to shared content, social support for even the most aggressive images can be generated. Personal identity can be enhanced by identifying with others and through social support given by others with whom you share interests on the Internet (Bennett, 2003).

As a distributed network, the Internet is not only very difficult to monitor or censor, but it allows for expression of an identity through participation in a group that shares your interests.

Identities can be made whole by participating with others in this interactive communication medium. Likewise the fact that identities can be changed and shielded is an import aspect of the following forms of aggression. Other Internet participants with whom a user can interact can come from nearly anywhere on earth. In addition, the aspect of the Internet that we identified as one person "fishing" for many people is critical here. Many of the forms of aggression we describe in this chapter involve one person contacting many others in order to eventually locate a particular target, such as a child, with the intention of aggression. Finally, the technical feature of the Internet that allows one computer to find many others is important. This feature allows the Internet to be used for accomplishing indirect violence on a large scale.

Certain extremist groups, such as those that advocate outgroup ethnic hate and aggression, may find the relatively uninhibited context of the Internet as a fertile ground for growth and expression. In a recent report by Reuters news (2010) it was noted that the Simon Wiesenthal Center found that the use of social networking sites such as Facebook, Twitter, and YouTube by militant and hate groups grew by almost 20% in the year 2010. The study, using research by the center and tips from the public, found more than 11,500 social networks, websites, forums, and blogs promoting violence, anti-Semitism, homophobia, hate music, and terrorism, an increase from 10,000 last year. Examples of hate on the Internet included videos of extremists appealing for recruits and showing how to make improvised explosive devices. Online games ranged from bombing Haitian earthquake survivors to shooting illegal immigrants and gays. Facebook groups included "national kick a ginger day" and "I love curry bashing."

In an investigation of hate crime with the Internet, Glaser et al. (2002) asked what makes racists advocate racial violence. They conducted semi-structured interviews with 38 participants in white racist Internet chat rooms. They examined the extent to which people would, in this unique environment, advocate interracial violence in response to purported economic and cultural threats. The authors experimentally manipulated the nature and proximity of the threats. Qualitative and quantitative analyses indicate that the respondents were most threatened by interracial marriage and, to a lesser extent, black people moving into white neighborhoods. In contrast, job competition posed by black applicants evoked very little advocacy of violence. Various supremacist groups in the US have also used the Internet for financial gain (Damphousse & Smith, 1998).

The technical feature of the Internet that allows one computer to find many others may also facilitate violence against oneself, via social support and conveying of information reducing potential inhibitory mechanisms. Information that may be nearly impossible to obtain by other means about methods of suicide may be obtained from the Internet. It is now extremely easy to access information about suicide from the Internet using search engines. Websites offering advice on suicide may be found by teenagers trawling the Internet for information on the best way to kill oneself (Beaston, Hosty, & Smith, 2000). These include websites such as Alt.Suicide.Holiday (ASH) suicide methods file (pro-suicide), Satan Service (pro-suicide), Suicide methods.net (pro-suicide).

One such site, now infamous, calling itself "Church of Euthanasia," advises people to "do a good job" when they commit suicide. It reads: "Suicide is hard work. It's easy to do it badly, or make rookie mistakes. As with many things, the best results are achieved by thorough research and careful preparation." The site goes on to discuss the pros and cons of death by shooting, hanging, crashing a car, jumping, slitting your wrists, drowning, freezing, overdosing, or gassing yourself with nitrous oxide, exhaust fumes, and oven gas. One site described using guns, overdosing, slashing one's wrists, and hanging as the "best methods to commit suicide." Other site titles suggested various suicide methods. One site illustrated various methods including lethal doses of poison, their availability, estimated time of death, and degrees of certainty.

In fact, 90% of hospital contacts resulting from self-harm involve self-poisoning. In 2000, Thompson found that information on how to commit suicide and the number of pro-suicide groups on the Internet are burgeoning (especially concerning self-poisoning) and the number of high-traffic news-groups encouraging suicide present on the Internet is increasing, compared to an earlier baseline. Thompson reports that details of how lethal chemicals can be purchased over the Internet, and lethal doses, are very explicit. However, the situation may be changing. In England rates of suicide among young (15–34-year-old) men and women, the age groups who make most use of the Internet, have been declining since the mid-1990s, a time when use of the Internet has expanded rapidly (Biddle, Brock, Brookes, & Gunnell, 2008). Cases of Internet-induced suicide may be offset by the potential beneficial effects or other suicide prevention activities contained in searches using suicide-related terms. Biddle et al. speculate that attempts are being made to clean up the web. They note that links to the pro-suicide Satan Service site were often unavailable.

Not everyone is equally affected by exposure to these sites, of course, and there is no suggestion among mental health experts that merely viewing suicide websites will instigate an attempt from an otherwise healthy individual (Adekola, Yolles, & Armenta, 2001). The problem, according to these authors, is that especially vulnerable individuals have been sharing information about suicide with one another. There are examples of interactive notes on the Internet followed by a suicide fatality (Baume, Cantor, & Rolfe, 1997). Adekola et al. (2001) caution that, although surfing the Internet for information may be useful for patients with other disorders, the potential hazard makes it inappropriate for use among those prone to extreme depression and suicide. These authors recommend that mental health care providers should counsel patients about alternatives to surfing the web at times of crisis. Staying off the web may be the best idea for these individuals. Instead they should seek help by calling crisis lines and talking to clinicians, friends, or family members.

Opportunity Aspects

Targets of Aggression are Readily Available

One of the various "opportunity" aspects provided by the Internet environment pertains to the ability of one person to "fish" or "troll" for many others. Many people can be contacted and stalked, and children can be contacted for aggressive purposes. Dempsey et al. (2011), for instance, found that the Internet does not create new aggressors, but provides the tools for already aggressive young people in the physical world to victimize a larger group of peers in cyberspace.

Stalking has often received attention from popular press, legal opinion, law enforcement, and social scientists (Best, 1999; Spitzberg & Cupach, 2003). Stalking is legally defined as the willful, malicious, and repeated following and harassing of another person (Sfiligoj, 2003). Typical stalking behavior involves physically following the victims, telephone harassment, and vandalism. Stalkers also often use binoculars, cameras, hidden microphones, and public records to keep track of the whereabouts of their victims.

Stalking is a major public health concern, primarily for women, and is associated with many adverse health outcomes, including death. Basile, Swahn, Chen, and Saltzman (2006) examined a cross-sectional sample of adults aged 18 years and older living in the US ($n = 9684$) who participated in a risk random-digit-dial telephone survey. In the US, 4.5% of adults reported having ever been stalked. Women had significantly higher prevalence (7%) of stalking victimization than did men (2%). People who were never married or who were separated, widowed, or divorced had significantly higher odds of being stalked than those who were married or had a partner. People aged 55 years or older and those who were retired were least likely to report stalking victimization.

This study shows that stalking affects many adults. Nearly 1 in 22 adults (almost 10 million, approximately 80% of whom were women) in the US were stalked at some time in their lives.

The development of the Internet and the rapid growth of digital communication have dramatically increased the efficiency and convenience of information gathering, exchange, and processing. However, many attributes of the Internet—low cost, ease of use, anonymity, ease of data gathering, and cross-referencing—make it also an attractive medium for stalkers. Given the enormous amount of personal information available through the Internet, a stalker can easily locate private information about a potential victim with a few mouse clicks or keystrokes, especially if victims volunteered private information on social network sites or blogs.

The use of the Internet, email, or other electronic communications devices to stalk another person or "cyber stalking" involves an array of activities; it shares important characteristics with offline stalking, including the desire to exert control over the victims. The Internet, though, provides new avenues for pursuit of a victim. A cyber stalker may send repeated, threatening, or harassing messages by the simple push of a button or use programs to send these messages without being physically in front of a computer terminal. A cyber stalker can also easily dupe other Internet users into harassing or threatening a victim by posting the name, phone number, or email address of the victim in public chat rooms, Internet bulletin boards or gossip platforms such as juicycampus.com which do not censor content posted by users. In addition to its ease of use, the anonymity of the Internet also makes cyberspace a place where stalkers can conceal their true identity from law enforcement agencies (see later).

Sfiligoj (2003) has found that whilst the majority of stalkers have been in relationships with their victims, some have never met their victim or they are merely acquaintances (e.g., neighbor, friend, or coworker). Scientific information on stalking has been limited, despite unprecedented media, legal, and legislative attention over the past 10 years.

Sometimes when individuals are seeking useful information on the Internet, they might increase the likelihood of being victimized by stalkers and/or other aggressors. For example, Finn and Banach (2000) have identified problems and dangers that may be encountered when females seek health and human services on the Internet, and the implications of these problems and dangers for human service organizations. Participation in online self-help groups may be harmful to some members for the following reasons:

◆ Members may encounter cyber stalkers.

◆ Communication may become disinhibited online, exposing participants to threats, profanity, seduction, and personal attacks.

◆ The qualifications of moderators are not regulated.

◆ The identity of members is unknown, which can cause problems in self-help groups concerned with issues of violence and abuse.

◆ Members may receive misinformation from other group members.

◆ Messages may be forwarded or archived and searched by search engines, resulting in a loss of privacy.

◆ *Identity can be easily disguised.*

The fact that interaction with others on the Internet enables the disguising of one's identity can contribute greatly to the potential of aggression, such as the sexual abuse of children, whereby pedophilic predators may have the opportunity to reach children who otherwise would be better protected (Quayle & Taylor, 2002a, 2000b, 2003). Barnitz (2001) discusses the need for a coordinated local and global response to the commercial sexual exploitation of children as one of the most destructive forms of child abuse. He stresses that although some efforts have been made to stop the trafficking in children and youth, they are far from sufficient. The scope of the child sex trade in physical and sexual violence for profit is outlined by Barnitz, and he notes that the Internet has made high-tech trade profitable.

The ability to hide identity has also enabled law enforcement agencies to conduct Internet stings directed at pedophiles (Fulda, 2002). After the Supreme Court upheld laws prohibiting child pornography in 1982, law enforcement agencies embarked on a large-scale effort to track and arrest purveyors of child pornography. With the rise of the Internet, child pornography proliferated. In the latter half of the 1990s, US law enforcement agencies began directing their efforts online. This era also witnessed the rise of greater cooperation between federal, state, and local law enforcement agencies and between nations. One such typical sting operation, "Operation Candyman" centered on a Yahoo! e-group that invited people to trade pictures of child pornography. The Federal Bureau of Investigation (FBI) estimates that there were more than 7000 subscribers to the group, with around 2400 living abroad.

Targets are Unseen

A social psychological feature of the Internet includes the remoteness of victim to perpetrator. Albert Bandura has written extensively about the ways in which we excuse or allow ourselves to engage in moral transgressions that would otherwise be repugnant to us. He notes that on the Internet, transgressive acts can be performed in anonymity toward depersonalized or faceless victims located thousands of miles away (Bandura, 1990a, 1990b, 2004). There are no consequences in terms of the victim's reactions. There is no ability for the victim to retaliate. The victim can be easily dehumanized. Bandura's writings on this topic emanate from his more general focus on moral disengagement.

Bandura (1990a, 1990b) has outlined a set of conditions that disinhibit people and make it possible for them to engage in immoral behavior such as destructive aggression. He identifies three submechanisms: Self-monitoring, judgmental, and self-reactive (Bandura, 1990a, 1990b, 2004). The first step to exercising control over one's conduct is self-monitoring. Actions give rise to self-reactions through a judgmental function in which the individual's conduct is evaluated against their internal standards and situational circumstances. If an internal standard is violated, a self-sanction may occur.

People usually do not engage in reprehensible conduct unless they have justified to themselves the rightness of their actions or disassociated themselves from the consequences of their actions. Social cognitive theory of moral agency identifies mechanisms by which moral self-sanctions are selectively disengaged from detrimental conduct (e.g., Bandura, 1996). Moral disengagement may center on the cognitive restructuring of transgressive conduct into a benign or worthy one by using the mechanism of moral justification. Other psychological restructuring mechanisms which may be employed to justify a moral construct are:

♦ sanitizing euphemistic language

♦ advantageous comparison

♦ disavowal of a sense of personal agency by diffusion or displacement of responsibility

♦ disregarding or minimizing the injurious effects of one's actions

♦ attribution of blame to, and dehumanization of, those who are victimized.

Most important for our discussion of the social psychological features of the Internet that facilitate aggression are the last three of these mechanisms. (We will return to the other mechanisms in the discussion later on "hacking.") Cyber crimes such as virus attacks, hacking, or identity theft are particular difficult to combat due to the unique environment of cyberspace. The accessibility of an immense audience, coupled with the anonymity of the subject, make the Internet a perfect vehicle for locating victims, and it provides an environment where the victims don't see or speak to the attackers (Joinson, 2003).

Research attention within this area has focused on the sequences of written exchanges on discussion topics that begin with a disagreement and get more heated. The exchange often involves character attacks and foul language (Douglas & McGarty, 2001). Wallace and others have speculated that flaming is attributable to the psychological state of "deindividuation" (i.e., people lose their identity or sense of uniqueness as individuals). According to the theory of deindividuation (Zimbardo, 1969), under some social and psychological conditions (e.g., being in a large crowd or being anonymous), individuals are not able to view themselves as distinct individuals (i.e., they are deindividuated). Deindividuation will lead to a reduction of self-evaluation because of a lack of self-awareness (Duval & Wicklund, 1972). Consequently, a decreased self-evaluation would be conducive to antinormative and uninhibited behavior (Zimbardo, 1969).

In considering the technological aspects, it is important to recall that the Internet was designed as a highly decentralized system that defies regulation. Because anybody can have access, and there is no central authority, Internet participants can use it for destructive purposes. The damage done may be enormously magnified because virtually all of the systems on which people depend in their everyday life are interdependently run by computer network systems. Therefore, hacking, virus attacks, and identity theft are becoming increasingly destructive and are forms of aggression made possible by features of the Internet, particularly those that increase depersonalization, lack consequences in terms of victim's reactions, and typically do not enable victims to retaliate.

At the same time, computer systems are vulnerable to a variety of forms of aggressive retaliation by disgruntled employees, former employees, or contractors. The Computer Security Institute/FBI Computer Crime and Security Survey between 1996 and 2000 found that insiders topped the list of likely sources of cyber attacks, with more than 80% of respondents citing them as a likely source. In the 2000 survey, 71% of the respondents reported insider unauthorized access incidents (Power, 2000). In 2001, a disgruntled employee was convicted of hacking into the computerized waste management system of Maroochy Shire, Queensland, causing millions of gallons of raw sewage to spill out into local rivers and parks (Tagg, 2001). The individual in question appears to have been acting alone. However, to the extent that other "insiders" are able and willing to act in concert with "outsiders" (potential terrorists or otherwise), vulnerabilities to aggressive hackers or saboteurs may be exponentially greater because of the deindividuation features of the Internet.

A person may steal someone else's identity or break into a computer in order to steal information for financial gain, but the same acts can also be committed purely for the purpose of sabotage. Unlike crimes in the physical world, such as a bank robbery, it is often difficult to identify and assess the nature of cyber crimes due to the technological features of the Internet.

A computer virus is a program or piece of code that is loaded on to a computer without its user's knowledge and runs against the user's wishes. Viruses can also replicate themselves: A simple virus can make a copy of itself over and over again, and is relatively easy to produce. All computer viruses are man-made. Even a simple virus can be dangerous, because it can quickly use all available memory and bring the system to a halt. An even more dangerous type of virus is one capable of transmitting itself across networks and bypassing security systems.

One of the most aggressive aspects of a virus attack is that one person can cause catastrophic damages and affect the lives of millions of people in a very short period of time. In 1999, the infamous "Melissa" virus infected thousands of computers in a few hours, causing an estimated US$80 million in damage. On December 4, 2000, a 23-year-old Filipino hacker "accidentally" sent out a very simple computer virus that was attached to an email message proclaiming "I LOVE YOU." It raced over the world via email, crashed email systems, and destroyed data on millions of computers in a few hours. This "love bug" caused an estimated US$10 billion in damage worldwide, and affected the White House, Congress, the Pentagon, and the British House of Commons, along with numerous corporations. Other, more recent, attacks have included the dissemination of computer worms such as "Slammer," a worm that brought much of the Internet to its knees in 2003 and "Blaster" a worm that triggered a payload that launched a denial of service attack against http://www.windowsupdate.com; "Sasser" (2004) which damaged the British Coast Guard and Delta Airlines, which had to cancel some flights after its computers became infected; "Storm" (2007) like "Blaster" and others before, this worm's payload performed a denial-of-service attack on http://www.microsoft.com.

Web page defacement is also a frequent form of aggressive cyber attack that is often perpetrated by hackers to express personal or political opinions. To deface a web page, a hacker first gains access to the system server on which the website is stored, and then changes the content of the website. In March 2001, on the second anniversary of the NATO bombing of the Chinese embassy in Belgrade, a hacking group defaced numerous US commercial and government websites with pro-Chinese and anti-American slogans. A more recent example involved Rupert Murdoch's Fox News Corporation web page in Summer 2011 on which he was reported dead after the *News of the World* phone hacking scandal.

Interviews with students who have engaged in web page defacement and other forms of hacking reveal that they engage in several forms of moral disengagement, including the cognitive restructuring of transgressive conduct into a benign or worthy act, by moral justification, sanitizing euphemistic language, and advantageous comparison. In Marc Roger's article, "Modern-day Robin Hood or moral disengagement: understanding the justification for criminal computer activity," he used moral disengagement as a foundation to hypothesize that hackers and computer criminals are employing moral disengagement mechanisms in an attempt to reduce self-censure (Chantler, 1996; Denning, 1998; Rogers, 1999).

Several studies and articles quote hackers as stating that their activities are purely an intellectual activity and that information should be freely available to everyone (e.g., Chantler, 1996). Individuals engaged in criminal computer activity routinely minimize or misconstrue the consequences (Chantler, 1996; Denning, 1998; Shaw, Post, & Roby, 1998). These individuals have stated that they never intentionally damage any files. They lay responsibility on the victims, claiming that besides, companies have or should have backups of their data and systems (Chantler, 1996). Other individuals dehumanize the victims and refer to them in terms such as multinational corporations, or just networks and systems. They usually do not comment on the impact to the end users and system administrators, the cost to potential consumers, or the long-term effects (Spafford, 1997). The attribution of blame to the victim is possibly the most common mechanism employed by computer criminals and hackers (Rogers, 1999). The majority of researchers, who have used interviews and self-report surveys, quote the hacker subjects as blaming the system administrators or programmers for lax security, and stating that the victims deserved to be attacked (Chantler, 1996). Stealing music is also justified with these moral disengagement tactics.

Cyberbullying

It is very important to acknowledge that since the first edition of this book the Internet has changed dramatically, especially with the appearance of social networks where people are not operating anonymously but are mostly identified. It is very important to see how aggression is related to the online identified world. Cyberbullying is an aggressive behavior that involves using the Internet, cell phones or other devices to send or post text or images intended to hurt or embarrass another person. Cyberbullying can range in seriousness from continuing to send emails to someone who has said they want no further contact with the sender, but it may also include threats, sexual remarks, pejorative labels (i.e., hate speech), ganging up on victims by making them the subject of ridicule in forums, and posting false statements as fact aimed at humiliation. Cyberbullies may disclose victims' personal data (e.g., real name, address, or workplace/schools) at websites or forums or may pose as the identity of a victim for the purpose of publishing material in their name that defames or ridicules them. Some cyberbullies may also send threatening and harassing emails and instant messages to the victims, while other post rumors or gossip and instigate others to dislike and gang up on the target. One element of cyberbullying that is considerably different from our previous discussion of social psychological factors is the degree to which this behavior is fueled not by anonymity but the use of social networks where people are identified—both bully and target—intentionally embarrass others, harass, intimidate, or make threats online to one another. This bullying occurs via email, text messaging, posts to blogs, and websites Facebook pages and other venues where victims and aggressors are likely to be fully identified.

Dehue, Bolman, and Völlink (2008) report on a survey of 1500 students between grades 4–8. The survey revealed that 42% of children have been bullied while online, one in four have had it happen more than once and 35% of children have been threatened online. Nearly one in five had had threats more than once. The survey also showed that 21% of children have received mean or threatening emails or other messages and 58% of children admit someone has said mean or hurtful things to them online. However, 58% have not told their parents or an adult about something mean or hurtful that happened to them online.

Cyberbullying has the same characteristics as indirect, traditional bullying: It happens more than once, it involves psychological violence, and it is intentional (Flemish Committee for Education, Training, Science and Innovation, 2004). However, cyberbullying also has some specific characteristics unique to the fact that it is carried out over the Internet. Most importantly, in contrast with traditional bullies, cyberbullies are often anonymous (Finkelhor, Mitchell, & Wolak, 2007; Ybarra and Mitchell, 2001). As we have stressed earlier, visual anonymity can increase the social influence exerted by group norms and depersonalization (Spears, Postmes, & Wolbert (2002). Another important difference is the lack of physical and social cues, which insure that cyberbullies are not personally confronted with the way their victims react and with the consequences of their harassments (Postmes & Spears, 1998). For the victims, the lack of social cues hampers the interpretation of the message (McKenna & Bargh, 2000). Finally, the encroachment on victims' formerly safe private space makes the cyberspace bullying message especially harmful compared to more traditional forms of bullying (van Puymbroek, 2006). A third important difference has to do with most parents. Many parents are unfamiliar with the Internet and therefore are often unaware of their child engaging in cyberbullying or being cyberbullied (British Broadcasting Corporation, 2004). In rare cases, even parents engage in cyberbullying: Lori Drew, an adult mother from Missouri, used a fake MySpace profile named "Josh Evans" in 2006 to cyberbully Megan Meier, age 13 at the time. The teenager hanged herself at home after receiving cruel messages from "Josh," including one stating the world would be better off without her.

Summary and Concluding Comments

The Internet is a human communication environment with certain unique characteristics that can activate and shape various psychological mechanisms, some of them pertaining to the potential for aggression. We have emphasized in this chapter that to analyze the conditions that contribute to aggression, it is essential to consider the role of interactive multiple factors, such as those creating the motivation to commit aggression, those reducing internal and external inhibitions that might prevent acting out of the desire to aggress, and those factors providing the opportunity for the act to occur. Within each of these categories, we have suggested that there are certain features of the Internet that are particularly relevant to increased risk for aggressive conduct.

For example, we have suggested that the Internet is ubiquitous and interactive and thus likely to often be particularly engaging. We have also emphasized that Internet content is unregulated and consumption of information is often private and unmonitored, so that contact with similar others provides social support, and the user is often anonymous. Concealment and depersonalization can bring out the worst in people by removing personal and social sanctions for pernicious conduct, particularly since targets are often readily available, unseen, and may be reached in ways not available via other communication media. Such characteristics can disinhibit aggressive tendencies.

References

Adekola, O. A. Yolles, J. C., & Armenta, J. (2001). The Internet and suicide. *Psychiatric* Bulletin *25*, 400.

Aiken, M., & Waller, B. (2000). Flaming among first-time group support system users. *Information and Management*, *37*, 95–100.

Alao, A. O., Yolles, J. C., & Armenta, W. R. (1999). Cybersuicide: the Internet and suicide. *American Journal of Psychiatry*, *156*, 1836–1837.

Anderson, C. A., Berkowitz, L., Donnerstein, E., Huesmann, L. R., Johnson, J. D., Linz, D.,… Wartella, E. (2003). The influence of media violence on youth. *Psychological Science in the Public Interest*, *4*, 81–110.

Anderson, C.A., & Bushman, B.J. (2001). Effects of violent video games on aggressive behavior, aggressive cognition, aggressive affect, physiological arousal, and prosocial behavior: a meta-analytic review of the scientific literature. *Psychological Science*, *12*, 353–359.

Anderson, C. A., & Bushman, B. J. (2002). Human aggression. *Annual Review of Psychology*, *53*, 27–51.

Anderson, C. A., Carnagey, N. L., Flanagan, M., Benjamin, A. J., Eubanks, J., & Valentine, J. C. (2004). Violent video games: Specific effects of violent content on aggressive thoughts and behavior. *Advances in Experimental Social Psychology*, *36*, 199–249.

Anderson, C. A., & Dill, K. (2000). Video games and aggressive thoughts, feelings, and behavior in the laboratory and in life. *Journal of Personality and Social Psychology*, *78*, 772–790.

Anderson, C. A., Sakamoto, A., Gentile, D. A., Ihori, N., Shibuya, A., Yukawa, S.,… Kobayashi, K. (2008). Longitudinal effects of violent video games on aggression in Japan and the United States. *Pediatrics*, *122*, e1067–e1072.

Anderson, C. A., Shibuya, A., Ihori, N., Swing, E. L., Bushman, B. J., Sakamoto, A.,… Saleem, M. (2010). Violent video game effects on aggression, empathy, and prosocial behavior in Eastern and Western Countries: A meta-analytic review. *Psychological Bulletin*, *136*, 151–173.

Anderson, J. & Bower, G. (1973). *Human associative memory*. Washington, DC: Winston.

Arquilla, J., & Karasik, T. (1999). Chechnya: a glimpse of future conflict? *Studies in Conflict & Terrorism*, *22*, 207–229.

Atkin, C. (1983). Effects of realistic TV violence vs. fictional violence on aggression. *Journalism Quarterly*, *60*, 615–621.

Atlas, R., Cornett, L., Lane, D. M., & Napier, H. A. (1997). The use of animation in soft-ware training: pitfalls and benefits. In M.A. Quinones and A. Ehrenstein (eds), *Training for a rapidly changing workplace: applications of psychological research* (pp. 281–302). Washington, DC: American Psychological Association.

Bandura, A. (1973). *Aggression: a social learning analysis*. Oxford, UK: Prentice Hall.

Bandura, A. (1977). *Social learning theory*. Oxford, UK: Prentice Hall.

Bandura, A. (1990a). Mechanisms of moral disengagement. In W. Reich (Ed.), *Origins of terrorism: psychologies, ideologies, theologies, states of mind* (pp. 161–91). New York, NY: Cambridge University Press.

Bandura, A. (1990b). Selective activation and disengagement of moral control. *Journal of Social Issues, 46,* 27–46.

Bandura, A. (1996). Moral disengagement in the perpetration of inhumanities. *Journal of Personality and Social Psychology, 71,* 364–374.

Bandura, A. (2002). Social cognitive theory in cultural context. *Applied Psychology, 51,* 269–290.

Bandura, A. (2004). The role of selective moral disengagement in terrorism and counterterrorism. In F. M. Moghaddam and A. J. Marsella (eds), *Understanding terrorism: psychosocial roots, consequences, and interventions* (pp. 121–150). Washington, DC: American Psychological Association.

Barnitz, L. (2001). Effectively responding to the commercial sexual exploitation of children: a comprehensive approach to prevention, protection, and reintegration services. *Child Welfare. Special Issue: International Issues in Child Welfare, 80,* 597–610.

Baron, R. A., & Bell, P. A. (1977). Sexual arousal and aggression by males: effects of type of erotic stimuli and prior provocation. *Journal of Personality and Social Psychology, 35,* 79–87.

Baron, R. A., & Richardson, D. R. (1994). Human aggression. *Perspectives in social psychology* (2nd ed.). New York, NY: Plenum Press.

Barron, M., & Kimmel, M. (2000). Sexual violence in three pornographic media: toward a sociological explanation. *Journal of Sex Research, 37,* 161–168.

Basile, K. C., Swahn, M. H., Chen, J., & Saltzman, L. E. (2006). Stalking in the United States: recent national prevalence estimates. *American Journal of Preventive Medicine, 31*(2), 172–175.

Baume, P., Cantor, C. H., & Rolfe, A. (1997). Cybersuicide: the role of interactive suicide notes on the Internet. *Crisis, 18,* 73–79.

Beaston, S., Hosty, G.S., & Smith, S. (2000). Suicide and the Internet. *Psychiatric Bulletin, 24,* 434.

Bennett, L. (2003). Lifestyle politics and citizen-consumers: identity, communication, and political action in late modern society. In J. Corner & D. Pels (Eds.), *Media and political style: essays on representation and civic culture* (pp. 137–151). Thousand Oaks, CA: Sage.

Berkowitz, L. (1989). The frustration-aggression hypothesis: Examination and reformulation. *Psychological Bulletin, 106,* 59–73.

Berkowitz, L. (1993). *Aggression: its causes, consequences and control.* New York, NY: McGraw–Hill.

Berkowitz, L., & Alioto, J.T. (1973). The meaning of an observed event as a determinant of its aggressive consequences. *Journal of Personality and Social Psychology, 28,* 206–17.

Best, J. (1999). *Random violence: how we talk about new crimes and new victims.* Berkeley, CA: University of California Press.

Biddle, L., Brock, A., Brookes, S., & Gunnell, D. (2008). Suicides rates in young men in England and Wales in the 21st century: time trend study. *British Medical Journal, 336,* 539–542.

Blunt, G. (2003). *Islam in the Digital Age: E-Jihad, Online Fatwas and Cyber Islamic Environments* (pp. 26–27). London, UK: Pluto Press.

British Broadcasting Corporation. (2004, July 21). Parents "unsure how kids use Net." CBBC Newsround. Retrieved from http://news.bbc.co.uk/cbbcnews/hi/sci_tech/newsid_3911000/3911957.stm

Buckley, K. E., & Anderson, C. A. (2006). A theoretical model of the effects and consequences of playing video games. In P. Vorderer & J. Bryant (Eds.), *Playing Video Games – Motives, Responses, and Consequences* (pp. 363–378). Mahwah, NJ: LEA.

Bushman, B.J., & Anderson, C.A. (2002).Violent video games and hostile expectations: a test of the general aggression model. *Personality & Social Psychology Bulletin, 28,* 1679–1686.

Bushman, B. J., Rothstein, H. R., & Anderson, C. R. (2010). Much ado about something: Violent video game effects and a school of red herring: Reply to Ferguson and Kilburn (2010). *Psychological Bulletin, 136,* 182–187.

Campbell, D. (2001, September 26). Internet gives peace a chance. *Guardian Unlimited.*

Castells, M. (2009). *The Rise of the Network Society: The Information Age: Economy, Society, and Culture.* Oxford, UK: Wiley-Blackwell.

Chambers, J. A., & Ascione, F. R. (1987). The effects of prosocial and aggressive videogames on children's donating and helping. *Journal of Genetic Psychology, 148*, 499–505.

Chantler, N. (1996). *Profile of a computer hacker.* Seminole, FL: Interpact Press.

Cohen, J. (1988). *Statistical power analysis for the behavioral sciences* (2nd ed.). Hillsdale, NJ: Lawrence Erlbaum Associate, Inc.

Daft, R. L., & Lengel, R. H. (1984). Information richness: a new approach to managerial behavior and organizational design. *Research in Organizational Behavior, 6*, 191–233.

Damphousse, K. R., & Smith, B. L. (1998). The Internet: a terrorist medium for the 21st century. In H. W. Kushner (Ed.), *The future of terrorism: violence in the new millennium* (pp. 208–224). Thousand Oaks, CA: Sage.

Dehue, F., Bolman, C., and Völlink, T. (2008). Cyberbullying: Youngsters' experiences and parental perception. *Cyberpsychology & Behavior, 11*(2), 217–233.

Demetriou, C., & Silke, A. (2003). A criminological Internet "Sting": experimental evidence of illegal and deviant visits to a website trap. *British Journal of Criminology, 43*, 213–222.

Dempsey, A. G., Sulkowski, M. L., Dempsey, J., & Storch, E. A. (2011). Has cyber technology produced a new group of peer aggressors? *Cyberpsychology, Behavior, and Social Networking, 14*(5), 297–302.

Denning, D. (1998). *Information warfare and security.* Reading, MA: Addison–Wesley.

Denning, D. (2000). *Cyberterrorism.* Testimony before the Special Oversight Panel on Terrorism Committee on Armed Services U.S. House of Representatives, May 23, 2000.

Dodge, K. A. (1980). Social cognition and children's aggressive behavior. *Child Development, 51*, 620–635.

Dodge, K. A. (1986). A social information processing model of social competence in children. In M. Perlmutter (Ed.), *The Minnesota Symposium onChild Psychology* (Vol. 18, pp. 77–125). Hillsdale, NJ: Erlbaum.

Douglas, K.M., & McGarty, C. (2001). Identifiability and self-presentation: computer-mediated communication and intergroup interaction. *British Journal of Social Psychology, 40*, 399–416.

Duval, S., & Wicklund, R.A. (1972). *A theory of objective self-awareness.* New York, NY: Academic Press.

Entertainment Software Association. (2009). *Essential facts about the computer and video games industry.* Washington, DC: Entertainment Software Association.

Ferguson, C. J. (2007). The good, the bad and the ugly: A meta-analytic review of positive and negative effects of violent video games. *Psychiatric Quarterly, 78*, 309–316.

Ferguson, C. J., & Kilburn, J. (2009). The public health risks of media violence: A meta-analytic review. *Journal of Pediatrics, 154*, 759–763.

Finn, J., & Banach, M. (2000). Victimization online: the downside of seeking human services for Women in the Internet. *CyberPsychology & Behavior, 3*, 785–96.

Finkelhor, D., Mitchell, K., & Wolak, J. (2000). *Online Victimisation: A report on the nation's youth.* Alexandria, VA: National Center for Missing & Exploited Children.

Fisher, W.A., & Barak, A. (2000). Online sex shops: phenomenological, psychological, and ideological perspectives on Internet sexuality. *CyberPsychology & Behavior, 3*, 575–589.

Flemming, P., & Stohl, M. (2001). Myth and realities of cyberterrorism. In A. Schmid (Ed.), *Countering Terrorism Trough Enhanced International Cooperation* (pp. 70–105), Vienna, Austria: ISPAC (International Scientific and Professional Advisory Council of the United Nations Crime Prevention and Criminal Justice Program).

Froomkin, A. M. (1999). Legal issues in anonymity and pseudoanonymity. *The Information Society, 15*, 113–127.

Fulda, J. S. (2002). Do Internet stings directed at pedophiles capture offenders or create offenders? And allied questions. *Sexuality & Culture: An Interdisciplinary Quarterly, 6*, 73–100.

Gackenbach, J. (Ed.). (1998). *Psychology and the Internet: intrapersonal, interpersonal, and* transpersonal implications. San Diego, CA: Academic Press.

Geen, R. G. (2001). *Human aggression* (2nd ed.). London, UK: Taylor & Francis.

Gentile, D. A., & Gentile, J. R. (2008). Violent video games as exemplary teachers: A conceptual analysis. *Journal of Youth & Adolescence, 9,* 127–141.

Gentile, D. A., Lynch, P. J., & Linder, J. R. (2004). The effects of violent video game habits on adolescent hostility, aggressive behaviors, and school performance. *Journal of Adolescence, 27,* 5–22.

Glaser, J., Dixit, J., & Green, D. P. (2002). Internet for self and society: is social life being transformed? *Journal of Social Issues. Special Issue, 58,* 177–193.

Gossett, J. L., & Byrne, S. (2002). A content analysis of Internet rape sites. *Gender and* Society, *16,* 689–709.

Graham, S., & Hudley, C. (1994). Attributions of aggressive and nonaggressive African-American male early adolescents – a study of construct accessibility. *Developmental Psychology, 30,* 365–373.

Hayne, S., & Rice, R. (1997). Attribution accuracy when using anonymity in group support systems. *International Journal of Human Computer Studies, 47,* 429–450.

Heinzl, T. (2003, October 23). Couple guilty in obscenity trial. *Dallas Star-Telegram.*

Huesmann, L. R. (1998). The role of social information processing and cognitive schema in the acquisition and maintenance of habitual aggressive behavior. In R. G. Geen & E. Donnerstein (Eds.), *Human aggression: Theories, research, and implications for social policy* (pp. 73–109). San Diego, CA: Academic Press.

Joinson, A. N. (2003). *Understanding the psychology of Internet behaviour: virtual worlds, real lives.* New York, NY: Palgrave Macmillan.

Kahn–Egan, C. N. (1998). *Pandora's boxes: children's reactions to and understanding of television and internet rules, ratings, and regulations.* Unpublished doctoral dissertation, Florida State University, FL.

Kiesler, S. (Ed.). (1997). *Culture of the Internet.* Mahwah, NJ: Erlbaum.

Kiesler, S., Siegel, J., & McGuire, T. W. (1984). Social psychological aspects of computer-mediated communication. *American Psychologist, 39,* 1123–1134.

Lagerspetz, K. M., Bjoerkqvist, K., & Peltonen, T. (1988). Is indirect aggression typical of females? Gender differences in aggressiveness in 11–12-year-old children. *Aggressive Behavior, 14,* 403–414.

Lea, M., O'Shea, T., Fung, P., & Spears, R. (1992). "Flaming" in computer-mediated communication: observations, explanations, implications. In M. Lea (Ed.), *Contexts of computer-mediated communication* (pp. 89–112). Hertfordshire, UK: Harvester Wheatsheaf.

Linz, D., Donnerstein, E., & Adams, S. (1989). Physiological desensitization and judgments about female victims of violence. *Human Communication Research, 15,* 509–522.

Malamuth, N., & Addison, T. (2001). Integrating social psychological research on aggression within an evolutionary-based framework. In G. J. O. Fletcher and M. S. Clark (Eds.), *Blackwell Handbook of Social Psychology: Interpersonal Process.* (pp. 129–161). Malden, MA: Blackwell.

Malamuth, N., Addison, T., & Koss, M. (2000). Pornography and sexual aggression: are there reliable effects and can we understand them? *Annual Review of Sex Research, 11,* 26–91.

McKenna, K. Y. A., & Bargh, J. A. (2000). Plan 9 from cyberspace: the implications of the Internet for personality and social psychology. *Personality & Social Psychology Review, 4,* 57–75.

Meloy, J. R. (1999). Stalking: an old behavior, a new crime. *Forensic Psychiatry, 22,* 85–99.

Miller, D. B., & DiGiuseppe, D. (1998). Fighting social problems with information: the development of a community database—the Violence Information Network. *Computers in Human Service, 15,* 21–34.

Möller, I., & Krahé, B. (2009). Exposure to violent video games and aggression in german adolescents: A longitudinal analysis. *Aggressive Behavior, 35,* 75–89.

Murphy, S. (2007). A social meaning framework for research on participation in social online games. *Journal of Media Psychology, 12*(3).

Parker, D. (1998). *Fighting computer crime: a new framework for protecting information.* New York, NY: John Wiley & Sons.

Polman, H., De Castro, B. O., & Van Aken, M. A. G. (2008). Experimental study of the differential effects of playing versus watching violent video games on children's aggressive behavior. *Aggressive Behavior, 34,* 256–264.

Post, J. (1996). The dangerous information system insider: psychological perspectives. Retrieved from http://www.infowar.com

Postmes, T., Spears, R., & Lea, M. (1998). Breaching or building social boundaries? Side-effects of computer-mediated communication. *Communication Research*, 25, 689–715.

Power, R. (2000). *Tangled WEB: tales of digital crime from the shadows of cyberspace*. Indianapolis, IN: Que/Macmillan.

Quayle, E., & Taylor, M. (2002a). Child pornography and the Internet: perpetuating a cycle of abuse. *Deviant Behavior*, 23, 331–362.

Quayle, E., & Taylor, M. (2002b). Paedophiles, pornography and the Internet: assessment issues. *British Journal of Social Work*, 32, 863–875.

Quayle, E., & Taylor, M. (2003). Model of problematic Internet use in people with a sexual interest in children. *CyberPsychology & Behavior*, 6, 93–106.

Rathmell, A. (1997). Cyber-terrorism: the shape of future conflict. *Royal United Service Institute Journal*, October, 40–46.

Rice, R. E. (1993). Media appropriateness: using social presence theory to compare traditional and new organizational media. *Human Communication Research*, 19, 451–484.

Rogers, M. (1999). Psychology of hackers: steps toward a new taxonomy. Retrieved from http://www.infowar.com

Rubin, A. M. (1994). Media uses and effects: a uses-and-gratifications perspective. In J. Bryant and D. Zillmann (Eds.), *Media effects: advances in theory and research. LEA's communication series* (pp. 417–436). Hillsdale, NJ: Erlbaum.

Rueters. (2010, March 15). *Militant and hate group Internet use grows*. New York, NY: Reuters.

Schneider, W., & Shiffrin, R. M. (1977). Controlled and automatic human information processing: I. Detection, search, and attention. *Psychological Review*, 84, 1–66.

Sfiligoj, T. M. (2003). A comparison of stalkers and domestic violence batterers. *Journal of Psychological Practice*, 8, 20–45.

Shaw, E., Post, J., & Roby, K. (1998). *Information terrorism and the dangerous insider*. Paper presented at the meeting of InfowarCon'98, Washington, DC.

Slater, M. D. (2003). Alienation, aggression, and sensation-seeking as predictors of adolescent use of violent film, computer, and website content. *Journal of Communication*, 53, 105–121.

Slater, M. D., Henry, K., Swaim, R. C., & Anderson, L. L. (2003). Violent media content and aggressiveness in adolescents: a downward spiral model. *Communication Research*, 30, 713–736.

Spafford, E. (1997). Are hacker break-ins ethical? In M. D. Ermann, M. B. Williams, & M. S. Shauf (Eds.), *Computers, Ethics, and Society* (pp. 77–88). New York, NY: Oxford University Press.

Smith, S. (2006). Perps, pimps, and provocative clothing. Examining negative content pattern in video games. In P. Vorderer & J. Bryant (Eds.), *Playing video games—motives, responses, and consequences* (pp. 64–87). Mahwah, NJ: Lawrence Erlbaum.

Spears, R., & Lea, M. (1994). Panacea or panopticon? The hidden power in computer-mediated communication. *Communication Research*, 21, 427–459.

Spears, R., Postmes, T., Lea, M., & Wolbert, A. (2002). When are net effects gross products? The power of influence and the influence of power in computer-mediated communication. *Journal of Social Issues*, 58, 91–107.

Spitzberg, B.H., & Cupach, W.R. (2003). What mad pursuit? Obsessive relational intrusion and stalking related phenomena. *Aggression & Violent Behavior*, 8, 345–375.

Stohl, M. (Ed.). (1988). *The politics of terrorism* (3rd ed.). New York, NY: Marcel Decker.

Tagg, L. (2001, November 1). Aussie hacker jailed for sewage attacks. Iafrica.com. Retrieved from http://cooltech.iafrica.com/technews/archive/november/837110.htm

Thompson, S. (2000) Suicide and the internet. *Psychiatric Bulletin*, 24, 434.

Todorov, A., & Bargh, J.A. (2002). Automatic sources of aggression. *Aggression & Violent Behavior*, 7, 53–68.

Tsfati, Y., & Weimann, G. (2002). www.terrorism.com: terror on the Internet. *Studies in Conflict & Terrorism, 25*, 317–332.

Valkenburg, P. M., & Soeters, K. E. (2001). Children's positive and negative experiences with the Internet: an exploratory survey. *Communication Research, 28*, 652–675.

van Puymbroek, J. (2005). Cyberpesten is cool. [Cyberbullyng is cool]. Retrieved from http://www. standaard.be/artikel/detail.aspx?artikelid=GLUE94PC

Vlaamse Commissie voor Onderwijs, Vorming en Wetenschapsbeleid [Flemish Committee for Education, Training, Science and Innovation]. (2004). *Advies 2003-2004-5.*

von Feilitzen, C. (2009). *Influences of Mediated Violence: A Brief Research Summary.* Gothenburg, Sweden: International Clearinghouse on Children, Youth and Media, NORDICOM, University of Gothenburg.

Wallenius, M., & Punamäki, R. -L. (2008). Digital game violence and direct aggression in adolescence: A longitudinal study of the roles of sex, age, and parent-child communication. *Journal of Applied Developmental Psychology, 29*, 286–294.

Walther, J. B. (1992). Interpersonal effects in computer-mediated interaction: a relational perspective. *Communication Research, 19*, 52–90.

Walther, J. B. (1994). Anticipated ongoing interaction versus channel effects on relational communication in computer-mediated interaction. *Human Communication Research, 20*, 473–501.

Walther, J. B. (1996). Computer-mediated communication: impersonal, interpersonal, and hyperpersonal interaction. *Communication Research, 23*, 3–43.

Walther, J. B., Anderson, J. F., & Park, D. W. (1994). Interpersonal effects in computer-mediated interaction: a meta-analysis of social and antisocial communication. *Communication Research, 21*, 460–487.

Weber, R., Behr, K. M., & Bates, C. (2011, May). *How video game interactivity moderates video game effects: An experimental study.* Paper presented at the annual meeting of the International Communication Association (ICA), Boston, MA.

Weber, R., Ritterfeld, U., & Mathiak, K. (2006). Does playing violent video games induce aggression? Empirical evidence of a functional magnetic resonance imaging study. *Media Psychology, 8*, 39–60.

Ybarra, M. L., & Mitchell, K. J. (2001). Youth engaging in online harassment: associations with caregiver-child relationships, Internet use and personal characteristics. *Journal of Adolescence, 27*, 319–336.

Zimbardo, P. G. (1969). The hyman choice: individuation, reason, and order vs. individuation, impulse and chaos. In W. J. Arnold & D. Levine (Eds.), *Nebraska symposium on motivation* (pp. 237–307). Lincoln, NE: University of Nebraska Press.

Chapter 8

The Kindness of Strangers: Prosocial Behavior on the Internet

Lee Sproull, Caryn A. Conley, and Jae Yun Moon

Introduction

I have found many people who are struggling with similar issues banding together to help each other. It is the best place in the world, and i couldn't think of another place to go to meet so many lovely people . . . (MDJunction Scheuermann's Disease support group.)

Dear Volunteers, . . .Your feedback gave me an objective and learned viewpoint that we knew was needed, but didn't understand how to evaluate internet media. . . . We are remedying that gap NOW via each of your expertise. It has been enlightening . . . You all made for a SUPER ADVISORY team effort. We were impressed and got so much more then we anticipated. THANK YOU! We're giving Gerard C another AWARD because his efforts were outstanding and helpful in very specific ways that benefited our ability to act upon everyone else's feedback. (Sparked, December 17, 2011; Antakarana Co-Creation Learning Project, http://www.sparked.com/ask/Our-Website-Needs-the-Wisdom-of-an-External-Eye.)

I can speak Hindi, Urdu, English, Sanskrit and Moroccan. But I can't read what's on my computer screen. Being blind online means I have to listen to all the text – including ads . . . Instead of ads, Wikipedia has a community of millions of volunteer editors double-checking every word and citation. I'm so grateful for them – their work makes learning online possible. The philosophy of Wikipedia is to make a sea from drops. And it applies to everyone who contributes, whether a few edits or a few dollars. Thank you, Aniruddha Kumar, Wikipedia Author. (https://wikimediafoundation.org, December 17, 2011.)

As many of you already know, a protein causing AIDS in rhesus monkeys that hadn't been solved for 15 years was resolved by Foldit players and confirmed by x-ray crystallography. That paper was selected for an Advance Online Publication (AOP) today in Nature Structural & Molecular Biology . . . We are so proud of everything that you Foldit players have accomplished already, and we hope that this article will show the world the power of citizen science! ("Nature Structural & Molecular Biology paper online!" Foldit blog, http://fold.it/portal/blog, September 18, 2011.)

These messages illustrate one of the most striking social aspects of the Internet, which is that every day hundreds of thousands of people voluntarily help strangers on the net with no expectation of direct reciprocity or reward. Yet the help is consequential and people are enormously grateful for it, as the messages illustrate. This chapter is about the kinds of generous behavior on the net referenced in the messages—prosocial behavior, defined as "voluntary intentional behavior that results in benefits for another" (Eisenberg & Miller, 1987).

People voluntarily help strangers in many ways on the net, including:

- donating funds to worthy causes through online charitable organizations

- donating idle computing power from their personal computers (PCs) to help scientists analyze large data files

♦ working on projects that create freely-available information products like open source software and encyclopedia articles

♦ working on projects organized for socially-worthwhile causes, such as electronically mentoring disadvantaged students or making public domain literature freely available on the web

♦ offering support to one another in discussion forums.

Prosocial behavior on the net can be found in private email lists, private social networks, and corporate intranets (e.g., Bock, Zmud, Kim, & Lee, 2005; Constant, Sproull, & Kiesler, 1996; Johnson, Haigh, Becker, Craig, & Wigley, 2008; Kankanhalli, Tan, & Wei, 2005; Olivera, Goodman, & Tan, 2008; Wasko & Faraj, 2005; Wellman & Gulia, 1999). While private helping is salutary, this chapter focuses on public helping, for two reasons: (1) Public contexts are more accessible to potential volunteers and researchers than are private ones; (2) public contexts offer an opportunity to understand behavior about which the offline world offers few opportunities for study, namely, social situations in which large numbers of people voluntarily help strangers with no expectation of direct reciprocity or reward.

Five sections follow. Section one introduces perspectives from offline research on prosocial behavior. Section two characterizes the electronic context for prosocial behavior. Section three examines why people engage in prosocial behavior on the net in the light of relevant theoretical perspectives on person attributes and interaction processes. Section four presents evidence about the social effects of electronic prosocial behavior. Section five offers implications, suggestions for future research, and final comments.

Perspectives from Research on Offline Behavior

In the offline world, prosocial behavior is found in a variety of social contexts, which can be characterized along two dimensions. One is the strength of the social relationship among participants. The other is the degree and type of the context's structural organization. Social psychologists have focused on social situations with minimal formal organizational structure and nonexistent interpersonal relations—for example, bystanders helping among strangers in emergency situations.[1] Sociologists have focused on more highly organized social contexts, such as the self-help group and the community or volunteer organization (e.g., Akera, 2001; Knoke, 1981; Penner et al., 2005 for a review; Popielarz & McPherson, 1995; Wellman & Wortley, 1990; Wilson, 2000 for a review).

In some ways, prosocial behavior on the net resembles bystanders helping strangers in the offline world. Helpers and beneficiaries usually have no pre-existing face-to-face relationship; there is no expectation of reciprocity or even of any continued relationship. Requests for help come at random times. However, in some ways prosocial behavior on the net resembles behavior in voluntary organizations in the offline world. Encounters with strangers occur in organized social contexts, in which helping is supported and rewarded over time. Often the beneficiary may be the generalized group, rather than specific individuals, as in, for example, contributing to a volunteer software project.

---

[1] Social psychologists also study helping within the context of strong and enduring friendship and family ties (e.g., Bolger, Zuckerman, & Kessler, 2000; Latané & Darley, 1970; Penner, Dovidio, Piliavin, & Schroeder, 2005 for a review). Those behaviors, which are embedded in ongoing expectations about reciprocity and reward, are outside the scope of this chapter.

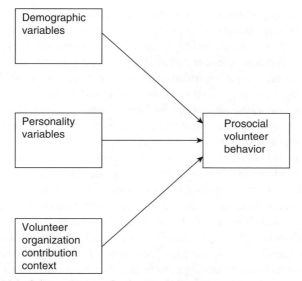

Fig. 8.1 Stylized model of determinants of volunteer behavior.

A general model of volunteerism in the offline world provides an orienting theoretical structure. (See Fig. 8.1 for stylized version and Penner (2002), for a more elaborated version of this model that synthesizes previous research and theorizing.) Three main classes of variables have been shown to affect volunteerism in the offline world: Attributes of the volunteer organization or context, demographic and personality variables, and motivations such as other-oriented empathy and helpfulness. The next section discusses attributes of the online context. The following one discusses person attributes and interaction processes among the variable classes.

Attributes of the Online Context for Prosocial Behavior

Technical and social components interact to form the context that supports prosocial behavior on the net. Technical components include hardware, software, data and file structures, and communications systems; social components include goals, roles, rules, and norms. Although no two contexts are exactly the same, many of them can be categorized broadly in terms of a dominant software application and the degree to which help is delivered via a direct connection to an identified person. Four main categories of prosocial contexts are: Support group discussion forums, service projects, open collaborative work projects, and citizen science projects.[2]

Throughout the history of the Arpanet and in the early days of the Internet, the support group discussion forum was the primary prosocial contribution context. In this context a combination of software and social norms organizes behavior in online discussion groups. Someone posts a message containing a question or request for help and others reply directly to the requester

---

[2] A fifth category of context where prosocial behavior may occur is social network sites such as Facebook. Unlike the previous four categories, social network sites support relationships among personally-known and identified people rather than strangers. Helping is not the dominant contribution to these sites; people mostly use these sites to satisfy their need to belong and need for self-presentation (e.g., Nadkarni & Hofmann, 2012).

with messages containing answers, comments, or suggestions. Software displays messages as "threads"—a seed message and all responses to it. Threads organize messages by topic so that everyone can view related messages, making it easy for potential contributors and beneficiaries to see what has already been contributed and where there are opportunities for further contribution. This contribution context offers an immediate connection between people needing help and those providing it. Initially, support group discussion forums had a relatively low degree of formal organization. Today, many are sponsored by formal organizations such as MDJunction or PatientsLikeMe and offer additional features like "Ask an Expert." But the primary means of asking for and giving help remains the question/response thread.

Electronic service projects are often sponsored by formal organizations that use a variety of software applications. Electronic mentoring projects (e.g., Mentornet) may use complex matching algorithms to pair mentors and protégés, but rely on simple email as the means for direct personal connection between them. Electronic community development projects (e.g., http://www.onlinevolunteering.org) may use collaborative software like wikis to support collaborative work such as building science curricula or developing funding proposals. In these cases and others like them, sponsoring organizations determine the goals, identify beneficiaries, and specify volunteer tasks. In 2010, the first charitable crowdfunding website, http://www.crowdrise.com, was launched that encourages volunteers to organize their own prosocial projects. Because people recruit friends to contribute to these projects, there may be a direct personal connection among contributors, but not between contributors and beneficiaries.

In open collaborative work contexts, the outcome is a freely-produced and freely-shared information product, such as open source software, encyclopedia articles, repair manuals, or uncopyrighted digital books. The supporting software typically includes mechanisms to record contributions, aggregate contributions across the product, and to keep track of changes to the product. The supporting software may also display contribution totals to the group as a whole and give members feedback on their contributions. Information product groups also typically support group interaction, using message boards and discussion forums. In contrast with support group discussion forums or service projects, the direct beneficiaries of open information projects are not usually specific people or groups who need help. The assumed beneficiary is "anyone who can use it."

In citizen science contexts, volunteers aid scientific projects in a variety of ways. People donate idle PC cycles in the service of large, distributed computing projects. Hobbyists contribute personally-collected data about the physical world, such as bird sightings or backyard weather information, to sites for ongoing scientific projects. These projects maintain databases for research and public distribution. People label words and images to improve search engine performance. People analyze galaxy data from space telescopes and investigate efficient folding structures for proteins. In all such projects, researchers benefit, but in most cases specific researcher identity is probably not particularly salient to volunteers. In their view, the beneficiary is "science."

Despite differences among them, all of these contexts share attributes that affect the online prosocial experience (Amichai-Hamburger, 2008). One is that transaction costs are substantially lower than they would be in an offline context. People can participate at any hour of the day or night from any place with technology and net access. They can fit their contributions into their own time schedule. The basic unit of contribution is often quite small—a message, an edit, a label, an upload, a "share-with-your-network" click, a monetary pledge. It consumes a small unit of time and attention and represents a voluntary micro-contribution to the community (Sproull & Arriaga, 2007). Some people may devote many hours a week to online prosocial activity, but they can do so in small units of time at their own convenience. Volunteers note that convenience and schedule flexibility are two common reasons for choosing to volunteer online (Mukherjee, 2010).

A second shared attribute is transparency. Requests for help and the results of help are visible to all. Everyone who goes to a support group discussion forum will see messages that ask for help and messages that give it. Everyone who goes to an electronic service project will see opportunities to help and helpful contributions prominently displayed. Many open collaborative projects and citizen science projects display leader boards or contribution tables that remind people that the sum total of all micro-contributions can be quite substantial.

Low transaction costs and transparency are two attributes of the electronic context that make it relatively easy to be helpful, but convenience is not the only determinant of prosocial behavior. Fig. 8.1 suggests that person variables and interaction processes are also important. The next section explores these attributes and processes.

Attributes of People and Interaction Processes

Visible Status Characteristics and Attribution

Those who need help: In the offline world, physically attractive people are more likely to be helped than are unattractive people (Athanasiou & Green, 1973; Byrne, Baskett, & Hodges, 1971; Chaiken, 1979; Dommeyer & Ruggiero, 1996; Harrell, 1978; Mims, Hartnett, & Nay, 1975; Piliavin & Piliavin, 1975; Scott, 1969; West & Brown, 1975; Wilson, 1978). Social similarity also affects helping in the offline world (Eagly & Crowley, 1986; Emswiller, Deaux, & Willits, 1971; Simon, Stürmer, & Steffens, 2000; Simon et al., 1998; Wellman & Wortley, 1990). In the online world, however, people seeing a request for help may have little or no information about the requester's physical appearance or social similarity conveyed by visible attributes such as age, gender, or race. In the offline world, one of the impediments to asking for help is the perceived threat to one's public self-image (Karabenick & Knapp, 1988). Physical invisibility may reduce that perceived threat in the online world; so, too, may the use of pseudonyms, screen names, or anonymous postings.

Those who give help: In the offline world, bystander helping is influenced by the number of other people available to provide help (Latané & Darley, 1970). If people see that others are available to help, their own motivation to help is diminished. In the online world, it is hard to know how many potential helpers are available. The combination of visible needs for help and unknown numbers of potential helpers may make the felt need to offer help more salient. Until one person actually offers help, every potential helper may assume that he or she is the only one who could help. Physical invisibility also reduces the barriers to offering help for people whose age, gender, race, or other visible attributes lead people to discount their contributions in the offline world, regardless of their actual usefulness. Help provided is not spurned on the basis of irrelevant physical or social attributes; it can be judged based solely on its quality.

Decision to Make an Initial Contribution

With the exception of bystander helping during an emergency, in the offline world the initial decision to volunteer is typically a planned one occurring over a period of time (Penner, 2002). Some research has investigated what influences people to ask for help online (Davison, Pennebaker, & Dickerson, 2000; Tanis, 2008; Ybarra & Suman, 2006), but there is no research on how people decide to make their first helpful contribution. Many initial volunteer acts may be more spontaneous in the online world than in the offline world because, as we have noted earlier, transaction costs are low and the unit of contribution is small. Not only is it easy to make a helpful contribution, it is also easy to control the extent of further involvement. In the offline world, an initial helpful act may serve as a "foot in the door" that will generate subsequent burdensome demands on one's time or emotional energy (Burger, 1999). In the online world, an initial volunteer contribution may generate less foot-in-the-door pressure, owing in part to the fact that contributors may not be easily identified and contacted for further assistance. Some contexts allow for anonymous contributions (e.g., Kane, 2011). The highly skewed distribution of contributions in many of the online prosocial contexts examined above (e.g., Kane, 2011; Moon & Sproull, 2008) suggests that many contributors make one-time only contributions to a particular context. For example, Kane (2011) found that 69% of contributors to a Wikipedia article contributed once or at most twice to a given article.

In the offline world, "volunteer social pressure," or "a potential volunteer's subjective perceptions of how significant others feel about him/her becoming a volunteer and his/her motivation to comply with these feelings" is an important determinant of the initial volunteering decision (Penner, 2002, pp. 461–462). Objectively speaking, social pressure is lower in online volunteering than in offline volunteering because online volunteering is typically done in the privacy of one's own computing environment rather than in the physical presence of others. Crowdfunding, a relatively new type of contribution platform, provides a contribution context in which social pressure may become salient. For example, the tag line for Crowdrise acknowledges the importance of social pressure with, "if you don't give back, no one will like you."

Motivation to Help

Prosocial behavior may be motivated by altruism or egoism and often by a combination of both (Batson, 1991; Batson & Powell, 2003; Nelson, 1999; Piliavin & Charng, 1990). Altruistic prosocial behavior is motivated purely by the desire to increase another person's welfare; egoistic prosocial behavior is motivated by the desire to increase one's own welfare or that of one's group or cause through helping others (Batson, 1998; MacIntyre, 1967). Both types of motivation are likely to be present in electronic contribution contexts and, to a greater or lesser degree, in the same person. In a number of studies, online help providers have attested to the altruistic motives of empathy, community interest, and generalized reciprocity, and egoistic motives of self-development, reputation enhancement, and fun (e.g., Butler, Sproull, Kiesler, & Kraut, 2007; Lakhani & von Hippel, 2003; Nov, 2007; Oreg & Nov, 2008; Pope, 2001; Schroer & Hertel, 2009; Wasko & Faraj, 2000). In a comparative study of personality attributes across different types of contribution context, Oreg and Nov (2008) found that egoistic motives and values were stronger in volunteer software project contributors and altruistic motives and values were stronger in Wikipedia contributors, but volunteers in both contexts reported both types of motives.

In electronic contexts, as in offline ones, a majority of the help is often provided by a minority of the members who incur substantial costs of their own time. Eighty percent of English language Wikipedia content is written by 10% of Wikipedians (Priedhorsky et al., 2007). Within a sample of online discussion forums for technical support, 11–15% of forum participants provided almost half the answers within a given time period (Moon & Sproull, 2008). About 88% of the code in the Apache server software project was contributed by 15 core developers (Mockus, Fielding, & Herbsleb, 2002). Occasional ad hoc positive feedback as well as intrinsic benefit is probably sufficient to offset the cost to the infrequent helper (Yang & Lai, 2010). However, when people repeatedly respond to requests for help, take on substantial duties, or contribute significantly to the group in other ways, even if they do so in small increments, then more systematic recognition as well as other forms of benefit will reinforce sustained helping behavior. That is, the greater the cost of the helping behavior, the greater the need for personal rewards if the helping is to be sustained (Field & Johnson, 1993; Omoto & Snyder, 1995).

In the offline world, motivation to advance the goals of the larger group is often associated with enhanced performance and commitment. (See Meyer, Stanley, Herscovitch, and Topolnytsky (2002) for a meta-analysis of the organizational commitment literature indicating that affective/normative commitment positively correlates with performance.) In the electronic context, participants who report being motivated by community or group interest often provide the most valuable contributions (Bateman, Gray, & Butler, 2011; Blanchard & Markus, 2004; Butler et al., 2007; Constant et al., 1996; Meyer et al., 2002). The site that supports donating idle PC cycles to scientific projects allows contributors to establish "teams," which are credited when a team member donates cycles. Team totals are posted in a leader board along with each team's top individual contributor. Team affiliation is positively related to a person's contribution level even though the contribution is merely idle PC cycles (Nov, Anderson, & Arazy, 2010). (Also, see the discussion in the "Social Identity Theory" section.)

Social Learning Theory

Social learning theory suggests that prosocial behavior is learned (Bandura, 1977; Bandura & McDonald, 1963; Batson, 1998, for a recent review). Observing loved and respected role models engaged in prosocial behavior demonstrates how people can and should behave prosocially. Rewards reinforce helping behavior; punishments reduce unhelpful or hurtful behavior. Within a group context, social recognition, not just private reward, increases prosocial behavior (Fisher & Ackerman, 1998). Observational modeling processes with reinforcement will result in learning over time (Compeau & Higgins, 1995; Lim, Ward, & Benbasat, 1997). Although social learning theory was developed within the context of physically colocated actors and observers, it can be applied within the electronic context to the extent that prosocial behavior is observable and socially reinforced in that context.

Electronic contribution contexts often explicitly encourage newcomers to observe others' behavior for awhile before they make their first contribution. The visibility of behavior on the net ensures that all observers will see examples of helpful contributions. Moreover, they will also see that some of these contributions are explicitly recognized as helpful. That is, sometimes a helpful reply to a question receives a thankful reply from the person who asked for help or a bug report or software contribution receives a commendation from another contributor or explicit recognition within the software credit files. These commendations are usually visible to everyone and thus constitute social recognition, not just private reward. Social recognition for helpful behavior can also go beyond ad hoc public acknowledgments. Some contexts use software that records and displays recognition points. People whose contributions receive the greatest number of recognition points for a given period of time are publicly acknowledged in leader boards or credit tables. MovieLens.org uses email newsletters to indicate to community members whether their performance is average, low, or high in comparison to other community members (Harper, Li, Chen, & Konstan, 2007). Question and answer communities such as Naver Knowledge-In adopt a point system and prominently feature top rated answerers for each topic category (Nam, Ackerman, & Adamic, 2009). In some open information project contexts, contribution quality may be assessed directly by software; in still other contexts, software lets human participants rate the quality of the contribution. In addition to helpful contributions, participants will occasionally see unhelpful or erroneous ones. These, too, may engender a visible response in the form of complaints or corrective edits. Visible recognition—whether textual or numeric, ad hoc or systematic, positive or negative—is a powerful learning reinforcement mechanism for both direct and vicarious learning. The combination of visible contributions with both ad hoc and systematic feedback suggests that the minimum criteria for learning how to engage in prosocial behavior in the electronic context are met (Moon & Sproull, 2008).

Social learning theory also suggests that low-cost trials are more effective than high-cost ones in the initial stages of learning. We have noted that the cost of a single micro-contribution is relatively low in the electronic context. Studies of various Internet discussion groups and volunteer work groups have reported a mean message length ranging from 8 to 30 lines of new text (Galegher, Sproull, & Kiesler, 1998; Sproull & Faraj, 1995; Wasko & Faraj, 2000; Winzelberg, 1997). They have also reported a mean participation time of 10–20 minutes per session (Boberg et al., 1995; Brennan, Moore, & Smyth, 1995; Lakhani & von Hippel, 2003). Approximately one-quarter of contributions to top-quality articles on Wikipedia consist of minor edits (Kane, 2011). The newcomer to a group can learn vicariously about prosocial behaviors by viewing small demonstrations of it. The newcomer can learn directly by making small prosocial contributions and receiving (small, easy-to-make, visible to all) positive reinforcements for doing so.

Social Identity Theory

Social identity theory and self-categorization theory (Tajfel & Turner, 1986; Turner, Hogg, Oakes, Reicher, & Wetherell, 1987) are helpful in understanding why some people exhibit sustained prosocial behavior. These theories were developed within the context of offline identity processes where people's identities are reinforced in part through interaction with specific other known people. They are relevant in the electronic context because identities are also reinforced through interaction with social groups. The electronic contribution context can serve as a reinforcing social group for its members even if they have no personal ties with any one member. Social identity theory is based on the premise that people identify with particular groups in order to enhance their self-esteem. Identification leads to selective social comparisons that emphasize intergroup differences along dimensions that favor the ingroup and confer positive distinctiveness on the ingroup when compared to the salient outgroup (Hogg & Abrams, 1988). Categorizing the self and others in terms of groups emphasizes group members' fit with the relevant group prototype or "cognitive representation of features that describe and prescribe attributes of the group" (Hogg & Terry, 2000, p. 123). The prototype guides the participants' understanding of the group and its expected behaviors and attitudes. People identified with a group will thus be more likely to exhibit behaviors (and more behaviors) that are consistent with shared group norms and cooperate with the group and its members. In a discourse analysis of electronic health support groups, Galegher et al. (1998) found that people legitimated their requests for help in their messages by describing their membership in the group and by appealing to the group's shared history. Even frequent posters framed their requests for help in terms that referenced the group. Requests that did not reference the group were much less likely to receive a reply. In a linguistic analysis of discussion groups, Sassenberg (2002) demonstrated that people in cohesive groups exhibited greater linguistic norm conformity than people in ad hoc groups. In sum, interactions among participants can both define and express the group norms. Group prototypes are negotiated and redefined through member interactions (McKenna & Green, 2002; Postmes, Spears, & Lea, 2000). In other words, participants collectively define who is an admired member and what is a high-quality contribution through comments and feedback provided in response to member contributions.

In both offline and online contexts, frequent participants are likely to form relational bonds with one another (Lawler, Thye, & Yoon, 2000), especially if they expect the group to persist over the long-term (Chidambaram, 1996; Walther, 2002). In electronic prosocial contexts, as people participate over time they become aware of other members who repeatedly provide valuable help. Moon (2004) suggests that, over time, active members will form a sense of community with other core members and become committed to this core subgroup of the larger group. These highly identified volunteers will help other members, not only as a service to those needing help and as a matter of self-interest, but also in order to demonstrate their identification with and commitment to the core group of volunteers who sustain the group as a whole. In a study of volunteer Linux developers, Hertel, Niedner, and Herrmann (2003) found that identification with the developers in the Linux subsystem in which the respondent was participating, but not identification with the Linux user community as a whole, was positively related to the number of hours spent on the Linux project. In an experimental study of contributions to an electronic movie review community, Rashid et al. (2006) found that subgroup identification, but not identification with the group as a whole, increased contribution rates. In an empirical investigation of two online communities, Ma and Agarwal (2007) found that the more a participant believes that other members correctly perceive their salient identities, the more likely they are to make a contribution and the more satisfied they are with their community experiences. Kittur, Pendleton, and Kraut (2009) found that volunteers who joined Wikipedia subgroups exhibited more prosocial behaviors than volunteers who did not join subgroups.

Group identification increases cooperative behaviors related to group maintenance and survival (Ashforth & Mael, 1989; Kramer, 1993; Mael & Ashforth, 1995; Tyler, 1999). Volunteerism studies in the offline world have generally found that participation in voluntary association management can foster commitment (Simon et al., 1998; Wilson, 2000). In this literature, "participation in management" refers to having an active role in the decisions made by the association, and not mere participation by showing up. A study of 212 voluntary email lists found that the volunteer who maintains a list, often called a list "owner," spends substantially more time than other members in infrastructure maintenance, social control, and external promotion (Butler et al., 2007). Typically, owners take responsibility for such time-consuming work as regular maintenance and upgrades of the technical infrastructure and dealing with problems such as viruses and junk email. Infrastructure administration also involves developing and maintaining components that are unique to the needs of the particular group, such as an up-to-date content archive, ancillary files such as group descriptions and frequently asked questions, and the list of people who have access to the group. Owners also take some responsibility for the social management of the group. They remind members about the rules and the norms of the group, manage disputes, prevent exploitation of individual members, chastise those who engage in inappropriate behavior, and deny serious offenders access to the group, usually as a last resort. Owners frequently encourage members and membership as well. They promote desirable behavior by recognizing people who contribute especially informative or supportive messages, and those who create interesting or useful group activities. Leaders in open collaborative work projects have been shown to model desirable behaviors, unblock bottlenecks, and establish productive subgroup structures (e.g., Kittur et al., 2009; Moon & Sproull, 2008; Vibbur, 2009).

Social learning processes and social identification processes help explain how prosocial behaviors can be learned and sustained on the net. Social identification processes are instrumental in the group's collective definition of what constitutes helpful, as opposed to harmful, behavior in the context of the group. Long-term participants identified with the core subgroup, including group owners or founders, are committed to enforcing these group norms. Just as people learn from respected authorities in the offline context, software that makes valued long-term contributors of the group visible and salient facilitates people's learning from members most representative of the respected group prototypical member.

The Value of Online Prosocial Behavior

Value to People Who Receive or Give Help

Many studies across a variety of online contexts report that participation is beneficial to participants.[3] Protégés in online mentoring report positive attitudinal and behavioral outcomes (Bennett, Tsikalas, Hupert, Meade, & Honey, 1998; Muller & Barsion, 2003; Watson, 2006). Some members of medical and psychological support groups derive health benefits from their participation in addition to information and social benefits. The evidentiary base for health benefits is small, but it comes from studies that use either random assignment or statistical procedures to control for other factors that could influence health status. Health-status benefits include shorter hospital stays (Gray et al., 2000), decrease in pain and disability (Lorig et al., 2002), decrease in social isolation (Galegher et al., 1998), decrease in depression (Glasgow, Boles, McKay, Feil, & Barrera, 2003; Rains & Young, 2009), increase in quality of life (Shaw, Hawkins, McTavish, Pingree, & Gustafson, 2006), increase in social support (Glasgow et al., 2003; Han et al., 2011), decrease in health-intervention program attrition (Richardson et al., 2010), and increase in self-efficacy and psychological well-being (Cummings et al., 2002; McKenna & Bargh, 1998; Rains & Young, 2009). Active members of online discussion groups and volunteer collaborative work groups report that information benefits are important to them (Baym, 1999; Lakhani & von Hippel, 2003; Lakhani & Wolf, 2005; Panciera, Masli, & Terveen, 2011; Wasko & Faraj, 2000). Some members also derive the social benefits that can come from interacting with other people: getting to know them, building relationships, making friends, having fun (Baym, 1999; Butler et al., 2007; Chiu, Hsu, & Wang, 2006; Cummings et al., 2002; Ellison, Steinfield, & Lampe, 2007; Kendall, 2002; Nov et al., 2011; Quan y Hasse, Wellman, Witte, & Hampton, 2002; Wasko & Faraj, 2005).

A few studies have focused specifically on benefits to those who help others. As predicted by social learning theory, people who devote substantial time and attention to helping others report receiving both egoistic and altruistic benefits, but relatively greater altruistic benefits than those who are less involved. In their study of 212 discussion groups, Butler et al. (2007) found that group owners (who spent more time helping the group than did other members) reported receiving different levels and types of benefits compared to other members. They reported lower levels of information benefits and higher levels of prosocial benefits, such as the satisfaction of helping other people and supporting the real world community associated with the group's topic. This finding is consistent with the role identity theory and research by Piliavin and her colleagues who suggest that in-role volunteer activity, which is behavior specified by a person's role as a volunteer, encourages an altruistic self-image and commitment to the community (see, for example, Callero, Howard, & Piliavin, 1987; Piliavin & Callero, 1991). Members of professional online communities

---

[3] Even "lurkers," people who read group messages but never post them, receive informational benefits from passive participation in electronic discussion groups (e.g., Butler et al., 2007; Nonnecke & Preece, 2000a, 2000b; Wasko & Faraj, 2000). Up to 90% of group members never post or do so less than once a month, with software discussion groups exhibiting up to 30% higher lurking than health support groups on average (Nonnecke & Preece, 2000a). Because lurkers may constitute a substantial fraction of electronic group membership, benefits to lurkers should not be ignored even if lurkers are invisible to the group and to researchers. Nevertheless, consonant with research on offline groups and communities, passive participants derive fewer benefits than do active ones (e.g., Callero, Howard, & Piliavin, 1987; Omoto & Snyder, 1995). Passive participants report mostly information benefits; their total level of benefits is lower than that for more active participants; they are more likely to drop out (Butler et al., 2007; Cummings, Sproull, & Kiesler, 2002).

report increased self-esteem, enhanced reputations, knowledge, self-efficacy, and enjoyment in helping others (e.g., Chiu et al., 2006; Wasko & Faraj, 2005). A study of people who help others by answering questions in an open-source software support group found that people who contributed help derived learning benefits, reputational benefits, and benefits related to advancing the group (Lakhani & von Hippel, 2003). A study of volunteer programmers found that people who donated code were more likely to report identification with the software development group, whereas people who only used the code were more likely to report only egoistic benefits from participation (Hertel et al., 2003). A study of a collaborative geographic wiki that provides useful information for bicyclists found that people who contributed to the wiki reported a sense of having benefited the local cycling community, whereas bicyclists who merely consumed the wiki information reported only personal information benefits (Panciera et al., 2011). A study of electronic mentoring of college undergraduates found that mentors reported they derived satisfaction from "helping the next generation move ahead" and insight into their own career experiences (Muller & Barsion, 2003). This finding is consistent with research on mentoring in the offline world, which finds that those who mentor derive both altruistic and egoistic benefits from so doing (Higgins & Kram, 2001). Because the Internet encourages users to share more intimate information about themselves, close and personal relationships may develop among users much faster than in offline relationships (Amichai-Hamburger, 2008). Internet technologies in general enable volunteers to explore, develop, and redefine their identities due to fewer physical constraints and increased control over the type of information shared in the online environment (Amichai-Hamburger, 2008; Williamson, Wright, Schauder, & Bow, 2001).

Value to Society

Extrapolating from studies that document benefits to individual people, we can speculate on broader social benefits although they have not yet been the focus of rigorous research. If members of health and lifestyle groups achieve improved health status, the cost of their medical or psychological care could decrease. (Alternatively, better-informed members may seek additional tests or treatments, thereby increasing the cost of their care.) If members of special populations like schoolteachers, female science students, or senior citizens derive cognitive, social, and emotional benefits from participating in electronic groups, then the larger society may benefit as well. Online volunteer discussion groups, in which people ask and answer questions about open source software, have received industry awards for providing high-quality help (Foster, 1998, 1999, 2000). All open source software users benefit indirectly from the resulting high-quality software.

Volunteer collaborative work groups enable free access to high-quality information of many different forms—an important societal benefit. For example, Project Gutenberg, whose goal is to make the world's public domain literature freely available online, relies upon volunteers to scan images of book pages, to proofread electronic pages, and to manage the consolidation and digital archiving of resulting texts. Project Gutenberg reports that these ebooks were downloaded more than four million times in a recent 30-day period. In another example, Wikipedia reports more than 78 million unique visitors a month read its more than 17 million articles written and edited by volunteers. Some of these articles in the health domain have been judged to display professional-level quality (Devgan, Powe, Blakey, & Makary, 2007; Giles, 2005). Some practicing physicians and pharmacists report using Wikipedia as a source of information in providing patient care (Brokowski & Sheehan, 2009; Hughes, Joshi, Lemonde, & Wareham, 2009). Some large open source software projects are used by millions of people: For example, Apache is estimated to power more than 65% of the world's websites (http://www.apache.org); the Tor Project enabled 36 million people to maintain their anonymity while online, protecting free online speech

(Noyes, 2011). The Internet infrastructure relies to a large extent on open source software such as sendmail, which enables people to communicate through email. The availability of open source solutions provided low-cost technical infrastructure for many electronic groups and citizen science projects.

Citizen science projects are beginning to benefit science in appreciable ways. Idle PC cycles donated by volunteers generate an average daily computing power of about 4 PetaFLOPs, more computing power than the world's largest supercomputer. Hundreds of thousands of volunteers have submitted millions of natural history records to scientific databases; hundreds of thousands of volunteers have contributed to improving the quality of other scientific databases. Scientists have published hundreds of scholarly papers resulting from these projects. In the Galaxy Zoo project, individual citizen contributions have been recognized through shared authorship on reports describing the discovery of a new astronomical object (Young, 2010).

Implications and Future Research

Prosocial behavior is widespread on the net. Evidence of its beneficial consequences for participants and the broader society is beginning to accumulate. As new types of electronic contribution contexts emerge and more people engage in online prosocial behavior, research opportunities abound for all components of the stylized model of Fig. 8.1.

Individual attributes: In the offline world, demographic variables like age, race, gender, education level, and family income are associated with volunteer behavior. Demographic data are not routinely reported in research on online prosocial behavior, so it remains an open question if the same demographic patterns are evident in the online context. Although validated personality scales are routinely used in offline research on volunteering—for example, to measure other-oriented empathy and helpfulness (e.g., Eisenberg & Fabes, 1990; Stiff, Dillard, Somera, Kim, & Sleight, 1988), they are not routinely employed in studies of online volunteering. Doing so would improve the cumulativeness of this research and would help connect it to research on offline volunteering (e.g., Amichai-Hamburger, Lamdan, Madiel, & Hayat, 2008). Similarly, investigations of motivations for offline volunteering routinely use validated multidimensional multi-item scales (e.g., Clary et al., 1998; Klandermans, 2003), whereas many measures of motivation in online settings are more ad hoc. (See Oreg & Nov, 2008; Schroer & Hertel, 2009 for recent counterexamples.)

Individual differences affect help-seeking and help-offering behaviors offline (Nadler & Fisher, 1986). For example, individual differences in self-esteem affect tendencies for asking and providing help. People with low self-esteem are less likely to ask for help because they feel threatened. The relative invisibility of many electronic contexts makes it psychologically less threatening for everyone, but this effect may be stronger for people with low self-esteem. Studies that do not control for individual differences when measuring the perceived benefits to individuals of the help provided and received online may lead to incomplete or even wrong conclusions. McKenna and Bargh (1998) found, for example, that although active participation in support groups was beneficial, the benefits accrued only to those for whom identity as a member of the group was important. Future research on the causes and consequences of prosocial behavior at the individual level should incorporate important individual personality variables.

Moreover, with few exceptions, studies that have focused on understanding individual attributes like motivations for helping have not assessed the quality of the help provided. However, the quality of help provided is what determines its value to individual recipients. (See Hoch, Norris, Lester, and Marcus (1999) for one exception that found that informational help provided in online public medical discussion groups is of comparable quality to expert medical advice.) We should also note that some types of "helping" behavior on the net, while rare, may be defined by many observers as antisocial rather than prosocial. A stark example of this can be found in volunteer "pro-ana" (pro-anorexia) online groups, whose members support one another in their "personal choice" to become dangerously thin. In sum, there is much research to be done at the individual level focusing on the determinants, costs, and benefits of online prosocial behavior.

Contribution context: Studies of offline helping have found that people help less when they see more people in the helping context (Latané & Darley, 1970). However, in the electronic context there may be few salient cues regarding group size. Research on the role of perceived group size could provide a fuller account of some of the situational determinants of helping behavior in the electronic context. Different contexts now present variation in cues to the presence and behavior of other volunteers—for example, through leader boards and credit tables, which may have an important effect on perceived group size.

Most research on online prosocial behavior has been conducted within a single contribution context. It is now possible and desirable to conduct comparative studies both within and across different types of contribution contexts. Comparative studies across different open collaborative software projects illuminate the influence of different software structures on the amount and quality of volunteer contributions (e.g., Conley, 2008). Similarly comparative research makes it feasible to understand the role of different types of feedback mechanisms (e.g., Moon & Sproull, 2008). Comparative studies also let us investigate how context type interacts with individual contributor attributes. Comparing open software contributors with Wikipedia contributors, for example, allowed Oreg and Nov (2008) to find that "software contributors placed a greater emphasis on reputation-gaining and self-development motivations, compared with content contributors, who placed a greater emphasis on altruistic motives" (p. 2055).

Methods: Studies using one-time (cross-sectional) questionnaires that ask people to self-report their motivations for helping others are problematic. Cross-sectional studies cannot distinguish the role of motivation from pre-existing group differences, such as the (possible) higher educational attainment of volunteers than non-volunteers. Researchers have made some progress in untangling people's *ex ante* motivations for helping from their post hoc justifications for helping by conducting laboratory experiments and longitudinal surveys. These methods can more accurately assess causal links among motivations, attributions, and contributions (e.g., Penner & Finkelstein, 1998). The archives of public discussion groups and open collaborative work groups offer the opportunity to design and conduct unobtrusive longitudinal studies of prosocial behavior. McKenna and Bargh (1998) demonstrate how positive responses to a first post increase the likelihood of the newcomer's subsequent active involvement in a group. More research on reinforcement processes is feasible and would be useful. A comparative content analysis of posts from frequent posters with those from infrequent posters could illuminate developmental processes associated with identification with a prosocial subgroup. Galegher et al. (1998) demonstrate how referencing group membership in a request for help increases the likelihood that help will be provided. See Sassenberg (2002) for an example of a cross-sectional linguistic analysis of conformity to group communication norms; see Moon (2004) for one of a longitudinal study of subgroup identification in open collaborative work groups.

Researchers are becoming more sensitive to ethical issues involved in conducting Internet research on any topic (e.g., Bruckman, 2002; Buchanan, 2010; Frankel & Siang, 1999; Nosek, Banaji & Greenwald, 2002; Thomas, 1996). Both archival and contemporary studies of prosocial behavior must attend to these ethical issues. Because public contribution contexts *are* public, it is easy to post an online questionnaire to the group as a whole or to the email addresses of people who have contributed to the group. As more and more social scientists and their students try to study prosocial behavior by using online questionnaires, the potential subjects of study may react negatively. It is important to remember that one person's research instrument is another person's spam.

Evolving technology: Developments in technology allow people to interact in new and different ways on the Internet. Web 2.0 and social media are moving away from traditional discussion boards towards richer interactions among users based on connections to other users rather than threads in a discussion board. These changes affect how people interact, and therefore will likely affect how people provide help, how people solicit help, and the type of help provided. For example, Twitter users use hashtag (#) conventions to form spontaneous online groups to help in particular events, such as following a disaster. For example, in 2007 people used Twitter to inform others about the wild fires in San Diego, California (Poulsen, 2007). More recently, people across the world have used Twitter and Facebook in the aftermath of the 2011 Japan earthquake and tsunami to connect with family and friends and get relief information such as emergency phone numbers and shelter information (Wallop, 2011). People have also used Twitter under normal circumstances to ask their government for help (Brice, 2010) and inform people about commuter issues (Purdy, 2008). While Facebook is not primarily a way for strangers to help one another, it certainly offers opportunities to investigate how research on strong-tie helping in the offline world (e.g., Bartlett & DeSteno, 2006; Bolger 2000; Kiesler, Zdaniuk, Lundmark, & Kraut, 2000) applies in the online world. New Internet tools for scientific resource sharing (e.g., BOINC) will make it possible to organize many more online citizen science projects. Future research should examine how asking for and giving help manifest themselves with these newer, more interactive, technologies.

In 2010, 62.8 million Americans contributed more than 8.1 billion hours of volunteer service in the offline world. As online prosocial behavior increases, it is likely that some fraction of those volunteers will turn to online volunteering instead of, or in addition to, making their contributions in the offline world. It is even more likely that the Internet will attract new people to new forms of volunteering so that the total number of volunteers and amount of volunteer service increases not just in the United States but also globally. Understanding the relationship between online and offline volunteering represents a new and important research challenge. In sum, the net offers the opportunity to engage in meaningful prosocial behavior, the opportunity to theorize about who engages in these behaviors and why they do, and the opportunity to study these behaviors in a wide variety of contexts.

References

Akera, A. (2001). Voluntarism and the fruits of collaboration: The IBM user group, SHARE. *Technology and Culture, 42*(4), 710–736. doi: 10.1353/tech.2001.0146

Amichai-Hamburger, Y. (2008). Potential and promise of online volunteering. *Computers in Human Behavior, 24*(2), 544–562. doi: 10.1016/j.chb.2007.02.004

Amichai-Hamburger, Y., Lamdan, N., Madiel, R., & Hayat, T. (2008). Personality characteristics of Wikipedia members. *CyberPsychology and Behavior, 11*(6), 679–681. doi: 10.1089/cpb.2007.0225

Ashforth, B. E., & Mael, F. (1989). Social identity theory and the organization. *Academy of Management Review, 14*(1), 20–39.

Athanasiou, R., & Green, P. (1973). *Physical attractiveness and helping behavior.* Paper presented at the 81st Annual Convention of the American Psychological Association, Montreal, Canada.

Bandura, A. (1977). *Social Learning Theory.* Englewood Cliffs, NJ: Prentice Hall.

Bandura, A., & McDonald, F. J. (1963). Influence of social-reinforcement and behavior of models in shaping children's moral judgments. *Journal of Abnormal and Social Psychology, 67*(3), 274–281. doi: 10.1037/h0044714

Bartlett, M. Y., & DeSteno, D. (2006). Gratitude and prosocial behavior: Helping when it costs you. *Psychological Science, 17*(4), 319–325. doi: 10.1111/j.1467-9280.2006.01705.x

Bateman, P. J., Gray, P. H., & Butler, B. (2011). The impact of community commitment on participation in online communities. *Information Systems Research, 22*(4), 841–854. doi: 10.1287/isre.1090.0265

Batson, C. D. (1991). *The Altruism Question: Toward a Social Psychological Answer.* Hillsdale, NJ: Lawrence Erlbaum.

Batson, C. D. (1998). Altruism and prosocial behavior. In D. T. Gilbert, S. T. Fiske, & G. Lindzey (Eds.), *Handbook of Social Psychology* (4th ed., Vol. II, pp. 282–316). New York, NY: McGraw-Hill.

Batson, C. D., & Powell, A. A. (2003). Altruism and prosocial behavior. In T. Millon & M. J. Lerner (Eds.), *Handbook of Psychology, Volume 5: Personality and Social Psychology* (pp. 463–484). Hoboken, NJ: Wiley.

Baym, N. K. (1999). *Tune in, Log on: Soaps, Fandom, and Online Community.* Thousand Oaks, CA: Sage.

Bennett, D., Tsikalas, K., Hupert, N., Meade, T., & Honey, M. (1998, September). The benefits of online mentoring for highschool girls: Telementoring young women in science, engineering, and computing project. Retrieved from http://www2.edc.org/CCT/admin/publications/report/telement_bomhsg98.pdf

Blanchard, A. L., & Markus, M. L. (2004). The Experienced "Sense" of a Virtual Community: Characteristics and Processes. *Database for Advances in Information Systems, 35*(1), 65–79.

Boberg, E. W., Gustafson, D. H., Hawkins, R. P., Chan, C. -L., Bricker, E., Pingree, S., & Berhe, H. (1995). Development, acceptance, and use patterns of a computer-based education and social support system for people with AIDS/HIV infection. *Computers in Human Behavior, 11*(2), 289–311. doi: 10.1016/0747-5632(94)00037-I

Bock, G. W., Zmud, R. W., Kim, Y. G., & Lee, J. N. (2005). Behavioral intention formation in knowledge sharing: Examining the roles of extrinsic motivators, social-psychological forces, and organizational climate. *MIS Quarterly, 29*(1), 87–111.

Bolger, N., Zuckerman, A., & Kessler, R. (2000). Invisible support and adjustment to stress. *Journal of Personality and Social Psychology, 79*(6), 953–961. doi: 10.1037/0022-3514.79.6.953

Brennan, P. F., Moore, S. M., & Smyth, K. A. (1995). The effects of a special computer network on caregivers of persons with Alzheimer's disease. *Nursing Research, 44*(3), 166–172.

Brice, A. (2010, July 20). Chavez says he's gotten nearly 288,000 help requests through Twitter. *CNN.* Retrieved from http://www.cnn.com/2010/WORLD/americas/07/20/venezuela.chavez.twitter/index.html?hpt=T2

Brokowski, L., & Sheehan, A. H. (2009). Evaluation of pharmacist use and perception of Wikipedia as a drug information source. *Annals of Pharmacotherapy, 43*(11), 1912–1913. doi: 10.1345/aph.1M340

Bruckman, A. (2002). Studying the amateur artist: A perspective on disguising data collected in human subjects research on the Internet. *Ethics and Information Technology, 4*(3), 217–231. doi: 10.1023/A:1021316409277

Buchanan, E. (2010). Internet research ethics: past, present, and future. In R. Burnett, M. Consalvo & C. Ess (Eds.), *The Handbook of Internet Studies* (pp. 83–108). Hoboken NJ: Wiley-Blackwell.

Burger, J. M. (1999). The foot-in-the-door compliance procedure: A multiple-process analysis and review. *Personality and Social Psychology Review, 3*(4), 303–325. doi: 10.1207/s15327957pspr0304_2

Butler, B., Sproull, L., Kiesler, S., & Kraut, R. (2007). Community effort in online groups: Who does the work and why? In S. P. Weisband (Ed.), *Leadership at a Distance: Research in Technologically Supported Work* (pp. 171–194). Mahwah, NJ: Lawrence Erlbaum.

Byrne, D., Baskett, G., & Hodges, L. (1971). Behavioral indicators of interpersonal attraction. *Journal of Applied Social Psychology, 1*(2), 137–149. doi: 10.1111/j.1559-1816.1971.tb00358.x

Callero, P. L., Howard, J. A., & Piliavin, J. A. (1987). Helping behavior as role behavior: Disclosing social structure and history in the analysis of prosocial action. *Social Psychology Quarterly, 50*(3), 247–256. doi: 10.2307/2786825

Chaiken, S. (1979). Communicator physical attractiveness and persuasion. *Journal of Personality and Social Psychology, 37*(8), 1387–1397. doi: 10.1037/0022-3514.37.8.1387

Chidambaram, L. (1996). Relational development in computer-supported groups. *MIS Quarterly, 20*(2), 143–165. doi: 10.2307/249476

Chiu, C. M., Hsu, M.-H., & Wang, E. T. G. (2006). Understanding knowledge sharing in virtual communities: An integration of social capital and social cognitive theories. *Decision Support Systems, 42*(3), 1872–1888. doi: 10.1016/j.dss.2006.04.001

Clary, E. G., Snyder, M., Ridge, R. D., Copeland, J., Stukas, A. A., Haugen, J., & Miene, P. (1998). Understanding and assessing the motivations of volunteers: A functional approach. *Journal of Personality and Social Psychology, 74*(6), 1516–1530. doi: 10.1037/0022-3514.74.6.1516

Compeau, D. R., & Higgins, C. A. (1995). Application of social cognitive theory to training for computer skills. *Information Systems Research, 6*(2), 118–143. doi: 10.1287/isre.6.2.118

Conley, C. A. (2008). *Design for Quality: The case of open source software development.* Unpublished doctoral dissertation, New York University, New York, NY.

Constant, D., Sproull, L., & Kiesler, S. (1996). The kindness of strangers: The usefulness of electronic weak ties for technical advice. *Organization Science, 7*(2), 119–135. doi: 10.1287/orsc.7.2.119

Cummings, J. N., Sproull, L., & Kiesler, S. (2002). Beyond hearing: Where real world and online support meet. *Group Dynamics: Theory, Research and Practice, 6*(1), 78–88. doi: 10.1037/1089-2699.6.1.78

Davison, K. P., Pennebaker, J. W., & Dickerson, S. S. (2000). Who talks? The social psychology of illness support groups. *American Psychologist, 55*(2), 205–217. doi: 10.1037/0003-066X.55.2.205

Devgan, L., Powe, N., Blakey, B., & Makary, M. (2007). Wiki-Surgery? Internal validity of Wikipedia as a medical and surgical reference. *Journal of the American College of Surgeons, 205*(3), S76–S77. doi: 10.1016/j.jamcollsurg.2007.06.190

Dommeyer, C. J., & Ruggiero, L. A. (1996). The effects of a photograph on a mail survey response. *Marketing Bulletin, 7*, 51–57.

Eagly, A. H., & Crowley, M. (1986). Gender and helping behavior: A meta-analytic review of the social psychological literature. *Psychological Bulletin, 100*(3), 283–308. doi: 10.1037/0033-2909.100.3.283

Eisenberg, N., & Fabes, R. A. (1990). Empathy: Conceptualization, measurement, and relation to prosocial behavior. *Motivation and Emotion, 14*(2), 131–149. doi: 10.1007/BF00991640

Eisenberg, N., & Miller, P. A. (1987). The relation of empathy to prosocial and related behaviors. *Psychological Bulletin, 101*(1), 91–119. doi: 10.1037/0033-2909.101.1.91

Ellison, N. B., Steinfield, C., & Lampe, C. (2007). The benefits of Facebook "friends": Social capital and college students' use of online social network sites. *Journal of Computer-Mediated Communication, 12*(4), 1143–1168. doi: 10.1111/j.1083-6101.2007.00367.x

Emswiller, T., Deaux, K., & Willits, J. (1971). Similarity, sex, and requests for small favors. *Journal of Applied Social Psychology, 1*(3), 284–291. doi: 10.1111/j.1559-1816.1971.tb00367.x

Field, D., & Johnson, I. (1993). Satisfaction and change: A survey of volunteers in a hospice organisation. *Social Science & Medicine, 36*(12), 1625–1633. doi: 10.1016/0277-9536(93)90351-4

Fisher, R. J., & Ackerman, D. (1998). The effects of recognition and group need on volunteerism: A social norm perspective. *Journal of Consumer Research, 25*(3), 262–275. doi: 10.1086/209538

Foster, E. (1998, February 2). Best Technical Support Award: Linux user community. *InfoWorld, 20*(5), S16.

Foster, E. (1999, November 29). Best technical support: It may not be the guy on the telephones anymore. *InfoWorld, 21*(48), 109.

Foster, E. (2000, January 14). Best customer support? The award goes to Sybase Internet newsgroups. *InfoWorld, 22*(3), 80.

Frankel, M. S., & Siang, S. (1999, November). Ethical and legal aspects of human subjects research on the Internet: A report of a workshop. Retrieved from http://www.aaas.org/spp/dspp/sfrl/projects/intres/main.htm

Galegher, J., Sproull, L., & Kiesler, S. (1998). Legitimacy, authority, and community in electronic support groups. *Written Communication*, *15*(4), 493–530. doi: 10.1177/0741088398015004003

Giles, J. (2005). Internet encyclopedias go head to head. *Nature*, *438*(7070), 900–901. doi: 10.1038/438900a

Glasgow, R. E., Boles, S. M., McKay, H. G., Feil, E. G., & Barrera, M. J. (2003). The D-net diabetes self-management program: Long-term implementation, outcomes, and generalization results. *Preventive Medicine*, *36*(4), 410–419. doi: 10.1016/S0091-7435(02)00056-7

Gray, J. E., Safran, C., Davis, R. B., Pompilio-Weitzner, G., JStewart, J. E., Zaccagnini, L., & Pursley, D. (2000). Baby CareLink: Using the Internet and telemedicine to improve care for high-risk infants. *Pediatrics*, *106*(6), 1318–1324. doi: 10.1542/peds.106.6.1318

Han, J. Y., Shah, D. V., Kim, E., Namkoong, K., Lee, S. Y., Moon, T. J.,... Gustafson, D. H. (2011). Empathic exchanges in online cancer support groups: Distinguishing message expression and reception effects. *Health Communication*, *26*(2), 185–197. doi: 10.1080/10410236.2010.544283.

Harper, F. M., Li, S. X., Chen, Y., & Konstan, J. A. (2007). Social comparisons to motivate contributions to an online community. In Y. de Kort, W. IJsselsteijn, C. J. H. Midden, B. Eggen & B. J. Fogg (Eds.), *Persuasive Technology, Second International Conference on Persuasive Technology, PERSUASIVE 2007* (pp. 148–159). New York, NY: Springer.

Harrell, W. A. (1978). Physical attractiveness, self-disclosure, and helping behavior. *The Journal of Social Psychology*, *104*(1), 15–17. doi: 10.1080/00224545.1978.9924033

Hertel, G., Niedner, S., & Herrmann, S. (2003). Motivation of software developers in open source projects: An Internet-based survey of contributors to the Linux kernel. *Research Policy*, *32*(7), 1159–1177. doi: 10.1016/S0048-7333(03)00047-7

Higgins, M. C., & Kram, K. E. (2001). Reconceptualizing mentoring at work: A developmental network perspective. *Academy of Management Review*, *26*, 264–288.

Hoch, D. B., Norris, D., Lester, J. E., & Marcus, A. D. (1999). Information exchange in an epilepsy forum on the World Wide Web. *Seizure*, *8*(1), 30–34. doi: 10.1053/seiz.1998.0217

Hogg, M. A., & Abrams, D. (1988). *Social Identifications: A Social Psychology of Intergroup Relations and Group Processes*. London, UK: Routledge.

Hogg, M. A., & Terry, D. J. (2000). Social identity and self-categorization processes in organizational contexts. *Academy of Management Review*, *25*(1), 121–140.

Hughes, B., Joshi, I., Lemonde, H., & Wareham, J. (2009). Junior physician's use of Web 2.0 for information seeking and medical education: A qualitative study. *International Journal of Medical Informatics*, *78*(10), 645–655. doi: 10.1016/j.ijmedinf.2009.04.008

Johnson, A. J., Haigh, M. M., Becker, J. A. H., Craig, E. A., & Wigley, S. (2008). College students' use of relational management strategies in email in long-distance and geographically close relationships. *Journal of Computer-Mediated Communication*, *13*(2), 381–404. doi: 10.1111/j.1083-6101.2008.00401.x

Kane, G. C. (2011). A multimethod study of information quality in Wikipedia collaboration. *ACM Transactions on Management Information Systems*, *2*(1), Article 4. Retrieved from http://portal.acm.org/tmis/archive:

Kankanhalli, A., Tan, B. C. Y., & Wei, K.-K. (2005). Contributing knowledge to electronic knowledge repositories: An empirical investigation. *MIS Quarterly*, *29*(1), 113–143.

Karabenick, S. A., & Knapp, J. R. (1988). Effects of computer privacy on help-seeking. *Journal of Applied Social Psychology*, *18*(6), 461–472. doi: 10.1111/j.1559-1816.1988.tb00029.x

Kendall, L. (2002). *Hanging Out in the Virtual Pub: Masculinities and Relationships Online*. Berkeley, CA: University of California Press.

Kiesler, S., Zdaniuk, B., Lundmark, V., & Kraut, R. (2000). Troubles with the Internet: The dynamics of help at home. *Human-Computer Interaction*, *15*(4), 323–351. doi: 10.1207/S15327051HCI1504_2

Kittur, A., Pendleton, B., & Kraut, R. (2009). *Herding the cats: the influence of groups in coordinating peer production.* Paper presented at the 5th International Symposium on Wikis and Open Collaboration (WikiSym "09), Orlando, FL.

Klandermans, B. (2003). Collective political action. In D. O. Sears, L. Huddy & R. Jervis (Eds.), *Oxford Handbook of Political Psychology* (pp. 670–709). New York: NY: Oxford University Press.

Knoke, D. (1981). Commitment and detachment in voluntary associations. *American Sociological Review, 46*(2), 141–158. doi: 10.2307/2094975

Kramer, R. M. (1993). Cooperation and organizational identification. In J. K. Murnighan (Ed.), *Social Psychology in Organizations: Advances in Theory and Research* (pp. 244–268). Englewood Cliffs, NJ: Prentice Hall.

Lakhani, K., & von Hippel, E. (2003). How open source software works: "Free" user-to-user assistance. *Research Policy, 32*(6), 923–943. doi: 10.1016/S0048-7333(02)00095-1

Lakhani, K. R., & Wolf, R. (2005). Why hackers do what they do: Understanding motivation and effort in free/open source software projects. In J. Feller, B. Fitzgerald, S. Hissam & K. R. Lakhani (Eds.), *Perspectives on Free and Open Source Software* (pp. 3–21). Cambridge, MA: MIT Press.

Latané, B., & Darley, J. M. (1970). *The Unresponsive Bystander: Why doesn't he Help?* New York, NY: Appleton-Century Crofts.

Lawler, E. J., Thye, S. R., & Yoon, J. (2000). Emotion and group cohesion in productive exchange. *American Journal of Sociology, 106*(3), 616–657. doi: 10.1086/318965

Lim, K. H., Ward, L. M., & Benbasat, I. (1997). An empirical study of computer system learning: Comparison of co-discovery and self-discovery methods. *Information Systems Research, 8*(3), 254–272. doi: 10.1287/isre.8.3.254

Lorig, K. R., Laurent, D. D., Deyo, R. A., Marnell, M. E., Minor, M. A., & Ritter, P. L. (2002). Can a back pain e-mail discussion group improve health status and lower health care costs?: A randomized study. *Archives of Internal Medicine, 162*(7), 792–796. doi: 10.1001/archinte.162.7.792

Ma, M., & Agarwal, R. (2007). Through a glass darkly: Information technology design, identity verification, and knowledge contribution in Online communities. *Information Systems Research, 18*(1), 42–67. doi: 10.1287/isre.1070.0113

MacIntyre, A. (1967). Egoism and altruism. In P. Edwards (Ed.), *The Encyclopedia of Philosophy* (Vol. 2, pp. 462–466). New York, NY: Macmillan.

Mael, F. A., & Ashforth, B. E. (1995). Loyal from day one: Biodata, organizational identification, and turnover among newcomers. *Personnel Psychology, 48*(2), 309–333. doi: 10.1111/j.1744-6570.1995.tb01759.x

McKenna, K. Y. A., & Bargh, J. A. (1998). Coming out in the age of the Internet: Identity "demarginalization" through virtual group participation. *Journal of Personality and Social Psychology, 75*(3), 681–694. doi: 10.1037/0022-3514.75.3.681

McKenna, K. Y. A., & Green, A. S. (2002). Virtual group dynamics. *Group Dynamics: Theory, Research and Practice, 6*(1), 116–127. doi: 10.1037/1089-2699.6.1.116

Meyer, J. P., Stanley, D. J., Herscovitch, L., & Topolnytsky, L. (2002). Affective, continuance, and normative commitment to the organization: A meta-analysis of antecedents, correlates, and consequences. *Journal of Vocational Behavior, 61*(1), 20–52. doi: 10.1006/jvbe.2001.1842

Mims, P. R., Hartnett, J. J., & Nay, W. R. (1975). Interpersonal attraction and help volunteering as a function of physical attractiveness. *The Journal of Psychology: Interdisciplinary and Applied, 89*(1), 125–131. doi: 10.1080/00223980.1975.9923913

Mockus, A., Fielding, R. T., & Herbsleb, J. D. (2002). Two case studies of open source software development: Apache and Mozilla. *ACM Transactions on Software Engineering and Methodology, 11*(3), 309–346. doi: 10.1145/567793.567795

Moon, J. Y. (2004). *Identification processes in distributed electronic groups: A study of voluntary technical support groups on the Net.* Unpublished doctoral dissertation, New York University, New York, NY.

Moon, J. Y., & Sproull, L. S. (2008). The Role of Feedback in Managing the Internet-Based Volunteer Work Force. *Information Systems Research*, *19*(4), 494–515. doi: 10.1287/isre.1080.0208

Mukherjee, D. (2010). An exploratory study of older adults' engagement with virtual volunteerism. *Journal of Technology in Human Services*, *28*(3), 188–196. doi: 10.1080/15228835.2010.508368

Muller, C. B., & Barsion, S. J. (2003). *Assessment of a large-scale e-mentoring network for women in engineering and science: Just how good is MentorNet?* Paper presented at the WEPAN (Women in Engineering Programs & Advocates Network) 2003 Conference, Chicago, IL.

Nadkarni, A., & Hofmann, S. G. (2012). Why do people use Facebook?. *Personality and Individual Differences*, *52*(3), 243–249. doi: 10.1016/j.paid.2011.11.007

Nadler, A., & Fisher, J. D. (1986). The role of threat to self-esteem and perceived control in recipient reaction to help: Theory development and empirical validation. *Advances in Experimental Social Psychology*, *19*, 81–122. doi: 10.1016/S0065-2601(08)60213-0

Nam, K. K., Ackerman, M. S., & Adamic, L. A. (2009). *Questions in, Knowledge iN? A study of Naver's Questions Answering Community.* Paper presented at the SIGCHI Conference on Human Factors in Computing Systems, Boston, MA.

Nelson, T. D. (1999). Motivational bases of prosocial and altruistic behavior: A critical reappraisal. *Journal of Research*, *4*(1), 23–31.

Nonnecke, B., & Preece, J. (2000a). *Lurker demographics: Counting the silent.* Paper presented at the the the SIGCHI Conference Human Factors in Computing Systems (CHI 2000), The Hague, Netherlands.

Nonnecke, B., & Preece, J. (2000b). *Persistence and lurkers in discussion lists: A pilot study.* Paper presented at the 33rd Hawaii International Conference on System Sciences, Maui, HI.

Nosek, B. A., Banaji, M. R., & Greenwald, A. G. (2002). E-Research: Ethics, security, design, and control in psychological research on the Internet. *Journal of Social Issues*, *58*(1), 161–176. doi: 10.1111/1540-4560.00254

Nov, O. (2007). What motivates Wikipedians? *Communications of the ACM*, *50*(11), 60–64. doi: 10.1145/1297797.1297798

Nov, O., Anderson, D., & Arazy, O. (2010). *Volunteer computing: A model of the factors determining contribution to community-based scientific research.* Paper presented at the 19th International World Wide Web Conference (WWW 2010), Raleigh, NC.

Nov, O., Arazy, O., & Anderson, D. (2011). *Dusting for science: Motivation and participation of digital science volunteers.* Paper presented at the iConference 2011, Seattle, WA.

Noyes, K. (2011, March 29). Awards highlight impact of open source software. *PCWorld*. Retrieved from http://www.pcworld.com/businesscenter/article/223482/awards_highlight_impact_of_open_source_software.html

Olivera, F., Goodman, P. S., & Tan, S. S.-L. (2008). Contribution behaviors in distributed environments. *MIS Quarterly*, *32*(1), 23–42.

Omoto, A. M., & Snyder, M. (1995). Sustained helping without obligation: Motivation, longevity of service, and perceived attitude change among AIDS volunteers. *Journal of Personality and Social Psychology*, *68*(4), 671–686. doi: 10.1037/0022-3514.68.4.671

Oreg, S., & Nov, O. (2008). Exploring motivations for contributing to open source initiatives: The roles of contribution context and personal values. *Computers in Human Behavior*, *24*(5), 2055–2073. doi: 10.1016/j.chb.2007.09.007

Panciera, K., Masli, M., & Terveen, L. (2011). *"How should I go from ___ to ___ without getting killed?": Motivation and benefits in open collaboration.* Paper presented at the 7th International Symposium on Wikis and Open Collaboration (WikiSym "11), Mountain View, CA.

Penner, L. A. (2002). Dispositional and organizational influences on sustained volunteerism: An interactionist perspective. *Journal of Social Issues*, *58*(3), 447–467. doi: 10.1111/1540-4560.00270

Penner, L. A., Dovidio, J. F., Piliavin, J. A., & Schroeder, D. A. (2005). Prosocial behavior: Multilevel perspectives. *Annual Review of Psychology*, *56*, 365–392. doi: 10.1146/annurev.psych.56.091103.070141

Penner, L. A., & Finkelstein, M. A. (1998). Dispositional and structural determinants of volunteerism. *Journal of Personality and Social Psychology, 74*(2), 525–537. doi: 10.1037/0022-3514.74.2.525

Piliavin, I. M., & Piliavin, J. A. (1975). Costs, diffusion, and the stigmatized victim. *Journal of Personality and Social Psychology, 32*(3), 429–438. doi: 10.1037/h0077092

Piliavin, J. A., & Callero, P. L. (1991). *Giving Blood: The Development of an Altruistic Identity.* Baltimore, MD: Johns Hopkins University Press.

Piliavin, J. A., & Charng, H.-W. (1990). Altruism: A review of recent theory and research. *Annual Review of Sociology, 16,* 27–65. doi: 10.1146/annurev.so.16.080190.000331

Pope, W. G. (2001). *The use of computer conferencing as an organizational knowledge transfer tool.* Unpublished doctoral dissertation, Pace University, New York, NY.

Popielarz, P. A., & McPherson, J. M. (1995). On the edge or in between: Niche position, niche overlap, and the duration of voluntary association memberships. *American Journal of Sociology, 101*(3), 698–720. doi: 10.1086/230757

Postmes, T., Spears, R., & Lea, M. (2000). The formation of group norms in computer-mediated communication. *Human Communication Research, 26*(3), 341–371. doi: 10.1111/j.1468-2958.2000.tb00761.x

Poulsen, K. (2007, October). Firsthand Reports From California Wildfires Pour Through Twitter. *Wired.* Retrieved from http://www.wired.com/threatlevel/2007/10/firsthand-repor/

Priedhorsky, R., Chen, J., Lam, S. K., Panciera, K., Terveen, L., & Riedl, J. (2007). *Creating, destroying, and restoring value in Wikipedia.* Paper presented at the 2007 International ACM Conference on Supporting Group Work, Sanibel Island, FL.

Purdy, K. (2008, February 12). Track Commuting Delays via Twitter with Commuter Feed. *Lifehacker.* Retrieved from http://lifehacker.com/#!355453/track-commuting-delays-via-twitter_with-commuter-feed

Quan y Hasse, A., Wellman, B., Witte, J., & Hampton, K. (2002). Capitalizing on the Internet: Social contact, civic engagement and sense of community. In B. Wellman & C. Haythornthwaite (Eds.), *The Internet in Everyday Life* (pp. 291–324). Oxford, UK: Blackwell.

Rains, S. A., & Young, V. (2009). A meta-analysis of research on formal computer-mediated support groups: Examining group characteristics and health outcomes. *Human Communication Research, 35*(3), 309–336. doi: 10.1111/j.1468-2958.2009.01353.x

Rashid, A. M., Ling, K., Tassone, R. D., Resnick, P., Kraut, R., & Riedl, J. (2006). *Motivating participation by displaying the value of contribution.* Paper presented at the the SIGCHI conference on Human Factors in computing systems, Montreal, Quebec, Canada.

Richardson, C. R., Buis, L. R., Janney, A. W., Goodrich, D. E., Sen, A., Hess, M. L.,... Piette, J. D. (2010). An online community improves adherence in an Internet-mediated walking program. Part 1: Results of a randomized controlled trial. *Journal of Medical Internet Research, 12*(4), e71. doi: 10.2196/jmir.1338

Sassenberg, K. (2002). Common bond and common identity groups on the Internet: Attachment and normative behavior in on-topic and off-topic chats. *Group Dynamics: Theory, Research and Practice, 6*(1), 27–37. doi: 10.1037/1089-2699.6.1.27

Schroer, J., & Hertel, G. (2009). Voluntary engagement in an open web-based encyclopedia: Wikipedians and why they do it. *Media Psychology, 12*(1), 96–120. doi: 10.1080/15213260802669466

Scott, R. A. (1969). *The Making of Blind Men: A Study of Adult Socialization.* New York, NY: Russell Sage Foundation.

Shaw, B. R., Hawkins, R., McTavish, F., Pingree, S., & Gustafson, D. H. (2006). Effects of insightful disclosure within computer mediated support groups on women with breast cancer. *Health Communication, 19*(2), 133–142. doi: 10.1207/s15327027hc1902_5

Simon, B., Loewy, M., Stürmer, S., Weber, U., Freytag, P., Habig, C.,... Spahlinger, P. (1998). Collective identification and social movement participation. *Journal of Personality and Social Psychology, 74*(3), 646–658. doi: 10.1037/0022-3514.74.3.646

Simon, B., Stürmer, S., & Steffens, K. (2000). Helping individuals or group members? The role of individual and collective identification in AIDS volunteerism. *Personality and Social Psychology Bulletin, 26*(4), 497–506. doi: 10.1177/0146167200266008

Sproull, L., & Arriaga, M. (2007). Online communities. In H. Bidgoli (Ed.), *Handbook of Computer Networks: Distributed Networks, Network Planning, Control, Management, and New Trends and Applications* (Vol. 3, pp. 898–914). Hoboken, NJ: John Wiley & Sons.

Sproull, L., & Faraj, S. (1995). Atheism, sex and databases: The net as a social technology. In B. Kahin & J. Keller (Eds.), *Public Access to the Internet* (pp. 62–81). Cambridge, MA: The MIT Press.

Stiff, J. B., Dillard, J. P., Somera, L., Kim, H., & Sleight, C. (1988). Empathy, communication, and prosocial behavior. *Communication Monographs, 55*(2), 198–213. doi: 10.1080/03637758809376166

Tajfel, H., & Turner, J. C. (1986). The social identity theory of intergroup behavior. In S. Worchel & W. G. Austin (Eds.), *Psychology of Intergroup Relations* (2nd ed., pp. 7–24). Chicago, IL: Nelson-Hall Publishers.

Tanis, M. (2008). Health-related on-line forums: What's the big attraction? *Journal of Health Communication, 13*(7), 698–714. doi: 10.1080/10810730802415316

Thomas, J. (1996). Introduction: A debate about the ethics of fair practices for collecting social science data in cyberspace. *Information Society, 12*(2), 107–117. doi: 10.1080/713856137

Turner, J. C., Hogg, M. A., Oakes, P. J., Reicher, S. D., & Wetherell, M. S. (1987). *Rediscovering the Social Group: A Self-Categorization Theory*. Oxford, UK: Basil Blackwell.

Tyler, T. R. (1999). Why people cooperate with organizations: An identity-based perspective. *Research in Organizational Behavior, 21*, 201–246.

Vibbur, B. (2009). *Community performance optimization: Making your people run as smoothly as your site*. Paper presented at the 5th International Symposium on Wikis and Open Collaboration (WikiSym "09), Orlando, FL.

Wallop, H. (2011, March 13). Japan earthquake: How Twitter and Facebook helped. The Telegraph. Retrieved from http://www.telegraph.co.uk/technology/twitter/8379101/Japan-earthquake-how-Twitter-and-Facebook-helped.html

Walther, J. B. (2002). Time effects in computer-mediated groups: Past, present and future. In P. Hinds & S. Kiesler (Eds.), *Distributed Work* (pp. 235–257). Cambridge, MA: MIT Press.

Wasko, M. M., & Faraj, S. (2000). "It is what one does": why people participate and help others in electronic communities of practice. *Journal of Strategic Information Systems, 9*(2–3), 155–173. doi: 10.1016/S0963-8687(00)00045-7

Wasko, M. M., & Faraj, S. (2005). Why should I share? Examining social capital and knowledge contribution in electronic networks of practice. *MIS Quarterly, 29*(1), 35–57.

Watson, S. (2006). Virtual mentoring in higher education: Teacher education and cyber-connections. *International Journal of Teaching and Learning in Higher Education, 18*(3), 168–179.

Wellman, B., & Gulia, M. (1999). Net surfers don't ride alone: Virtual community as community. In B. Wellman (Ed.), *Networks in the Global Village* (pp. 331–367). Boulder, CO: Westview Press.

Wellman, B., & Wortley, S. (1990). Different strokes from different folks: Community ties and social support. *American Journal of Sociology, 96*(3), 558–588. doi: 10.1086/229572

West, S. G., & Brown, T. J. (1975). Physical attractiveness, the severity of the emergency and helping: A field experiment and interpersonal simulation. *Journal of Experimental Social Psychology, 11*(6), 531–538. doi: 10.1016/0022-1031(75)90004-9

Williamson, K., Wright, S., Schauder, D., & Bow, A. (2001). The Internet for the blind and visually impaired. *Journal of Computer Mediated Communication, 7*(1). Retrieved from http://jcmc.indiana.edu/vol7/issue1/williamson.html

Wilson, D. W. (1978). Helping behavior and physical attractiveness. *The Journal of Social Psychology, 104*(2), 313–314. doi: 10.1080/00224545.1978.9924081

Wilson, J. (2000). Volunteering. *Annual Review of Sociology, 26*, 215–240. doi: 10.1146/annurev.soc.26.1.215

Winzelberg, A. (1997). The analysis of an electronic support group for individuals with eating disorders. *Computers in Human Behavior, 13*(3), 393–407. doi: 10.1016/S0747-5632(97)00016-2

Yang, H.-L., & Lai, C.-Y. (2010). Motivations of Wikipedia content contributors. *Computers in Human Behavior, 26*(6), 1377–1383. doi: 10.1016/j.chb.2010.04.011

Ybarra, M. L., & Suman, M. (2006). Help seeking behavior and the Internet: A national survey. *International Journal of Medical Informatics, 75*(1), 29–41. doi: 10.1016/j.ijmedinf.2005.07.029

Young, J. R. (2010, May 28). Crowd science reaches new heights. *The Chronicle of Higher Education.* Retrieved from http://chronicle.com/article/The-Rise-of-Crowd-Science/65707/

Chapter 9

Groups and Computer-Mediated Communication

Joseph B. Walther

Introduction

Although computer-mediated communication (CMC) has become central to the performance of numerous social activities, its research origins lie in the study of online groups. The social and psychological dynamics of group collaboration have lead to the development and refinement of most theories of CMC. Research in wide-ranging domains, from knowledge-sharing to online personal relationships, have their roots in the dynamics of group interaction in online settings.

A common rationale for the use of groups for decision-making and problem solving—whether groups work offline or online via the Internet—is that groups make better decisions than individuals when facing complicated problems (Schweiger & Sandberg, 1989). High-quality decisions by groups facing complex, ambiguous situations often require multiple perspectives (Hoffman & Maier, 1961; Triandis, Hall, & Ewen, 1965), the expression of contrary viewpoints (Nemeth, 1986), and the evaluation of multiple alternatives (Schweiger, Sandberg, & Ragan, 1986). Online groups are employed, among other reasons, to take advantage of individuals' disparate perspectives and divergent information resulting from differences in their local contexts.

It is therefore critical for online groups, formed in order to capitalize on diversity, not only to share the information contributed by all members, but to process this information effectively, in order to realize these potential benefits. A major thrust of research and development has focused on whether CMC might offer an effective substitute for face-to-face (FtF) meetings. After all, the thinking went, if people could meet online, without leaving their offices, obviating the need for FtF meetings and the considerable time, money, effort, and travel that often accompanied them, people would be better off—provided that online meetings were just as effective as traditional ones. Moreover, if meetings could be conducted asynchronously—with people leaving and reading each other's messages at times of their own choosing rather than in "real time"—even more efficiency could be realized.

Today, the idea of groups working together online has become a commonplace. *Virtual groups* spread across cities and even continents are suggested to offer many advantages to corporations and other organizations. "Flash mobs" and large protest groups coordinate themselves spontaneously, converging on a geographic location and transmitting records of their activities to their associates. All these possibilities, of course, are enabled by digital communication technology. Yet communication technologies may pose their own challenges to a group's communication. Aspects of technological systems may interact with or exacerbate the kinds of communication difficulties that groups face even when groups are not distributed among a variety of places. Therefore, the study of online groups offers important questions and answers that tell us about group communication generally, and help guide decisions about how to compose and manage groups when they are virtual. Among these questions, theory and research have focused on such issues as the formation of impressions in groups, the exchange of task-oriented and socioemotional communication, the development of trust in group members, and how groups process disparate information in their decision-making and problem-solving discussions. Accompanying research on these phenomena in traditional groups, research over the last three decades has examined how CMC affects these processes. This chapter reviews research on these issues, and addresses how communication media dampen group processes or lead groups to accommodate the challenges of new communication media in original ways.

Group Formation and Impression Development

Traditionally, groups form (or are formed by someone) in order to solve a problem or make a decision. When groups first meet, their members form initial impressions of one another based on their nonverbal characteristics and the content of their self-disclosures, that is, how they look and sound, and what they say about themselves, such as their interests or expertise. First impressions tend to be fairly stereotypical, and they tend to develop into different degrees of attraction among members. There are several forms of attraction that vary in relationships, including group relationships: Physical attraction, or how good-looking people find one another to be; social attraction, or how much individuals desire friendly relations between them; and task attraction, or how reliable and dependable someone appears to be in relation to their potential contributions to the group's task (McCroskey & McCain, 1974).

Online groups may not have access to members' physical and vocal characteristics, and without having them, impression formation processes are transformed. One approach to impression formation in online groups suggests that the absence of nonverbal cues about one another's physical characteristics actually has the potential to magnify the attraction members experience toward one another. The social identification model of deindividuation effects (see Lea, Spears, Watt, & Rogers, 2000), or SIDE model, argues that when groups operate through CMC such as email or a real-time, text-based discussion system, the absence of visual cues about one another promotes a feeling of depersonalization: They cannot see, and therefore do not apprehend, that people are different from one another. This would be especially likely when people jump into a group discussion quickly and with very little opportunity to discuss personal issues rather than the focus of the group's task (Walther & Carr, 2010).

Early research on CMC suggested that the absence of nonverbal cues in online groups should interfere with impression formations, and that such groups would be impersonal and sterile (Kiesler, Siegel, & McGuire, 1984; Siegel, Dubrovsky, Kiesler, & McGuire, 1986). Another approach suggests something quite the opposite. If online group members experience depersonalization, and if the group members are aware of some common characteristic they all share, or they know that they are all a certain type of people—for instance, they are all psychology students, or they are all lawyers, or they are all concerned with arthritis research—then this overarching social identity leads them to experience a common link. The combination of not sensing interindividual differences, and sensing an overarching similarity to one another by virtue of belonging to a supergroup identity, may lead online group members to form exceptionally strong attraction to the group, even though members have, at best, vague impressions about the individuals in the group aside from their overarching similarity.

Research on the SIDE model has generally involved experiments manipulating the two factors, visual anonymity and type of identification, in online groups. Half of the groups of CMC users in an experiment would communicate with one another using a text-based chat system only, whereas another half would use the chat system and be shown photos that were supposed to represent the members. The former condition provides visual anonymity presumably instigating depersonalization, whereas the latter condition involves visual identification and individuation. The second factor, group identification, is altered by prompting participants explicitly either to look for the unique and distinctive characteristics of the *group* in which they were involved, rather than, alternatively, to try to detect what made the *individuals* with whom they were conversing unique and different from one another. Such research has produced predicted interaction effects of visual anonymity/identifiability by group/personal identity, with conditions involving both visual anonymity and group identity providing the greatest scores on attraction (Lea, Spears, & de Groot, 2001).

An interesting study by Weisband and Atwater (1999) compared the bases for liking in FtF and computer-mediated groups. In CMC groups, the more frequently a group member participated (by sending messages), the more the others liked the member. In FtF groups, there was no significant relationship between participation frequency and liking. It appears that liking, in FtF interactions, may be based on idiosyncratic characteristics, whereas in online groups, the more prototypical a member is (by being the ultimate, participating virtual group member) the more well liked that person is.

As recent research (Walther & Carr, 2010) has pointed out, there are many times when the SIDE approach explains how online groups develop a group-based impression. At other times, this level of impression formation may be insufficient. Perhaps there are inconsistencies among the members' communications and apparent orientations to the task or to one another. Perhaps a member writes something particularly amusing or inspiring. Perhaps there are such clear differences in the frequency and quality of contributions that a unified impression of the group, as a group, does not remain viable. The question then becomes how, without nonverbal cues to individual characteristics, do online group members sort out who's who? In this case, an alternative explanation seems warranted.

The social information processing (SIP) theory of CMC (Walther, 1992) describes how people get to know one another individually online despite the absence of nonverbal cues that otherwise help do the job, and accrue impressions of others online that achieve the level of development that is expected through offline communication. The SIP theory proposes that when nonverbal cues are unavailable, communicators adapt their interpersonal (as well as instrumental) communication to whatever cues remain available through the channel that they are using. In text-based CMC, the theory expects individuals to adapt the encoding and decoding of social information into language and the timing of messages. Although many readers of the theory have interpreted this argument to refer to emoticons (typed-out smiles, frowns, and other faces; Derks, Bos, & von Grumbkow, 2007), the theory focuses primarily on language content and style characteristics as more primary cues to interpersonal information.

Despite the capability of CMC to foster interpersonal impressions, SIP also argues that CMC operates at a different rate than FtF communication in terms of users' speed of sending and receiving messages, and the time it takes to extract information from these messages in order to build impressions. Because verbal communication with no nonverbal cues conveys a fraction of the information of FtF communication, CMC should require a longer time to do the same job as FtF encounters do.

Several studies have supported SIP's idea that the process of forming impressions of group members takes longer when it occurs through CMC than FtF communication (e.g., Walther, 1993). Recent studies have confirmed that time affects impression formation online using asynchronous communication such as email (Peter, Valkenburg, & Schouten, 2005; Ramirez, Zhang,

McGrew, & Lin, 2007), or using real-time chat episodes repeated over several consecutive days (Hian, Chuan, Trevor, & Detenber, 2004; Wilson, Straus, & McEvily, 2006). Even the photos on social media like Facebook, and its Dutch counterpart Hyves, offer insufficient information about others. One study that investigated whether people formed impressions of one another by perusing users' photos and self-descriptions on Hyves found that impressions were formed more strongly using dynamic, interactive text-based CMC than they were by relying on the static materials on Hyves (Antheunis, Valkenburg, & Peter, 2010).

Which factor is the stronger, the SIDE-based group identification-type impression of others, or the SIP-like approach to learning about group members as individuals online? An experiment recently tested both dynamics in a single setting in order to address this very question. Visually-anonymous online groups involved assignment of four members into two distinct subgroups (Wang, Walther, & Hancock, 2009), following the methods of SIDE-theoretic research: One sub-group was told that the members had common zodiac signs and personalities, which differed from the other subgroup's. The researchers further prompted one member of each four-person group to enact interpersonally friendly (or unfriendly) behaviors toward the rest of the members. Initial tests showed that the zodiac indoctrination led members to believe that the two subgroups were different, and that they identified more strongly with their common subgroup member than with the other subgroup. In spite of that, however, participants evaluated the deviants in each group on the basis of the individuals' interpersonal behaviors and not on the basis of those individuals' membership with respect to other subgroup members. These results suggest that SIP provides a more robust explanation for impression development in cases in which there are marked differences among group members' actions.

Task and Socioemotional Communication

A variety of perspectives on small group interaction point out that group decision-making requires a balance of at least two types of communication. The first, task-oriented communication, includes messages by which group members advance the exchange of information they need, to define the problem and its requirements, to articulate potential solutions, and to deliberate over the relative merits of alternatives. Task-oriented messages include asking for or providing information, or asking for or providing opinions. The second type of communication, socioemotional communication, focuses on the emotional and social processes in groups, such as expressing agreement or disagreement, adding levity, and negative exchanges such as blaming or insults. Whether theorists refer to these message types as task versus socioemotional (Bales, 1950) or instrumental versus maintenance messages (McGrath, 1984), most approaches to small group interaction specify that both types are necessary for a productive and cohesive group.

The extent to which online groups exhibit socioemotional communication was a contentious issue in early research on CMC. Many theorists suspected that, as mentioned earlier, communicating online without nonverbal cues or a sense of individuality might dampen users' emotional orientation, leading them to forego socioemotional communication in online groups (e.g., Hiltz, Johnson, & Turoff, 1986). Indeed, when online groups meet using real-time, text-based discussion systems, and they are provided little time to reach a group decision, members exhibit less socioemotional communication, and generate task-oriented messages almost exclusively. While some researchers suggested that meetings of such a nature would provide great efficiency, most studies found that the lack of socioemotional responses in short-term, online groups was associated with reduced frequency and/or quality of decision-making (see for review, Walther, 1996).

How people manage to express socioemotional communication in online groups has been discovered largely through investigations of the SIP theory, discussed earlier. This research establishes that group members take the emotional impulses they would normally express via nonverbal cues on a FtF basis, and translate them into verbal (language) behaviors online. Walther, Loh, and Granka's (2005) research shows this point most directly. The researchers had individuals discuss a controversial issue FtF or via real-time computer chat. Prior to their discussions, researchers privately prompted one of the members to increase or decrease his or her friendliness by whatever means that person chose to do so. Others rated the same individual's demeanor. Coders then analyzed recordings of the FtF participants for the physical as well as verbal behaviors that corresponded to variations in demeanor. Among physical behaviors, a number of vocal cues provided the greatest influence on demeanor ratings, followed by a group of specific kinesic behaviors (including body movements and facial expressions); the participants' language had no significant influence on perceptions of their demeanor. In contrast, in the CMC transcripts, several specific verbal behaviors bore significant association with differences in demeanor. It seems that CMC users quite naturally adapt to the change in channels when it comes to expressing socioemotional messages.

The SIP theory and its accompanying research has led many researchers to recognize that CMC is not inherently bereft of socioemotional communication. When interaction time is constrained, online groups tend to exhibit more task orientation than social orientation. Moreover, the amount of time pressure that online groups experience is directly related to the proportion of socioemotional communication their members exchange: When online groups perceive they have little time to reach a decision, they exchange less socioemotional messages, to a greater extent than time pressure effects socioemotional communication in FtF groups (Reid, Ball, Morley, & Evans, 1997). However, when online groups are allowed to develop over time, levels of social communication increase, and become similar to those found in FtF group discussions.

Trust in Small Group Relations

Small groups breed interdependence, and therefore groups that function well develop a good degree of trust among members. Interdependence refers to the state that exists in which one individual must rely on others in order to complete a task and to complete it well. It is rare that group decisions or tasks could be solved by one person alone. Even when such a possibility exists, groups tend to allocate portions of the groups' efforts among their members so that no one person has to do a disproportionate amount of work, and once such allocations have been made, members are vulnerable to each other as they anticipate each member's completion of his or her respective responsibilities (Mayer, Davis, & Schoorman, 1995). In other words, even if one person could have done the job independently, groups create situations in which members must trust one another to get the pieces of the work completed, since doing the whole job by oneself becomes more difficult the closer to deadline the group waits on itself. Whether the wait will be aversive or acceptable is mediated by the degree of trust a group has. How conflict is managed within a group is also affected by trust.

Research on trust in FtF groups recognizes that groups are often comprised of strangers who have no history with one another and hence, no actual basis to trust one another. This can stall some groups' progress. On the other hand, groups whose members get going immediately seem to act *as though they can trust each other*. Researchers refer to this state as "swift trust"; Meyerson, Weick, and Kramer (1996) argue that, even before group members get to know one another, members make judgments about the categorical similarity of other members (i.e., whether others seem to be the same kinds of persons as themselves, such as "psychology majors" or "conscientious students"). When these judgments connote positive stereotypes, members take action on their group's task as if they knew one another interpersonally and as if they were aware of one another's dedication and skills with regard to their joint activity. Through time and interaction, group members learn about each other as individuals in terms of members' skills and abilities, the pace at which each other works, and their relative reliability. When these characteristics are positive, groups may transition from "swift trust" to "enduring trust." When these characteristics are not positive, a climate of trust does not develop, and in such cases, groups tend not to perform as well, as individuals tend to look after their own unique contributions but not the contributions of others.

The notion of swift trust is especially valuable for online groups. In online groups, members initially have even less information about one another at an interpersonal level due to the absence of vocal and physical appearance information that is present in FtF settings. Yet, as SIDE theory (discussed previously) suggests, CMC users are likely (in some circumstances) to make categorical judgments about online group members, and over-attribute the degree of similarity between other members and themselves. On that basis, some online groups exhibit swift trust, and jump into their group tasks without reservation, according to Jarvenpaa and Leidner's (1998) research, which also found that only when long-term online groups initially exhibit swift trust are they able to maintain the level of commitment and demeanor that they need to be successful throughout the completion of their task.

Although swift trust appears to be important, it is not sufficient to propel a group to successful completion of its task; enduring trust, as mentioned earlier, is needed. Researchers have questioned the ability of online groups to develop this form of trust. Pessimistic accounts point, again, to the lack of nonverbal information about group members, suggesting that people cannot get to know each other online the way they do offline. Without getting to know one another, they argue, developing enduring trust cannot be possible (e.g., Handy, 1995).

Two opposing positions counter the claim that online groups cannot develop trust. The first position suggests that the behaviors that group members need to exhibit, and observe from one another, are not the ones that physical appearance and vocal cues convey. Rather, group members make judgments about one another's trustworthiness from behavioral exhibitions of trustworthy group behavior. For instance, Iacono and Weisband (1997) focused on a set of messages that prompted actions, and responses to such messages that provided validation for the individuals who had ventured suggestions, as messages that should promote trust in online groups. More specifically, they focused on (1) group members' messages that suggested initiating work processes (asking a specific question or proposing action, implicating a response from others), and (2) messages by other group members responding directly to and thereby confirming such initiations. Iacono and Weisband studied 14 virtual teams comprised of students at several universities who worked together for 3 weeks. They coded groups' messages for initiations and responses in several categories: work process, work content, technical aspects, contact regulation, and fun. They also evaluated the quality of the groups' collaborative papers as a measure of performance. Results showed that initiations and responses in the categories of work process (how to work as a group) and work content (substantive contributions to the project) were significantly associated with the quality of performance. These findings reinforce the notion that certain forms of messages breed trust in online groups—despite the absence of nonverbal cues—and that trust relates to the quality of groups' performances.

The second claim to counter the notion that online groups cannot develop trust came in the results of a study that asked the question, what can be done to help online groups accomplish what they would normally do using nonverbal communication, and what forms of online communication can help make up for the information deficits that CMC presents to online groups? Walther and Bunz (2005) devised a set of rules for virtual groups, adherence to which, they hypothesized, would help online groups make up for the decrements in information and rate of communication in CMC compared to FtF communication, and foster trust in online groups. Moreover, the researchers tested the utility of these rules in an experiment involving interuniversity groups of students.

The first rule of virtual groups is *start immediately*. Because information exchange in CMC operates at a slower rate than FtF communication, according to SIP theory, and in order to foster swift trust, online groups have no time to waste in order to be able to generate sufficiently frequent exchanges to start their projects and to start getting to know each other. The second rule, *communicate frequently*, also emphasizes the need for virtual groups to make up for the relatively slow information exchange in CMC, and compensate for that effect by communicating a great deal. Rule three is to *multitask* getting organized and generating substantive contributions. FtF groups tend to spend the first portion of their interaction defining a task, identifying its subcomponents, and allocating work among members (Gersick, 1988). Although these steps are important, a virtual group often "burns up" too much precious time trying to settle these issues, leaving insufficient time for the reading, fact-finding, writing, and integration of their substantive contributions that they need for successful task completion. Although jumping into substative work before a group settles who does what risks that there may be some duplication of effort, duplication of effort does not reduce the quality of a job, only its efficiency.

The fourth rule of virtual groups is *overtly acknowledge having read one another's messages*. In FtF group meetings one can be relatively certain that one's colleagues have heard what one says. Online, such certainty requires partners to reply explicitly. Not knowing whether partners have gotten one's message can lead to (false) assumptions that they got it and agreed, got it and didn't like it so said nothing, didn't get the message altogether, or that they have quit the project altogether. Needless to say, this kind of uncertainty is worrisome, and degenerates trust. Group members should reply that they have gotten a message, even if only to say that they will read it again and act on it at some specific time later. The fifth rule recommends *be explicit about what you are thinking and doing*. In FtF communication, one may nod, shake one's head, or turn away from others to signify disagreement. In CMC, one must learn to transform these vague forms of feedback into verbal statements in order for partners to understand one's reservations and take them into account in improving their work. Although people often feel they should not criticize one another verbally, in CMC there is no other method, and the expression of disagreement is critical to group decision-making. Finally, rule six suggests *make interim deadlines and stick to them*. Nothing tells a group that a member can be counted upon more than a member fulfilling commitments early on in a group's development; failing to meet a preliminary deadline signifies to everyone that they have been vulnerable to an unreliable partner.

Research has verified the utility of most of these rules. Walther and Bunz (2005) assigned a third of their four-member interuniversity student groups (whose task was to write an integrative synopsis of five research articles) to the rule, *communicate frequently*. That is, a significant proportion of these students' grades were determined by the frequency of their online communication with each other. Another third of the groups were assigned the *multitasking* rule. The final third of the groups were graded completely with respect to the quality of their paper, and had no specific rule assignment. Results showed that any groups with a rule assignment tended to follow all six rules more so than did groups with no rule assignment. Results also showed that adherence to each of the six rules for virtual groups was strongly correlated with the amount of trust members expressed toward their groups. Finally, following five of the six rules also predicted the quality of the groups' papers (with the multitasking rule affecting trust but not affecting paper quality).

These results have implications at a variety of levels. They demonstrate the utility of the rules for virtual groups, at one level. At another level they show that online groups can accommodate for the information gaps that CMC imposes, relative to FtF communication, by invoking alternative, compensatory behaviors. At another level, they show that virtual groups benefit from some kind of management—an authority or a set of structures that lead them to reflect certain group behaviors, from which they benefit. Traditionally research shows that offline groups, too, benefit from structured conversations such as meeting agendas and other interaction techniques (Poole, 1991; Sunwolf & Seibold, 1999). The *rules of virtual groups* seem especially suited to the particular information management needs of people working online.

Information Processing in Groups and the Effects of Distance on Social Influence

This chapter began by discussing the benefits of groups and of virtual, online groups in particular. These benefits included the notion that groups can make better decisions and solve complex problems more effectively than individuals can, by nature of the different perspectives and information that respective group members may have. Online groups, in particular, should capitalize on being able to include far-flung members from different locations contributing unique information. All of this is well and good provided that groups make effective use of disparate information. There is ample evidence, however, that group discussion in general inhibits effective exchange of information. The nature of distributed online groups complicates the question of who influences whom in online decision-making. This last section of the chapter focuses on two issues: How hidden profile exercises show some limitations on group decision-making, and second, how these dynamics are complicated when online groups are comprised of members at different locations.

The assumption that group members' unique contributions will lead to a better decision than any one individual would make alone depends on pooling the group's overall information elements, which are heterogeneous in at least some parts. In an examination of the pooling of information in decision-making groups, Stasser and his associates developed an experimental paradigm in which groups would seem almost certain to outperform individuals (e.g., Stasser & Titus, 1985). This "hidden profile paradigm" provides a method of studying group interaction experimentally, but in a way that resembles the kinds of information problems that real-world groups face when different members know different things. In a hidden profile exercise, groups can arrive at a correct decision only by pooling information that members individually have. Information sets are given to group members prior to discussion, such that each member sees a number of information bits favoring one alternative, and a majority of these bits are distributed to all members; all members see the same information favoring alternative #1. Also among the individuals' information sets, however, are unique pieces of information (i.e., information not known to other members) which favor a different decision alternative. If all information bits are exchanged, the preponderance of information would favor alternative #2 rather than alternative #1. When members do not pool critical information, however, the superiority of alternative #2 remains hidden, and the quality of decisions is poorer.

Despite the necessity of exchanging unique information, groups tend to discuss common information to a greater extent than unique information and therefore the superiority of the preferable alternative does not become evident to the group. A number of studies have shown that group discussions are dominated by commonly-held information (see Stasser, 1992; Wittenbaum & Stasser, 1996, for review). Not only is more common than unique information mentioned in group discussions, but once it has been mentioned, group members repeat common information more often than unique information.

The literature on information pooling in the hidden profile paradigm offers different explanations for poor information exchange. One explanation contends that it is simply, mathematically more probable for members to mention common information, and as a result, it has greater impact (Larson, Foster-Fishman, & Keys, 1994; Stasser, Taylor, & Hanna, 1989; Stasser & Titus, 1987). Alternatively, researchers attribute information exchange deficits to social-psychological processes such as mutual enhancement (Wittenbaum, Hubbell, & Zuckerman, 1999), in which people are more likely to notice and remember others' information which complements their own (misplaced) opinion. Another approach focuses on the biasing effect of members' initial preferences: According to Gigone and Hastie (1993, 1997), shared information has a large impact on the group members' initial, pre-discussion preferences, and these preferences, in turn, promote members' tendencies to consider additional information that supports their initial position, and disregard information that challenges it. Because common information is misleading, and, consequently, no group member can detect the best alternative on the basis of his or her individual information, group members typically enter the discussion with suboptimal decision preferences. Since group members do not like to change their initial preferences once they formed them, hidden profiles which lead to incorrect initial preferences also lead members to misinterpret new information that is inconsistent with their initial preferences (Brodbeck, Kerschreiter, Mojzisch, Frey, & Schulz-Hardt, 2002; Greitemeyer & Schulz-Hardt, 2003). Various strategies have been investigated that mitigate the deleterious effects of a hidden profile somewhat, but few interventions seem to diminish its effects completely.

Research on the effects of CMC in hidden profile discussions has produced mixed results. Some researchers suggested that CMC makes matters worse than FtF group discussions. Hollingshead (1996a, 1996b) suggested that a hidden profile discussion via CMC would result in even worse decisions than in FtF settings, by invoking the notion (which we have now encountered many times) that group members need nonverbal cues to be able to communicate effectively. Using a relatively short time period for FtF and CMC group discussions of a hidden profile case, Hollingshead (1996a) indeed found more reduced information exchange and poorer group decisions in CMC compared to FtF groups. She attributed these results to an "information suppression effect" where less information is shared when people are communicating through technology than when they are interacting face-to-face (Hollingshead, 1996b).

An alternative approach invoked SIP theory's notion that CMC groups require more time than FtF groups to communicate as effectively. Campbell and Stasser (2006) gave groups a hidden profile in a short FtF meeting, a short CMC meeting, or an hour-long CMC meeting. As they hypothesized, decisions were worse in the short CMC than in the short FtF meetings, but decisions in the long CMC meetings were superior to all the other conditions. Apparently time and technology are a good combination for mitigating the effects of hidden profile information dilemmas.

When members of a small group sit around a table, FtF, working on a decision-making problem like a hidden profile dilemma, at least they all know they are part of the same group, and they tend (somewhat wrongly) to assume they know the same things. These conditions and assumptions would seem to present a real dilemma for virtual groups that are comprised specifically to take advantage of having members in different places who have different information than one another. Do groups assume that people in the same location know the same things and that remote members know differently? Do virtual group members trust close members and distrust members who are farther away? Do these issues affect whose information and opinions they pay attention to as they make decisions? These questions about virtual groups were examined using hidden profile discussions in which one member had a set of information that differed substantially from the others, among several types of online groups: Completely colocated (all members from the same college), completely distributed (each member at a different college), or mixed (two members from one college, and other members at two other places) (Bazarova, Walther, & McLeod, 2012).

Previous research suggested a variety of different predictions about the patterns of influence in these virtual groups, that is, when the person with the minority information set would get the others to change their minds. The first predictions are about the potential influence on the group of an individual from a remote location who has unique information. One prediction, the *double-minority effect*, suggested that a member from a different location who also had information that suggested a different conclusion than other group members, is too different from others. Someone so unlike the rest of the group would be regarded negatively, and therefore such a person's information would be ignored. The double-minority effect would be that a when a person with a minority information set was at a remote location relative to others, that member would not influence the group.

A second prediction, based on *congruity theory*, made the opposite hypothesis: Because we expect people who are different from us to know different information than we do, we pay attention to people who are different. So when a member from a remote location offers information that is different from the rest of the group's, that member influences others' opinions (Phillips, 2003).

The next predictions regarded the influence of a minority opinion member who was colocated with at least one other group member. The *black sheep effect* occurs when we expect people who are similar to one another to agree with one another, and when someone who should be similar disagrees with her or his kind, that person is perceived by others as disloyal and disliked. In offline groups, the black sheep effect predicts that ingroup members "react so strongly against fellow group members who are deviant . . . often derogating and rejecting (deviant) ingroup members significantly more strongly than outgroup members" (Marques, Abrams, Paez, & Hogg, 2001, p. 400). Therefore, when a colocated member of a virtual groups expresses information that contradicts his her colocated partner, that person is not only uninfluential, she or he may invoke a boomerang effect and influence the group's opinion in the direction opposite of what the member is trying to advocate. Finally, a complex prediction is called the *minority contract leniency model* (Crano, 2001). This explanation suggests that when a similar (in this case, colocated) group member disagrees somewhat, but does not disagree to an extreme extent, others want to know why that individual is acting differently than they expected. In that case, the rest of the group pays particular attention to the "mild deviant" and, as a result, that member's information is especially influential.

The experiment using colocated, distributed, or mixed groups provided 2 weeks on an online discussion board to each group. Researchers established what each member's initial opinion was before the discussion, and after the discussion, and the researchers analyzed what information pieces were exchanged online in order to see whether minority members' information exchanges differed mildly or strongly from others' information. The results supported three of the four predictions.

When a minority information member was remote to others, the pattern consistent with the *congruity* prediction emerged, and not the *double-minority* hypothesis. Remote, minority information members influenced the groups' decisions, which, in a hidden profile, lead to better results.

When a minority information member was colocated to another member or all members, both the *minority leniency contract* model and the *black sheep effects* emerged. That is, when a colocated member offered some information that differed from others, the group's decision was influenced by that information; other members changed their opinions more, and the group made better decisions. However, when a colocated member wrote a great number of information items that differed with other members', the information was apparently rejected, and the other members' decisions were unaffected by the minority information set.

Obviously, the information the minority set members had was not of their own creation, and whether they were colocated to or distributed from others has no rational impact on the information's importance or utility. The manner in which other group members attended to or ignored the information reflects systematic biases to which virtual groups are subject, leading to different attributions rather than real differences about members.

Strong Ties, Weak Ties, Virtual Communities, and Coups

The discussion so far has focused on small groups and CMC. Although there is no specific number of members that makes a group small, we usually think of anywhere between a handful and a dozen or so people. Traditionally, this has been because this size provides for relatively easy communication. The Internet has changed what a group can be, and now immensely large groups—from dozens to hundreds or thousands—exchange information and guide their activities using CMC. New forms of social media, like Twitter and Facebook, allow CMC users to broadcast information widely, but in a way that focuses on specific topics which others can choose to track or follow. Arranging information transmission to anyone who wishes to receive it by organizing its dissemination following topics, rather than sending messages to specific persons, has enabled the creation of huge online collectives, or virtual communities. These communities exchange of information about specific issues, offer social support, and enable the coordination of social movements.

One of the advantages that virtual communities offer is the spread of information among "weak tie" social connections. The notion of strong ties and weak ties was developed by Grannovetter (1973), and they describe two different types of relationship one may have with others, at least in traditional (pre-Internet) settings. Strong ties are those people who spend time with one another and communicate directly with each other, like families and close friends. People in a network of strong ties tend to possess similar information and knowledge as one another. Weak ties, on the other hand, are other people who an individual does not know directly. Rather, they may be reached through an intermediary (such as a strong tie). In other words, a friend of your friend, who is not known directly to you, is a weak tie. Granovetter demonstrated that weak ties tend to have access to different kinds of information than one's network of close ties possesses, and therefore, connecting to weak tie(s) expands the flow of diverse information across different social groups.

With this notion in mind, researchers are beginning to understand the benefits of Facebook and similar social network sites. Although the broad classification of "friends" on Facebook does not distinguish strong from weak ties, one's aggregation of Facebook friends tends to contain both types. Although we tend to have met a vast majority of our Facebook friends in some offline context, many of these people are no longer close to us or in frequent contact; they now travel in different social circles than we do, and as a result they may be considered to reflect the properties of weak ties as discussed earlier, rather than strong ties. Research has demonstrated the number of Facebook friends one has is associated with one's self-reported level of social capital, that is, the feeling that one could find help and resources from others when needed (Steinfield, Ellison, & Lampe, 2008).

Aside from contacting one's own friends, the Internet, some researchers argue, now functions as the intermediary between an individual and his or her prospective weak ties (e.g., Wellman & Gulia, 1996). That is, rather than asking one's friends if they have friends who might provide information one needs or who might feel like-minded about a social issue, individuals can now search the Internet for communication about the topic of concern, and discover a virtual community discussing the topic. Because the participants in those communities are not personally known to each other, and travel in different social circles, they tend to converge on topics about which they feel strongly (rather than connect for interpersonal reasons) and they possess diverse information on the topic, as weak ties tend to do.

These kinds of online groups take many forms. One of these forms is online social support groups, a phenomenon occupying a separate chapter in this volume. The most recent form of virtual communities are flash mobs and protest groups. A flash mob is a group of people who plan via social media to converge on a specific location. Sometimes these mobs do nothing more than amuse and entertain, by breaking into a song or performance in a public place such as a train station. In other versions, a flash mob meets to launch a protest or cause disruption. Numerous reports suggest that the "Arab Spring" revolts in several Middle Eastern countries in 2011—the Tunisian revolt that toppled its government, the coup in Cairo that deposed Egypt's president, the Libyan uprising that removed its dictator from power, and elsewhere—were originally organized as flash mobs. Leaders send messages via mobile media telling people where to converge and when, and to call for reinforcements if needed. For instance, if police meet protestors in a specific location and in sufficient number to suppress the protest, protestors use social media to draw other protesters from other locations in order to outnumber police. Such anecdotes describing the utility of social media have emerged from protests and "occupy" efforts (like Occupy Wall Street) around the world (see for review, Wasik, 2012). At the same time, authorities are aware of these Internet-based efforts as well. One strategy to suppress a protest in San Francisco in 2011 involved suspending cell phone and Internet capability in the city's subway system, which had been suspected to be the target for social unrest (Murphy, 2011).

Last Word

Research continues to explore the benefits and the tribulations that CMC brings to group discussions. There seems to be a tendency for new technologies to develop that offer more and more features that resemble FtF communication. Yet audioconferencing and videoconferencing systems are hardly new at all, and each has a spotty history in research on their respective effectiveness (see Gergle, Kraut, & Fussell, 2004). Obviously more cues or interfaces more like FtF are not the answer to the challenges of online group communication. Learning what biases to expect, how to dissipate them, and how to encourage groups to adapt most effectively to CMC systems—as this chapter has tried to highlight—may offer more promise in the long run.

Acknowledgments

The author wishes to thank Poppy McLeod, Natalya Bazarova, and Ulla Bunz for their contributions to the research described in this chapter.

References

Antheunis, M. L., Valkenburg, P. M., & Peter, J. (2010). Getting acquainted through social network sites: Testing a model of online uncertainty reduction and social attraction. *Computers in Human Behavior*, 26, 100–109.

Bales, R. F. (1950). A set of categories for the analysis of small group interaction. *American Sociological Review*, 15, 257–263.

Bazarova, N. N., Walther, J. B., & McLeod, P. L. (2012). Minority influence in computer-mediated groups: A comparison of four theories of minority influence. *Communication Research*, 39, 295–316.

Brodbeck, F. C., Kerschreiter, R., Mojzisch, A., Frey, D., & Schulz-Hardt, S. (2002). The dissemination of critical, unshared information in decision-making groups: The effects of prediscussion dissent. *European Journal of Social Psychology*, 32, 35–56.

Campbell, J., & Stasser, G. (2006). The influence of time and task demonstrability on decision-making in computer-mediated and face-to-face groups. *Small Group Research, 37,* 271–294.

Crano, W. D. (2001). Social influence, social identity, and ingroup leniency. In C. K. W. de Dreu & N. K. de Vries (Eds.), *Group consensus and minority influence: Implications for innovation* (pp. 122–143). Oxford, UK: Blackwell.

Derks, D., Bos, A. E. R., & von Grumbkow, J. (2007). Emoticons and social interaction on the Internet: The importance of social context. *Computers in Human Behavior, 23,* 842–849.

Gergle, D., Kraut, R. E., & Fussell, S. R. (2004). Language efficiency and visual technology: Minimizing collaborative effort with visual information. *Journal of Language and Social Psychology, 23,* 491–517.

Gersick, C. J. G. (1988). Time and transition in work teams: Toward a new model of group development. *Academy of Management Journal, 31,* 9–41.

Gigone, D., & Hastie, R. (1993). The common knowledge effect: Information sharing and group judgment. *Journal of Personality and Social Psychology, 65,* 959–974.

Gigone, D., & Hastie, R. (1997). The impact of information on small group choice. *Journal of Personality and Social Psychology, 72,* 132–140.

Grannovetter, M. S. (1973). The strength of weak ties. *American Journal of Sociology, 78,* 1360–1380.

Greitemeyer, T., & Schulz-Hardt, S. (2003). Preference-consistent evaluation of information in the hidden profile paradigm: Beyond group-level explanations for the dominance of shared information in group decisions. *Journal of Personality and Social Psychology, 84,* 322–339.

Handy, C. (1995). Trust and the virtual organization. *Harvard Business Review, 73*(3), 40–50.

Hian, L. B., Chuan, S. L., Trevor, T. M. K., & Detenber, B. H. (2004). Getting to know you: Exploring the development of relational intimacy in computer-mediated communication. *Journal of Computer-Mediated Communication, 9*(3). Retrieved January 3, 2007 from http://jcmc.indiana.edu/vol9/issue3/detenber.html

Hiltz, S.R., Johnson, K., & Turoff, M. (1986). Experiments in group decision making: Communication process and outcome in face-to-face versus computerized conferences. *Human Communication Research, 13,* 225–252.

Hoffman, L., & Maier, N. R. F. (1961). Quality and acceptance of problem solving by mere bets of homogeneous and heterogeneous groups. *Journal of Abnormal and Social Psychology, 62,* 401–407.

Hollingshead, A. B. (1996a). The rank-order effect in group decision making. *Organizational Behavior and Human Decision Processes, 68,* 181–193.

Hollingshead, A. B. (1996b). Information suppression and status persistence in group decision making: The effects of communication media. *Human Communication Research, 23,* 193–219.

Iacono, C. S., & Weisband, S. (1997, January). *Developing trust in virtual teams.* Paper presented at the 30th Hawaii International Conference on System Sciences, Maui, HI.

Jarvenpaa, S. L., & Leidner, D. E. (1998). Communication and trust in global virtual teams. *Journal of Computer-Mediated Communication, 3*(4). Retrieved from http://jcmc.indiana.edu/vol3/issue4/jarvenpaa.html

Kiesler, S., Siegel, J., & McGuire, T. W. (1984). Social psychological aspects of computer-mediated communication. *American Psychologist, 39,* 1123–1134.

Larson, J. R., Jr., Foster-Fishman, P. G., & Keys, C. B. (1994). Discussion of shared and unshared information in decision-making groups. *Journal of Personality and Social Psychology, 67,* 446–461.

Lea, M., Spears, R., Watt, S. E., & Rogers, P. (2000). The InSIDE story: Social psychological processes affecting on-line groups. In T. Postmes, M. Lea, R. Spears, & S. D. Reicher (Eds.), *SIDE issues centre stage: Recent developments in studies of de-individuation in groups* (pp. 47–62). Amsterdam, the Netherlands: KNAW.

Lea, M., Spears, R., & de Groot, D. (2001). Knowing me, knowing you: Anonymity effects on group polarization in CMC within groups. *Personality and Social Psychology Bulletin, 27,* 526–537.

Marques, J. M., Abrams, D., Paez, D., & Hogg, M. A. (2001). Social categorization, social identification, and rejection of deviant group members. In M. A. Hogg & S. Tindale (Eds.), *Blackwell handbook of social psychology: Group processes* (pp. 400–424). Malden, MA: Blackwell.

Mayer, R. C., Davis, J. H., & Schoorman, F. D. (1995). An integrative model of organizational trust. *Academy of Management Review, 20,* 709–734.

McCroskey, J., & McCain, T. (1974). The measurement of interpersonal attraction. *Speech Monographs, 41,* 261–266.

McGrath, J. (1984). *Groups: Interaction and performance.* Englewood Cliffs, NJ: Prentice-Hall.

Meyerson, D., Weick, K. E., & Kramer, R. M. (1996). Swift trust and temporary groups. In R. M. Kramer & T. R. Tyler (Eds.), *Trust in organizations: Frontiers of theory and research* (pp. 166–195). Thousand Oaks, CA: Sage.

Murphy, D. (2011, August 13). To prevent protests, San Francisco subway turns off cell signals. *PCMag.com.* Retrieved from http://www.pcmag.com/article2/0,2817,2391046,00.asp

Nemeth, C. (1986). Differential contributions of majority and minority influence. *Psychological Review, 93,* 23–32.

Peter, J., Valkenburg, P. M., & Schouten, A. P. (2005). Developing a model of adolescent friendship formation on the Internet. *Cyberpsychology and Behavior, 8,* 423–430.

Phillips, K. W. (2003). The effects of categorically based expectations on minority influence: The importance of congruence. *Personality and Social Psychology Bulletin, 29,* 3–13.

Poole, M. S. (1991). Procedures for managing meetings: Social and technological innovation. In R. A. Swanson & B. O. Knapp (Eds.), *Innovative meeting management* (pp. 53–109). Austin, TX: 3M Meeting Management Institute.

Ramirez, A., Jr., Zhang, S., McGrew, K., & Lin, S.-F. (2007). Relational communication in computer-mediated interaction: A comparison of participant-observer perspectives. *Communication Monographs, 74,* 492–516.

Reid, F. J. M., Ball, L. J., Morley, A. M., & Evans, J. S. B. T. (1997). Styles of group discussion in computer-mediated decision making. *British Journal of Social Psychology, 36,* 241–262.

Schweiger, D. M. & Sandberg, W. R. (1989). The utilization of individual capabilities in group approaches to strategic decision making. *Strategic Management Journal, 10,* 31–43.

Schweiger, D. M., Sandberg, W. R. & Ragan, J.W. (1986). Group approaches for improving strategic decision making: A comparative analysis of dialectical inquiry, devil's advocacy, and consensus. *Academy of Management Journal, 29,* 51–71.

Siegel, J., Dubrovsky, V., Kiesler, S., & Mcguire, T. W. (1986). Group processes in computer-mediated communication. *Organizational Behavior and Human Decision Processes, 37,* 157–187.

Stasser, G. (1992). Information salience and the discovery of hidden profiles by decision-making groups: A "thought experiment." *Organizational Behavior and Human Decision Processes, 52,* 156–181.

Stasser, G., Taylor, L. A., & Hanna, C. (1989). Information sampling in structured and unstructured discussions of three- and six-person groups. *Journal of Personality and Social Psychology, 57,* 67–78.

Stasser, G., & Titus, W. (1985). Pooling of unshared information in group decision making: Biased information sampling during discussions. *Journal of Personality and Social Psychology, 48,* 1467–1478.

Stasser, G., & Titus, W. (1987). Effects of information load and percentage of common information on the dissemination of unique information during group decision making. *Journal of Personality and Social Psychology, 53,* 81–93.

Steinfield, C., Ellison, N. B., & Lampe, C. (2008). Social capital, self-esteem, and use of online social network sites: A longitudinal analysis. *Journal of Applied Developmental Psychology 29,* 434–445.

Sunwolf, & Seibold, D. R. (1999). The impact of formal procedures on group processes, members, and task outcomes. In L. Frey, D. S. Gouran, & M. S. Poole (Eds.), *The handbook of group communication theory and research* (pp. 395–431). Thousand Oaks, CA: Sage.

Triandis, H. C., Hall, E. R. & Ewen, R. B. (1965). Member homogeneity and dyadic creativity. *Human Relations*, *18*, 33–54.

Walther, J. B. (1992). Interpersonal effects in computer-mediated interaction: A relational perspective. *Communication Research*, *19*, 52–90.

Walther, J. B. (1993). Impression development in computer-mediated interaction. *Western Journal of Communication*, *57*, 381–398.

Walther, J. B. (1996). Computer-mediated communication: Impersonal, interpersonal, and hyperpersonal interaction. *Communication Research*, *23*, 3–43.

Walther, J. B., & Bunz, U. (2005). The rules of virtual groups: Trust, liking, and performance in computer-mediated communication. *Journal of Communication*, *55*, 828–846.

Walther, J. B., & Carr, C. T. (2010). Internet interaction and intergroup dynamics: Problems and solutions in computer-mediated communication. In H. Giles, S. Reid, & J. Harwood (Eds.), *The dynamics of intergroup communication* (pp. 209–220). New York, NY: Peter Lang.

Walther, J. B., Loh, T., & Granka, L. (2005). Let me count the ways: The interchange of verbal and nonverbal cues in computer-mediated and FtF affinity. *Journal of Language and Social Psychology*, *24*, 36–65.

Wang, Z., Walther, J. B., & Hancock, J. T. (2009). Social identification and interpersonal communication in computer-mediated communication: What you do versus who you are in virtual groups. *Human Communication Research*, *35*, 59–85.

Wasik, B. (2012). Crowd control. *WIRED*, *20*(1), 76–83, 112–113.

Weisband, S., & Atwater, L. (1999). Evaluating self and others in electronic and face-to-face groups. *Journal of Applied Psychology*, *84*, 632–639.

Wellman, B., & Gulia, M. (1996). Net surfers don't ride alone: Virtual communities as communities. In M. A. Smith & P. Kollack (Eds.), *Communities in cyberspace* (pp. 167–194). Berkeley, CA: University of California Press.

Wilson, J. M., Straus, S. G., & McEvily, W. J. (2006). All in due time: The development of trust in computer-mediated and face-to-face groups. *Organizational Behavior and Human Decision Processes*, *99*, 16–33.

Wittenbaum, G. M., Hubbell, A. P., & Zuckerman, C. (1999). Mutual enhancement: Toward an understanding of the collective preference for shared information. *Journal of Personality and Social Psychology*, *77*, 967–978.

Wittenbaum, G. M., & Stasser, G. (1996). Management of information in small groups. In J. L. Nye & A. M. Brower (Eds.), *What's social about social cognition? Research on socially shared cognition in small groups* (pp. 3–28). Thousand Oaks, CA: Sage.

Chapter 10

Leadership within Virtual Contexts

Crystal L. Hoyt

Introduction

Leadership is a critical component of group life, one necessary for directing the behavior of group members in pursuit of common goals. Using social influence processes, leaders transform the individual action of group members into collective action in pursuit of common goals (Chemers, 2000). Scholars throughout history, from early philosophers to more contemporary social scientists, have set out to explore the nature of effective leadership. At present, the context in which leadership occurs is rapidly changing, thus opening up a new frontier for leadership researchers (Avolio, Kahai, & Dodge, 2000; Zaccaro & Klimoski, 2002). The ever-increasing use of information and communication technologies allows people, organizations, and ideas to be interconnected while spanning geographic boundaries. These changes bring with them exciting opportunities as well as new challenges and questions regarding leadership. Given the vital role of leadership in group and organizational life, empirical investigations into leadership within this new virtual context are indispensable (Weisband, 2008) yet in surprisingly short supply (Fjermestad, Kahai, Zhang, & Avolio, 2007).

The goal of this chapter is to provide an overview of leadership within virtual contexts by focusing on relevant theories and empirical research. First, I start by reviewing some of the changes, opportunities, and challenges for leadership ushered in with the proliferation of advanced information technologies. Next, I briefly review classic theories of leadership in traditional face-to-face (FtF) contexts followed by a review of various theories relevant to leadership within virtual contexts. After the theoretical review, I turn to overviewing the extant empirical research examining leadership within virtual contexts. Finally, I end with a brief discussion of other promising theoretical approaches for future research in this cutting-edge field of research.

The New Virtual Age: Changes, Challenges, and Opportunities

Organizations have been decentralized by the advent of virtual technologies. This has given new opportunities to and placed new demands upon leaders. Leaders are more frequently charged with leading virtual groups, groups of individuals who are geographically dispersed and who are using electronic communication to work together. The leadership literature clearly shows that the effects of leadership vary across situations (Howell, Dorfman, & Kerr, 1986; Podsakoff, Mackenzie, Ahearne, & Bommer, 1995), thus making it imperative to gain a better understanding of how the changes brought about by these new and varying virtual contexts influence leadership effectiveness. Avolio et al. (2000) chose the term e-leadership to refer to leadership in these new virtual contexts driven by advanced information technologies. They define e-leadership as "a social influence process mediated by advanced information technologies to produce a change in attitudes, feelings, thinking, behavior, and/or performance with individuals, groups, and/or organizations" (p. 617).

The proliferation of advanced information technologies, ranging from the use of email to the use of computer-mediated virtual groups that are dispersed over location and time, brings with it a number of changes that have the potential to influence how effective leadership is practiced (Avolio & Kahai, 2003; Kahai & Avolio, 2004). The changes to our communication processes brought about from these technologies range from minor to fundamental, with messages being spread faster and broader than ever, thus helping break down the geographical and organizational boundaries that were once present. This offers the potential for developing greater social capital, or the quality of social relationships that people form in their working environment (Zaccaro & Bader, 2003). Leaders now have greater contact with their followers. However, the nature of this contact has changed. With people meeting virtually, as opposed to FtF, they can find themselves in virtual meetings with individuals they have never met in person and leaders can have difficulty monitoring group members' behaviors. These changes have brought about greater access to information which can lead to more transparency throughout organizations and alter the influence of leaders as well as power relations amongst individuals. This can ultimately lead to a migration of leadership both lower within an organization and beyond the boundaries of the organization.

These and other changes brought about by new information technologies can present a number of challenges for leaders (Cascio & Shurygailo, 2003). Many of the functions of leadership in traditional FtF settings may need to be redefined in these new settings. Leaders in these new virtual workplaces need to work on establishing new norms and procedures both for their groups as well as themselves, particularly as it pertains to boundaries between work and home. It can be difficult for leaders to monitor progress toward goals in these new virtual environments. One of the biggest challenges for e-leaders is establishing trust and cultivating cohesion with and amongst their group members who are not physically colocated (Cascio & Shurygailo, 2003; Zaccaro & Bader, 2003). In addition to this, effective leaders in virtual contexts must serve as the liaison, direction setter, and operational coordinator of the group (Zaccaro & Bader, 2003). Doing so entails effectively coordinating and integrating team members, cultivating efficacy as well as shared understandings of the task, promoting information and idea sharing, managing team conflict and affect, and nurturing social and human capital among the team members.

Theoretical Approaches to Leadership: A Brief Review

There is a long history to the social scientific study of leadership (Hoyt, Goethals, & Forsyth, 2008; Northouse, 2010). This rich body of research attempts to uncover the traits, abilities, behaviors, and/or situational factors that contribute to leadership effectiveness (Yukl, 2002). Over the years both the conceptualization of leadership and the corresponding research approaches have evolved greatly (Hunt, 1999). Here I briefly review the broad strokes of the evolution of leadership studies.

The Great Person Approach

The first social scientists interested in scientifically studying leadership apparently took their cue from great philosophers such as Plato and Plutarch by asking what traits and characteristics make an individual fit for leadership. This great person, or trait, approach wherein theorists sought personality, social, physical, or intellectual traits and skills that differentiated leaders from nonleaders was dominant for several decades. For example, compared to nonleaders, leaders were often assumed to be more intelligent, taller, more self-confident, to have a greater need for achievement, and to come from a higher social status. This approach can be seen in many biographical and autobiographical accounts of great leaders and it contributes to a "common sense" approach to leadership which suggests that leaders must have certain traits to be effective. Contemporary leadership theorists who have revisited the importance of traits and skills generally agree that while certain crucial traits or skills alone are not enough to make an effective leader, they are indeed an important precondition for effective leadership (Northouse, 2010; Yukl, 2002). The reemergence of this perspective has been associated with more sophisticated models as well as acknowledgments of the deficiencies in this approach (Zaccaro, 2007).

The Behavioral Approach

Next, for a variety of reasons, including the growing emphasis on studying observable behaviors in psychology, scholars began taking a look at what leaders *actually do*. Taking a behavioral approach, researchers stress the importance of the constancy and predictability of the leader's behavior across leadership situations. Some of the first and most well-known studies focused on comparing authoritarian, democratic, and laissez-faire leadership styles (Lewin, Lippitt & White, 1939). These styles vary in the extent to which the leader is involved in making decisions: From being the primary decision-maker (authoritarian), to involving the group members (democratic), to having minimal involvement in decision-making (laissez-faire). The most prominent behavioral leadership studies were those undertaken by the University of Michigan and by Ohio State University. Interestingly, both lines of research, conducted concurrently and independently, arrived at similar conclusions. Both research camps concluded that leadership behaviors could be classified into two groups: Task- and relationship-oriented behaviors. In general, task-oriented behaviors are focused on facilitating goal achievement whereas relationship-oriented behaviors are focused on developing positive interpersonal relationships. Although there are certainly limitations to this approach—for example, it might not effectively describe leader behaviors in more collectivist societies (Ayman & Chemers 1983)—this line of research has contributed to our understanding of leadership in a number of ways and has clearly identified the importance of both task and relationship behaviors for effective leadership (Fleishman & Harris, 1962; Yukl, 2002).

The Situational Contingency Perspectives

The behavioral approach gave way to the integrative situational contingency perspective after a number of researchers began calling for a more inclusive approach to understanding leadership by examining situational factors, such as task requirements, situational constraints, or type of work group, when determining which leader behaviors (or traits) will be most effective. Thus, leadership theorists began moving from the simplistic leader-centric models to more complex models attempting to understand the relationship between behaviors (or traits) and situations. For example, Fiedler's Contingency Model (Fiedler, 1964) suggests that whereas task-oriented leaders are most effective in extreme situations (either favorable or unfavorable), relationship-oriented leaders are most effective in moderately favorable situations. Other prominent contingency models include Path–Goal Theory (House & Mitchell, 1974), Hersey–Blanchard Situational Theory (Hersey & Blanchard, 1969), and Cognitive Resources Theory (Fiedler & Garcia, 1987). The primary assumption of the various models is that the effectiveness of the various behaviors or traits of leaders is dependent on the requirements of the particular leadership situation, and this framework still dominates a large portion of leadership research. This approach has expanded our understanding of leadership by acknowledging that there is no single best way to lead, different behaviors and traits are more and less effective in various situations, and that people can learn to be effective leaders. The very premise of this chapter, examining leadership within virtual contexts, is grounded in the situational approach.

The Relational Perspectives

Another approach to understanding leadership emphasizes the relationship between leaders and followers (Hoyt & Goethals, 2010). Edwin Hollander's (1993) exchange theory of leadership maintains that leaders and followers provide benefits to each other. In exchange for leader competence and conformity, followers give leaders legitimacy, or idiosyncrasy credits, allowing them some credit to deviate or innovate on behalf of the group. Tom Tyler (Tyler & Lind, 1992) contends that a leader's legitimacy is largely dependent on "procedural justice": treating followers fairly regardless of actual instrumental advantages. Graen and colleagues' (Graen & Uhl-Bien, 1995) Leader–Member Exchange (LMX) theory identifies the leader–member dyadic relationship as the fundamental component of the leadership process. According to LMX theory, the dyadic relationships between leaders and followers are important; high-quality relationships are associated with a great variety of positive outcomes including enhanced organizational performance, job satisfaction, and career progress.

Transformational and Transactional Leadership

Fueled by a focus on leader–follower relationships as the heart of leadership, there was a paradigm shift in the 1970s to "new leadership" (Conger, 1999; Hunt, 1999). This shift was aided by House's (1977) work on charismatic leadership and Burns's (1978) now classic work on leadership which had a profound impact on the field of leadership studies by introducing two new concepts: Transactional and transforming leadership. Originally articulated as transforming leadership (Burns, 1978) but later expanded and substantially modified into transformational leadership (Bass, 1985), this complex and powerful style of leadership focuses on motivating, mentoring, inspiring, and empowering followers to fully develop their abilities to contribute to their organization. This approach to understanding leadership investigates processes that transform followers' views of themselves and their work, and it spotlights the important role of follower emotions and leader–follower relationships (Chemers, 1997; Hunt, 1999). Transformational leadership is often contrasted with transactional leadership, which focuses on exchanges between leaders and followers focusing on the followers' self-interest, such as a business leader rewarding an employee's excellent performance with a large bonus. Substantial empirical evidence highlights the role of both transformational and transactional leadership in leadership effectiveness, although the relationship with transformational leadership is stronger (Bass, 1990, 1997; Lowe, Kroeck, & Sivasubramaniam, 1996).

Theoretical Approaches to Leadership in Virtual Contexts

I now turn to briefly reviewing a variety of theories, including theories focused on communication and advanced technologies, which are relevant to understanding leadership within virtual contexts.

Adaptive Structuration Theory

Adaptive structuration theory (DeSanctis & Poole, 1994) is an adaptation of Giddens's (1979) structuration theory, which attempts to move beyond the dualism of structure (fixed aspects of our social institutions) versus agency (capacity for volitional individual action) when explaining human behavior by acknowledging the importance of both. Structuration theory maintains that human action is at least in part determined by the rules and norms that govern the pre-existing social structures in the context where the action takes place. This human action, in turn, can reaffirm, modify, or even transform social structure, making social structure both the instrument and outcome of social action. The context in which groups interact is defined by many structures from a variety of sources including the environment, the group task, as well as advanced technology. Adaptive structuration theory was developed by researchers in an attempt to understand the interaction of groups using advanced information technology. According to this theory, the perceptions that users have regarding the role and utility of the technology can influence how the technology is used and ultimately group outcomes. Group process is determined by the nature of how people interpret and use the structures (termed appropriation). Appropriations that are consistent with the spirit of the technology, promote positive attitudes, and help the group in task attainment are most likely to result in positive group outcomes.

Avolio et al. (2000) developed a broad conceptual framework for research on leadership processes in virtual contexts based on adaptive structuration theory. In their framework, they consider a group's internal system another social structure. A group's internal system includes factors such as leadership style, group member relations, members' expertise, perceptions of others and the group, shared mental models, identification with the group, and diversity of membership, experience, and backgrounds. According to Avolio et al., leadership can be viewed as a subsystem of a larger social organizational system and this subsystem can be seen as a source of structures that guide group member actions. The system of leadership encompasses the quality of interactions between leaders and followers (Graen & Uhl-Bien, 1995), people's lay, or implicit, theories regarding what constitutes leadership (Lord & Maher, 1991), group interactions (Sivasubramaniam, Murry, Avolio, & Jung, 2002), the leadership culture (House & Aditya, 1997), as well as both individual and collective leadership behavior throughout levels of organizations (Avolio, 1999). This framework highlights the importance of examining the interconnectedness of leadership with the virtual information technologies within a greater social organizational system.

Zaccaro's Model of Leadership and Virtual Team Processes

Zaccaro, Ardison, and Orvis (2004) offer another model of leader–team dynamics within virtual contexts. According to Zaccaro, Rittman, and Marks (2001), leaders are effective by influencing five team processes; leaders influence motivational processes (members' choices regarding task engagement and the resources put forth), affective processes (expression of emotion and affect), cognitive processes (collective information processing, transactive memory, and generating shared knowledge), coordination processes (synchronization of activities), and boundary spanning processes (outreach and environmental scanning activities). According to this model of leadership and virtual team processes, various aspects of working in a virtual context can influence how leaders help manage these processes including the geographic and temporal dispersion of the team members, the duration of the team's existence, and the level of technological sophistication. These characteristics of virtual group life can have a particularly important influence on the collective motivation of the team that stems from the team's cohesion, collective efficacy, and trust. Importantly, these characteristics of working virtually have the potential to both impair and improve group processes and organizational effectiveness. Accordingly, Zaccaro et al. (2004) offer a number of prescriptions for effectively leading virtual teams such as recommending that these leaders focus on developing quick trust and encouraging complete exchange of information amongst group members.

Social Identity Model of Deindividuation Effects

This next model offers a perspective on group functioning and leadership within virtual contexts that provide for anonymity. The social identity model of deindividuation effects (Reicher, Spears,

Postmes, 1995; Spears & Lea, 1994) advances an alternative explanation for the effects of anonymity and deindividuation offered in the traditional deindividuation model (Diener, 1979; Festinger, Pepitone, & Newcomb, 1952). The traditional views of deindividuation claim that when individuals are anonymous and deindividuated, they are fully immersed in the group, they feel low accountability, have low self-awareness, and are more likely to behave anti-normatively. A meta-analysis of the literature, however, revealed little support for either the occurrence of anti-normative behavior or the existence of the proposed deindividuated state. Rather, the findings support the social identity model of deindividuation effects by showing that when individuals and groups are "deindividuated" they conform more to local norms. According to this model, anonymity can result in depersonalization where people do not have information regarding others in the group and this dearth of information results in people being more sensitive to information about their personal or their social identity (Postmes & Spears, 1998; Spears, Postmes, Lea, & Watt, 2001). If the information makes a social identity salient, individuals will be more likely to behave in accordance with group norms and standards whereas information highlighting individuality will result in people adhering to their internal personal standards and norms. For example, when social, rather than personal, identities are salient in deindividuated settings, group members are more likely to shift their individual opinions in the direction of the perceived attitude of the group at large. Thus, anonymity can change the relative salience of one's personal or social identity, resulting in important effects on behavior.

This perspective points to the importance of leadership in virtual, particularly anonymous, settings. There are a number of leadership approaches suggesting that it is precisely those challenging, confusing, and uncertain situations that present prime opportunities for leaders to have a notable impact. For example, Shamir and Howell (1999) as well as Waldman and Yammarino (1999) suggest that weak and uncertain situations provide the opportunity for charismatic and transformational leaders to be particularly influential. They can do so by inspiring and motivating their followers, instilling confidence in them, and appealing to their self-concepts and values. Furthermore, Sosik, Avolio, and Kahai (1997) argue that transformational leaders' focus on collective action can work to make collective, rather than individual, identities salient.

Media Richness Theory

Another theoretical approach to understanding how virtual contexts can influence leadership is media richness theory. According to Daft and Lengel (1986) the richness of a medium refers to the ability of that medium to enable people to develop a shared understanding in ambiguous situations. Rich communication mediums allow for quicker shared understanding to be developed by way of capacity for immediate feedback, number of cues available, language variety, and degree to which intent is focused on the recipient. For example, an online threaded discussion is considered a very lean medium whereas a FtF interaction is deemed a rich medium. Originally this theory purported that a medium had a set level of richness. However, empirical studies have provided mixed support. In response to the inconsistent findings, researchers began to examine social factors that can contribute to the effectiveness of various media. Researchers have shown, for example, how lean media can provide for rich interactions amongst people who know each other. Walther (1995) showed how the exchange of information over lean media became as effective as richer media over time. In a similar vein, Chidambaram (1996) found that the perceived social presence amongst group members communicating via text-based technology increased as people spent greater time with their communication partners. In a theoretical extension of media richness theory, Carlson and Zmud (1999) proposed channel expansion theory. This theory contends that the following experiential factors can lead to higher perceived media richness: Experience with the medium, the communication topic, the communication partners, and the organizational context. Media richness theory and its extensions provide important insights for understanding leadership in virtual contexts. Indeed, according to adaptive structuration theory (Avolio et al., 2000), media richness can influence the appropriation of new technology. Furthermore, a leadership style that focuses on making group identities salient (such as transformational leadership; see the "Social Identity Model of Deindividuation Effects" section) becomes even more important in lean media, rather than rich media, contexts. Varying levels of media richness ultimately create different situations with which leaders must contend (Huang, Kahai, & Jestice, 2010).

Empirical Research Examining Leadership in Virtual Contexts

Although virtual technologies have placed new opportunities as well as new demands on leadership practices, the study of leadership within these virtual settings is still very much in its infancy. There is a significantly larger literature examining group processes and development within virtual contexts from which we can generalize implications for leaders. However, this chapter will center exclusively on research focusing on leadership. Researchers have taken a variety of approaches to studying leadership in virtual contexts (Avolio et al., 2000). These approaches range from field research comparing processes and outcomes across groups that already have structures and leaders to experimental research involving controlled laboratory studies. Furthermore, research in the field ranges from simply collecting survey data to manipulating factors such as leadership. Similarly, in the laboratory a variety of factors have been manipulated including the presence of leadership, the style of leadership, the context (virtual or FtF) of the group interaction, and other situational and contextual variables.

The research presented in this section is organized as follows: First, I review research examining the impact of leadership on group interactions and effectiveness within virtual contexts by presenting research undertaken in the field as well as experimental investigations. Next, I turn to reviewing the ample research investigating a particular theoretical approach to leadership: Transformational leadership. After considering how transformational leadership influences a variety of leadership outcomes in virtual contexts, I discuss the literature examining transformational leadership across contexts. Finally, I end by reviewing research on leadership within virtual contexts that takes sundry theoretical approaches.

Leadership in Virtual Contexts: Research Explorations in the Field

Some researchers have set out to simply establish the importance of leadership in virtual environments. In one study examining groups with existing structures and leaders, Harmon, Schneer, and Hoffman (1995) investigated the impact of information technology (audio-conferencing) on group decision performance as well as the status structure, and thus the leadership, of well-established decision teams. This initial research supported the important role that leaders can have in virtual contexts by showing that the group structure and the leader's influence remained stable across virtual and FtF contexts. Indeed, leaders can play a significant role in ensuring group success in virtual contexts. In another study showing the relevance of leadership in virtual groups, Butler, Sproull, Kiesler, and Kraut (2008) examined intact virtual groups by contacting Internet listserve leaders and members. Although both leaders and members contributed to community building work, leaders made more contributions toward sustaining successful online groups. Furthermore, in addition to playing an important role in maintaining the infrastructure, leaders also played a prominent role in social community building.

Other researchers have set out to investigate what makes for effective leader behaviors in virtual contexts. Hambley, O'Neill, and Kline (2007) used qualitative techniques in a descriptive field study examining intact virtual groups and their results reveal four important findings relevant to virtual group leader effectiveness. First, it was clear that strong leadership is critical in virtual teams. Second, it is crucial for leaders to run effective, regular, and well-organized team meetings. Next, developing strong social relationships and cohesion amongst group members is essential. Finally, the leader and group members need to learn how to use various media effectively and the leader needs to set the norms for their use. In another field study dedicated to studying a 20-month collaboration amongst engineers, Bradner and Mark (2008) found that from the perspective of team leaders, one important predictor of success of the virtual collaboration is a FtF interaction at the beginning of the collaboration. In addition, identifying interdependencies amongst group members helps the leaders coordinate themselves as well as the team.

Another approach to studying leadership in the field is to assign leaders to virtual groups and analyze the behaviors of the leaders in concert with their relative effectiveness. Using this approach, Kayworth and Leidner (2002) examined leaders in 13 global teams. In their research the most effective leaders displayed high levels of behavioral complexity. Specifically, the effective leaders were able to express empathy and serve as effective mentors while at the same time effectively asserting their authority. These leaders communicated with their followers on a regular basis and were prompt and detailed in their communications. In addition, they made all members' roles and responsibilities in the group clear. The importance of effective communication for leaders of virtual groups has also been underscored by the research of Cummings (2008). Studying 129 work groups in a global organization, he found that within-group communication by the leader plays an important role in group effectiveness and that leaders can help mitigate the negative consequences of geographic dispersion by ensuring frequent informal contact.

Leadership can take on many forms in virtual contexts from one centralized leader to a greater dispersion of leadership throughout group members. The importance of centralized versus decentralized leadership can depend on many factors including the goals and size of the virtual groups. Examining online communities designed to respond to the disaster following Hurricane Katrina, Torrey et al. (2008) found a difference in leadership amongst small blog communities and large forums. The small blog communities had a centralized leader and were successful more immediately in terms of developing trust and managing information compared to the more decentralized large forums. However, the larger forums were longer lasting groups; the moderated blogs began to dissolve once the moderator turned her or his attention away from the blog.

In sum, these basic field studies confirm the importance of leadership in virtual contexts: Existing leadership and group structures can persist in virtual environments and leadership, whether centralized or decentralized, can play a critical role in group success. Leaders who are effective in these environments focus on giving structure and organization to their group in part by making sure roles and responsibilities are clear, frequently and regularly communicate with group members, and they ensure all members can effectively engage with the technology. Furthermore, effective leaders need to focus on the socioemotional needs of their group members and tactics such as meeting FtF before using advanced information technologies can be useful to that end.

Leadership in Virtual Contexts: Experimental Explorations of Group Interactions and Effectiveness

In another research approach, researchers manipulate the presence of leadership, often in addition to situational variables, in order to gain a better understanding of the role that leadership plays in group interactions and effectiveness. Using the approach of manipulating elected leadership, Ho and Raman (1991) also manipulated the type of decision aid, or support, provided (no support, support in a FtF context, support in an electronic context) in small decision-making groups. In the electronic context they used a group decision support system (GDSS) which is an interactive network of computer terminals through which group members interact through communication of text-, graphics-, video-, or voice-based information. These information technology-based environments facilitate the interactive sharing and use of information among group members. Although they found differences in group consensus based on the decision support, this study found no significant effects of leadership. They did, however, see nonsignificant trends indicating that the presence of a leader was associated with more unequal influence within the group. Using a similar approach, Lim, Raman, and Wei (1994) did find evidence of leadership effects with a virtual context. Specifically, examining decision-making groups using a GDSS, they found that the elected leader exercised greater influence than the other members of the group whereas in the condition without a leader there were more equal levels of participation amongst group members.

In further support of how leaders in virtual contexts can contribute to unequal levels of participation of group members, George, Easton, Nunamaker, and Northcraft (1990) manipulated the communication medium (a virtual context using GDSS or a FtF context using manual support), leadership, and anonymity. Although there were no main effects of leadership, leadership did interact with anonymity and context. Specifically, the most satisfied group members were those who were anonymous and had a leader and those who were identified and did not have a leader. Additionally, the most unequal levels of participation were found in FtF groups without a leader and virtual groups with a leader. In addition to contributing to unequal participation, leaders can have a hard time influencing members to exchange information in virtual environments. In Barkhi, Jacob, Pipino, and Pirkul's (1998) study, groups performed a mixed-motive task while interacting either FtF or virtually. Their results supported media richness theory in that FtF groups performed better than virtual groups. However, leadership did not appear to have any substantive effects on performance. But, they did find that the leader was more successful in influencing members to exchange truthful information in the FtF compared to the virtual context.

Other experimental studies show the importance of leadership for improving group performance. Hiltz, Johnson, and Turoff (1991) manipulated both leadership and feedback in virtual groups working on a complex ranking problem. In this study leadership played a role in improving the quality of decisions. Leadership also interacted with feedback such that when group members were given feedback, they had lower levels of agreement when there was a leader compared to when there was no leader. These findings indicate that suggestions by the leader may have contradicted the implications from the feedback. In another study, Kim, Hiltz, and Turoff (2002) investigated the effects of leadership (or not) in virtual groups completing a semistructured task who were in parallel coordination mode (all discussion topics presented from the beginning of the study) or sequential discussion mode (discussion topics opened sequentially). They found that groups with leaders had greater objective decision quality, higher levels of participation, and greater satisfaction with the decision process. They also found an interaction between leadership and coordination on satisfaction with the decision process such that in the sequential discussion mode, members with a leader were more satisfied than those without a leader.

Overall, this general experimental literature suggests that leadership can play an important role in group processes and outcomes in virtual contexts. Some research has pointed to the difficulties leaders have in encouraging group members to contribute equally and engage in truthful exchanges in virtual contexts. However, others have found that leaders contribute to increased participation amongst group members as well as better decision quality from the group and greater levels of trust. The discrepancies regarding the influence of leaders on followers in virtual groups can likely be attributed to the different communication technologies employed and the varying leadership behaviors across studies.

Transformational Leadership in Virtual Contexts

In another approach to examining leadership in virtual contexts, researchers systematically manipulate specific leadership behaviors or styles. The one theoretical approach to leadership that has garnered the most attention by theorists interested in advanced communications technologies is transformational leadership. Burns's (1978) original conceptualization of transforming leadership was renamed transformational leadership and reconceptualized by Bass and colleagues (Bass & Avolio, 1993). Four behavioral components comprise the dimensions of transformational leadership: Charisma or idealized influence (followers trust in, identify with, and want to emulate the leader), inspirational motivation (leaders communicate high expectations to their followers often by using symbols or emotional appeals), intellectual stimulation (followers are encouraged to be creative and innovative, and to challenge their own beliefs and values as well as those of the leader and the organization), and individualized consideration (the leader demonstrates a high degree of personal concern for the followers' needs).

Sosik and colleagues undertook the initial empirical investigations into the effects of transformational leadership in virtual groups by examining the effects of leadership style on group potency and effectiveness of work groups performing a creativity task using a GDSS (Sosik, 1997). Their research demonstrated that groups working under high, compared to low, transformational leadership generated more original solutions, solution clarifications, supportive remarks, and questions about solutions in addition to reporting higher levels of perceived performance, extra effort, and satisfaction with the leader (Sosik, 1997). Again looking at high and low levels of transformational leadership, Sosik, Kahai, and Avolio (1998) studied group creativity under anonymous and identified electronic brainstorming conditions. They found that participants in the high transformational condition demonstrated greater originality and higher levels of elaboration compared to those under low transformational leadership. Furthermore, in the identified condition high, as opposed to low, transformational leadership was associated with greater flexibility. The leadership effects disappeared, however, in the anonymous condition; the authors suggest that anonymity may substitute for leadership by encouraging flexible thinking.

In addition to comparing high and low transformational leadership, they also compared transformational to transactional leadership. Compared to transactional leadership, transformational leadership was shown to more strongly impact group potency, the group's collective belief that it can be effective (Sosik, Avolio, Kahai, & Jung, 1998; Sosik et al., 1997). The positive effects of transformational leadership on group potency were amplified when participants were anonymous during the group writing session (relying on collective effort). Furthermore, anonymity also enhanced the positive effects of transformational, relative to transactional, leadership on group effectiveness (Sosik, et al., 1997). Looking more specifically at elements of transformational and transactional leadership, Sosik, Avolio, and Kahai (1998) examined group creativity in electronic brainstorming across leadership (transformational/transactional) and anonymity (anonymous/identified) conditions. Elements of both transactional and transformational leadership (goal setting and inspirational leadership) were positively associated with group creativity whereas intellectual stimulation and individualized consideration were negatively related to creativity. These effects (except the intellectual stimulation effect) were stronger under the anonymous conditions.

This research points to the importance of contextual factors, such as anonymity of follower inputs, in leadership effectiveness. According to Kahai and Avolio (2004), this research suggests that anonymity might enhance the impact of transformational leaders by creating a situation consistent with their emphasis on the collective as opposed to the individual. This is consistent with the social identity model of deindividuation effects (Reicher, et al., 1995). Using electronic meeting systems with software designed to facilitate group problem solving and decision-making, Kahai, Sosik, and Avolio (2003) demonstrated that transformational leadership, but not transactional leadership, helped overcome the social loafing effects demonstrated by those whose input was anonymous and pooled with a group for rewards. Additionally, although transactional leadership was associated with higher group efficacy and satisfaction with the task when individual input was identified, in the anonymous condition transformational leadership overcame those advantages of transactional leadership. The important role of anonymity in enhancing the effects of leadership style was also shown in another study by Sosik, Kahai, and Avolio (1999). Examining small work groups using a GDSS for a creativity task, they found that flow, a psychological state characterized by concentration, enjoyment, and intrinsic motivation, mediated perceptions of transformational and transactional leadership in the anonymous condition. Anonymity led to marginally more positive effects of perceptions of transformational leadership on flow. These studies point to the particularly beneficial impact of transformational leadership on groups working under conditions of anonymity.

Researchers then turned their attention to examining the role of transformational versus transactional leadership style on ethical decision-making in an electronic meeting system (Kahai & Avolio, 2006). In this research, the authors manipulated leadership style (transformational or transactional) and had participants engage in the task of discussing the ethical issues surrounding copying software that is copyrighted. They found that participants working with a transformational, compared to transactional, leader were more likely to make arguments against copying the software and the group members exposed to these arguments had a greater variance in their reported intentions to copy the software. The participants working with a transactional leader were less likely to make arguments against copying and they reported greater intentions to illegally copy the software. Thus, the important role of leadership style in fostering ethical decision-making is evident within a virtual context.

In sum, these studies examining transformational leadership within virtual contexts point to the importance of leadership behaviors in making a difference in these virtual groups. Leadership style has been shown to have an impact on a variety of important outcomes such as group effectiveness, group potency, creativity, and ethical decision-making. Furthermore, a variety of situational factors including task structure, anonymity, and others, have been shown to interact with leadership style to impact outcomes.

Transformational Leadership across Contexts

Other research examines and compares the impact of leadership styles across FtF and virtual contexts. Hoyt and Blascovich (2003) examined the effects of transformational leadership across virtual and FtF environments and found no differences in the effectiveness of leadership style across contexts. Compared to transactional leadership, transformational leadership was associated with decreases in quantitative performance but increases in qualitative performance, leadership satisfaction, and group cohesiveness across contexts (FtF, intercom, and immersive virtual environment). Furthermore, trust mediated the effects of leadership style on satisfaction and group cohesiveness. However, while group performance and cohesiveness were similar across virtual and nonvirtual group settings, group members were most satisfied with their leader when inter-acting FtF.

Hambley et al. (2007) examined the effects of transformational and transactional leadership on group interactions styles and outcomes across three contexts: FtF, videoconference, or text-based chat. Similar to Hoyt and Blascovich (2003) they found that the impact of leadership style did not vary across contexts. However, unlike Hoyt and Blascovich, they did not find differences in the impact of transformational and transactional leadership on their outcomes variables. Both leader-ship styles were equally effective in the teams completing the problem-solving tasks. However, the type of media used did have an impact on their interactions and cohesiveness. Specifically, they found that constructive interaction was higher in FtF compared to videoconference and chat teams and that team cohesion was higher in FtF and videoconference compared to chat teams.

Contrary to these studies, other research has shown differences in the effectiveness of various leadership styles across contexts. For example, Whitford and Moss (2009) conducted a survey study demonstrating that elements of transformational leadership—visionary leadership and per-sonal recognition—differentially predict job satisfaction and work engagement across virtual and FtF contexts. In another demonstration of the differing effects of transformational leadership across contexts, Purvanova and Bono (2009) had participants serve as leaders in both FtF and virtual team contexts with the goal of developing a business project proposal. Their results indi-cated that the most effective leaders were those who used greater transformational leadership in the virtual compared to the FtF environment. Furthermore, the impact of transformational lead-ership on group performance was greater in the virtual compared to the FtF environment. Thus, this study suggests that transformational leadership, focused on socioemotional factors, is more important in virtual contexts where information is lean and the situation is often more ambigu-ous, in support of predictions from the social identity model of deindividuation effects. Other researchers, using field research techniques, have supported these findings. Using a survey of employees working in geographically dispersed teams, Joshi, Lazarova, and Liao (2009) found that inspirational leadership predicted team members' trust and commitment to the team and that these relationships were stronger in teams that were more geographically dispersed. Furthermore, perceptions of trust and commitment were predictors of team level performance. These findings support the social identity model of deindividuation effects as well as a social identity perspective to leadership (see later) by pointing to the important role of leaders in facilitating a collective identity orientation amongst the followers by drawing on socialized relationships, particularly in dispersed settings.

Another set of researchers set out to directly test media richness theory by examining the impact of leadership style across high and low media-rich virtual environments (Huang et al., 2010). Specifically, they manipulated transformational and transactional leadership style with participants working on a decision-making task either in a virtual world or with instant messag-ing. They found a direct relationship between transactional leadership and task cohesion whereas transformational leadership improved the cooperative climate which positively influences task cohesion. Task cohesion and cooperative climate also played important roles in group function-ing. Specifically, task cohesion was shown to positively predict group consensus and member satisfaction with the discussion, and cooperative climate predicted member satisfaction as well as decreasing the time spent on the task. Importantly, they also found that the effects of leadership depended on the context, or media richness, such that they only occurred when media richness was low. These findings are in line with those of Purvanova and Bono (2009) suggesting that low media richness presents a challenging situation in which leadership takes on greater importance than less challenging situations.

Like the research in the previous section, this research examining transformational leadership across contexts demonstrates the powerful role of both transformational and transactional leadership in influencing group outcomes in virtual contexts. The relative effectiveness of the two styles depends on the task and outcomes being observed. In examining these styles across contexts some studies show similar effects across contexts whereas others point to the particularly powerful influence of transformational leadership in virtual and media lean contexts. This is likely due, at least in part, to the important role of transformational leadership in cultivating trust, cooperation, and social relationships which are particularly important for groups interacting in these environments.

Other Approaches to Leadership within Virtual Contexts: Participative, LMX, and Emergent Leadership

Although transformational leadership is the primary theoretical approach researchers have taken to investigate leadership within virtual contexts, some researchers have taken other theoretical approaches. For example, researchers have examined participative versus directive leadership. Participative leaders increase followers' participation by consulting with them and integrating their input during decision-making whereas directive leaders do not seek this input and rather they guide their followers' participation by giving them clear directions on how to complete their task (Northouse, 2010). Kahai, Sosik, and Avolio (2004) researched the effects of participative and directive leadership on creativity in electronic (GDSS) groups. They found that perceptions of both leader participativeness and directiveness were positively related to the followers' levels of participation which in turn positively related to performance but negatively related to satisfaction. In another study examining participative versus directive leadership in virtual groups (Kahai, Sosik, & Avolio, 1997), the researchers found that overall participants made more supportive remarks under participative than directive leadership. Furthermore, they found that the relative effectiveness of the different leadership styles in promoting solution proposals was dependent on the nature of the task: Participative leadership was more effective for semistructured problems whereas directive leadership was more important for more structured problems.

Another theoretical approach to understanding leadership that has recently garnered the attention of researchers examining leadership in virtual groups is LMX, an approach that regards the interactions and relationships among leaders and followers to be central to the leadership process. Using a survey technique, Golden and Veiga (2008) assessed the degree to which their participants' work was virtual, the quality of their LMXs, and their levels of commitment, job satisfaction, and performance. Their results indicated that the quality of the relationships is a significant predictor of all three outcomes. Specifically, better quality relationships are associated with greater levels, and conversely low-quality relationships are associated with lower levels, of organizational commitment, satisfaction, and performance. Furthermore, these relationships are strongest for those who work extensively within virtual contexts.

Increasingly, researchers have started to conceptualize leadership within virtual contexts as distributed amongst group members who are more likely to share or rotate the leadership roles compared to those in FtF contexts (Avolio, 1999; Zigurs, 2003). In response to this, researchers are beginning to study emergent leadership within these electronically-mediated contexts. Carte, Chidambaram, and Becker (2006) examined emergent leadership in virtual teams by studying virtual student groups over a semester. Their data point to the importance of leadership in these virtual groups as the better performing groups also displayed more leadership behaviors compared to the lower performing groups. More specifically, well-performing teams displayed higher levels of individual performance-focused leadership behaviors as well as greater levels of collective leadership concentrated on monitoring the group to keep it on track.

When comparing emergent leadership across FtF and virtual teams, research points to some difficulties that can be encountered in virtual contexts. Balthazard, Waldman, and Atwater (2008) had small groups perform a team-based task either FtF or virtually. They had each member assess each group member on transformational leadership, and their results showed greater levels of emergent transformational leadership in the FtF, compared to virtual, groups. Furthermore, they found that groups had greater cohesion, synergy, and solution acceptance as well as a more constructive, and less defensive, interaction style when performing FtF versus virtually. In addition, both the team member interaction style and the group leadership mediated the effects of context (FtF vs. virtual) on cohesion and solution acceptance.

Researchers are also examining and comparing assigned versus emergent leadership in virtual groups. In their laboratory study, Wickham and Walther (2007) had small groups discuss a decision-making task in a virtual context with either an assigned leader or not. They found that most of the virtual groups had more than one leader emerge, perhaps because of the different role requirements in the group. Furthermore, groups with assigned leaders were *less* likely to have a consensual leader than nonassigned groups, likely because participants felt compelled to still identify the assigned leader as a group leader even when another individual emerges as group leader. Importantly emergent leaders (whether assigned or not) were those who communicated the most, were perceived to be the most intelligent, and were both encouraging and authoritarian in their actions. These findings are consistent with findings regarding emergent leadership in FtF groups. There is strong empirical support for the "babble hypothesis," arguing that people who talk the most in groups are most likely to emerge as group leaders (Mullen, Salas, & Driskell, 1989; Sorrentino & Boutillier, 1975). Furthermore, this research corroborates a substantial literature showing that leaders tend to be more intelligent than nonleaders (Zaccaro, Kemp, & Bader, 2004) and it provides support for the importance of both task- and relationship-oriented behaviors in the group. The findings do not support the social identity model of deindividuation effects perspective, which would maintain that members should recognize and support the assigned leader as opposed to favoring effective behaviors from any member.

Other studies support these findings. For example, Yoo and Alavi (2004) conducted a longitudinal study of senior executives of a United States federal government agency and found a number of factors that predict emergent leadership in the virtual teams. Specifically, group members who sent more messages, especially task-oriented messages, and longer messages to the group were more likely to emerge as leaders than those who did not. In yet another approach, researchers have sought to examine the emergence of a particular type of leadership in virtual environments: Transformational leadership. Balthazard, Waldman, and Warren (2009) looked at the predictors of transformational leadership in both virtual and FtF groups. In accordance with previous research in traditional contexts, in the FtF context the emergence of transformational leadership was predicted by the personality variables of extraversion and emotional stability. However, these variables were not strong predictors of emergent transformational leadership in the virtual contexts. But further analyses showed findings similar to those mentioned earlier: Both the quantity and quality of participants' written communication were predictors of emergent leadership.

In sum, other approaches to conceptualizing leadership beyond transformational leadership can be beneficial to understanding leadership in virtual contexts. Both participative and directive leadership are important in these contexts and their relative effectiveness depends on factors such as the type of task. It is also important for leaders to develop high-quality relationships with their followers since the impact of these relationships on outcomes appears to be intensified within virtual contexts. Finally, emergent leadership, whether concentrated in a single individual or shared with a collective, has also been shown to be important for group success although it is not

always easy to cultivate within virtual contexts. Furthermore, supporting research from traditional FtF contexts, people who communicate the most in the virtual contexts are most likely to
emerge as leader.

Promising Theoretical Approaches and Future Research

A common theme across many definitions of leadership is that leadership involves interpersonal
processes between individuals in a group working toward a common goal. Thus, relations between
leaders and followers and social influence processes are integral to the understanding of leadership (Hoyt, 2008; for a comprehensive review see Hoyt, Goethals, & Riggio, 2006). Because virtual
contexts have the potential to fundamentally change interactions between people, taking a relational perspective to the study of leadership in these contexts is a promising avenue of research.
The transformational leadership framework is one such relational approach, but there are many
more that hold great promise for understanding leadership in virtual contexts. In addition to
focusing more on the leader–follower relations theories discussed earlier in the chapter (e.g.
exchange theories, justice, LMX), another approach would be to examine how leaders and group
members influence and persuade one another within virtual contexts. Leadership processes often
involve changing others behaviors and thoughts in order to help achieve the group's goals. Indeed,
effective leaders often have a remarkable capacity for using social influence tactics. Importantly,
social influence works both ways with both followers and leaders attempting to influence each
other. For example, followers are more likely to use ingratiation and blocking tactics with authoritarian leaders and rational persuasion with participative leaders (Ansari & Kapoor, 1987). There
has been a great deal of foundational research focused on understanding the dynamics of social
influence tactics in traditional settings (Kipnis, Schmidt, & Wilkinson, 1980; Yukl & Falbe, 1990)
and more recent research examining some of these processes within virtual contexts. These
streams of research have paved the path for a fruitful research program focusing on understanding leadership-related social influence processes within virtual contexts.

As is the case with research on leadership generally, work on leadership in virtual contexts could
certainly benefit from theoretical perspectives that acknowledge or highlight the critical role of
followers in the leadership process. One such perspective is the social-cognitive approach to
understanding perceptions of leaders. This approach highlights the importance of the follower as
perceiver in relational leadership processes. Leadership is, arguably, largely in the eye of the
beholder. At one extreme, theorists have argued that leadership stems directly from cognitive and
attributional processes that lead people to perceive people as leaders (Lord & Maher, 1991).
According to Lord and Maher, leadership begins with "the process of being perceived by others as
a leader" (1991, p. 11). Individuals are deemed leaders to the extent that their traits and behaviors
are compatible with lay notions of what it means to be a leader. These widely held and shared
beliefs are referred to as implicit leadership theories or leadership prototypes and people's perceptions and evaluations of leaders are guided by these theories. Such implicit theories commonly
revolve around task-oriented and people-oriented traits and behaviors, such as being determined
and influential as well as being caring and open to others' ideas (Forsyth & Nye, 2008; Kenney,
Schwartz-Kenney, & Blascovich, 1996; Lord & Maher, 1991).

Undoubtedly, the changes brought about by advanced information technologies have the
potential to change the perceptions that individuals have of others. For example, this altered context requires a renewed focus on cultivating social relations. This may ultimately serve to alter
people's implicit theories to contain more relationship-oriented images. This may change who
people see fit to be qualified leaders and ultimately change the bias people have in their perceptions

and evaluations of others who do or do not fit the image of a leader (Hoyt & Chemers, 2008). For example, the leadership role has generally been thought to require agentic, masculine qualities, such as independence and assertiveness, and these agentic qualities are perceived to be incompatible with the communal, feminine qualities stereotypically associated with women (Eagly & Karau, 2002). Empirical evidence confirms that these masculine expectations regarding leaders can result in less favorable attitudes toward female leaders and greater difficulty for them to reach top roles and be viewed as effective in these top roles (Eagly & Carli, 2007; Heilman & Eagly, 2008). However, if interacting within virtual contexts serves to alter people's implicit notions of leadership to include more communal qualities, this will likely serve to alter these biases.

Another perception-based approach to understanding leader–follower relations is the social identity theory of leadership (Hogg, 2001). This approach argues that leadership is a result of normal processes associated with group membership. According to this perspective, when individuals strongly identify with their group, they are more likely to base their perceptions and evaluations of the leader on how representative, or prototypical, the leader is of the group's values, attitudes, and behavior. Combining this model with the social identity model of deindividuation effects suggests different leadership processes in virtual, compared to FtF, environments. According to the social identity model of deindividuation effects, these new technologies have the potential to change the relative salience of one's personal or social identity. This can have a profound impact on people's identification with their group and, according to the social identity theory of leadership, their perceptions and evaluations of their group leaders.

In addition to focusing more on leader–follower relations, with a particular emphasis on the followers, research on leadership in virtual contexts can benefit from comparing processes and outcomes across virtual and FtF contexts. If the goal is to better understand, theoretically, how these new information and communication technologies influence leadership processes, then cross-context comparisons are imperative. Furthermore, rather than simply adopting theoretical approaches developed in traditional settings, researchers should focus on modifying these theories or developing new theories. Avolio's conceptual framework based on adaptive structuration theory and Zacarro's model of leadership in virtual teams are good examples of such approaches. Further empirical work using these frameworks can help in the development of a systematic theory of leadership in virtual contexts.

The expansion of virtual technologies throughout organizations has revolutionized social relations and organizational processes. Many important social interactions, including leadership processes, are now mediated in some way by advanced information technology. Leaders are effective to the extent that they establish credibility and influence, build relationships amongst and with followers, cultivate a sense of collective competence amongst the followers, and appropriately match their leadership strategies to their environment (Chemers, 1997). The changes brought about by the rise in information technologies have generated exciting opportunities as well as new challenges for leaders. This new frontier of empirical research into leadership in virtual contexts will help elucidate these processes as well as strengthen our theoretical understanding and practice of leadership in this new virtual era.

References

Ansari, M. A., & Kapoor, A. (1987). Organizational context and upward influence tactics. *Organizational Behavior and Human Decision Processes, 40*, 39–49.

Avolio, B. (1999). *Full leadership development: Building the vital forces in organization.* Thousand Oaks, CA: Sage Publications.

Avolio, B., & Kahai, S. (2003). Adding the "E" to E-leadership: How it may impact your leadership. *Organizational Dynamics, 31*, 325–338.

Avolio, B. J., Kahai, S., & Dodge, G. E. (2000). E-leadership: Implications for theory, research, and practice. *The Leadership Quarterly, 11*, 615–668.

Ayman, R., & Chemers, M. M. (1983). Relationship of supervisory behavior ratings to work group effectiveness and subordinate satisfaction among Iranian managers. *Journal of Applied Psychology, 68*, 336–341.

Balthazard, P., Waldman, D., & Atwater, L. (2008). The mediating effects of leadership and interaction style in face-to-face and virtual teams. In S. Weisband (Ed.), *Leadership at a Distance: Research in technologically supported work* (pp. 127–150). Mahwah, NJ: Lawrence Erlbaum Associates.

Balthazard, P. A., Waldman, D. A. and Warren, J. E. (2009) Predictors of the emergence of transformational leadership in virtual decision teams. *The Leadership Quarterly, 20*, 651–663.

Barkhi, R., Jacob, V. S., Pipino, L., & Pirkul, H. (1998). A study of the effect of communication channel and authority on group decision processes and outcomes. *Decision Support System, 23*, 205–226.

Bass, B. M. (1985). *Leadership and performance beyond expectations*. New York, NY: Free Press.

Bass, B. M. (1990). From transactional to transformational leadership: Learning to share the vision. *Organizational Dynamics, 18*, 19–31.

Bass, B. M. (1997). Does the transactional-transformational leadership paradigm transcend organizational and national boundaries? *American Psychologist, 52*, 130–139.

Bass, B. M., & Avolio, B. J. (1993). Transforming leadership: A response to critiques. Leadership theory and research: Perspectives and directions. In M. M. Chemers, & R. Ayman (Eds.), *Leadership theory and research: Perspectives and directions* (p. 49–80). San Diego, CA: Academic Press.

Bradner, E., & Mark, G. (2008). Designing a tail in two cities: Leaders' perpectives on collocated and distance collaboration. In S. Weisband (Ed.), *Leadership at a Distance: Research in technologically supported work* (pp. 51–69). Mahwah, NJ: Lawrence Erlbaum Associates.

Burns, J. M. (1978). *Leadership*. New York, NY: Harper & Row Publishers.

Butler, B., Sproull, L., Kiesler, S., & Kraut, R. (2008). Community effort in online groups: Who does the work and why? In S. Weisband (Ed.), *Leadership at a Distance: Research in technologically supported work* (pp. 171–193). Mahwah, NJ: Lawrence Erlbaum Associates.

Carlson, J. R., & Zmud, R. W. (1999). Channel expansion theory and the experiential nature of media richness perceptions. *Academy of Management Journal, 42*, 153–170.

Carte, T., Chidambaram, L., and Becker, A., (2006). Emergent leadership in self-managed virtual teams: A longitudinal study of concentrated and shared leadership behavior. *Group Decision & Negotiation, 15*, 323–343.

Cascio, W. F., & Shurygailo, S. (2003). E-leadership and virtual teams. *Organizational Dynamics, 31*, 362–376.

Chemers, M. M. (1997). *An integrative theory of leadership*. Mahwah, NJ: Lawrence Erlbaum Associates Publishers.

Chemers, M. M. (2000). Leadership research and theory: A functional integration. *Group Dynamics: Theory, Research, and Practice, 4*, 27–43.

Chidambaram, L. (1996). Relational developmental in computer-supported groups. *MIS Quarterly, 20*, 143–165.

Conger, J. A. (1999). Charismatic and transformational leadership in organizations: An insider's perspective on these developing streams of research. *The Leadership Quarterly, 10*, 145–179.

Cummings, J. N. (2008). Leading groups from a distance: How to mitigate consequences of geographic dispersion. In S. Weisband (Ed.), *Leadership at a Distance: Research in technologically supported work* (pp. 33–50). Mahwah, NJ: Lawrence Erlbaum Associates.

Daft, R. L., & Lengel, R. H. (1986). Organizational information requirements, media richness and structural design. *Management Science, 32*, 554–571.

DeSanctis, G., & Poole, M. S. (1994). Capturing the complexity in advanced technology use: Adaptive structuration theory. *Organization Science, 5*, 121–147.

Diener, E. (1979). Deinividuation, self-awareness, and disinhibition. *Journal of Personality and Social Psychology, 37*, 1160–1171.

Eagly, A. H., & Carli, L. L. (2007). *Through the labyrinth: The truth about how women become leaders.* Boston, MA: Harvard Business School Press.

Eagly, A. H., & Karau, S. (2002). Role congruity theory of prejudice toward female leaders. *Psychological Review, 109*, 573–598.

Festinger, L., Pepitone, A., & Newcomb, T. (1952). Some consequences of de-individuation in a group. *The Journal of Abnormal and Social Psychology, 47*, 382–389.

Fiedler, F. E. (1964). A contingency model of leadership effectiveness. *Advances in Experimental Social Psychology, 1*, 149–190.

Fiedler, F. E., & Garcia, J. E. (1987). *New approaches to effective leadership: Cognitive resources and organizational performance.* Oxford, UK: John Wiley & Sons.

Fjermestad, Kahai, Zhang, & Avolio. (2007). Virtual team leadership: Beginnings and directions. *International Journal of e-collaboration, 3*, i–ix.

Fleishman, E. A., & Harris, E. F. (1962). Patterns of leadership behavior related to employee grievances and turnover. *Personnel Psychology, 15*, 43–56.

Forsyth, D. R., & Nye, J. L. (2008). Seeing and being a leader: The perceptual, cognitive, and interpersonal roots of conferred influence. In C. L. Hoyt, G. R. Goethals, & D. R. Forsyth (Eds.), *Leadership at the crossroads: Leadership and Psychology* (Vol. 1, pp. 116–131). Westport, CN: Praeger.

George, J. F., Easton, G. F., Nunamaker, J. F., & Northcraft, G. B. (1990). A study of collaborative group work with and without computer-based support. *Information Systems Research, 1*, 394–415.

Giddens, A. (1979). *Central problems in social theory: Action, structure and contradiction in social analysis.* London, UK: MacMillan.

Golden, T.D., & Veiga, J. F. (2008). The impact of superior-subordinate relationships on the commitment, job satisfaction, and performance of virtual workers. *The Leadership Quarterly, 19*, 77–88.

Graen, G. B., & Uhl-Bien, M. (1995). Relationship-based approach to leadership: Development of leader-member exchange (LMX) theory of leadership over 25 years: Applying a multi-level multi-domain perspective. *The Leadership Quarterly, 6*, 219–247.

Hambley, L. A., O'Neill, T. A., & Kline, T. J. (2007). Virtual team leadership: Perspectives from the field. *International Journal of e-Collaboration, 3*, 40–64.

Harmon, J., Schneer, J. A., & Hoffman, L. R. (1995). Electronic meetings and established decision groups: Audioconferencing effects on performance and structural stability. *Organizational Behavior and Human Decision Processes, 61*, 138–147.

Heilman, M., & Eagly, A. H. (2008). Gender stereotypes are alive, well, and busy producing workplace discrimination. *Industrial and Organizational Psychology: Perspectives on Science and Practice, 1*, 393–398.

Hersey, P., & Blanchard, P. (1969). The life cycle theory of leadership. *Training and Development Journal, 23*, 26–34.

Hiltz, S. R., Johnson, K., & Turoff, M. (1991). Group decision support: The effects of designated human leaders and statistical feedback in computerized conferences. *Journal of Management Information Systems, 8*, 81–108.

Ho, T. H., & Raman, K. S. (1991). The effect of GDSS and elected leadership on small group meetings. *Journal of Management Information Systems, 8*, 109–133.

Hogg, M. A. (2001). A social identity theory of leadership. *Personality and Social Psychology Review, 5*, 184–200.

Hollander, E. P. (1993). Legitimacy, power and influence: A perspective on relational features of leadership. In M. M. Chemers, & R. Ayman (Eds.), *Leadership Theory and Research: Perspectives and Directions* (pp. 29–46). New York, NY: Academic Press.

House, R. J. (1977). A 1976 theory of charismatic leadership. In J. Hunt, & L. L. Larson (Eds.), *The cutting edge* (pp. 189–207). Carbondale, IL: Southern Illinois University Press.

House, R. J., & Aditya, R. N. (1997). The social scientific study of leadership: Quo vadis? *Journal of Management, 23*, 409–473.

House, R. J., & Mitchell, T. R. (1974). Path-goal theory of leadership. *Contemporary Business, 3*, 81–98.

Howell, J. P., Dorfman, P. W., & Kerr, S. (1986). Moderator variables in leadership research. *The Academy of Management Review, 11*, 88–102.

Hoyt, C. L. (2008). Leader-follower relations. In A. Marturano & J. Gosling (Eds.), *Leadership: The key concepts* (pp. 90–94). Oxford, UK: Routledge.

Hoyt, C. L. & Blascovich, J. (2003). Transformational and transactional leadership in virtual and physical environments. *Small Group Research, 34*, 678–715.

Hoyt, C., & Chemers, M. M. (2008). Social stigma and leadership: A long climb up a slippery ladder. In C.L. Hoyt, G. R. Goethals, & D.R. Forsyth (Eds.) *Leadership at the crossroads: Leadership and psychology* (Vol. 1, pp. 165–180). Westport, CT: Praeger.

Hoyt, C. L., & Goethals, G. R. (2010). Leader-member exchange theory. In J. M. Levine, & M. A. Hogg (Eds.), *Encyclopedia of Group Processes and Intergroup Relations*. Thousand Oaks, CA: Sage.

Hoyt, C. L., Goethals, G. R., & Forsyth, D. R. (2008). A contemporary social psychology of leadership. In C. L. Hoyt, G. R. Goethals, & D. R. Forsyth (Eds.), *Leadership at the crossroads: Leadership and psychology* (Vol. 1, pp. 1–10). Westport, CT: Praeger.

Hoyt, C. L., Goethals, G. R. & Riggio, R. (2006). Leader-follower relations: Group dynamics and the role of leadership. In G. R. Goethals & G. Sorenson (Eds.), *A quest for a general theory of leadership: A multidisciplinary experiment* (pp. 96–122). Cheltenham, UK: Edward Elgar Publishing.

Huang, R., Kahai, S., & Jestice, R. (2010). The contingent effects of leadership on team collaboration in virtual teams. *Computers in Human Behavior, 26*, 1098–1110.

Hunt, J. G. (1999). Transformational/charismatic leadership's transformation of the field: A historical essay. *The Leadership Quarterly, 10*, 129–144.

Joshi, A., Lazarova, M. B., & Liao, H. (2009). Getting everyone on board: The role of inspirational leadership in geographically dispersed teams. *Organization Science, 20*, 240–252.

Kahai, S., & Avolio, B. (2004). E-leadership. In G.R. Goethals, G. Sorenson, & J. M. Burns (Eds.), *The Encyclopedia of Leadership* (pp. 417–425). Thousand Oaks, CA: Sage.

Kahai, S. & Avolio, B. (2006). Leadership style, anonymity, and the discussion of an ethical issue in an electronic context. *International Journal of e-Collaboration, 2*, 1–26.

Kahai, S. S., Sosik, J. J., & Avolio, B. J. (1997). Effects of leadership style and problem structure on work group processes and outcomes in an electronic meeting system environment. *Personnel Psychology, 50*, 121–136.

Kahai, S. S., Sosik, J. J., & Avolio, B. J. (2003). Effects of leadership style, anonymity, and rewards on creativity-relevant processes and outcomes in an electronic meeting system context. *The Leadership Quarterly, 14*, 499–524.

Kahai, S. S., Sosik, J. J., & Avolio, B. J. (2004). Effects of participative and directive leadership in electronic groups. *Groups & Organization Management, 29*, 67–105.

Kayworth, T., & Leidner, D. (2002). Leadership effectiveness in global virtual teams. *Journal of Management Information Systems, 18*, 7–40.

Kenney, R.A., Schwartz-Kenney, B. M., & Blascovich, J. (1996). Implicit leadership theories: Defining leaders described as worthy of influence. *Personality and Social Psychology Bulletin, 22*, 1128–1143.

Kim, Y., Hiltz, S. R., & Turoff, M. (2002). Coordination structures and system restrictiveness in distributed group support systems. *Group Decision and Negotiation, 11*, 379–404.

Kipnis, D., Schmidt, S. M., Wilkinson, I. (1980). Intraorganizational influence tactics: Explorations in getting one's way. *Journal of Applied Psychology, 65*, 440–452.

Lewin, K., Lippitt, R., & White, R. (1939). Patterns of aggressive behaviour in experimentally created "social climates". *Journal of Social Psychology, 10*, 271–299.

Lim, L. H., Raman, K. S., & Wei, K. K. (1994). Interacting effects of GDSS and leadership. *Decision Support Systems, 12*, 199–211.

Lord, R. G., & Maher, K. J. (1991). *Leadership and information processing: Linking perceptions and performance.* Boston, MA: Unwin Hyman.

Lowe, K. B., Kroeck, K. G., & Sivasubramaniam, N. (1996). Effectiveness correlates of transformation and transactional leadership: A meta-analytic review of the MLQ literature. *The Leadership Quarterly, 7*, 385–425.

Mullen, B., Salas, E., & Driskell, J. E. (1989). Salience, motivation, and artifact as contributions to the relation between participation rate and leadership. *Journal of Experimental Social Psychology, 25*, 545–559.

Northouse, P. (2010). *Leadership: Theory and Practice* (5th ed.). Thousand Oaks, CA: Sage Publications.

Podsakoff, P. M., MacKenzie, S. B., Ahearne, M., & Bommer, W. H. (1995). Searching for a needle in a haystack: Trying to identify the illusive moderators of leadership behaviors. *Journal of Management, 21*, 423–470.

Postmes, T., & Spears, R. (1998). Deindividuation and antinormative behavior: A meta-analysis. *Psychological Bulletin, 123*, 238–259.

Purvanova, R.K., & Bono, J.E. (2009). Transformational leadership in context: Face-to-face and virtual teams. *The Leadership Quarterly, 20*, 343–357.

Reicher, S., Spears, R., & Postmes, T. (1995). A social identity model of deindividuation phenomena. *European Review of Social Psychology, 6*, 161–198.

Shamir, B., & Howell, J. M. (1999). Organizational and contextual influences on the emergence and effectiveness of charismatic leadership. *The Leadership Quarterly, 10*, 257–283.

Sivasubramaniam, N., Murry, W. D., Avolio, B. J., & Jung, D. I. (2002). A longitudinal model of the effects of team leadership and group potency on group performance. *Group & Organization Management, 27*, 66–96.

Sorrentino, R. M., & Boutillier, R. G. (1975). The effect of quantity and quality of verbal interaction on ratings of leadership ability. *Journal of Experimental Social Psychology, 11*, 403–411.

Sosik, J.J. (1997). Effects of transformational leadership and anonymity on idea generation in computer-mediated groups. *Group & Organization Management, 22*, 460–487.

Sosik, J. J., Avolio, B. J., & Kahai, S. S. (1997). Effects of leadership style and anonymity on group potency and effectiveness in a group decision support system environment. *Journal of Applied Psychology, 82*, 89–103.

Sosik, J. J., Avolio, B. J., & Kahai, S. S. (1998). Inspiring group creativity: Comparing anonymous and identified electronic brainstorming. *Small Group Research, 29*, 3–31.

Sosik, J. J., Avolio, B. J., Kahai, S. S., & Jung, D. I. (1998). Computer-supported work group potency and effectiveness: The role of transformational leadership, anonymity and task interdependence. *Computers in Human Behavior, 14*, 491–511.

Sosik, J. J., Kahai, S. S., & Avolio, B. J. (1998). Transformational leadership and dimensions of creativity: Motivating idea generation in computer-mediated groups. *Creativity Research Journal, 11*, 111–121.

Sosik, J.J., Kahai, S.S., & Avolio, B.J. (1999). Leadership style, anonymity, and creativity in group decision support systems: The mediating role of optimal flow. *Journal of Creative Behavior, 33*, 1–30.

Spears, R., & Lea, M. (1994). Panacea or panopticon? The hidden power in computer-mediated communication. *Communication Research, 21*, 427–459.

Spears, R., Postmes, T., Lea, M., & Watt, S. E. (2001). A SIDE view of social influence. In J. P. Forgas, & K. D. Williams (Eds.) *Social Influence: Direct and indirect processes* (pp. 331–350). Philadelphia, PA: Psychology Press.

Torrey, C., Burke, M., Lee, M., Dey, A., Fussell, S., & Kiesler, S. (2008). Approaches to authority in online distaster relief communities after Hurricane Katrina. In S. Weisband (Ed.), *Leadership at a Distance: Research in technologically supported work* (pp. 223–245). Mahwah, NJ: Lawrence Erlbaum Associates.

Tyler, T. R., & Lind, E. A. (1992). A relational model of authority in groups. Advances in experimental social psychology. In M. P. Zanna (Ed.), *Advances in experimental social psychology* (Vol. 25, p. 390). San Diego, CA: Academic Press.

Waldman, D. A., & Yammarino, F. J. (1999). CEO charismatic leadership: levels of management and levels of analysis effects. *Academy of Management Review, 24,* 266–285.

Walther, J. B. (1995). Relational aspects of computer-mediated communication: Experimental observations over time. *Organization Science, 6,* 186–203.

Weisband, S. (2008). *Leadership at a Distance: Research in technologically supported work.* Mahwah, NJ: Lawrence Erlbaum Associates.

Whitford, T., & Moss, S. A. (2009). Transformational leadership in distributed work groups: The moderating role of follower regulatory focus and goal orientation. *Communication Research, 36,* 810–837.

Wickham, K., & Walther, J. B. (2007). Perceived behaviors of emergent and assigned leaders in virtual groups. *International Journal of e-Collaboration, 3,* 1–17.

Yoo, Y., & Alavi, M. (2004). Emergent leadership in virtual teams: what do emergent leaders do? *Information and Organization, 14,* 27–58.

Yukl, G. (2002). *Leadership in Organizations.* Upper Saddle River, NJ: Prentice Hall.

Yukl, G.A., & Falbe, C. M. (1990). Influence tactics and objectives in upward, downward, and lateral influence attempts. *Journal of Applied Psychology, 75,* 132–140.

Zaccaro, S. J. (2007). Trait-based perspectives of leadership. *American Psychologist, 62,* 6–16.

Zaccaro, S. J., Ardison, S. D., & Orvis, K. L. (2004). Leadership in virtual teams. In D. V. Day, S. J. Zaccaro, & S. M. Halpin (Eds.), *Leader development for transforming organizations: Growing leaders for tomorrow* (pp. 267–292). Mahwah, NJ: Erlbaum.

Zaccaro, S. J., & Bader, P. (2003). E-leadership and the challenges of leading E-teams: Minimizing the bad and maximizing the good. *Organizational Dynamics, 31,* 377–387.

Zaccaro, S. J., Kemp, C., & Bader, P. (2004). Leader Traits and Attributes. In J. Antonakis, A. T. Cianciolo & R. J. Sternberg (Eds.), *The Nature of Leadership* (pp. 101–124). Thousand Oaks, CA: Sage Publications.

Zaccaro, S. J., & Klimoski, R. J. (2002). The nature of organizational leadership: An introduction. In S. J. Zaccaro, R. J. Klimoski (Eds.), *The nature of organizational leadership: Understanding the performance imperatives confronting today's leaders* (pp. 3–41). San Francisco, CA: Jossey-Bass.

Zaccaro, S. J., Rittman, A. L., & Marks, M. A. (2001). Team leadership. *The Leadership Quarterly, 12,* 451–483.

Zigurs, I. (2003). Leadership in virtual teams: Oxymoron or opportunity? *Organizational Dynamics, 31,* 339–351.

Chapter 11

Online Prejudice and Discrimination: From Dating to Hating

Kimberly Barsamian Kahn, Katherine Spencer, and Jack Glaser

Introduction

A man seated at his computer opens the Google Internet search engine and starts to type. "Why are Blacks…," he begins entering into the search box. This is not the first time that an individual has started a search on Google using these particular words, and "Google Suggest" offers a drop-down list of phrases to complete the search. The suggestions displayed are computer-generated by Google using an algorithm that relies on the popularity of each search term. The sentences that appear are the most common ways that Google users have finished searches beginning with those specific phrases. In this instance, the Google Suggest drop-down list might suggest completing the phrase with "… so lazy," "… so unintelligent," or "… so good at basketball." The user finds what he was about to type—or some other result of interest—already listed in the drop-down menu, clicks on the suggested phrase, and views the search results. He then continues on to surf the web pages he is interested in, navigating cyberspace anonymously from the comfort of his home. He is unaware that his search choices, like the ones that preceded his, will shape the experiences of those who follow.

What can this seemingly commonplace example tell social scientists about prejudice and discrimination on the Internet? To begin, researchers have studied the existence of racial, ethnic, and national stereotypes based on these Google Suggest searches, which demonstrate how people experience and express biases even when seeking information (Dunnell, 2010). By initiating a Google search with question words such as "why are" and then an ethnicity, race, nationality, or gender, web users express at least a tacit belief that group differences are real and explicable. Google Suggest brings forth the most commonly entered phrases which represent a list of common cultural stereotypes (Dunnell, 2010). The results can be highly unpleasant, offensive, and even disgusting, revealing the type of overt stereotyping and prejudice that is rarely openly expressed in modern-day society. These cultural bias indexes are updated in real time, based on the number of searches that involve those terms, which allows for researchers to track both long- and short-term changes in stereotypes (Dunnell, 2010). For instance, a newsworthy attack by a Muslim in the United States (US) might lead to a surge in searches such as, "Why are Muslims…" and return words such as "evil," "terrorists," or "full of hate." The ability for researchers to study such changes in real time—without needing to conduct intensive or obtrusive original surveys—is a valuable research tool that is distinctive to the Internet.

How else can the Internet, with its unique characteristics and attributes, inform us about prejudice and discrimination in modern-day society? What do scientists know about online prejudice and discrimination, and what do we have still to learn? The following chapter delves deeper into these questions.

Social Psychology, Prejudice, Discrimination, and the Internet: A Review

As a field, social psychology broadly focuses on situational determinants of behavior and how mental processes influence social behavior (Allport, 1985). Mental processes include individual level psychological attitudes, which are further divided into a three-part structure of affect, cognition, and behavior (Hilgard, 1980). Within the domain of intergroup attitudes, prejudice represents the affective component, stereotyping the cognitive component, and discrimination the behavioral component (Allport, 1954). For the sake of simplicity for the current writing, we will treat prejudice and stereotyping—both internal mental processes—as bias that is differentiated from discrimination—which is the external, behavioral component (Glaser & Kahn, 2005). Therefore, we will refer to prejudice and to discrimination in the online world, with these terms representing internal mental processes versus external observed behavior, respectively.

When the Internet was a newer medium, we reviewed a burgeoning literature on the social psychology of prejudice and discrimination on the Internet (Glaser & Kahn, 2005). At that time, the Internet and Internet use were growing rapidly and, being a constantly evolving and changing new medium, much of our thoughts regarding the impact of the Internet on prejudice and discrimination were exploratory. The thesis that was posited was that the Internet had the possibility to decrease discriminatory effects, but also to increase expressions of prejudice. Specifically, we argued that the anonymity of the Internet would allow for freer expression of thoughts, beliefs, and feelings by reducing the influence of social desirability concerns, resulting in less self-censoring of prejudicial attitudes. Furthermore, the vast reach of the Internet would allow prejudiced individuals to access hate groups or easily contact like-minded others.

Simultaneously, we theorized, the anonymity of the Internet, despite its possibility to increase prejudice, might lead to a reduction in the behavioral component of intergroup bias—that of discrimination. The anonymity of the Internet, with the potential to hide social category cues, could allow for stigmatized group members to receive more equitable treatment in traditionally discriminated domains, such as housing, insurance, and health care. By purchasing and obtaining services online, where social identity cues are hidden, instead of in person, stigmatized group members would be less likely to receive discriminatory treatment (Glaser & Kahn, 2005).

Now, approximately 7 years later, has the Internet produced these hypothesized differential results regarding prejudice and discrimination? The evidence, like the thesis itself, appears to be mixed. In this chapter, we continue the discussion of group differences regarding who is on the Internet and what they are doing on it—the so-called "digital divide." Next, we address the distinctive characteristics of the Internet, including anonymity, perceived privacy, legitimacy, and permanency, and the effects of such characteristics on online prejudice and discrimination. We then examine the new trends of communication on the Internet, focusing on the explosion of social networking sites, and the implications of these forums for online prejudice and discrimination. Finally, we close with a discussion of how researchers, as in the opening Google Suggest scenario, can harness the unique properties of the Internet to study prejudice and discrimination.

Who Is (and Isn't) on the Internet and How Are They Using It? The Digital Divide

When considering the impact of the online world on prejudice and discrimination, one must first have an understanding of who is online, and whether disparities exist at this most basic level. The digital divide separates those who have access to the Internet from those who do not (National

Telecommunications and Information Administration, 1995; see Selwyn, 2004 for a review). In 2011, approximately one in five adults in the US did not have Internet access, and this gap was disproportionately distributed across the US population (James, 2011). Research on the digital divide has shown that one of the major disparities in Internet access is racial, such that White people are more likely to have access to the Internet than racial minorities (Hoffman & Novak, 1998; Hoffman, Novak, & Scholsser, 2001; James, 2011; Jones, Johnson-Yale, Millermaier, & Pérez, 2009). In addition to race, digital divides have also been identified based on age (Loges & Jung, 2001), gender (Wilson, Wallin, & Reiser, 2003), socioeconomic status (Ginossar & Nelson, 2010; Lorence & Greenberg, 2006), education (Bucy, 2000), and urban versus rural locations (Hale, Cotten, Drentea, & Goldner, 2010; Hindman, 2000; Wei & Zhang, 2008), all in the predictable directions (lower status and rural locations are associated with lesser access). These factors naturally add together, with some studies suggesting that Hispanics, and low-income Hispanics in particular, are the most digitally isolated group in the US (Ginossar & Nelson, 2010; James, 2011).

However, this type of digital divide regarding Internet access may be shrinking. Public access to the Internet has greatly expanded with the advent of wireless connectivity. Coffee shops, public libraries, and many other public spaces such as parks are increasingly offering free, or very low-cost, wireless Internet access. Gaining access to the Internet via smart phones—called leapfrogging—has also been particularly popular among those who lack other forms of access (James, 2011).

More recently, scholars have noted a shift in the nature of the digital divide from one based on lack of access to one based on usage patterns, redefining the term as "inequalities in the meaningful use of information and communication" (Wei & Hindman, 2011, p. 217). The original conception of the digital divide has now been updated as the "first digital divide," which was based on differential *access*. With access to the Internet increasing, the subsequent digital divide—termed the "second digital divide"—focuses on differences in Internet *use* between high- and low-status group members (Attewell, 2001; Wei & Hindman, 2011). Specifically, examining usage patterns of the Internet reveals that marginalized or low-status groups are less likely to use the Internet for "capital-enhancing" activities, such as reading international and local news, finding job opportunities, and obtaining pertinent health information (Hargittai & Hinnant, 2008). They are more likely to use the Internet for gaming or social reasons instead, which is less likely to advance career opportunities or knowledge. Therefore, while access might be increasing to a near ceiling that would preclude substantial differences between groups, the digital divide in type of use might continue to promote disparities.

Unique Characteristics of the Internet: The Relationship to Prejudice and Discrimination

Anonymity

The anonymity of the Internet is one of the medium's central characteristics which distinguishes it from previous forms of communication. Anonymity is also hypothesized to be one of the primary mechanisms responsible for the potential of the Internet to increase prejudice but decrease discrimination (Glaser & Kahn, 2005). Before we consider whether this proposition is supported by modern-day Internet use, we must ask the question, are people still anonymous on the Internet?

Recent research and trends indicate that anonymity has been declining as Internet use expands (Stelter, 2011). While the Internet has the possibility for its users to remain relatively anonymous when interacting with other users, it has become increasingly personal with the use of social media like blogs, Facebook, Twitter, and YouTube, encouraging, or even requiring, users to present more real aspects of their selves online. Indeed, impression management is still a key factor in the presentation of online selves, such that the online expressions might reflect more idealized versions of oneself than an entirely unbiased presentation (Bargh, McKenna, & Fitzsimons, 2002). Nonetheless, there has been a trend toward revealing more aspects of the self online, as opposed to fictional identities, avatars, or fake personalities. For example, the social network site Facebook, boasting more than 845 million active members (Facebook, 2012), has made it mandatory for its members to use their real identities on their site (Stelter, 2011). This requirement is also implicitly monitored and reinforced by other users, who label those who break the rule "Fakesters" (boyd & Ellison, 2008). LunarStorm, another online social networking site, scores users based on the authenticity of their profiles (boyd & Ellison, 2008). Furthermore, users of social networking sites are increasingly using the services to post and share photographs with friends, which also undermines anonymity and reinforces these authenticity norms. Many of these sites employ facial recognition technology, such that they automatically identify individuals in online photographs with their full names, based on information provided by users in previous photograph postings. One of the most influential and perhaps lasting impacts of social networking sites might be its impetus in expanding users' notions of what personal information should be public and changing beliefs about what should be private on the Internet (Stelter, 2011).

The Internet has also been used as a tool to discover the real identities of individuals, both online and offline—that is, making anonymous individuals "nonymous." The advent of cameras on mobile devices has allowed individuals to capture images of others and use the Internet community later to identify them (Stelter, 2011). Finally, a reduction in anonymity may also be caused by users habituating to the "presence" of the Internet. Similar to what subjects of documentary films do with cameras, Internet users may have become more accustomed to the medium and have let their proverbial guard down. This greater comfort level with the Internet could lead them to reveal more of their personal selves online.

Perceived Privacy

One of the most significant aspects of the Internet is that, despite the fact that nearly all Internet activity leaves a trace—if not a very visible record—people still *perceive* there to be privacy on the Internet. Similar to how deindividuation occurs in crowds or mobs, individuals may believe, with considerable justification, that they are merely one individual among masses on the Internet, making them feel unlikely to be individually identified. Research has demonstrated that individuals report more racial bias when filling out questionnaires in a large classroom setting—where they feel more anonymous and private—than when alone with an experimenter in the lab (Fazio, Jackson, Dunton, & Williams, 1995). Similarly, the Internet may increase perceived privacy simply because of the presence of a "crowd" of millions of fellow users worldwide.

Perceived privacy can encourage the expression of prejudice on the Internet, particularly with the new popular uses of the Internet (see Glaser & Kahn, 2005, for a discussion). For instance, personal blogs, in which individuals post their thoughts and experiences online, are often an outlet for prejudicial comments or bigotry. Despite the fact that these blogs are often tied to individuals' real-life identities and contain highly personal material, the fact that they are written on the Internet may make users feel that their thoughts are private, as they would be in a personal journal.

Furthermore, the combination of instantaneous access to Internet blogging and tweeting mediums, the informal nature of most web posts, and the perception of privacy can lead individuals to blurt out initial prejudicial responses to real world events. For example, in 2011, protestors at the Wisconsin state capitol building were fighting against the loss of collective bargaining rights for employees. When news broke that the police had been authorized to remove the protestors, a prominent Wisconsin deputy attorney general tweeted, "Use live ammunition" (Weinstein, 2011). Examining his past tweets and his personal blog illuminated his use of the blogging medium to express instantaneous reactions of bigotry, xenophobia, and racism (Weinstein, 2011). Once the prejudicial blogs were exposed (notably also via the Internet), the deputy lost his job with the state.

Are these informal Internet mediums, such as Twitter and blogging, windows into individuals' true attitudes? These Internet mediums might lead users to express their beliefs in less self-monitored or regulated ways. Existing research tends to support such notions. In a study comparing the expression of bias over different mediums, participants reported more bias when an interview occurred on the Internet than through more traditional, face-to-face interactions (Evans, Garcia, Garcia, & Baron, 2003). The Internet, therefore, may not just be a forum for the expression of bias, but actually be a cause in itself.

Legitimacy

Another related key characteristic regarding the Internet and its relationship to prejudice and discrimination is the perceived legitimacy of online media. Internet-based mediums, similar to many other written communication platforms, capitalize on the perception that information that is published—in seemingly any form—is seen as legitimate. Individuals may think written text is more intentional and thoughtful than spoken word—even with little evidence supporting this belief. Despite the fact that anyone with access and basic understanding can "publish" a blog, or article, or even a book online, the perception of legitimacy granted the published word gives credibility to writers' thoughts and attitudes. Individuals might mistake a blogger with no legitimate credentials for an expert on a particular topic. For instance, a large controversy erupted in 2011 when the author of a popular blog titled, "A Gay Girl in Damascus," supposedly a Syrian American lesbian named Amina living in Damascus, was revealed to be a heterosexual White male from the US (Addley, 2011). After "Amina" claimed to be kidnapped by Syrian security forces, the news media, US Embassy, and Facebook friends began searching for her, ultimately exposing the fraud. While this incident is also notable for the use of anonymity in order to expose injustices and rights violations across the world, it also highlights how blog posts on the Internet are seen as legitimate news, even when writers' identities or credentials are unverified. In fact, many respected news organizations, including the UK's *The Guardian*, had been in contact with "Amina" and reported her "news," with some real correspondents in the field risking their safety to attempt to meet her in Syria (Addley, 2011). Despite not having any credentials, this blogger had gained acceptance as a legitimate news source regarding the events in Syria simply by publishing thoughts on an Internet blog. Less spectacular examples no doubt abound, with bloggers speaking authoritatively despite lack of expertise.

Recent research has delved into the notions of legitimacy on the Internet, and its relationship to prejudice and racism. In a study assessing the credibility and legitimacy of various Internet communication mediums, Melican and Dixon (2008) found that nontraditional Internet news sources, such as blogs, not surprisingly, were viewed as less credible than other types of Internet news, such as online outlets of newspapers. However, interestingly, viewing these nontraditional sources as credible was associated with higher racial prejudice beliefs. While a causal argument cannot yet be made, the results suggest that relatively prejudiced individuals are more likely to trust and view nontraditional Internet sources as legitimate, perhaps because these sources are more likely to contain content supporting their beliefs. This pattern relates to the social psychological phenomenon of confirmation bias, in which individuals are likely to seek out information that confirms their pre-existing beliefs (see Nickerson, 1998, for a review). It is also possible that the content of these blogs promotes racial prejudice; those who view them as most legitimate could be more influenced by them.

Permanency

We lastly consider the permanent nature of information posted on the Internet, and discuss its impact on the expression of online prejudice and discrimination. Due to a variety of the characteristics of the Internet described earlier—anonymity, perceived privacy, and legitimacy—individuals may post thoughts, feelings, or reactions that they later would rather have removed. While original posts, pictures, videos, and blogs can be deleted, there is potentially a permanent record of anything posted on the Internet in the past. Through screen captures by other users, downloading of online material, and IP (Internet protocol) address tracing, once material makes its way onto the Internet, a record of its existence may always remain, despite the potential wishes of its original authors. The permanency of Internet material necessitates that individuals who post prejudicial thoughts or blogs may never be able to undo these actions, even if they no longer hold or wish to express those views. In contrast to more traditional public displays of bias, where apologies, explanations, and the passage of time can help an episode fade from memory, Internet-based incidents leave a trace that can serve as constant reminders.

New Trends on the Internet: Social Networking Sites

We now turn to a more detailed discussion of the newest trends of communication and usage of the Internet. Clearly, the rise of online social networks has been one of the most significant—and arguably most important—developments of the Internet over the last few years. In the following sections, we examine the most prominent online social networks and their implications for prejudice and discrimination.

Facebook

Facebook may be the most important online social network to study for several reasons, not the least of which being that it is the largest and most popular social networking platform (Kreutz, 2009). Social network sites similar to Facebook that target specific ethnicities or racial groups have also seen a dramatic expansion in usage. Examples of these networking sites include Black Planet for African Americans, AsianAvenue for Asian Americans, and MiGente for Latinos (boyd & Ellison, 2008). Furthermore, Facebook provides researchers with unique opportunities for studying human behavior in a naturalistic setting, particularly for behaviors that are otherwise hard to observe unobtrusively (Wilson, Gosling, & Graham, 2012). The merging of online Facebook social networks and offline friend networks—and the interaction between these two worlds—allows for new and innovative empirical examinations. We therefore ask the question, what can Facebook tell us about prejudice and discrimination on the Internet?

In studying online social networks like Facebook, it is important to consider how representative Facebook users are of more general populations. A recent study of 77,954 U.S. Facebook profiles demonstrated that the diversity of Facebook users has increased over time, currently paralleling the racial breakdown of the US population (Chang, Rosenn, Backstrom, & Marlow, 2010). The diversity of Facebook users might reflect the population, but are they using the medium to accurately represent and express their social identities? While self-presentation concerns and impression management issues are still present in Internet-based communication, there remains a trend for more nonymous presentation of the selves on social media. Following the trend of declining anonymity on the Internet, Grasmuck, Martin, and Zhao (2009) have found that Facebook users' ethnic and racial identities are salient, personal, and highly detailed on their profiles. Interviews and observational techniques confirmed the accuracy of users' profiles relative to their actual identities. Grasmuck et al. (2009) further suggest that ethnic and racial minorities may use Facebook as a way to vividly express their social identities, which may be devalued in broader society, in a free and unencumbered manner. We see here that, despite the lack of anonymity, minorities may view Facebook as a way to celebrate their social identities while being shielded from offline discrimination.

However, while users may feel that Facebook is a safe domain for social identity expression, it may result in increased offline discrimination. Employers, for example, have begun to use Facebook to screen potential job applicants, examining profiles to gain confidential information that is prohibited by equal opportunity laws in the US (Kluemper & Rosen, 2009). This information can then be used to discriminate against potential job candidates. Therefore, employers may commit this discriminatory act without ever having to admit that they received or where they found this confidential social identity information. Some employers have gone so far as to require potential job applicants' passwords to their social networking profiles, making this process even more explicit (Valdes & McFarland, 2012).

It has been compellingly demonstrated that employers continue to discriminate on the basis of race (Bertrand & Mullainathan, 2004). The extent to which racial minorities are freely and strongly expressing their identities online could leave them particularly vulnerable to discrimination. Furthermore, psychological research has demonstrated that highly identified minorities (Kaiser & Pratt-Hyatt, 2009) and highly stereotypic minorities (Eberhardt, Davies, Purdie-Vaughns, & Johnson, 2006; Kahn & Davies, 2011) are more likely to be targets of discrimination and prejudice. If employers glean such details from Facebook, highly identified and physically stereotypical minority individuals may be most likely to experience offline discrimination.

The practice of employers seeking Internet-based information about applicants has become so widespread that companies have formed that specialize in discovering and detailing applicants' online profiles (Mandell, 2011). One such company is Social Intelligence, which will search potential employees' Facebook, Twitter, MySpace, and online photosharing site accounts, as well as Google, for damaging information to report. Any questionable material, which may be taken out of context from years in the past, may harm job seekers by labeling them homophobic, prejudicial, or sexist. To the extent that companies like Social Intelligence are formalizing this process, and to the extent that they are not sharing information about race, ethnicity, religion, etc., this trend could mitigate discriminatory effects. However, to the extent that the existence of such companies is merely a reflection of a much greater tendency to seek online information about applicants for jobs, loans, etc., it may reflect a problematic trend.

Experimental research has also provided evidence for at least one type of discriminatory tendency based on users' online profiles. Peluchette and Karl (2008) had participants evaluate potential job applicants by viewing their online profiles. The results demonstrated that, among applicants who posted questionable material on their profiles, female applicants were less likely to be hired compared to male applicants. That is, potential employers were more accepting of males' profiles and online material, and were more stringent with those of females, resulting in gender discrimination in hiring.

Facebook can also be used as a tool to study the development and expression of attitudes and social norms, including prejudice. For example, Facebook users frequently post news articles they find interesting, and fellow users can express their approval of a posted item by clicking on the "Like" button. Users can also flag items that violate particular rules or norms as inappropriate. Researchers have mimicked this Facebook paradigm in investigations of racial attitudes and online discrimination. A study by Tynes and Markoe (2010) had participants view social media pages that contained pictures of the ostensible profile holder at a racially offensive party. The participants, both Black and White, then wrote a comment on the user's "wall"—a public forum where friends can write short messages—in response to the photographs. They found that White participants who believed society should be colorblind, as opposed to multicultural, were more likely to approve of the racially inappropriate content and support the user by making encouraging posts, laughing at the photographs, and affirming the pictures. In contrast, participants who were low in endorsement of colorblind ideology were more likely to respond by negatively evaluating and disagreeing with the racially biased content, with many saying that they would remove this person from their online social network. From this study, it is apparent how individuals use Facebook features, including the public wall, to both express their own beliefs and monitor their friends' posts and actions. Posting or liking a racially offensive picture or news story can lead to "defriending" in the cyberworld, potentially followed in the offline world as well, but it can also engender support from some, perhaps reinforcing bigoted norms.

Just as Facebook facilitated the social protests that led to regime change in Egypt (Ali, 2011), social media can be used to organize groups fighting against prejudice and discrimination or in response to specific polarizing racial incidents. One wonders what the American Civil Rights movement of the 1950s–1960s might have looked like had social media and Facebook been present. Indeed, researchers have examined the ability of social networking sites to promote civic engagement amongst the African American community using Black Planet, a Facebook-like social media forum that is targeted at the African American community (Byrne, 2007). While Byrne (2007) found that Black Planet promoted dialogue about racial prejudice and discrimination, she did not find an increase in civic engagement amongst these participants. Future research can continue to promote better understanding of the ways that online social media can be used to fight injustice and promote lasting offline change.

Twitter

While many of the same notions regarding prejudice and discrimination that apply to Facebook also are relevant for other forms of online social networking sites, there are also unique aspects of other prominent social networking platforms that relate to bias online. Twitter, launched in 2006, is a microblogging service that has a 140-character limit for each sent message, called a *tweet*. Representing a form of online text messaging, Twitter enables users to follow different members and receive their tweets, while also sending out their own tweets to their followers. This short character limit encourages quick—and potentially less thought-out—responses by its users. Messages on Twitter also instantly reach their group of followers, and it is often used to express sudden reactions to ongoing real world events. This format seems to encourage, or at least make more likely, prejudicial expressions. Numerous professional athletes, celebrities, comedians, and politicians have apologized for racially or ethnically insensitive tweets, with some losing their jobs or decreasing their popularity. Furthermore, because people can be, or at least *feel*, more anonymous on Twitter than on Facebook, since less real information is generally posted on a Twitter account, prejudice may be more likely to be expressed on Twitter.

Despite the potential for individuals to remain more anonymous on Twitter, researchers have found that a poster's location can be determined based on the dialect used in their tweets (Eisenstein, O'Connor, Smith, & Xing, 2010). Researchers analyzed 380,000 tweets by 9500 US users over a 1-week period in March 2010, and were able to detect regional differences in language expression. These different dialects then allowed researchers to predict users' locations within 300 miles (Eisenstein et al., 2010). Determining their race or ethnicity, even if not explicitly stated, might not be far away. Making users' social categories nonymous brings with it the potential for discrimination, particularly when considering employers' examination of the social media presence of potential job candidates.

YouTube

YouTube is an online broadcasting forum onto which users can upload video content for others to view. YouTube videos are often third-person representations of others' actions, including a full range of subjects, from talking cats to news broadcasts. Often, people post YouTube videos of their own statements and/or actions. Similar to blogging their written thoughts and paralleling the trends in other forms of online communication sites, users often reveal highly personal thoughts in this very open public forum (Lange, 2007). These videos can then go "viral" and be viewed by millions of users worldwide. When these online videos involve prejudice and bias, their existence can be double-edged swords, such that they promote the spread of intolerant attitudes while also exposing them and spreading the norm of condemnation of bias. One such incident that demonstrates the potential for YouTube to simultaneously spread prejudice while also allowing for its public condemnation occurred in 2010 when a White UCLA student posted a bigoted, 3-minute video rant against Asian American students, in which she mocked their accent and spoke derogatorily about their culture. The video went viral, with more than one million views in the following days, and caused a national uproar, heightened by the fact that it was posted after the tsunami in Japan. The student received death threats in response. Ultimately, the student removed the video and issued statements of apology, but it still remains available online—another example of permanency of the Internet—and the incident serves as a vivid example of how quickly a prejudicial rant can reach a very large audience on YouTube.

On the other hand, YouTube videos can also help reduce discrimination by documenting and publicizing discriminatory events that might otherwise have gone unnoticed. YouTube has been an effective venue for individuals who capture real-life video of controversial events using cell phone cameras. This method has been especially useful for citizens to document police brutality against minorities, such as the case of alleged police brutality against an Asian college student by the San Jose Police Department in 2009 (Baker, 2009). A cell phone video that captured this interaction was uploaded to YouTube, which was then watched by thousands and likely contributed to a police investigation. Thus, while YouTube may spread prejudice by making bigoted rants instantly accessible to millions of people worldwide, it may reduce discrimination by documenting offline incidents and holding individuals responsible for such actions.

Community Forums and Chat Rooms

Among the earlier forms of online communication, chat rooms and community forums are also common ways for individuals to connect with each other on the Internet, and to potentially transmit prejudice in both subtle and blatant ways. Chat rooms might encourage the social psychological phenomenon of groupthink, such that cohesive groups increase the likelihood of agreement among participants (Janis, 1972). This process can encourage the expression of, and agreement with, prejudicial beliefs. For example, Wikipedia is an online encyclopedia in which individuals are responsible for entering and maintaining the content. As an open forum, anyone on the Internet has the ability to change, add, or delete information on a Wikipedia page. Because Wikipedia is an open forum, it is susceptible to distortions that may be driven by ideology, including bigotry (Cohen, 2011). While this open strategy has significant benefits, users have taken advantage of this democratic approach to alter pages to include racist comments or prejudicial statements. These types of comments are normally detected and deleted, but their existence shows how individuals may be trying to use these online public forums to shape public discourse about given topics.

Similar to the altering of Wikipedia to support ideological beliefs, sports fans seek to shape and influence cultural understandings of events to match their perspectives using online chat rooms.

An interesting study by Sanderson (2010) delved into the use of online communication by fans to debate the existence of racism in sport, specifically focusing on racism in NCAA (National Collegiate Athletic Association) college football hiring of coaches. Examining discussion forums on the ESPN website (http://www.espn.com) revealed that fans' comments reproduced cultural ideology that denied the existence of racism, blamed victims, and even claimed reverse-racism against White coaches (Sanderson, 2010). Thus, fans took to the Internet to express their cultural ideologies about racism in society and to support the societal system.

Chat rooms can also help reduce the negative influences of prejudice and discrimination on stigmatized targets by providing an outlet to discuss sensitive racial issues. In a study about inter-racial interactions online, teenagers engaged in "racialized role taking" when interacting with members of other racial groups (Tynes, 2007). That is, teenagers used chat rooms to learn about other races or ethnicities and understand those unique perspectives. Through communicating their racial attitudes and identities in a positive setting, interaction partners learned about what it meant to be a member of the other racial group.

While the results of this study are encouraging, chat room discussions are not always positive regarding race, and can be detrimental when they take place in non-moderated chat rooms. A content and discourse analysis of adolescents' use of online chat rooms found that race and ethnicity were regular discussion topics amongst teens (Tynes, Reynolds, & Greenfield, 2004). The majority of these mentions of race were positive or neutral; however, negative remarks were frequent as well, particularly in unmonitored chat rooms. Monitored chat rooms had a substantially lower rate of negative racial comments, indicating how an online authoritative presence can reinforce norms of tolerance (Tynes et al., 2004). Although it is important to note that selection effects might be influencing these patterns, such that less biased individuals might be more likely to opt for moderated chat rooms, the results are nonetheless informative to consider regarding the expression on bias in online forums

Extremist Websites

Probably the most vitriolic type of online prejudice is the use of the Internet by racist extremists to communicate messages of intolerance. Since the web became a common societal medium, online hate groups have existed, leading to psychological research on these sites. The online presence of these groups has persisted in modern day (e.g., see Glaser, Dixit, & Green, 2002; Glaser & Kahn, 2005; see Brown, 2009, for a recent analysis of White supremacist discourse on the Internet). Countering the promulgation of racial and religious hatred on the Internet, numerous websites dedicated to tolerance and equality are also prevalent. UnderstandingPrejudice.org is one of the more comprehensive examples of a site aimed at disseminating scientific research to the public regarding current understanding of prejudice and how to reduce its many forms. The site contains links to 2000 prejudice-related resources, exercises, and demonstrations, and a database of scientific experts and organizations that focus on promoting tolerance.

Racial and Ethnic Preferences and Segregation Reflected in (and Promoted By?) Internet-Based Dating Sites

One area in which the Internet has dramatically affected offline social lives is through web-based dating and romantic matching programs like eHarmony.com and Match.com. By conservative estimates, tens of millions of Americans (and doubtless many millions more from other countries) have used online dating services (Madden & Lenhart, 2006). Like so many aspects of the Internet as it relates to prejudice and discrimination, online dating services afford a twofold analysis. First, they offer us relatively unobtrusive insight into patterns of preference and discrimination because Internet-based interactions leave a clear and accurate record of actual (if computer-mediated) behavior. Second, the very processes engendered by Internet-based communications and social relations can affect racial and ethnic relations. Examinations of online dating services and the specific postings people put on them allow us to survey race- and ethnicity-based preferences for romantic partners, and to estimate the rate at which people are finding partners of same versus other race or ethnicity, a factor that is influential with regard to racial and ethnic integration.

Given that the current "leader of the free world," the president of the US, is of mixed African and European ancestry, one might expect that intergroup dating and marriage is now widely accepted. Empirically, however, approval of interracial relationships is not exactly overwhelming. Schuman, Steeh, Bobo, and Krysan's (1997) review of twentieth-century surveys showed that White Americans' approval of interracial marriage increased steadily from nearly zero in 1958 to more than 60% approving in 1995. But even as recently as 2004, 24% of White Americans surveyed disapproved of interracial marriage (Institute of Government & Public Affairs at the University of Illinois). Putting these attitudes to a more behavioral test in the year 2000, voters in the state of Alabama elected to officially overturn a state antimiscegenation law (already rendered moot by a Supreme Court ruling), but only by a 60 to 40 margin. Interracial and interethnic romantic relationships are still relatively rare in most parts of the world.

As noted, online dating services offer an insight into patterns of racial and ethnic preferences. They are, of course, only representative of those who seek partners online, but there is no reason to suspect that such individuals are any less open to interracial or interethnic relationships than others. To the contrary, because many relationships are forged in environments (e.g., social clubs, places of worship, colleges, geographical locations, etc.) that are already relatively segregated, it is plausible that online matches would be *less* prone to such selectivity.

Studies have found, in fact, that those seeking romantic partners online do tend to express preferences for those within their racial and ethnic group. One early study seemed to contradict this, however. A survey of dating "personal ads" that had been posted by men on Yahoo.com found that only a small proportion (3–8%) of men seeking women spontaneously expressed a preference for partners from their own race, with White men being the least likely to do so relative to Asian, Black, and Hispanic men (Phua & Kaufman, 2003). For men seeking men, the expression of own-race preferences was higher (4–19%), with Black men being the most likely. The Phua and Kaufman (2003) study looked at the more old-fashioned personal ad type of online partner-seeking, where partner race/ethnicity preference was not included in the information requested by the service. Consequently, it may have underestimated the rate of race preference in partner-seeking.

More recently, Sweeney and Borden (2009) surveyed postings by Black and White men seeking women and women seeking men on an undisclosed, popular dating site. They found that both Black and White people overwhelmingly expressed preferences for dating partners from their own race, with 59% and 67%, respectively, indicating they desired a partner within their race and expressly not indicating a willingness to consider partners from the other group.

Robnett and Feliciano (2011), in a survey of thousands of Yahoo! personal ads from around the US, found that White posters exhibit the highest rate of racial/ethnic exclusion, and Black posters the least, and that for most racial or ethnic groups, women are more likely than men to express a preference for their own group. Similarly, Hitch, Hortaçsu, and Ariely (2010) find strong intragroup preferences among both men and women that varied little across age, income, and education levels. In sum, intraracial and intraethnic preferences are the norm in online dating, but there is also considerable intergroup partner-seeking occurring.

Race-Specific sites

Another indicator of racial and ethnic segregation in Internet dating services is the prevalence of race- and religion-specific sites for people exclusively seeking partners within their own group. In fact, the very existence of these sites may cause estimates of intragroup preferences based on activity on the generic sites (e.g., eHarmony.com and Match.com) to be artificially low because some of the individuals inclined to seek only ingroup partners are opting only for group-specific sites.

Race- and religion-specific sites are not just an indicator of ethnocentric preferences, but also may promote (or at least delay the decline) of such preferences. Specifically, they very directly promote intragroup partnering, but they also promote a norm that it is acceptable to seek partners only within one's group.

These sites are ubiquitous. eHarmony, one of the biggest providers, for example, has special sections for Asians, Black people (but not White), Christians, Jews, and Hispanics (and gays and lesbians, see discussion in "Antihomosexual Discrimination in Internet Dating Sites" section). The absence of a Whites-only section on eHarmony appears to reflect a general trend, perhaps reflecting a sensitivity that the hegemonic group should not overtly exclude others. In fact, the sole White-only dating service we could find on the Internet was operated by the notorious White supremacist website, Stormfront. It could also be the case that White people seeking White partners do not particularly need, nor think they need, a specific dating site for that purpose, because, being in the majority group, there are likely to be many White singles with whom to match on a generic site.

Group-specific dating sites are far more commonplace for minority groups. There are a large number of sites that are for Black people (e.g., blacksingles.com, blackpeoplemeet.com, soulsingles.com, datingblacksingles.com, blackpeoplelove.com/dating), Hispanics (e.g., allhispanicdating.com, latinsinglesconnection.com, latinopeoplemeet.com, latinlovesearch.com), and Asians (chineselovelinks.com, asiansingles.com).[1]

On the other hand, there are also sites that expressly promote intergroup dating (e.g., blackandwhitesingles.com, afroromance.com, interracialdatingcentral.com, whitewomenblackmen.com). These should serve to increase both the number of intergroup relationships and acceptance of them.

Religion-Specific Sites

Perhaps because religion has historically played a central role in both matchmaking and marrying, religion-based dating sites appear to be more prevalent than race-based sites (see http://www.free-mind-body-spirit.com/spiritualdating.html for a compendium of hundreds of religion-based dating sites). There are sites for Jews (e.g., jdate.com, jewishfriendfinder.com, ajewishdatingsite.com); Muslims (e.g., singlemuslim.com, muslima.com, muslimdatingwebsite.com); Buddhists, although there appear to be relatively few (e.g., buddhistconnect.com, buddhistdatingservice.com); Hindus (e.g., hindufaces.com, indiandating.com, hinduconnections.com); and many sites for Christians (e.g., BigChurch.com, christianmingle.com, christiansingles.com, christiancafe.com, christianmatchmaker.com), including sites for specific Christian denominations (e.g., Catholicmatch.com, catholicpeoplemeet.com, LDSmingle.com, LDSsingles.com, Episcopalsingles.org). Perhaps not surprisingly, the availability of religion-based dating sites resembles the pattern in race-based sites, which is that there appears to be a dearth of Protestant sites. In the US, where Internet dating services appear to be most common, Protestants are by far

---

[1] This section is not by any means intended to provide an exhaustive listing of group-specific sites.

the largest single denomination. Perhaps this religious hegemony engenders the same kind of reservation, or confidence, about intragroup partner seeking that being White does vis-à-vis race in America.

Antihomosexual Discrimination in Internet Dating Sites

While the Internet-based dating record is mixed with regard to interracial and interethnic relations, it has a more openly discriminatory history with regard to same-sex relations. One of the largest and most successful online dating sites, eHarmony, was sued in multiple states for explicitly excluding same-sex listings. Eventually, eHarmony settled a lawsuit in New Jersey in 2008, and reached a larger settlement in a California suit in 2010, ultimately setting up a companion site for gay and lesbian users, "compatiblepartners.net." Interestingly, for the racial and ethnic subsites eHarmony provides, it offers a format that is identical to the standard eHarmony format, but compatiblepartners.net is a separate site altogether, merely linked to the eHarmony main page. Perhaps more telling is the record of statements from eHarmony about this matter. Initially, the company's cofounder, Neil Clark Warren, stated that the exclusion of gay and lesbian participants was due to the lack of research on homosexual relationships that would enable eHarmony to derive the matching algorithms it would need. But Warren later indicated that eHarmony wishes to promote heterosexual marriages, eventually stating at a forum of the antigay rights organization, Focus on the Family, an express opposition to same-sex marriage (Wikipedia, 2011). An increasing number of dating sites include options for same-sex partners, which, eHarmony's record notwithstanding, may serve to both promote successful gay and lesbian matching while also promoting more accepting norms regarding homosexuality, by virtue of its inclusion in this growing trend.

As in so many domains (e.g., the ability to promote both isolation and connection), the Internet's effects on romantic relations is a double-edged sword, perhaps exacerbating the effects of preferences that would otherwise be played out more subtly. In this case, those who wish to draw from a diverse pool of potential partners have an unparalleled opportunity to do so; and those who seek to remain focused on their own group can do so more efficiently and even discretely.

Studying Prejudice and Discrimination on the Internet: New Techniques

As it continues to develop and expand its reach, the Internet brings social science researchers a new laboratory and tool with which to study racial prejudice and discrimination. Many researchers, as we predicted, have taken advantage of the various possibilities of the Internet to study bias in ways not previously feasible. Specifically, the Internet has helped increase research on prejudice and discrimination by providing access to more representative, diverse, and large samples and by allowing researchers to study sensitive phenomena unobtrusively and in naturalistic settings. Furthermore, the advent of social networking sites has added a new forum in which to study these psychological phenomena. We now detail some of the newer methods that have emerged regarding the study of online prejudice and discrimination (see Glaser & Kahn, 2005, for additional discussion).

Project Implicit is the most productive venture on the Internet to study implicit prejudice. It was developed and is run by social psychological researchers at Harvard University, the University of Virginia, and University of Washington (http://www.projectimplicit.net, 2011) and includes collaborators from all over the world. Project Implicit administers online Implicit Association Tests (IATs) in order to examine implicit stereotyping and prejudice using the web. Specifically, the IAT is designed to assess attitudes that are less consciously accessible to the participant—and therefore less likely to be consciously controlled—with the consistent finding that most individuals hold implicit biases against racial minorities relative to White populations. Visitors to Project Implicit's website may participate for free in a variety of IAT tests which include racial and ethnic group IATs, and, in doing so, receive feedback about their individual-level implicit racial attitudes and beliefs, and educational information about implicit social cognition. The collected data then helps researchers further study and understand implicit bias (e.g., the IAT's psychometric properties, implicit bias' relations to other constructs, etc.). Nearly 4.5 million tests have been taken on Project Implicit's site since it opened in 1998, and it is currently averaging over 15,000 tests each week (http://www.projectimplicit.net/generalinfo.php).

Based on data from the hundreds of thousands of visitors who have consented to participate in research, Project Implicit has yielded numerous important findings. Studies conducted utilizing Project Implicit have examined a wide variety of implicit biases, such as racism (Baron & Banaji, 2006; Joy-Gaba & Nosek, 2010; Schmidt & Nosek, 2010), sexism (Lemm, Dabady, & Banaji, 2003), ageism (Levy & Banaji, 2002), ethnocentrism (Cunningham, Nezlek, & Banaji, 2004), antifat bias (Schwartz, Vartanian, Nosek, & Brownell, 2006), and stigma of mental illness (Peris, Teachman, & Nosek, 2008). Importantly, the extremely large samples amassed by Project Implicit, possible only through Internet-based data collection, have allowed for analysis of the psychometric properties and predictive validity of the IAT itself (Greenwald, Nosek, & Banaji, 2003; Nosek, Greenwald, & Banaji, 2005; Nosek & Smyth, 2007). For example, Nosek and Smyth (2007) used Project Implicit data to explore moderators of the strength of correlations between implicit and explicit measures of the same attitudes, finding that, despite generally strong correlations, they tap distinguishable constructs.

Project Implicit stands out from other Internet-based research tools because, rather than relying on observation or administering questionnaire-style surveys, it utilizes a "virtual laboratory" in which simple experiments may be conducted. Because these same experiments can be conducted in laboratories or in the field under nearly identical circumstances, Project Implicit supplements and expands traditional offline, lab-based research by accessing populations, geographic areas, and even dates and times that offline research can miss.

In addition to Project Implicit, the advent of social networking sites has also provided an opportunity to study online prejudice. As discussed earlier, researchers have turned to Facebook to sift through its wealth of social information, but Facebook also lends itself well to recruiting participants for psychological studies, thereby allowing researchers to target specific geographic areas or racial populations. Some researchers have created Facebook-specific applications such as MyPersonality, with which users can fill out information on Facebook to learn about their personality profile (Wilson et al., 2012). Others have created data-crawling applications, which unobtrusively scroll through users' profiles and collect publicly available information (although the ethics of this practice in regard to violating privacy rules have been questioned; see Gjoka, Kurant, Butts, & Markopoulou, 2010, for a review). Others have taken to observing and coding Facebook profiles, with some researchers bringing participants into the lab to inform them of the study purposes before viewing their Facebook pages (Wilson et al., 2012). A meta-analysis by Wilson et al. (2012) summarized 202 relevant articles that used Facebook in research, with the studies falling into five major categories: Detailing participant usage patterns, reasons for using Facebook, presentation of social identities, how Facebook influences social interactions, and privacy and information sharing. The potential to study prejudice and/or discrimination exists in each of these topics on Facebook. Social networking sites will continue to be an interesting and innovative way to approach the study of online bias.

In addition to Facebook, other online services offer researchers access to diverse and more representative samples using the Internet. Of particular note is Knowledge Networks, a major polling firm that conducts web-based surveys that are of very high quality. Knowledge Networks provides a more representative sample of the US demography than most phone-based surveys or surveys sampling from the Internet alone because they provide both computers and Internet access to individuals who might not have it otherwise. In exchange, members agree to complete a minimum number of research surveys per month. Although Knowledge Networks provides one of the better samples currently available to researchers, like most professional survey firms, its service can be expensive and thus researchers are sometimes left searching for cheaper, alternative means of accessing participants.

One such alternative that has become popular with researchers is Mechanical Turk (a.k.a., MTurk), which is run through Amazon.com. MTurk is a type of online marketplace where individuals can post "hits," which are tasks that require human participants to complete, such as a survey. Users can sign up as a "worker" and view the lists of tasks that are currently offered, along with their approximate time to complete and compensation rates. The advantages of MTurk include its ease of use, its ability to collect a large amount of data in a short time span (e.g., within hours for hundreds of survey responses), its inexpensive nature (with some tasks only paying a few pennies), and its flexibility to accommodate almost any online task. Research has assessed the quality of the MTurk sample, finding higher levels of diversity than among US college participant pools or some Internet samples, as well as demonstrating good internal consistency and test–retest reliabilities among participant responses (Buhrmester, Kwang, & Gosling, 2011). While this represents an exciting new tool for prejudice researchers to access diverse pools of participants inexpensively, the ethics of such low payment levels have been debated, and it is unclear under what circumstances (i.e., how casually and distractedly), MTurk participants are carrying out tasks. In all, MTurk provides an affordable option for scientists to study prejudice via the Internet, but researchers may wish to rely on resources like MTurk for more preliminary studies, and conduct primary hypothesis tests on more formal samples, (see more on MTurk and other online research methods in Chapter 13).

Conclusions: The Future of Prejudice and Discrimination and the Internet

In some ways, predicting the future of online prejudice and discrimination is as difficult as predicting the future of the Internet itself. Prejudice and discrimination online will naturally respond to changes in the new ways in which the Internet is integrated into our lives. In our initial writing on the topic in 2005, we hypothesized that the Internet had the possibility to increase prejudice (or at least expressions of it) but decrease discrimination. In the years that have followed, our thesis regarding online prejudice and discrimination appears to still hold, *insomuch as people remain anonymous.* The recent trend for Internet users to become more nonymous—through the use of social networking sites, YouTube, blogs, and other more personal online communication forums— complicates these notions for both prejudice and discrimination. Declining anonymity will lessen the potential decrease in discrimination on the Internet, while simultaneously mitigating the expected increase in the expression of prejudice. From the potential target's perspective, becoming more nonymous online may make an individual more likely to experience discrimination, as social identity cues are more visible. However, becoming more nonymous may lessen a potential perpetrator's willingness to express prejudice, as they are more likely to be identified by and tied to the comments. Making individuals more identifiable may dissuade them from publicly expressing prejudice, but it also makes discriminatory actions more risky. It may be the case that reducing anonymity has a stronger impact on the expression of prejudice compared to the acts of discrimination. Many discriminatory acts, particularly online, are more passive in nature (e.g., the failure to give a minority a home loan), and thus individuals might be less concerned about identification. The expression of prejudicial attitudes, in contrast, tends to be a more active and obvious act, making identification a more salient and meaningful deterrent.

So, what is the future of discrimination and prejudice on the Internet? If these patterns continue, online prejudice and discrimination might more closely mimic the offline field, as users' identities becoming more salient online. In a more nonymous Internet world, we may also observe a trend such that individuals *strategically* use and seek out anonymity, once it is no longer the norm, when it is believed to be advantageous to their particular goals. These situations might include perpetrators seeking anonymity when expressing racism or prejudice, or traditional targets of discrimination hiding their social category in situations when it might be disadvantageous. Despite our inability to predict its future direction, the Internet remains a uniquely influential, potent, and far-reaching medium for both users and researchers alike to understand prejudice and discrimination, along with numerous other aspects of the human psychological experience.

References

Addley, E. (2011, June 13). Gay girl in Damascus hoaxer acted out of "vanity." *The Guardian*. Retrieved from http://www.guardian.co.uk/

Ali, A. H. (2011). The power of social media in developing nations: New tools for closing the global digital divide and beyond. *Harvard Human Rights Journal, 24*, 185–220.

Allport, G. W. (1954). *The nature of prejudice*. Oxford, UK: Addison-Wesley.

Allport, G. W. (1985). The historical background of social psychology. In G. Lindzey & E. Aronson (Eds.), *Handbook of Social Psychology* (3rd ed., Vol. 1, pp. 1–46). New York, NY: Random House.

Attewell, P. (2001). The first and second digital divides. *Sociology of Education, 74*, 252–259.

Baker, D. R. (2009, October 26). San Jose police to investigate brutality claim: Cell phone video shows man being hit with baton, tasered. *San Francisco Chronicle*. Retrieved from http://articles.sfgate.com/2009-10-26/bay-area/17184735_1_roommate-officer-kenneth-siegel-steak-knife

Bargh, J. A., McKenna, K. Y., & Fitzsimons, G. M. (2002). Can you see the real me? Activation and expression of the "'true self'" on the Internet. *Journal of Social Issues, 58*, 33–48.

Baron, A. S., & Banaji, M. R. (2006). The development of implicit attitudes: Evidence of race evaluations from ages 6 to 10 and adulthood. *Psychological Science, 17*, 53–58.

Bertrand, M., & Mullainathan, S. (2004). Are Emily and Greg more employable than Lakisha and Jamal? A field experiment on labor market discrimination. *The American Economic Review, 94*, 991–1013.

boyd, d.m., & Ellison, N. B. (2008). Social network sites: Definition, history, and scholarship. *Journal of Computer-Mediated Communication, 13*, 210–230.

Brown, C. (2009). www.hate.com: White supremacist discourse on the Internet and the construction of Whiteness ideology. *Howard Journal of Communications, 20*, 189–208.

Bucy, E. P. (2000). Social access to the Internet. *The Harvard International Journal of Press Politics, 5*, 50–61.

Buhrmester, M., Kwang, T., & Gosling, S. D. (2011). Amazon's Mechanical Turk: A new source of inexpensive, yet high-quality, data? *Perspectives on Psychological Science, 6*, 3–5.

Byrne, D. N. (2007). Public discourse, community concerns, and civic engagement: Exploring Black social networking traditions on BlackPlanet.com. *Journal of Computer-Mediated Communication, 13*, 319–340.

Chang, J., Rosenn, I., Backstrom, L., & Marlow, C. (2010, May). ePluribus: Ethnicity on social networks. Paper presented at the Fourth International AAAI Conference on Weblogs and Social Media,

Washington, DC. Retrieved from http://www.aaai.org/ocs/index.php/ICWSM/ICWSM10/paper/view/1534

Cohen, N. (2011, June 13). Shedding hazy light on a midnight ride. *The New York Times*. Retrieved from http://www.nytimes.com/

Cunningham, W. A., Nezlek, J. B., & Banaji, M. R. (2004). Implicit and explicit ethnocentrism: Revisiting the ideologies of prejudice. *Personality and Social Psychology Bulletin, 30*, 1332–1346.

Dunnell, T. (2010). Common stereotypes—list generated using Google Search. Retrieved from http://suite101.com/article/common-stereotypes--lists-generated-using-google-search-a261384

Eberhardt, J. L., Davies, P. G., Purdie-Vaughns, V. J., & Johnson, S. L. (2006). Looking deathworthy: Perceived stereotypicality of Black defendants predicts capital-sentencing outcomes. *Psychological Science, 17*, 383–386.

Eisenstein, J., O'Connor, B., Smith, N. A., & Xing, E. P. (2010, January). *A latent variable model for geographic lexical variation*. In *Proceedings of the 2010 Conference on Empirical Methods in Natural Language Processing* (pp. 1277–1287). Boston, MA.

Evans, D. C., Garcia, D. G., Garcia, D. M., & Baron, R. S. (2003). In the privacy of their own homes: Using the internet to assess racial bias. *Personality and Social Psychology Bulletin, 29*, 273–284.

Facebook (2012, March 1). Fact sheet. Retrieved from http://newsroom.fb.com/

Fazio, R. H., Jackson, J. R., Dunton, B. C., & Williams, C. J. (1995). Variability in automatic activation as an unobtrusive measure of racial attitudes: A bona fide pipeline? *Journal of Personality and Social Psychology, 69*, 1013–1027.

Free Mind Body Spirit (n.d.). Spiritual dating. Retrieved from http://www.free-mind-body-spirit.com/spiritualdating.html

Ginossar, T., & Nelson, S. (2010). Reducing the health and digital divides: A model for using community-based participatory research approach to e-health interventions in low-income Hispanic communities. *Journal of Computer-Mediated Communication, 15*, 530–551.

Gjoka, M., Kurant, M., Butts, C. T., & Markopoulou, A. (2010, March). Walking in Facebook: A case study of unbiased sampling of OSNs. In *Proceedings of INFOCOM*. San Diego, CA.

Glaser, J., Dixit, J., & Green, D. P. (2002). Studying hate crime with the internet: What makes racists advocate racial violence? *Journal of Social Issues, 58*, 177–193.

Glaser, J., & Kahn, K. B. (2005). Prejudice and discrimination and the Internet. In Y. Amichai-Hamburger (Ed.), *The Social Net: Human behavior in cyberspace* (pp. 247–274). Oxford, UK: Oxford University Press.

Grasmuck, S., Martin, J., & Zhao, S. (2009). Ethno-racial identity displays on Facebook. *Journal of Computer-Mediated Communication, 15*, 158–188.

Greenwald, A. G., Nosek, B. A., & Banaji, M. R. (2003). Understanding and using the Implicit Association Test: I. An improved scoring algorithm. *Journal of Personality and Social Psychology, 85*, 197–216.

Hale, T. M., Cotten, S. R., Drentea, P., & Goldner, M. (2010). Rural-urban differences in general and health-related internet use. *American Behavioral Scientist, 53*, 1304–1325.

Hargittai, E., & Hinnant, A. (2008). Digital inequality: Differences in young adults' use of the Internet. *Communication Research, 35*, 602–621.

Hilgard, E. R. (1980). Consciousness in contemporary psychology. *Annual Review of Psychology, 31*, 1–26.

Hindman, D. B. (2000). The rural-urban digital divide. *Journalism and Mass Communication Quarterly, 77*, 549–560.

Hitch, G.J., Hortaçsu, A., & Ariely, D. (2010). Matching and sorting in online dating. *American Economic Review, 100*, 130–163.

Hoffman, D. & Novak, T. (1998). Bridging the racial divide on the Internet. *Science, 280*, 390–1.

Hoffman, D., Novak, T., & Scholsser, A. (2001). The evolution of the Digital Divide: Examining the relationship of race to Internet access and usage over time. In B. Compaine (Ed.), *The Digital Divide: Facing a crisis or creating a myth?* (pp. 47–98). Cambridge, MA: MIT Press.

Institute of Government and Public Affairs at the University of Illinois (n.d.). Racial Attitudes: Updated Data, Table 3.1b. Retrieved from http://igpa.uillinois.edu/programs/racial-attitudes/data/white/t31b.

James, S. (2011, June 17). Hispanics rank high on Digital Divide. *The New York Times.* Retrieved from http://www.nytimes.com/

Janis, I. L. (1972). *Victims of groupthink: A psychological study of foreign-policy decisions and fiascos.* Boston, MA: Houghton Mifflin.

Jones, S., Johnson-Yale, C., Millermaier, S., & Pérez, F. S. (2009). U.S. college students' Internet use: Race, gender, and digital divides. *Journal of Computer-Mediated Communication, 14,* 244–264.

Joy-Gaba, J. A., & Nosek, B. A. (2010). The surprisingly limited malleability of implicit racial evaluations. *Social Psychology, 41,* 137–146.

Kahn, K. B., & Davies, P. G. (2011). Differentially dangerous? Phenotypic racial stereotypicality increases implicit bias among ingroup and outgroup members. *Group Processes and Intergroup Relations, 14,* 569–580.

Kaiser, C. R., & Pratt-Hyatt, J. S. (2009). Distributing prejudice unequally: Do Whites direct their prejudice toward strongly identified minorities? *Journal of Personality and Social Psychology, 96,* 432–445.

Kluemper, D. H., & Rosen, P. A. (2009). Future employment selection methods: Evaluating social networking web sites. *Journal of Managerial Psychology, 24,* 567–580.

Kreutz, C. (2009). The next billion—The rise of social network sites in developing countries. Retrieved from http://www.web2fordev.net/component/content/article/1-latest-news/69-social-networks

Lange, P. G. (2007). Publicly private and privately public: Social networking on YouTube. *Journal of Computer-Mediated Communication, 13,* 361–380.

Lemm, K. M., Dabady, M., & Banaji, M. R. (2003). *Evidence for gender picture priming.* Unpublished manuscript, Western Washington University, Bellingham, WA.

Levy, B., & Banaji, M. R. (2002). Implicit ageism. In T. Nelson (Ed.), *Ageism: Stereotyping and prejudice against older persons* (pp. 49–75). Cambridge, MA: MIT Press.

Loges, W. E., & Jung, J. (2001). Exploring the digital divide: Internet connectedness and age [Special issue]. *Communication Research, 28,* 536–562.

Lorence, D. P., & Greenberg, L. (2006). The zeitgeist of online health search: Implications for a consumer-centric health system. *Journal of General Internal Medicine, 21,* 134–139.

Madden, M., & Lenhart, A. (2006). *Online Dating.* Washington, DC: Pew Internet & American Life Project.

Mandell, L. J. (2011). Now you could lose a job because of something you "liked" on Facebook. Retrieved from http://jobs.aol.com/articles/2011/06/29/now-you-could-lose-a-job-over-something-you-liked-on-facebook/?ncid=txtlnkuscare00000002

Melican, D. B., & Dixon, T. L. (2008). News on the net: Credibility, selective exposure, and racial prejudice. *Communication Research, 35,* 151–168.

National Telecommunications and Information Administration (1995). *Falling through the Net: A survey of the "have nots" in rural and urban America.* Washington, DC: U.S. Department of Commerce.

Nickerson, R. S. (1998). Confirmation bias: A ubiquitous phenomenon in many guises. *Review of General Psychology, 2,* 175–220.

Nosek, B. A., Greenwald, A. G., & Banaji, M. R. (2005). Understanding and using the Implicit Association Test: II. Method variables and construct validity. *Personality and Social Psychology Bulletin, 31,* 166–180.

Nosek, B. A., & Smyth, F. L. (2007). A multitrait-multimethod validation of the Implicit Association Test: Implicit and explicit attitudes are related but distinct constructs. *Experimental Psychology, 54,* 14–29.

Peluchette, J., & Karl, K. (2008). Social networking profiles: An examination of student attitudes regarding use and appropriateness of content. *CyberPsychology and Behavior, 11,* 95–97.

Peris, T. S., Teachman, B. A., & Nosek, B. A. (2008). Implicit and explicit stigma of mental illness: Links to clinical care. *Journal of Nervous and Mental Disease, 196,* 752–760.

Phua, V. C., & Kaufman, G. (2003). The crossroads of race and sexuality: Date selection among men in internet "personal" ads. *Journal of Family Issues*, *24*, 981–994.

Project Implicit (2011). What is Project Implicit? Retrieved from http://projectimplicit.net/

Robnett, B., & Feliciano, C. (2011). Patterns of racial-ethnic exclusion by Internet daters. *Social Forces*, *89*, 807–828.

Sanderson, J. (2010). Weighing in on the coaching decision: Discussing sports and race online. *Journal of Language and Social Psychology*, *29*, 301–320.

Schmidt, K., & Nosek, B. A. (2010). Implicit (and explicit) racial attitudes barely changed during Barack Obama's presidential campaign and early presidency. *Journal of Experimental Social Psychology*, *46*, 308–314.

Schuman, H., Steeh, C., Bobo, L., & Krysan, M. (1997). *Racial attitudes in America: Trends and interpretations* (Rev. ed.). Cambridge, MA: Harvard University Press.

Schwartz, M. B., Vartanian, L. R., Nosek, B. A., & Brownell, K. D. (2006). The influence of one's own body weight on implicit and explicit anti-fat bias. *Obesity*, *14*, 440–447.

Selwyn, N. (2004). Reconsidering political and popular understandings of the digital divide. *New Media Society*, *6*, 341–362.

Southern Poverty Law Center (2004). All-White dating service planned. *Intelligence Report*, Summer 2004, 114.

Stelter, B. (2011, June 21). Upending anonymity: These days the web unmasks everyone. *The New York Times*. Retrieved from http://www.nytimes.com

Sweeney, K. A., & Borden, A. L. (2009). Crossing the line online: Racial preference of internet daters. *Marriage and Family Review*, *45*, 740–760.

Tynes, B. M. (2007). Role taking in online "classrooms": What adolescents are learning about race and ethnicity. *Developmental Psychology*, *43*, 1312–1320.

Tynes, B., Reynolds, L., & Greenfield, P. M. (2004). Adolescence, race, and ethnicity on the internet: A comparison of discourse in monitored vs. unmonitored chat rooms [Special issue]. *Journal of Applied Developmental Psychology*, *25*, 667–684.

Tynes, B. M., & Markoe, S. L. (2010). The role of color-blind racial attitudes in reactions to racial discrimination on social network sites. *Journal of Diversity in Higher Education*, *3*, 1–13.

Valdes, M., & McFarland, S. (2012, March 20). Employers ask job seekers for Facebook Password. Retrieved from http://www.sfgate.com

Wei, L., & Hindman, D. B. (2011). Does the digital divide matter more? Comparing the effects of new media and old media use on the education-based knowledge gap. *Mass Communication and Society*, *14*, 216–235.

Wei, L., & Zhang, M. (2008). The adoption and use of mobile phone in rural China: A case study of Hubei, China. *Telematics and Informatics*, *25*, 169–186.

Weinstein, A. (2011). Indiana official: "Use live ammunition" against Wisconsin protesters. Retrieved from http://motherjones.com/politics/2011/02/indiana-official-jeff-cox-live-ammunition-against-wisconsin-protesters

Wikipedia (2011). eHarmony. Retrieved from http://en.wikipedia.org/wiki/EHarmony#cite_note-24

Wilson, R. E., Gosling, S. D., & Graham, L. T. (2012). A review of Facebook research in the social sciences. *Perspectives on Psychological Science*, *7*(3), 203–220.

Wilson, K. R., Wallin, J. S., & Reiser, C. (2003). Social stratification and the digital divide. *Social Science Computer Review*, *21*, 133–143.

Chapter 12

Online Intergroup Contact

Béatrice S. Hasler & Yair Amichai-Hamburger

Introduction

In our globalized world we live and work in close contact with people from various backgrounds. However, globalization does not necessarily cause homogenization; quite the opposite in fact: We now have to deal with differences between ethnic, racial, and religious groups in a more direct way (Nolan, 1999). It has become crucial to everyday life to accept differences in values, beliefs, and interests between various social groups while building on commonalities. Nonetheless, we are witnessing a growing trend toward segregation and separatism in many places in the world (Hoter et al., 2009). Prejudice and discrimination against rival groups often result in conflict, ranging from mild hostility to all-out war, leading to the loss of thousands of lives each year. Especially in areas of intractable conflict, intergroup bias is characterized and reinforced by "antagonistic group histories, exclusionist myths, demonizing propaganda and dehumanizing ideologies" (Ramsbotham et al., 2011, p. 103).

The preamble to the United Nations Educational, Scientific and Cultural Organization (UNESCO) Constitution states that "since wars begin in the minds of men, it is in the minds of men that the defenses of peace must be constructed" (UNESCO Constitution, 1945). The challenge of reducing intergroup bias within the human mind lays a great necessity upon social psychological research. Many social psychologists have attempted to understand the complex phenomenon of intergroup conflict, and to provide solutions to end it. One of the leading theories advocated to reduce intergroup conflict is the Contact Hypothesis proposed by Allport (1954). The Contact Hypothesis specifies the key conditions needed to reduce intergroup bias and improve the relations between rival groups. These conditions have received empirical support in numerous intergroup contact studies (see Pettigrew, 1998; Pettigrew & Tropp, 2000, 2006 for reviews). In recent years, research attention has shifted from *what* conditions are important to *when* and *how* intergroup contact leads to positive outcomes (Pettigrew & Tropp, 2008). These studies explore the mediating processes underlying intergroup interactions, as well as moderators that facilitate or inhibit the success of intergroup contact (Dovidio et al., 2003). While earlier contact studies were mainly conducted in face-to-face (FtF) settings, more recent studies report on intergroup encounters using computer-mediated communication (CMC) (Harwood, 2010).

The Internet has become an accessible and important medium of communication. It provides ample opportunities for social interactions across geographical and time boundaries, and has the ability to break down barriers between members of rival groups (Amichai-Hamburger & Furnham, 2007; Ruesch, 2011). One of the greatest advantages of the Internet lies in its inherent ability to allow for tailoring and tweaking of various features in order to create optimal conditions for a specific contact situation (Amichai-Hamburger & McKenna, 2006). We argue in the current chapter that online intergroup contact may be easier to establish, and in some cases may be even more successful than FtF meetings.

Previous online intergroup research was mostly based on disembodied, textual forms of CMC. Although text-based CMC continues to be the dominant modality in which people interact with each other on the Internet, newer and more diversified forms of CMC have emerged that move beyond traditional text-only modes. These newer forms of CMC include multimedia and multi-user applications, such as video-conferencing and social media (e.g., social networking sites). Another notable trend is the use of shared three-dimensional virtual environments in which participants interact as avatars (i.e., graphical representations of themselves) (Lee, 2009). Avatar-based interactions are considered to be a form of re-embodiment in online environments, which resemble some characteristics of FtF interaction in the physical world. However, CMC is still very different from FtF contact, and has a different impact on the way people present themselves, interact, and perceive each other. Despite the relatively new emergence of embodied forms of CMC, several studies have already explored its potential for intergroup interactions. We integrate these empirical findings on embodied online interaction into our discussion of how the Internet can be used to reduce intergroup bias.

The chapter builds on established theoretical models of disembodied and embodied forms of CMC, and on previous intergroup contact research conducted in both FtF and CMC contexts. We start with a brief explanation of intergroup bias and conflict. Then we present the key conditions outlined in the Contact Hypothesis (Allport, 1954) for intergroup contact to be successful. We summarize and extend the arguments proposed by Amichai-Hamburger and McKenna (2006) in their Internet Contact Hypothesis that explains how Allport's (1954) conditions can be applied to online contact. Following the newer developments in contact research, we describe the most extensively studied moderator and mediator variables and how they may influence the success or failure of online intergroup encounters. We illustrate how the respective moderators and mediators of contact effects can be practically implemented (e.g., in educational games and community websites). Then we discuss the design and evaluation results of field studies conducted with members of rival groups in conflict regions. We conclude with an agenda for future research on online intergroup contact and conflict resolution.

Explaining Intergroup Bias and Conflict

Social (Self-) Categorization Theory (SCT) (Tajfel & Turner, 1979, 1986; Turner, 1975; Turner et al., 1987) addresses the fundamental role of social group identities in the development of intergroup bias and conflict. According to SCT, people identify themselves not only as individuals, but also as parts of a social group that they belong to (i.e., ingroup). This ingroup is distinguished from an outgroup (i.e., a group that an individual does not belong to) regarding distinct social categories, such as religion, race, or culture. Social categorization regarding ingroup versus outgroup membership accounts for cognitive, affective, and behavioral aspects of intergroup bias (Dovidio et al., 2003). Intergroup bias is especially pronounced if rival social groups differ in values, beliefs, and interests. Although ingroup/outgroup categorization and subsequent intergroup bias may result from any kind of social characteristic, such as age or gender, the focus of the current chapter lies on interethnic conflicts.

Cognitive Components of Intergroup Bias

People generally believe that their ingroup is a heterogeneous group, whereas the outgroup is perceived as relatively homogeneous (Linville & Jones, 1980; Linville et al., 1989). This leads to the tendency to stereotype members of the outgroup, and to generalize that they are all, for example, hostile, liars, or lazy. In addition, outgroup members are often perceived as being different from one's ingroup (Dion, 1973; Wilson & Kayatani, 1968). This "us versus them" perception serves to enhance the stereotypical—oftentimes negative—perception of outgroup members regarding a variety of traits, physical characteristics, and expected behavior. Stereotyping occurs automatically and unintentionally most of the time (Devine, 1989). It requires conscious effort and training to overcome the activation of stereotypes within intergroup encounters (Kawakami et al., 2000; Sassenberg & Moskowitz, 2005).

Affective Components of Intergroup Bias

Intergroup relations are often characterized by perceptions that the outgroup poses an actual or imagined threat to ingroup interests or survival. Intergroup anxiety may be augmented when there are negative stereotypes and prejudice toward the outgroup, and a history of protracted conflict (Stephan & Stephan, 1985). Prejudice held against members of the outgroup can simultaneously increase positive affect, sympathy, and trust toward other members of the ingroup. People consequently show greater attachment to, and preference for, their ingroup than to the outgroup (Brewer, 1999; Otten & Moskowitz, 2000). Since people are mostly unaware of their attitudes, it is challenging to change outgroup prejudices (Amichai-Hamburger, 2008).

Behavioral Components of Intergroup Bias

Intergroup bias is behaviorally manifested in overt or covert discrimination against the outgroup, which may occur intentionally or unintentionally. People are generally more helpful toward ingroup members than toward outgroup members (Dovidio et al., 1997), and work harder for their ingroup in the presence of an outgroup (Worchel et al., 1998). Furthermore, there is a strong tendency for people to treat outgroup members in line with their preconceived perceptions of them, while disregarding the way in which they actually behave. This is likely to make outgroup members respond in accordance with their expected, stereotypical behavior, which in turn provides confirming evidence that the initial negative stereotypes held against them were correct. This self-fulfilling prophecy creates a closed cycle of negative conduct from which it is hard to break (Word et al., 1974).

The Contact Hypothesis in Face-to-Face and Online Settings

The goal of positive intergroup contact is to enhance the relations between members of rival groups by reducing intergroup bias. Thus, intergroup contact is considered successful if it reduces negative stereotypes, prejudice, and discriminatory behavior toward members of the outgroup. The Contact Hypothesis (Allport, 1954) posits that mere contact between rival groups is unlikely to be sufficient. Rather, for contact to be successful, certain conditions must be fulfilled. These optimal conditions are (1) equal status between group members, (2) intergroup cooperation, (3) superordinate goals, and (4) support of authorities. Several other conditions were later added; among which "acquaintance potential" (Cook, 1962) that permits participants to build meaningful interpersonal relationships has been proposed as one of the most important (Pettigrew, 1998).

Pettigrew and Tropp's (2000, 2006) meta-analytic reviews of more than 500 studies showed that contact which meets the conditions outlined in the Contact Hypothesis has significantly decreased intergroup bias for various types of social groups, beyond racial and ethnic groups, for which it has been originally formulated. The more conditions applied, the more likely it was for contact to reduce intergroup bias (Pettigrew & Tropp, 2006). However, they also noted that these conditions are not essential, and that contact can be effective without all being fulfilled. Instead of treating them as necessary conditions, the authors suggested that they act as facilitating factors.

While Allport's (1954) conditions are difficult to implement in some FtF settings, the Internet is uniquely suited to set out these conditions, and may be even more effective in putting the Contact Hypothesis into practice (Amichai-Hamburger, 2008; Amichai-Hamburger & McKenna, 2006). We describe each of Allport's (1954) conditions in the following sections, identify the challenges associated with their implementation in organized FtF contact between rival groups in conflict, and discuss the opportunities that the Internet offers to overcome related difficulties.

Equal Status

According to the Contact Hypothesis, successful intergroup contact requires the establishment of equal social status between ingroup and outgroup members. McClendon (1974) argued that equal status increases the likelihood for perceived similarities between ingroup and outgroup members, which helps to reduce fixed stereotypes and prejudice (Pettigrew, 1971). However, status differences often exist in reality, that is, outside of an organized contact situation. Especially in the case of oppressed minority groups, extreme status differences can be predominant characteristics inherent to the nature of the conflict.

People are sensitive to very subtle cues of status that are transmitted through nonverbal channels in FtF interactions, such as dress code, body language, use of personal space, and seating positions (Amichai-Hamburger & McKenna, 2006). Therefore, equality of status is often difficult to establish in FtF meetings. In contrast, many of the nonverbal and social context cues that are indicative of a person's status are typically not in evidence when people communicate online. According to the Equalization Hypothesis (Dubrovsky et al., 1991), individuals appear as more equal in text-based CMC due to their visual anonymity. Consequently, potential disadvantages of low-status group members are expected to diminish in online contact. Spears et al. (2002) argued that CMC provides lower-status individuals with more confidence to "speak up" when status differences, which may have an intimidating effect in FtF interactions, are not visually salient. Thus, even when status differences of participating individuals are known, CMC tends to ameliorate some of the "real world" status differences by removing their visual salience. Therefore, it may be easier to establish equality of status in online intergroup encounters.

Cooperation Toward Superordinate Goals

One of the key conditions proposed by the Contact Hypothesis is that group members collaborate on a task, which is of equal importance to both groups. The task should be designed in a way that requires them to work toward a superordinate goal under which they need to combine their efforts. Cooperation, as opposed to competitive relationships, is expected to shift the focus more on the shared identity of the superordinate group. Based on their Common Ingroup Identity Model, Gaertner and Dovidio (2000) argue that the more integrated members of rival groups become into a newly created superordinate group, the less they perceive one another as members of an ingroup versus an outgroup. In other words, cooperation toward common goals reduces subgroup categorization, and transforms perceptions of "us" versus "them" into a more inclusive "we" (Gaertner et al., 2000). In order to establish a superordinate group identity, participants are required to find and rely on cross-cutting categories, which can be achieved by emphasizing shared interests and common goals (Brewer, 2000).

The formation of a superordinate group, which members of both sides can identify with and are willing to collaborate in, may be difficult to achieve in FtF settings. According to the Fault-line Theory (Lau & Murnighan, 1998), hypothetical dividing lines split members of a heterogeneous work group into subgroups along social categories. For instance, gender fault-lines would divide a team into male and female subgroups. The division into subgroups is likely to impair team functioning as indicated by increased subgroup conflict, and lower levels of group performance and cohesion (Lau & Murnighan, 2005; Molleman, 2005; Sawyer et al., 2006). Subgrouping is likely to occur in heterogeneous groups because people generally prefer to cooperate with similar (i.e., ingroup members) than with dissimilar others (i.e., outgroup members). It is important to note that subgrouping is caused by the *salience* of social categories, and is not due to differences between group members per se (Lau & Murnighan, 1998; van Knippenberg et al., 2010). In the presence of an outgroup, the salience of typical social categories may exaggerate dissimilarities between ingroup and outgroup members.

Online collaboration may be the key solution in overcoming the challenges that diverse groups often confront when they collaborate FtF. There has been a growing amount of empirical evidence for an advantage of group diversity in online collaboration (Staples & Zhao, 2006). It has been found that more diversity among members of virtual teams (both regarding demographic variables and geographic distributions) was correlated with lower levels of interpersonal conflict and higher group performance (Mortensen & Hinds, 2001; Polzer et al., 2006). The less members of a virtual team had in common, the more they united through collaboration on their task, which facilitated identification with a superordinate group (Walther & Carr, 2010).

Support of Authorities

As one of the preconditions outlined in the Contact Hypothesis for successful intergroup contact, participants from both groups should receive support from their respective authorities. Approval by an authority is likely to create positive expectations regarding the contact, and helps to establish positive social norms for the contact situation. Support of authorities is of particular significance if the differences between the groups are deep-seated or potentially explosive (Amichai-Hamburger & McKenna, 2006). However, institutions that are willing to organize or support a FtF intergroup meeting may encounter practical obstacles. For instance, organizers may face challenges when it comes to finding a suitable physical meeting place, transporting the participants, and compensating them for their time and travel expenses. This is particularly true when the members of opposing groups live at some distance from another. In this case, participation in intergroup contact may be limited to those who have the financial resources and flexibility to travel to the meeting or to those who live in close proximity to the meeting location. In other cases, members of rival groups are precluded from meeting FtF by social norms, segregation, or threats to safety (Hoter et al., 2009). Hence, the size and number of possible contacts are severely restricted when intergroup meetings take place in physical locations, and can sometimes be difficult or dangerous to arrange (Amichai-Hamburger & McKenna, 2006).

Online contact is an attractive alternative to FtF meetings, as it helps to overcome logistical and financial issues. The Internet makes it possible to bring together a large number of participants without time or physical constraints. Online meetings are neither costly to set up nor time consuming for the participants. Therefore, online contact is more likely to be approved by authorities. Institutions may consider participation in an online intergroup contact setting as taking lower risk than FtF contact since it is less likely to have repercussions (Amichai-Hamburger & McKenna, 2006). Since the social costs for participating in online encounters are marginal, it may also be easier for institutions to support intergroup contacts that take place on the Internet.

Acquaintance Potential

An optimal contact situation provides the opportunity for personal acquaintance between the members of opposing groups, and for developing cross-group friendships (Cook, 1962).

The contact has to create a context in which participants can closely interact, and engage in mutual self-disclosure in order to properly get to know the other side. Individuals who engage in self-disclosure reveal significant aspects of themselves to the other person, and make them understand how they see themselves (Worthy et al., 1969). Self-disclosure personalizes an intergroup interaction in a way that the interacting individuals focus their attention on individuating characteristics. The more people reveal about themselves, the more detailed knowledge they acquire about the outgroup. Thus, self-disclosure helps to see outgroup members as more diverse, which is likely to reduce the application of stereotypes (Fiske & Neuberg, 1990). Disclosure of emotions, rather than merely exchanging facts and information, has been found to increase intimacy, and help to establish mutual trust and cross-group friendships (Laurenceau et al., 1998). In contrast, if the contact is restricted to casual encounters, stereotypes are likely to remain unchanged. In order to develop close interpersonal bonds, and to establish a sense of belonging and acceptance, extensive and repeated contact is required. Cook (1962) has suggested that the more intimate an intergroup relationship becomes, the more favorable the attitudes will be toward the outgroup.

Earlier research on CMC stated that visually anonymous online interactions, in which nonverbal and social context cues are filtered out, would result in shallow, impersonal, and even hostile relationships (Kiesler et al., 1984, 1985; Sproull & Kiesler, 1986). However, the Reduced Social Cues approach has been criticized for its rigid focus on the technologically determined limitations of CMC (Lea & Spears, 1991). More recent CMC theories, such as the Social Information Processing (SIP) theory (Walther, 1992), shifted the focus toward the social and psychological processes in online communication. Research following the SIP approach claims that visual anonymity in text-based CMC does not necessarily lead to negative consequences, but may enhance (rather than reduce or restrict) communication in online groups. The visual anonymity in CMC provides individuals with more control over how they present themselves. According to Walther's (1996) Hyperpersonal Model, online communication may enhance impression formation by allowing participants to emphasize specific personal characteristics while hiding others, which is impossible in FtF communication. Indeed it has been found that participants who engaged in online group interactions employed deeper self-disclosures, asked more intimate questions (Joinson, 2001; Tidwell & Walther, 2002), and liked their group members more than those who interacted FtF (Bargh & McKenna, 2004).

These contradictory findings can be explained by artifacts of laboratory experiments in which online groups only interacted for a short amount of time, rather than effects of the communication medium (Hobman et al., 2002). It has been found that when given enough time, online contact was equally suitable to promote cross-group friendships, and often resulted in more intimate relationships over time than FtF contact (Tidwell & Walther, 2002; Walther, 1992, 1997; Wilson et al., 2006). Online intergroup contact should therefore aim for long-term collaboration instead of a single meeting of ad hoc groups, which are prone to insults and negative relations (Walther, 2009). Moreover, online contact may be advantageous regarding the development of sustainable intergroup relations as follow-up intergroup meetings are easier and less expensive to organize over the Internet than FtF.

Intergroup Contact Effects in Physical and Online Environments

One of the main critiques on the Contact Hypothesis is that it only predicts *what* conditions lead to positive outcomes of intergroup encounters, but does not specify *when* these facilitating conditions are important, and *how* contact works (Pettigrew, 1998). More recent contact research addresses the underlying processes that mediate the relationship between contact and intergroup

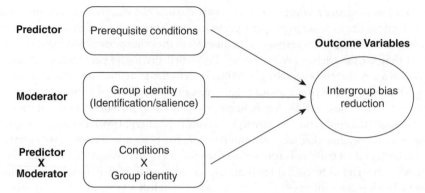

Fig. 12.1 A schematic model of moderators between contact and intergroup bias.

bias, and the factors that moderate (i.e., facilitate or inhibit) positive outcomes (Dovidio et al., 2003). Both moderators and mediators are third variables that influence the relation between independent and dependent variables, but they refer to different concepts (see Baron & Kenny, 1986). Moderators affect the direction and/or strength of the relationship between an independent variable and a dependent variable (see Fig. 12.1). Mediators refer to the mechanism through which an independent variable influences a dependent variable (see Fig. 12.2). In the context of intergroup relations, contact between rival groups constitutes the independent variable, and bias reduction the dependent variable.

Moderators of Contact Effects

The greatest challenge to the Contact Hypothesis is whether the results of a positive intergroup contact remain limited to the context of the meeting and the participants involved, or will be generalized to other situations and to the outgroup as a whole (Pettigrew, 1998). Generalization is crucial if intergroup contact is to have broad and lasting effects. If positive contact effects do not generalize further, bias against the outgroup will remain unchanged (Hewstone & Brown, 1986). The salience of an individual's group membership during an intergroup contact, and the extent to which the individual identifies with his or her ingroup, appear to be the most important moderators of generalization effects (Crisp & Beck, 2005; Dovidio et al., 2003). Fig. 12.1 shows a schematic moderator model of contact effects.

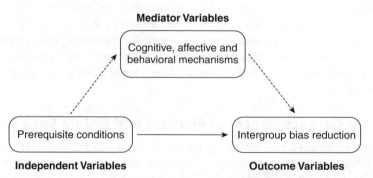

Fig. 12.2 A schematic model of mediators between contact and intergroup bias.

Group salience determines the extent to which individuals are perceived as representatives of their social group. Salience of social categories can be activated by various factors that emphasize the common characteristics of a group of people, such as religion, race, or culture. However, there is much debate among researchers about whether the salience of group membership should be high or low.

Hewstone and Brown (1986) argued that if a member of an outgroup is perceived only as an individual rather than also as a representative of his or her social group, then any change in attitude will remain target-specific. They claimed that outgroup identity must be highly salient for positive contact effects to generalize. Furthermore, individuals should be perceived as typical (rather than atypical) members of their group (Rothbart & John, 1985). If group salience is high, self-perception is dominated by the group membership, which leads to stronger ingroup identification and people's attitudes tend to shift toward the norm of their ingroup (e.g., majority opinion) (Sassenberg & Boos, 2003). This phenomenon illustrates the importance of creating a common ingroup identity, which integrates the values of both ingroup and outgroup members (Gaertner & Dovidio, 2000).

Conversely, Brewer and Miller (1984) among others have argued that group salience should be low as it could otherwise lead to activation of negative stereotypes during the contact. Miller (2002) claimed that personalized representations in which the focus of attention is directed toward participants' individual identities (i.e., high personal salience), while holding group salience low, would produce more favorable attitudes toward members of the outgroup (within and outside the given contact situation). This assumption is supported by studies on intergroup friendship, which stressed the value of personalized interactions (Pettigrew, 1997).

The question remains as to which level of group identity versus personal identity salience is optimal for bias reduction and generalization to occur, and how a superordinate group identity can be established and maintained in intergroup contact. Gaertner and Dovidio (2000) proposed a trade-off hypothesis according to which high personal salience was beneficial in initial contact, whereas group salience should be heightened in subsequent meetings in order to foster generalization. Dovidio et al. (2003) further suggested that the relative effectiveness of each of these strategies was moderated by situational and temporal factors, as well as individual differences.

One of the main advantages of CMC is that the degree of which personal identity versus group identity is salient can be easily manipulated depending on the particular needs of a given contact situation in order to achieve a desired outcome (Amichai-Hamburger & McKenna, 2006). In experimental studies using text-based CMC, high group salience is typically evoked by instructions that repeat the word "group," and encouraging participants to look for distinct attributes that are characteristic of their group (Walther & Carr, 2010). In anonymous CMC interactions, any social category can be magnified as the most important characteristic that distinguishes ingroup and outgroup members. High group salience can be achieved by using anonymous names that are evocative of the groups that participants are representing (e.g., Pakistan 1, Pakistan 2, India 1, etc.). On the other hand, high personal salience can be attained by instructions that frequently use the word "individuals," and prompt participants to look for diversifying characteristics of their group members (Walther & Carr, 2010). While participants are visually anonymous in text-based CMC, their personal or group identity can be visually represented and transformed in avatar-based CMC. Avatar appearance can be easily modified, and different attributes of participants' identities can be emphasized or hidden. Moreover, avatars can be used to create an online identity that does not need to correspond to a person's actual (offline) identity (Lee, 2009).

The Social Identity Model of Deindividuation Effects (SIDE) (Postmes et al., 1998; Reicher et al., 1995) presents a theoretical framework that explains how CMC triggers different identification processes as a consequence of participants' anonymity in online interactions. SIDE posits that anonymity leads to depersonalization and de-individuation, which increases participants' awareness of social categories, if they are made salient during an online group interaction. SIDE theorists have suggested that high salience of group membership in anonymous, text-based CMC would magnify social attraction toward the ingroup, and at the same time increase negative responses toward the outgroup.

Research on intergroup dynamics in CMC showed inconsistent results (Walter & Carr, 2010). CMC experiments that led participants to believe that the opposing group consisted of participants from a social group that was different from their own (e.g., being from different countries or rival universities), have not produced the predicted ingroup/outgroup effects (Lea et al., 2001; Postmes et al., 2002). The failure to generate these effects could be interpreted in a positive light. It appears that anonymous online groups comprised of members from distinctive subgroups are not as prone to ingroup/outgroup bias, as compared to equivalent intergroup contact situations in FtF settings. Instead, online groups may relate to all participants as members of a superordinate ingroup, while disregarding the fact that they represent different social groups (Amichai-Hamburger & McKenna, 2006).

This constitutes a beneficial effect for intergroup encounters, which can be used in a purposeful way in order to enhance an online contact situation. CMC can both heighten the perception of individual members as representatives of their respective social groups (in case of high group identity salience), and foster the formation of interpersonal relationships (in case of high personal identity salience), while simultaneously increasing attachment to a newly created superordinate ingroup (Amichai-Hamburger & McKenna, 2006; Thompson & Nadler, 2002). Such settings can enhance the desired balance of both "us" and "them" among participants, which facilitates acceptance and generalization (Amichai-Hamburger & McKenna, 2006).

Recent studies also tested ingroup/outgroup effects as predicted by SIDE theory in avatar-mediated interactions. Kim and Park (2011) used groups of participants that were represented either as identical or dissimilar avatars in online discussions. They predicted that uniform appearance would lead to higher group identification and increase participants' willingness to conform to the group norm. Conversely, it was expected that participants may experience a threat to their individuality due to uniform appearances, and would therefore diverge from the group norm in order to restore their uniqueness. This contradictory hypothesis is based on Optimal Distinctiveness Theory (Brewer, 1991, 1993), which states that individuals desire to attain an optimal balance of inclusion and distinctiveness both within and between social groups. These two conflicting motives are simultaneously activated in social interactions, resulting in compensation effects in case of a perceived threat to individuality as opposed to assimilation to group norms in order to satisfy the need for belonging. Indeed, both disparate processes were found to be activated and negated the impact of visual similarity on participants' intention to conform to the group norm (Kim, 2011; Kim & Park, 2011). Thus, too much visual similarity may inhibit potentially beneficial processes in avatar-based intergroup interactions. However, it remains unclear where the equilibrium between similarity and uniqueness in avatar appearance should be for an optimal outcome of online intergroup encounters.

Mediators of Contact Effects

One key concern in the current contact research is related to mediators of contact effects; that is, the question of *how* contact reduces intergroup bias. Fig. 12.2 shows a schematic mediator model of contact effects.

Several potential mediators have been investigated that translate contact into positive intergroup relations, including cognitive and affective mediator variables (Dovidio et al., 2003;

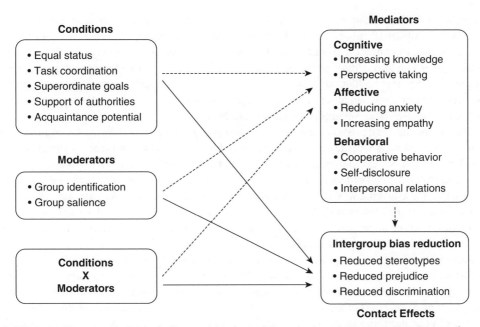

Fig. 12.3 An integrated model of Allport's (1954) conditions, and moderators and mediators of intergroup contact effects.

Pettigrew & Tropp, 2008). There are also a number of behavioral or communication-related mediators discussed in the contact literature, which determine the way in which members of opposing groups interact with one another. For example, it has been found that cooperative behavior mediates the relationships between other conditions (i.e., equal status, goal interdependence, and authority support) and intergroup bias (Koschate & van Dick, 2011). Self-disclosure has also been found to be a behavioral mediator between contact and intergroup bias (Turner et al., 2007). While these factors have already been discussed earlier as part of the facilitating conditions for successful intergroup contact, we focus here on the cognitive and affective mediators that have been most extensively studied, and received empirical support in FtF and CMC contexts.

Increasing knowledge about the outgroup is one of the most widely discussed cognitive mediators. Affective mediators include reducing negative emotions, such as anxiety and uncertainty, and increasing positive emotions, such as empathy through perspective-taking. We discuss how these mediating variables operate in intergroup interactions in FtF settings and on the Internet. Figure 12.3 shows an integrated model of the facilitating conditions for successful intergroup contact, and the moderator and mediator variables of contact effects.

Increasing Knowledge about the Outgroup

Based on the assumption that ignorance promotes prejudice (Stephan & Stephan, 1984), learning about the outgroup is considered to be a critical step in how intergroup bias can be reduced through contact (Pettigrew, 1998). With more information about outgroup members, people are more likely to see each other in individuated and personalized ways, which allows for the creation of new, nonstereotypic perceptions of the outgroup (Kawakami et al., 2000). Increased knowledge may also reveal similarities between different social groups, which are expected to lead to more favorable perceptions of outgroup members (Pettigrew, 1998). A better understanding, for example, of the beliefs and values of an outgroup, may further reduce uncertainty about how to interact with others (Stephan & Stephan, 1985). Reduced uncertainty in turn, is likely to reduce the avoidance of contact with outgroup members and discomfort in intergroup interactions (Gaertner & Dovidio, 1986). Such cognitive mediators may also be effective when there are opportunities to learn about others when an individual is not directly involved in an intergroup contact; for example, when observing or reading about interactions between other ingroup members with members of an outgroup (Dovidio et al., 2011).

The Internet makes it possible for everyone to access large amounts of information from various sources, such as news websites, blogs, or forums. Information can be found about the history of conflicts, reports on current political and social events, along with different viewpoints and opinions. Information about different types of social groups can be presented on the Internet in a more interactive and engaging way, especially with a higher level of self-involvement than traditional mass media channels (Harwood, 2010). Such online knowledge bases are available for educational purposes in order to prepare for an intergroup contact, or can be created by members of the involved social groups as a collaboration task.

Social networking sites, like Facebook, are popular examples of online cross-border communication and information sharing. Facebook explicitly states that it "is proud to play a part in promoting peace by building technology that helps people better understand each other. By enabling people from diverse backgrounds to easily connect and share their ideas, we can decrease world conflict in the short and long term" (Facebook, 2011). Other Internet services are particularly designed for rapid information sharing, such as Twitter, a micro-blogging network used by millions of people worldwide. Social networking and information sites also exist for particular conflict regions, for example the MidEast Web,[1] as well as for global peace communities, such as the Peace and Collaborative Development Network.[2]

A great potential for self-paced and collaborative learning is provided by social and educational virtual worlds, online learning games, and training simulations, which do not only disseminate information about other cultures, but enable the learner to acquire language and culture-specific nonverbal communication skills. A good example is the educational game series *Global Conflicts*,[3] which provides educators with game-based learning tools and additional course materials for teaching about different conflicts throughout the world. *Global Conflicts* games present interactive, immersive role-play scenarios to explore and learn about various topics, such as democracy, human rights, globalization, terrorism, climate, and poverty. Several role-play and simulation games have been developed specifically about the Israeli–Palestinian conflict. For example, the *PeaceMaker*[4] game simulates the Israeli–Palestinian conflict in a virtual environment, including footage and photographs from actual events. Players are confronted with information about political processes and facts about the conflict, and learn about the various social, economical, and moral issues involved in this multifaceted conflict.

Other interesting examples of educational virtual worlds can be found in *Second Life*.[5] For example, the Second China island in *Second Life* has been built to facilitate the learning of Chinese culture using immersive scenarios, buildings, and interaction with virtual humans (i.e., nonplayer characters controlled by artificial intelligence) (Fishwick et al., 2008).

----

[1] http://mideastweb.org

[2] http://www.internationalpeaceandconflict.org

[3] http://www.globalconflicts.eu

[4] http://www.peacemakergame.com

[5] http://secondlife.com

Second China offers spaces for culturally relevant "edutainment" as well as spaces for exploring news and current affairs. Another *Second Life* project called Understanding Islam through Virtual Worlds shows how people can get to know more about Muslim culture in an authentic, experiential way by visiting historical places, mosques, houses, and museums inside the virtual world that are built according to real-world examples, and to interact with others while learning about religious rituals, Islamic customs and values (King & Fouts, 2009). The authors noted that virtual worlds are ideal instruments for immersive story-telling that offer new opportunities for greater first-hand understanding of Islam for policy-makers, diplomats, and people worldwide.

Alelo[6] delivers a set of training tools to promote better intercultural communication. Most of the training tools have been developed to prepare military soldiers for operations in different cultural environments. For example, Alelo's Virtual Cultural Awareness Trainer (VCAT) has been designed for cultural skills training to effectively master social interactions between culturally diverse populations (Johnson, 2009). VCAT utilizes simulations of intercultural situations that trainees are likely to encounter while carrying out their jobs or missions. These training systems give trainees the opportunity to practice conversations in realistic, animated settings by utilizing interactive dialogues in which they interact as avatars with nonplayer characters. Trainees are required to make choices in the context of the situation and thereby learn how to behave in culturally appropriate ways in respect to specific social encounters. These scenarios include greetings, introductions, arranging meetings, and discussing business with counterparts.

While these information sites and training systems mainly prepare individuals for intergroup contact, increased knowledge is also likely to occur as a result of an online intergroup contact. However, it has been found that knowledge alone is not sufficient in order to reduce intergroup bias (Pate, 1981). Meta-analytic tests of contact studies showed that the mediating value of cognitive variables generally appears to be weaker than affective mediators (Pettigrew & Tropp, 2008).

Reducing Anxiety about Intergroup Contact

Initial intergroup encounters are often accompanied with anxiety (Pettigrew, 1998). Anxiety may result in negative responses toward the outgroup *during* contact, and lead to *anticipatory* anxiety about future meetings (Plant & Devine, 2003; Stephan et al., 1999). In a state of anxiety, people experience uncertainty about how they should act or how they might be perceived by others (Stephan & Stephan, 1985), and are more likely to apply stereotypes (Bodenhausen, 1990). Intergroup anxiety may to lead to miscommunication and distrust toward outgroup members (Dovidio et al., 2002), or even result in avoidance of intergroup contact (Plant & Devine, 2003; Shelton & Richeson, 2005). Consequently, intergroup anxiety and uncertainty hinders the formation of harmonious intergroup relations (Dovidio et al., 2003). A number of contact studies have demonstrated that reduced anxiety operates as a mediator between intergroup contact and reduced prejudice toward the outgroup (Pettigrew & Tropp, 2008). While FtF contact may lead to high levels of anxiety among participants, online intergroup encounters are expected to evoke less anxiety both in anticipation of and during the contact situation (Amichai-Hamburger, 2008).

The Internet creates a protected environment in which participating individuals meet while staying within their familiar physical surroundings. People are more likely to feel comfortable and less anxious when interacting with outgroup members from the privacy of their homes. Although the Internet is considered to be a public sphere, it still evokes a private feel for participants (McKenna, 2007; McKenna & Bargh, 2000). Research that has shown an increased activation and use of stereotypes (especially those tied to racial prejudice) in the public as opposed to private

---

[6] http://www.alelo.com

places where people are more open and willing to alter their habitual responses (Lambert et al., 2003; Zajonc, 1965). Thus, online intergroup contact is expected to inhibit the activation of stereotypes and may mitigate the anxiety that often accompanies FtF meetings (Amichai-Hamburger & McKenna, 2006; Walther, 2009).

Many of the social factors that lead to feelings of anxiety and uncertainty in FtF encounters (e.g., having to respond on the spot or being under visual scrutiny) are absent in online interactions. Online intergroup contact provides participants with a higher level of control over how they present themselves and their views. Participants may feel better able to express themselves in online intergroup encounters, and feel more at ease with their online partners than they would if they were interacting FtF (Amichai-Hamburger, 2005). They choose when to start and finish an online interaction by logging on and off, and have more time to compose their text messages. Thus, the high degree of control over the communication process creates stronger feelings of security and power in online contact compared to FtF encounters (Amichai-Hamburger & Furnham, 2007). At the same time, immediacy of feedback is given as online interactions can take place in real-time, providing the participants with a sense of co-presence. In particular, avatar-based interactions in shared virtual environments are said to increase the feeling of being together in the same (virtual) room, despite of the physical distance between participants (Schroeder, 2006).

However, it has been found that anxiety especially mediated the relationship between contact and prejudice when group salience was high. Mediation effects were less pronounced when the salience of group identity was low (Voci & Hewstone, 2003), and may only occur for members who strongly identify with their ingroup (Tausch et al., 2007). These limitations on the mediating role of anxiety demonstrate the importance of considering group identification and salience of group identity as a moderator.

Virtual worlds bear a great potential for realistic intergroup interactions in which group identity can be made visually salient (e.g., by using avatars with ethnic connotations). On the other hand, transferring the physical characteristics of outgroup members into the virtual environment is likely to provoke high levels of anxiety as in equivalent FtF encounters. For example, Dotsch and Wigboldus (2008) found that Dutch participants who approached Moroccan avatars showed higher levels of stress as measured by increased skin conductance levels than if they approached White avatars. Indicators of implicit prejudice were also found in participants' behavior as they kept larger distances from Moroccan avatars than from White avatars. Thus, it appears that merely moving intergroup contact to online media may not be sufficient for a reduction in anxiety. Additional factors that influence the experience of an online intergroup interaction need to be considered, such as a means to increase positive emotions in preparation for and during the contact situation.

Increasing Empathy through Perspective-Taking

Intergroup bias has been found to be reduced by perspective-taking and enhancing empathic concern toward members of the outgroup (Pettigrew & Tropp, 2008). In studies of perspective-taking and empathic role-playing, participants were asked to imagine themselves or act as another person (e.g., an outgroup member with specific attributes). Especially when participants were requested to focus their attention on the feelings, as opposed to facts about the other person's situation, perspective-taking increased empathy. Participants who empathized with outgroup members expressed more positive feelings and attitudes toward members of the outgroup, and showed more prosocial behaviors (Batson et al., 1997; Galinsky & Moskowitz, 2000; Peng et al., 2010; Todd et al., 2011).

While empathy is clearly an affective mediator between contact and intergroup bias reduction, perspective-taking may also operate on a cognitive level (Galinsky & Moskowitz, 2000). Taking over the perspective of another person is assumed to activate neural processes that are typically being used to evaluate the self (Ames et al., 2008). The provoked overlap of the self and the other person may increase the perceived similarity between the individual and the respective outgroup member, which in turn is expected to lead to a reduction of stereotypes regarding the outgroup (Davis et al., 1996; Galinsky & Moskowitz, 2000).

Role-play and case studies have been found to be highly effective tools for empathic learning and promoting social change (Mezirow, 1997). Nonetheless, role-play can be difficult and expensive to organize if human actors are required. Using film or written case studies may be a more practical alternative. Narrative story-telling has been found to be an effective method of conflict reconciliation, which is widely used to promote various causes over the Internet (Kampf, 2011). The Internet is particularly suitable for this task because it enables practically everyone to post stories documenting their view on a conflict and its impact on their daily lives (e.g., via blogs), and to share photographs and video messages (e.g., via YouTube). Still, such case studies greatly limit the level of interactivity, and do not allow for a dialogue with the portrayed person. The observer is being placed in a rather passive position, and the empathy-evoking potential of such case studies greatly rely on the observer's ability to imagine being in the situation of the other person. A possible way to overcome the limited level of interactivity is collaborative story-telling, which makes use of the possibility to post comments and discuss stories with others online. Such collaborative story-telling approaches are expected to enhance mutual understanding and empathy (Stock et al., 2009).

While case studies make it possible to imagine an outgroup member's lived experience, role-playing enables participants to take over someone else's perspective. There is a great variety of computer and video games, which provide highly interactive and immersive role-play environments. In online role-playing games, players have the ability to literally act as someone else through the use of virtual characters (i.e., avatars), and directly experience social situations from their perspective. Such role-play interactions can take place in a simulation of the other person's physical environment. Interacting in virtual environments has the great advantage of allowing participants to experience being in remote locations without having to leave home. Moreover, virtual environments make it possible to design a neutral place for intergroup encounters, whereas FtF meetings always take place in a culture-specific environment (Hasler, 2011; Hasler & Friedman, in press).

In the *PeaceMaker* game, players can choose to take on the role of the Israeli Prime Minister or the President of the Palestinian Authority. The game provides players with opportunities to resolve the Israeli–Palestinian conflict (i.e., establishing a two-state solution) by choosing political, economic, and security actions (Kampf, 2011). Players have to respond to in-game events like suicide bombings, army raids, and the demands of various interest groups, while interacting with political leaders and authorities (Burak et al., 2005). Players lose or win points depending on the effects of their actions. The goal is to achieve a balanced and positive score for both the Israeli and the Palestinian groups (Gonzalez & Saner, in press).

The first-person nature of computer games has been found to increase people's identification with the character they play and its actions, compared to merely observing a character in a film (Eastin et al., 2009; Fischer et al., 2010; Klimmt et al., 2009). The appearance of one's avatar plays a crucial role in perspective-taking and identification processes. Avatars make it possible to transform people's real-world identities, and to let them temporarily adopt an outgroup member's identity and appearance in a virtual environment. People have been found to evaluate themselves in ways an imaginary third party would while observing their own behavior in a virtual body with physical characteristics of an outgroup member (e.g., race). The phenomenon that people infer their expected behaviors and attitudes from observing their avatar's appearance has been termed the Proteus Effect (Yee & Bailenson, 2007). Through a series of studies, Yee and his colleagues demonstrated that such altered self-representations can have significant and instantaneous impacts on how people interact with others (Yee & Bailenson, 2006, 2007; Yee et al., 2009). Changes in behavior not only occurred during the embodiment in a virtual environment, but also persisted through subsequent social interactions in the real world (Yee et al., 2009). Such transfer effects from the virtual into the physical world are of crucial importance for lasting outcomes of inter-group contact interventions.

Empirical findings on embodied perspective-taking are inconsistent. Yee and Bailenson (2006) conducted a virtual reality (VR) experiment in which participants were embodied as an elderly avatar. Participants reduced their prejudice and reported more positive attitudes toward elderly people afterwards. Gonzales et al. (2010) found in their study on racial prejudice in *Second Life* that White participants who were represented as Black avatars lessened their racist attitudes. Both men and women showed reduced implicit negative attitudes (as measured through a linguistic analysis of chat protocols) toward Black people after playing Black avatars. After being embodied as a Black avatar, compared to those who were represented as a White avatar, only female participants reported more explicit positive attitudes toward Black people in a post-experiment questionnaire.

In contrast, Groom et al. (2009) found in their VR study that regardless of participants' actual race, those who were represented as Black avatars had their stereotypes activated and showed greater racial bias than participants who were represented as White avatars. Eastin et al. (2009) also found that White players showed more hostile thoughts after playing a violent video game as a Black character than after playing a White character. Players may have activated their stereotypes of Black people as being more aggressive, which may have led not only to having more aggressive thoughts, but also unconsciously acting out the violent stereotype by playing more aggressively. A similar study was conducted by Peña et al. (2009) who found a negative priming effect of avatar appearance. Participants who were represented as avatars wearing black cloaks showed more aggressive attitudes than those who were represented as white-cloaked avatars. This effect was replicated in a second experiment in which participants that were represented as Ku Klux Klan avatars developed more aggression than those using avatars dressed as doctors. Thus, the act of observing oneself embodied as a prototypical outgroup member may either enhance empathy and promote the extension of positive concepts of the self, or could, on the other hand, prime or activate pre-existing negative stereotypes. It has yet to be investigated under which conditions each effect may occur and how it can be positively tweaked.

These ambiguous effects are also reflected in the evaluation results of the *PeaceMaker* game. Several studies evaluated the impact of the *PeaceMaker* game on increased factual knowledge, changes in attitudes and perceptions, and decision-making strategies depending on players' personalities, religious and political affiliations, and trust attitudes (Gonzalez & Czlonka, 2010; Martin & Gonzalez, 2010). Game behavior and players' subjective reports have been compared across different groups of participants, and different game play settings have been evaluated, such as collaborative play versus single player (Kampf, 2011). The main findings show that players are biased regarding their game strategy and in-game decision-making, depending on which side they are favoring. However, it has been found to be advantageous if the game was played in dyads composed of players from the different groups. Such tandem playing resulted in higher game scores, and players learned more about each other on a personal level during game play (Kampf, 2011).

Field Studies on Online Intergroup Contact in Conflict Regions

Although many social scientists have promoted the potential of the Internet for intergroup contact and conflict resolution, the majority of published work in this area is based on laboratory experiments using artificially created in/outgroups instead of participants from actual rival groups. Nevertheless, there are some notable exceptions of empirical field studies using means of CMC to facilitate intergroup contact among populations in conflict. Most of the documented field work on online intergroup contact has been conducted in regions with protracted conflict, such as between Catholics and Protestants in Northern Ireland (Austin, 2006), and between Israelis and Arabs/Palestinians in the Middle East (McKenna et al., 2009; Mollov, 2006).

Israeli Jews and Palestinians have difficulties meeting FtF due to security issues. They typically have to navigate checkpoints in contentious territories in order to meet. Movement restrictions and the severity of the violence in the Middle East often make it dangerous, and in some cases impossible, to organize FtF meetings. Online contact therefore becomes an attractive alternative, and is a hopeful option for constructive dialogues between rival sides (Ellis & Moaz, 2007). Other field studies focused on the tension between majority and minority groups within Israel, including participants from the Arab and Jewish sections (Hoter et al., 2009; Yablon, 2007). Although these two groups are not geographically separated but live in the same area or neighborhoods in mixed cities, they show a great psychological distance imposed by prejudice and stereotypes held against one another (Hoter et al., 2009). A similar social divide exists in Northern Ireland in which a deeply-rooted rivalry between Catholic and Protestant communities strongly affects almost every aspect of life (Trew, 1986). The religious polarization has a long and violent history, resulting in a deeply segregated society in an unstable political and social environment.

All of these online intergroup contact projects were designed based on the theoretical foundation of the Contact Hypothesis (Allport, 1954), and share similar goals. They aim to decrease intergroup bias, and increase mutual understanding in order to improve the relationship between rival groups. Most of these projects have been designed as peace-building interventions within educational contexts, while others examined online communities formed on social networking sites involving participants of rival groups (McKenna et al., 2009; Ruesch, 2011). The design and evaluation methods of these projects are summarized in Table 12.1. We note that many of these projects (at least partially) met the conditions proposed by the Contact Hypothesis (Allport, 1954), and found (sometimes very creative) ways to implement some of the moderator and mediator variables of contact effects discussed in the current chapter.

Online Contact between Catholics and Protestants in Ireland

The most extensively studied and well-documented online intergroup contact project is the Dissolving Boundaries program in Ireland, which aims to bridge Catholic and Protestant schools (Austin, 2006). The program facilitates cross-community links through collaborative online activities between small groups of pupils, which were paired with another group of similar ages and abilities from their partner schools.

Contact Effects

The evaluation results show an overall positive impact of the curricular and social intergroup interactions (Austin, 2006). The teachers reported an increased mutual understanding as well as respect and tolerance for opposing views. Austin also observed an increase in perceived ingroup/outgroup similarity, which was found to be stronger for primary school pupils than for the older secondary school pupils. Younger pupils also reported that the program helped them to develop cross-group friendships more so than the older pupils did.

Lessons Learned

Facilitative recommendations have been derived based on the lessons learned from several iterations of the program (Austin, 2006). An important concern has been the successful integration of the conditions proposed by the Contact Hypothesis (Allport, 1954) with theories of collaborative online learning. Although equal status within the contact situation has been achieved by creating student groups of similar age and ability, the evaluation reports also indicate successful contact that involves students with special needs. Austin (2006) further discussed the issue of finding a suitable collaboration task for online intergroup projects. He recommends avoiding sensitive topics—at least in an initial phase. Support of both the schools as institutions and the teachers as authorities has been identified as one of the most crucial factors. Austin (2006) stressed that the teachers' enthusiasm is critical for the success of an online intergroup encounter, but is insufficient if the aspirations of the program are not supported by the participating schools.

Online Contact between Israeli Jews and Arabs

Hoter et al. (2009) described an educational online project involving religious and secular Jewish and Arab teacher colleges within Israel organized by the Center for Multiculturalism and Technology. The project aimed at teaching prospective educators to master educational technologies effectively, and to provide them with the opportunity to develop multicultural views with intended carry-over effects in their own futures as school teachers. The center's approach is based on collaborative online learning in small multicultural groups, each of which is supervised by trained local instructors.

Contact Effects

The initial evaluation of the project revealed a high level of satisfaction with the course, particularly regarding the multicultural learning experience (Hoter et al., 2009). Based on participants' qualitative responses, the authors remarked that many had formed strong bonds with their group members on an interpersonal level, and appeared to value their newly developed empathy for one another. The qualitative analysis also revealed indicators of group-level effects regarding an increase in perceived ingroup/outgroup similarity. The authors concluded that structured online intergroup contact interventions "can reduce bias, stigmas, and ethnic prejudice among prospective teachers" (Hoter et al., 2009, p. 10).

Lessons Learned

In addition to the conditions proposed in the Contact Hypothesis (Allport, 1954), the authors identified specific factors based on their experiences and evaluation results that further facilitate a successful online intergroup contact in an educational context (Hoter et al., 2009). The project appeared to benefit from (1) dealing with general subjects instead of conflicts (e.g., history or politics), (2) focusing on long-term collaboration, (3) gradually progressing over media from text-based CMC to audio/video channels, and finally FtF meetings, as well as (4) employing team teaching by course instructors from different cultural groups. In particular, the gradual increase in media richness of the intergroup contact has been regarded as an effective way to reduce anxiety in initial phases of the contact. Although mediated contact facilitated the perception of equal status, the authors noted a disadvantage for Arab students when communicating in Hebrew with native-speaking Israeli Jews. In order to overcome language barriers, the authors introduced a policy in the curriculum that spelling or grammar errors would be disregarded.

Another online contact project between Israeli Jews and Arabs called Feeling Close from a Distance has been described by Yablon (2007). The project was designed as an after school program for high school students, and aimed at establishing positive relationships between the opposing groups through long-term online interactions.

Contact Effects

While the project's evaluation results have not been published yet, Yablon (2007) refers to the evaluation of an earlier project on online intergroup contact using an equivalent setting. Yablon and Katz (2001) concluded that chat and email exchange between the two groups was suitable for the establishment of positive interpersonal relationships and to bring about attitudinal change. However, an increase in positive attitudes toward the outgroup has only been observed in the group of Jewish students, while the Arab students maintained their a priori higher level of positive attitudes toward their Jewish counterparts throughout the contact. The failure to detect a statistically significant increase in the Arabs' attitudes has been explained by a "ceiling effect," which left little room for the measurement of potential improvements.

Lessons Learned

Yablon and Katz (2001) particularly stressed the importance of organizing *intra*group meetings in addition to *inter*group encounters. Intragroup workshops, in which participants had the opportunity to clear up potential misconceptions within their own ethnic group, led to deeper and more thorough intergroup discussions, which also touched the most sensitive issues of the conflict. In contrast to other studies, in which conflict-related topics were avoided, Yablon and Katz (2001) considered this openness and inclusion of sensitive topics as crucial for an effective online intergroup contact.

Israeli–Palestinian Online Contact

Mollov (2006) provides an evaluation of an Arab–Jewish online dialogue organized by an Israeli university in cooperation with a Palestinian counterpart. The project facilitated email-based one-on-one contacts between Jewish Israeli and Palestinian students. The online dialogue focused specifically on Jewish and Islamic religious practices, and was carried out over a period of 2 months.

Contact Effects

A pre–post comparison revealed an increase in participants' knowledge about the practices and holidays of the two religions, but no statistically significant change in attitudes toward the respective outgroup (Mollov, 2006). The missing change in mutual perceptions has been attributed to the fact that participants' attitudes were already positive prior to the contact, and remained positive throughout the dialogue encounter. Thus, the failure to detect attitudinal changes should not be interpreted as a negative result, but rather as a consequence of a "ceiling effect" in the measurements, which has also been the case in Yablon and Katz's (2001) study. A qualitative analysis of the messages showed that students did not only exchange topic-related information about their religions, but also engaged in mutual self-disclosure.

Lessons Learned

Mollov (2006) concluded that an intergroup dialogue may be most effective when both online and offline meetings are combined as in the reported project. He further stressed the importance of choosing a topic, such as religion, that both sides can relate to. The religious dialogue resulted in a constructive and positive discussion, and made it possible for participants to discover similarities between themselves—not only on an interpersonal level but also on an intergroup level. The assumption that political or historical topics may have led to less favorable outcomes is supported by Ellis and Moaz's (2007) study of an online argument between Israelis and Palestinians. They found that online dialogues that focused on political issues exacerbated the culturally-specific argument styles that promote conflict. Thus, focusing on a less sensitive topic, which makes it easier for both sides to converge and find commonalities, is likely to lead to more positive outcomes than discussing conflict-related issues.

In a similar attempt to bridge conflict groups in the Middle East through online contact, McKenna et al. (2009) set up a Good Neighbors Blog for intercultural exchange. The project aimed at including invited blog authors who represented all of the major regions of the Middle East including the various religious and political factions within each region.

Contact Effects

McKenna et al. (2009) observed positive trends among those who were willing to participate. A content analysis of the blog entries indicated (sometimes radical) changes in attitudes over time. Some of the blog authors' opinions and argument styles shifted toward commonly held values, goals, and world-views. They also observed increased knowledge and mutual understanding, an increased level of perceived similarity, and generalization from the positive interpersonal contacts between blog authors toward the respective outgroup as a whole. However, these newly developed positive perceptions have often been challenged—and even negated—by real-life events (e.g., acts of violence on either side). Thus, it remains unclear how robust and sustainable such changes in attitudes would be.

Lessons Learned

McKenna et al. (2009) reported great difficulties in recruiting blog authors from the various sides as active participants for their project. They identified three main reasons: Fear, language insecurity (i.e., communicating in English), and unwillingness to interact with the "enemy". Guaranteed anonymity and a neutral server location did not appear to be sufficient for reducing participants' fears associated with potential risks of taking part in an intergroup contact that is not embraced by their respective societies.

Intergroup Contact in Uncontrolled Virtual Spaces

All of the field studies discussed so far were conducted in controlled virtual spaces with conflict resolution and peace-making as their primary goals. However, there are also numerous intergroup interactions taking place on the Internet (e.g., in forums, social networking sites, etc.) that are not initiated by institutions or guided by facilitators. Ruesch (2011) analyzed 770 Facebook groups about the Israeli–Palestinian conflict as an example of naturally-occurring intergroup contacts in an uncontrolled virtual space. Ruesch's (2011) case study revealed a "highly fragmented, polarized virtual sphere with little intergroup contact" (p.11). One of her major observations was the considerable number of extremist groups as opposed to only 14.4% of groups that self-identified as "peace groups" dedicated to intergroup dialogue and peace initiatives. Thus, it appears that Facebook groups are more often used for intragroup mobilization and self-expression than for intergroup contact. Members of the extremist groups tended to express hateful, antagonistic opinions with little tolerance for the outgroup's positions or more moderate views.

This finding is in line with the conclusions from Ellis and Moaz's (2007) study on online arguments between Israelis and Palestinians, which showed that unstructured political online dialogues are unlikely to be successful in terms of reducing intergroup biases. Ruesch's (2011) observation also provides supporting evidence for the issues raised by Kahn et al. (see Chapter 11), which illustrated the negative potential consequences of social networking sites for intergroup relations. The Internet provides an easy way for prejudiced individuals to find like-minded others and build online hate groups. However, the extremist groups in Ruesch's (2011) case study were found to be less active in their discussion forums than the moderate or neutral groups. Although these results challenge the utopian views of the inherently positive nature of the Internet, Ruesch (2011) acknowledged that the mere fact that peaceful Facebook groups exist shows the potential for its positive use within intergroup contact and conflict resolution.

An Agenda for Further Research on Online Intergroup Contact

In regard to publications, there are few empirical field studies on online intergroup contact available, which makes it difficult to draw reliable conclusions. Despite their higher ecological validity than laboratory experiments using artificially created in/outgroups, field studies have methodological drawbacks. Online intergroup encounters examined in field studies often lack representativeness due to a self-selection bias of participants. Those who are willing to participate in an intergroup contact may not be representative of other members of their group, or only represent a specific subgroup that holds more moderate views. It also remains unclear to what extent the results obtained for a specific group of participants can be generalized to other conflict populations. For instance, ceiling effects are likely to occur if those who are willing to participate in an intergroup contact project already hold relatively positive a priori attitudes toward the outgroup. This tendency is reflected in Pettigrew and Tropp's (2006) meta-analytic study, which involved the factor of whether or not participants had a choice in taking part in an intergroup contact. They found that studies with coerced participation reported higher effect sizes of contact effects than studies in which participation was voluntary. Although voluntary participation has been stated as an important prerequisite for successful intergroup contact (Amir, 1969), the trade-off effect associated with participants' choice and selection bias deserves further research. Future empirical field studies would greatly benefit from evaluating the outcome of an online intergroup contact against a "no contact" control condition. None of the field studies discussed earlier involved a control group design or tested experimental variations, which makes it difficult to interpret their evaluation results.

The evaluation results of the field studies discussed in the current chapter also have to be interpreted with caution since they are often based on observations of individual participants and the authors' subjective experiences. Nonetheless, these studies are important first steps toward a theory-driven design of online intergroup contacts. They illustrate how Allport's (1954) conditions can be implemented in online meetings, and (implicitly or explicitly) address some of the cognitive, affective, and behavioral variables that have been identified as moderators or mediators of contact effects (see Table 12.1 for a summary). In addition, some facilitating factors and issues are emerging from these studies that deserve special consideration in future research: (1) The role of facilitators or instructors as supporting authorities, (2) the issue of topic sensitivity, (3) language barriers as hindrances of intergroup interactions, and (4) the relationship between the duration and impact of an intergroup contact.

Some hindrances of online intergroup contacts could be resolved in the near future through technological advancements. For instance, machine-translation systems are a promising technical solution to overcome the issues associated with language barriers in multicultural online encounters (Aiken et al., 2011). Other factors, such as the choice of an appropriate topic, the design of a collaboration task, and the guidance of participants during a contact project are unlikely to be

Table 12.1 Overview of online intergroup contact projects in conflict regions.

Project title (website)	Participating groups	Contact modes/ media	Conditions	Moderators	Mediators	Evaluation methods	References
Dissolving Boundaries (http://www. dissolvingboundaries. org)	Pupils from Catholic and Protestant schools of Northern Ireland and the Republic of Ireland	Various asynchronous collaboration tools; video-conferencing for synchronous communication	Support of authorities; equal status; cooperation and common goals; acquaintance potential	Emphasis on intergroup rather than interpersonal contact (interactions between paired small groups) Manipulation of group/ personal identity salience by sharing personal or group photographs and self-descriptions	Facilitating *cross-group friendships* through information exchange in an "online student cafe"	Ethnographic study (including questionnaires and interviews) of teachers' and students' perceptions	Austin (2006)
Center for Multiculturalism and Technology (http:// tak.macam.ac.il)	Students from religious and secular Arab and Jewish teachers' colleges in Israel	Gradual process from asynchronous textual CMC to synchronous audio/ video communication, and final FtF meetings	Support of authorities; equal status;[a] cooperation and common goals; acquaintance potential	Manipulation of group/ personal identity salience by gradually progressing from visually anonymous textual CMC to real-time video/FtF contact	Encouraging *cooperative behavior* by providing both individual and group grades *Reducing anxiety* through initial contact in asynchronous textual form	Quantitative evaluation of course satisfaction; qualitative analysis of self-reports in blog posts and FtF meetings	Hoter et al. (2009)
Feeling Close from a Distance	Afterschool interaction program between Arab and Jewish teenagers in Israel	Online group discussions (chat, email) with initial and final FtF meetings	Support of authorities; equal status;[a] cooperation and common goals; acquaintance potential	Ingroup meetings in addition to intergroup contact, in which students discussed issues related to their self-identity, ingroup relationships, as well as to the Israeli–Arab conflict	Encouraging *cooperative behavior* through earning "group money" Fostering *self-disclosure* through personal homepages *Increasing knowledge* through weekly quizzes Facilitating trust and *relationship building* through long-term interaction (1 year)	Descriptive analysis of online interactions; amount of "group money" collected (as a measure of cooperation)	Yablon (2007)

Project for Arab-Jewish Dialogue	Israeli-Jews and Palestinian university students	Email exchange with initial and final FtF meetings	Support of authorities; equal status;[a] acquaintance potential	Salience of personal identity through interpersonal dialog; salience of group identity through discussion of religions as group-specific characteristics	*Increasing knowledge* through one-to-one religious dialogs	Quantitative pre–post assessment of knowledge acquisition and attitude change; qualitative evaluation of email messages	Mollov (2006)
Good Neighbors Blog	Bloggers who represent different national, political, and religious groups in the Middle East	Anonymous, public blog posts by invited authors (with comments from visitors), email exchange and FtF meeting among some of the bloggers	Acquaintance potential (at least among bloggers; not including anonymous visitors)	Salience of group identity using flag icons of each member's country Heightened common ingroup identity by using terms like "we," "us," "our" on the informational pages of the website; visitors are invited to "join our neighborhood"	Fostering *self-disclosure* through personal "introduction" posts by the bloggers *Reducing fear* of participation by guaranteeing anonymity and neutral server location	Ethnographic study of blog entries	McKenna et al. (2009)

[a] The condition of "equal status" within the contact situation was given in these projects by pairing students of the same educational level and study background. However, status differences exist in real life (i.e., outside of the organized contact situation) due to considerable power asymmetry between the opposing groups (i.e., discrimination of the Arab minority in Israel, and oppression of people in the Palestinian territories).

resolved solely by technological advancements, but instead require the efforts of trained human facilitators. More research is needed regarding the specific strategies that are effective in moderating online discussions between groups in conflict, and group-specific topics and collaboration tasks. Facilitators and instructors may play a crucial role, especially when sensitive (i.e., conflict-related) issues are discussed in an intergroup encounter (Yabon & Katz, 2001). Both experimental laboratory studies (e.g., Walther, 2009) and the field studies discussed in the current chapter indicate that long-term collaboration tends to result in more positive outcomes. However, research should also focus specifically on how technical solutions and human forces need to be combined for successful outcomes of short-term interventions, as long-term interactions may not always be feasible. There is a great potential in methodological advancements that would further develop empirical research on online intergroup contact.

Methodological Advancements

More sensitive measurements are required in order to effectively evaluate the success of online intergroup contacts. These measurements need to be able to detect rather small changes in each of the three components of intergroup bias (i.e., affective, cognitive, and behavioral). Importantly, they would be designed in ways that do not interfere with the intergroup interaction and attention of participants.

Sensitive Measurements

Hamburger (1994) suggested that in order to assess the impact of intergroup contacts, it is vital to employ very sensitive measurements. Participants are highly unlikely to change the central tendency of their stereotype perceptions immediately after contact, especially when this negative label is very much a cultural component. Instead, the change in the variability of the stereotype, which is likely to be more sensitive to change, should be measured. This is particularly important when two opposing groups have a deeply-rooted history of conflict. In such cases any changes in the attitudes of group members will initially be very slight, and will be missed by any assessment method that is not highly sensitive. Hamburger (1994) points out that if such assessments are not in place, effective intergroup projects may be abandoned for a seemingly lack of progress, despite an actual change; but the mechanism employed to measure such a modification was not sensitive enough to pick it up. This assumption has been supported by a number of intergroup contact studies (Garcia-Marques & Mackie, 2001; Hewstone & Hamberger, 2000; Paolini et al., 2004).

One of the challenges is to develop sensitive measurements that are capable of detecting the smallest changes in the stereotype perception before the individual is even aware of the change. For example, these measurements may relate to physiological indicators of which the participant is unaware. Previous studies have suggested that although implicit and explicit attitudes are related, they operate on different levels of awareness and may therefore lead to different evaluation results of an intergroup contact project (Yabar et al., 2006). Explicit measures collected in questionnaires and interviews may be especially influenced by social desirability factors. Measures of explicit prejudice, such as the Affective Thermometer (Abelson et al., 1982), require participants to indicate their feelings toward an ingroup or outgroup on a "very positive" to "very negative" scale. While evaluation results based on such explicit measurements are likely to be biased, implicit measures may provide a more valid assessment of changes in participants' attitudes beyond their conscious awareness. A variety of tests have been developed and validated that provide implicit measures of prejudice and stereotypes, such as the Implicit Association Test (IAT) (Greenwald et al., 1998). The IAT presents positive and negative attributes that are paired with prototypical names or photographs of ingroup and outgroup members, and measures the speed and accuracy of associative judgments. There are many versions of the IAT available as computer-based tests[7] for various kinds of social groups, which can be easily administered to assess whether an online intergroup contact reduced participants' implicit bias against their outgroup.

Another methodological issue is concerned with the sensitivity of coding instruments for content analysis of intergroup communications. In this regard we agree with Ellis and Moaz (2007), who stressed the importance of taking cultural differences in communication styles into account when analysing online discussions to avoid a "Western bias" in evaluating results. Moreover, cultural differences also add error variance in the coding and analysis of an interethnic contact dialogue as they are another source of variance in statements. This additional cultural variance could undermine the statistical power of the tests used to evaluate the success of an intergroup contact.

Unobtrusive Measurements

Instead of treating online contact as a substitute for FtF interactions, the advantages brought about by the distinct features of CMC need to be exploited to a greater extent. Researchers should take advantage of the fact that interacting in digital media generates a large amount of data, which can be easily recorded and used for behavior-based analysis. Collecting observational data on social behavior in physical environments often requires invasive and expensive methods, such as the placement of sensors or cameras at various locations, or involvement of human observers. In contrast, online environments make it possible to unobtrusively track and monitor participants' behavior in an extremely precise and automated way that does not interfere with the social interaction.

Kampf (2011) pointed to various unobtrusive measures for the purpose of studying intergroup interactions in virtual worlds and simulation games, as well as on social networking sites. She further stressed the importance of such unobtrusive measurement techniques because they make it possible to study intergroup encounters on a longitudinal basis. Based on such long-term observations of intergroup interactions, behavioral indicators of attitudinal changes may be detected that participants are not necessarily aware of; thus, they would not be captured in self-reports. While participants of an organized intergroup contact may seek social desirability and provide more positive responses in questionnaires and interviews, behavior-based observations are more likely to reveal an objective and valid assessment of contact effects.

Research on Moderator Variables of Contact Effects

Once such sensitive and unobtrusive measurement techniques are in place, they would be extremely useful not only for a post hoc analysis of intergroup behavior, but also as monitoring tools during the contact itself. Ideally, such tools would give an immediate indication of participants' perceptions of the contact, both on the interpersonal and intergroup levels. Online contact organizers would have an awareness of the participants' perceptions, and would be able to intervene in real time. For instance, such interventions could involve a careful adjustment of group versus personal identity salience without disturbing the flow of the positive processes of the contact. By following these two levels of intergroup contacts closely, we would also be able to advance our understanding of the components that affect both levels in either positive or negative ways. Thus, it would be possible to build a range of manipulations of the salience of group identity and personal identity, which can then be employed during a contact situation in ways that are both

---

[7] https://implicit.harvard.edu/implicit/

subtle and appropriate. These tools would also enable organizers to constantly verify the degree of change taking place on the interpersonal level and the impact on the intergroup level. For instance, in a situation where a positive impression on the interpersonal level has already been achieved, group salience has to be enhanced very gently. These unobtrusive measurements and real-time interventions would help us bring about a generalization from a positive interpersonal contact to the perception of the whole outgroup, which is the aim of an intergroup contact as promoted by the Contact Hypothesis (Hewstone & Brown, 1986).

Research on Mediator Variables of Contact Effects

As affective variables have been identified as the most crucial mediator variables of intergroup contact effects, special consideration is required for future studies of how empathy and perspective-taking can be fostered in online intergroup encounters—either by technological means or human facilitators. Moreover, we argue that a more refined view of affective variables is needed. Prejudice against outgroups may be based on different types of negative affect; that is, different types of emotion, such as anger, fear, guilt, envy, or disgust (Cottrell & Neuberg, 2005; Glick, 2002; Mackie & Smith, 2002). These different types of affect may result in different kinds of discrimination against the outgroup. For example, prejudice based on fear is likely to cause a defensive reaction in order to defend the ingroup status (Neuberg & Cottrell, 2002), whereas prejudice derived from guilt from the distress of being in the presence of the outgroup is likely to lead to avoidance (Glick, 2002). Any attempt to reduce prejudice must tackle the relevant affect. If efforts are mistakenly concentrated on an irrelevant affect, for example, the diminution of outgroup fears, when in fact the relevant affect is guilt, an intergroup contact intervention is unlikely to prove effective. For example, the facilitators (i.e., instructors or supervisors) of an online intergroup encounter can analyze the sources of a dominant affect and ensure that the task instructions or information in a knowledge database about the respective groups addresses these specific negative emotions. Facilitators may also address the specific conflict-related emotions in intragroup meetings in order to make sure that the participants transfer information to the other side in a way that will counteract this process.

Conclusions

The Internet has an enormous potential for providing tools to create effective intergroup contacts that may overcome many of the challenges associated with FtF meetings between rival groups in conflict. Its unique characteristics provide an excellent basis to put the Contact Hypothesis into practice, and to implement the various moderator and mediator variables of contact effects, as demonstrated in the current chapter. There are clearly potential obstacles in putting together an intergroup contact over the Internet (see Chapter 11). While taking the challenges fully into account, it is our belief that online contact is an exceptionally powerful tool that can improve interpersonal and intergroup relations.

However, the mere potential of the Internet is clearly not sufficient to bring about changes in prejudice, stereotypes, and discrimination toward outgroup members. Whether the Internet will in the long-term emerge as an effective tool for intergroup contact and conflict resolution largely depends on what we, as humans, make out of it (Ruesch, 2011). Although the facilitation of intergroup contact through technology (i.e., the Internet) has gained momentum in recent years, the number of empirical field studies that evaluate these efforts is still limited (Kampf, 2011). We strongly encourage further research that moves beyond explaining and understanding intergroup behavior in laboratory settings. A greater focus on fieldwork in conflict regions that makes use of CMC for intergroup encounters would augment existing theories concerned with inter-group relations, and has the potential to bridge the gap between academic research and policy-makers (Power, 2011). By applying the theoretical models and integrating the findings of empirical studies in contexts outside of the laboratory (where actual intergroup conflict is occurring), social psychological research will have a greater impact on conflict resolution.

References

Abelson, R. P., Kinder, D. R., Peters, M. D., & Fiske, S. T. (1982). Affective and semantic components in political person perception. *Journal of Personality and Social Psychology, 42*, 619–630.

Aiken, M., Wang, J., Gu, L., & Paolillo, J. (2011). An exploratory study of how technology supports communication in multilingual groups. *International Journal of e-Collaboration, 7*, 17–29.

Allport, G. W. (1954). *The nature of prejudice*. New York, NY: Addison-Wesley.

Ames, D. L., Jenkins, A. C., Banaji, M. R., & Mitchell, J. P. (2008). Taking another person's perspective increases self-referential neural processing. *Psychological Science, 19*, 642–644.

Amichai-Hamburger, Y. (2005). Personality and the Internet. In Y. Amichai-Hamburger (Ed.), *The social net: Human behavior in cyberspace* (pp. 27–55). New York, NY: Oxford University Press.

Amichai-Hamburger, Y. (2008). The contact hypothesis reconsidered: Interacting via Internet: Theoretical and practical aspect. In A. Barak (Ed.), *Psychological aspects of cyberspace: Theory, research, applications* (pp. 209–227). Cambridge, UK: Cambridge University Press.

Amichai-Hamburger, Y., & Furnham, A. (2007). The positive net. *Computers in Human Behavior, 23*, 1033–1045.

Amichai-Hamburger, Y., & McKenna, K. Y. A. (2006). The contact hypothesis reconsidered: interacting via the Internet. *Journal of Computer-Mediated Communication, 11*, 825–843.

Amir, Y. (1969). Contact hypothesis in ethnic relations. *Psychological Bulletin, 71*, 319–342.

Austin, R. (2006). The role of ICT in bridge-building and social inclusion: theory, policy and practice issues. *European Journal of Teacher Education, 29*, 145–161.

Bargh, J. A., & McKenna, K. Y. A. (2004). The Internet and social life. *Annual Review of Psychology, 55*, 573–590.

Baron, R. M., & Kenny, D. A. (1986). The moderator-mediator variable distinction in social psychological research: conceptual, strategic, and statistical considerations. *Journal of Personality and Social Psychology, 51*, 1173–1182.

Batson, C. D., Polycarpou, M. P., Harmon-Jones, E., Imhoff, H. J., Mitchener, E. C., Bednar, L. L.,... Highberger, L. (1997). Empathy and attitudes: can feeling for a member of a stigmatized group improve feelings toward the group? *Journal of Personality and Social Psychology, 72*, 105–118.

Bodenhausen, G. V. (1990). Stereotypes as judgmental heuristics: evidence of circadian variations in discrimination. *Psychological Science, 1*, 319–322.

Brewer, M. (1991). The social self: on being the same and different at the same time. *Personality and Social Psychology Bulletin, 17*, 475–482.

Brewer, M. (1993). The role of distinctiveness in social identity and group behavior. In M. A. Hogg & D. Abrams (Eds.), *Group motivation: Social psychological perspectives* (pp. 1–16). New York, NY: Harvester-Wheatsheaf.

Brewer, M. B. (1999). The psychology of prejudice: ingroup love or outgroup hate? *Journal of Social Issues, 55*, 429–444.

Brewer, M. B. (2000). Reducing prejudice through cross-categorization: effects of multiple social identities. In S. Oskamp (Ed.), *Reducing prejudice and discrimination* (pp. 165–184). Mahwah, NJ: Lawrence Erlbaum.

Brewer, M. B., & Miller, N. (1984). Beyond the contact hypothesis: theoretical perspectives on desegregation. In N. Miller & M. B. Brewer (Eds.), *Groups in contact: The psychology of desegregation* (pp. 281–302). Orlando FL: Academic Press.

Burak, A., Keylor, E., & Sweeney, T. (2005). PeaceMaker: a video game to teach peace. In M. Maybury, O. Stock, & W. Wahlster (Eds.), *Intelligent Technologies for Interactive Entertainment* (LNCS 3814, pp. 307–310). Berlin, Germany: Springer.

Cook, S.W. (1962). The systematic analysis of socially significant events: a strategy for social research. *Journal of Social Issues, 18*, 66–84.

Cottrell, C. A., & Neuberg, S. L. (2005). Different emotional reactions to different groups: a sociofunctional threat-based approach to "prejudice". *Journal of Personality and Social Psychology, 88*, 770–789.

Crisp, R. J., & Beck, S. R. (2005). Reducing intergroup bias: the moderating role of ingroup identification. *Group Processes & Intergroup Relations, 8*, 173–185.

Davis, M. H., Conklin, L., Smith, A., & Luce, C. (1996). Effect of perspective taking on the cognitive representation of persons: a merging of self and other. *Journal of Personality and Social Psychology, 70*, 713–726.

Devine, P. G. (1989). Stereotypes and prejudice: their automatic and controlled components. *Journal of Personality and Social Psychology, 56*, 5–18.

Dion, K. L. (1973). Cohesiveness as a determinant of ingroup-outgroup bias. *Journal of Personality and Social Psychology, 28*, 163–171.

Dotsch, R., & Wigboldus, D. H. J. (2008). Virtual prejudice. *Journal of Experimental Social Psychology, 44*, 1194–1198.

Dovidio, J. F., Eller, A., & Hewstone, M. (2011). Improving intergroup relations through direct, extended and other forms of indirect contact. *Group Processes & Intergroup Relations, 14*, 147–160.

Dovidio, J. F., Gaertner, S. L., & Kawakami, K. (2003). Intergroup contact: the past, present, and the future. *Group Processes & Intergroup Relations, 6*, 5–21.

Dovidio, J. F., Gaertner, S. L., Kawakami, K., & Hodson, G. (2002). Why can't we just get along? Interpersonal biases and interracial distrust. *Cultural Diversity and Ethnic Minority Psychology, 8*, 88–102.

Dovidio, J. F., Gaertner, S. L., Validzic, A., Matoka, K., Johnson, B., & Frazier, S. (1997). Extending the benefits of recategorization: evaluations, self-disclosure, and helping. *Journal of Experimental Social Psychology, 33*, 401–420.

Dubrovsky, V. J., Kiesler, S., & Sethna B. N. (1991). The equalization phenomenon: status effects in computer-mediated and face-to-face decision-making groups. *Human-Computer Interaction, 6*, 119–146.

Eastin, M. S., Appiah, O., & Cicchirllo, V. (2009). Identification and the influence of cultural stereotyping on postvideogame play hostility. *Human Communication Research, 35*, 337–356.

Ellis, D., & Maoz, I. (2007). Online argument between Israeli Jews and Palestinians. *Human Communication Research, 33*, 291–309.

Facebook (2011). Peace on Facebook. [Online] Retrieved November 22 2011 from http://peace.facebook.com

Fischer, P., Kastenmüller, A., & Greitemeyer, T. (2010). Media violence and the self: the impact of personalized gaming characters in aggressive video games on aggressive behavior. *Journal of Experimental Social Psychology, 46*, 192–195.

Fishwick, P. A., Henderson, J., Fresh, E., Futterknecht, F., & Hamilton, B. D. (2008). Simulating culture: an experiment using a multi-user virtual environment. In *Proceedings of the 40th Conference on Winter Simulation*, Miami, FL, December 7–10, 2008.

Fiske, S. T., & Neuberg, S. L. (1990). A continuum model of impression formation from category-based to individuating processes: influences of information and motivation on attention and interpretation. In M. P. Zanna (Ed.), *Advances in experimental social psychology* (pp. 1–74). San Diego, CA: Academic Press.

Gaertner, S. L., & Dovidio, J. F. (1986). The aversive form of racism. In J. F. Dovidio & S. L. Gaertner (Eds.), *Prejudice, discrimination, and racism* (pp. 61–89). Orlando, FL: Academic Press.

Gaertner, S. L., & Dovidio, J. F. (2000). *Reducing intergroup bias: The Common Ingroup Identity Model.* Philadelphia, PA: Psychology Press.

Gaertner, S. L., Dovidio, J. F., Banker, B. S., Houlette, M., Johnson, K. M., & McGlynn, E. A. (2000). Reducing intergroup conflict: from superordinate goals to decategorization, recategorization, and mutual differentiation. *Group Dynamics: Theory, Research, and Practice*, 4, 98–114.

Galinsky, A. D., & Moskowitz, G. B. (2000). Perspective-taking: decreasing stereotype expression, stereotype accessibility, and in-group favoritism. *Journal of Personality and Social Psychology*, 78, 708–724.

Garcia-Marques, L., & Mackie, D. M. (2001). Not all stereotype-incongruent information is created equal: the impact of sample variability on stereotype change. *Group Processes & Intergroup Relations*, 4, 5–19.

Glick, P. (2002). Sacrificial lambs dressed in wolves' clothing: Envious prejudice, ideology, and the scapegoating of Jews. In L. S. Newman & R. Erber (Eds.), *Understanding genocide: The social psychology of the Holocaust* (pp. 113–142). New York, NY: Oxford University Press.

Gonzales, A. L., Falisi, A., & Hancock, J. T. (2010). Decreasing racist attitudes through virtual play: Evidence of verbal perspective taking by White students when playing Black avatars in Second Life chat. Paper presented at the *2010 Annual Convention of the National Communication Association*. San Francisco, CA.

Gonzalez, C., & Czlonka, L. (2010). Games for peace: Empirical investigations with PeaceMaker. In J. Cannon-Bowers & C. Bowers (Eds.), *Serious game design and development: Technologies for training and learning* (pp. 134–149). Hershey, PA: IGI Global Information Science Reference.

Gonzalez, C., & Saner, L. (in press). Thinking or feeling? Effects of decision making personality in conflict resolution. In J. V. Brinken, H. Konietzny, & M. Meadows (Eds.), *Emotional gaming*.

Greenwald, A. G., McGhee, D. E., & Schwarz, J. L. K. (1998). Measuring individual differences in implicit cognition: the Implicit Association Test. *Journal of Personality and Social Psychology*, 74, 1464–1480.

Groom, V., Bailenson, J. N., & Nass, C. (2009). The influence of racial embodiment on racial bias in immersive virtual environments. *Social Influence*, 4, 231–248.

Hamburger, Y. (1994). The contact hypothesis reconsidered: effects of the atypical outgroup member on the outgroup stereotype. *Basic and Applied Social Psychology*, 15, 339–358.

Harwood, J. (2010). The contact space: a novel framework for intergroup contact research. *Journal of Language and Social Psychology*, 29, 147–177.

Hasler, B. S. (2011). Intercultural collaborative learning in virtual worlds. In R. Hinrichs & C. Wankel (Eds.), *Transforming virtual world learning*. Cutting-edge technologies in higher education (Vol. 4, pp. 271–310). Bingley, UK: Emerald Publishing.

Hasler, B. S., & Friedman, D. A. (in press). Sociocultural conventions in avatar-mediated nonverbal communication: a cross-cultural analysis of virtual proxemics. *Journal of Intercultural Communication Research*.

Hewstone, M., & Brown, R. (1986). Contact is not enough: an intergroup perspective. In M. Hewstone & R. Brown (Eds.), *Contact and conflict in intergroup encounters* (pp. 3–44). Oxford: Blackwell.

Hewstone, M., & Hamberger, J. (2000). Perceived variability and stereotype change. *Journal of Experimental Social Psychology*, 36, 103–124.

Hobman, E. V., Bordia, P., Irmer, B., & Chang, A. (2002). The expression of conflict in computer-mediated and face-to-face groups. *Small Group Research*, 33, 439– 465.

Hoter, E., Shonfeld, M., & Ganayim, A. (2009). Information and communication technology (ICT) in service of multiculturalism. *The International Review of Research in Open and Distance Learning*, 10, 1–15.

Johnson, W. L. (2009). A simulation-based approach to training operational cultural competence. In *Proceedings of ModSIM 2009*, Virginia Beach, VA.

Joinson, A. N. (2001). Self-disclosure in computer-mediated communication: the role of self-awareness and visual anonymity. *European Journal of Social Psychology*, 31, 177–192.

Kampf, R. (2011). Internet, conflict and dialogue: The Israeli case. *Israel Affairs*, 17, 384–400.

Kawakami, K., Dovidio, J. F., Moll, J., Hermsen, S., & Russin, A. (2000). Just say no (to stereotyping): effects of training in the negation of stereotypic associations on stereotype activation. *Journal of Personality and Social Psychology, 78*, 871–888.

Kiesler, S., Siegel, J., & McGuire, T. (1984). Social psychological aspects of computer-mediated communication. *American Psychologist, 39*, 1123–1134.

Kiesler, S., Zubrow, D., Moses, A. M., & Geller, V. (1985). Affect in computer-mediated communication: an experiment in synchronous terminal-to-terminal discussion. *Human-Computer Interaction, 1*, 77–104.

Kim, J. -H. (2011). Two routes leading to conformity intention in computer-mediated groups: matching versus mismatching virtual representations. *Journal of Computer-Mediated Communication, 16*, 271–287.

Kim, J., & Park, H. S. (2011). The effect of uniform virtual appearance on conformity intention: social identity model of deindividuation effects and optimal distinctiveness theory. *Computers in Human Behavior, 27*, 1223–1230.

King, R., & Fouts, J. S. (2009). Digital Diplomacy: understanding Islam through virtual worlds. Project Report of the Carnegie Council: The Voice for Ethics and International Affairs. [Online] Retrieved November 22, 2011 from http://www.carnegiecouncil.org/resources/articles_papers_reports/0014.html

Klimmt, C., Hefner, D., & Vorderer, P. (2009). The video game experience as "true" identification: a theory of enjoyable alterations of players' self-perception. *Communication Theory, 19*, 351–373.

Koschate, M., & van Dick, R. (2011). A multilevel test of Allport's contact conditions. *Group Processes & Intergroup Relations, 14*, 1–19.

Lambert, A. J., Payne, B. K., Jacoby, L. L., Shaffer, L. M., Chasteen, A. L., & Khan, S. R. (2003). Stereotypes as dominant responses: on the "social facilitation" of prejudice in anticipated public contexts. *Journal of Personality and Social Psychology, 84*, 277–295.

Lau, D. C., & Murnighan, J. K. (1998). Demographic diversity and faultlines: the compositional dynamics of organizational groups. *Academy of Management Review, 23*, 325–340.

Lau, D. C., & Murnighan, J. K. (2005). Interactions within groups and subgroups: the effects of demographic faultlines. *Academy of Management Journal, 48*, 645–659.

Laurenceau, J. -P., Feldman Barrett, L., & Pietromonaco, P. R. (1998). Intimacy as an interpersonal process: the importance of self-disclosure, partner disclosure, and perceived partner responsiveness in interpersonal exchanges. *Journal of Personality and Social Psychology, 74*, 1238–1251.

Lea, M., & Spears, R. (1991). Computer-mediated communication, de-individuation and group decision making. *International Journal of Man-Machine Studies, 39*, 283–301.

Lea, M., Spears, R., & de Groot, D. (2001). Knowing me, knowing you: anonymity effects on social identity processes within groups. *Personality and Social Psychology Bulletin, 27*, 526–537.

Lee, J. -E. R. (2009). To reveal or cloak? Effects of identity salience on stereotype threat responses in avatar-represented group contexts. *International Journal of Internet Science, 4*, 34–49.

Linville, P. W., & Jones, E. E. (1980). Polarized appraisals of out-group members. *Journal of Personality and Social Psychology, 38*, 689–703.

Linville, P. W., Fischer, G. W., & Salovey, P. (1989). Perceived distributions of the characteristics of in-group and out-group members: empirical evidence and a computer simulation. *Journal of Personality and Social Psychology, 57*, 165–188.

Mackie, D. M., & Smith, E. R. (Eds.) (2002). *From prejudice to intergroup emotions: Differentiated reactions to social groups.* Philadelphia, PA: Psychology Press.

Martin, J., & Gonzalez, C. (2010). *The cultural determinants of strategic bias in conflict resolution.* Paper presented at the 23rd Annual International Association of Conflict Management Conference, Boston, MA, June 24–27, 2010.

McClendon, M. J. (1974). Interracial contact and the reduction of prejudice. *Sociological Focus, 7*, 47–65.

McKenna, K. Y. A. (2007). Through the Internet looking glass: Expressing and validating the self. In A. Joinson, K. Y. A. McKenna, T. Postmes, & U.-D. Reips (Eds.), *Oxford Handbook of Internet Psychology* (pp. 205–221). New York, NY: Oxford University Press.

McKenna, K. Y. A., & Bargh, J. A. (2000). Plan 9 from cyberspace: the implications of the Internet for personality and social psychology. *Personality and Social Psychology Review, 4*(1), 57–75.

McKenna, K. Y. A., Samuel-Azran, T., & Sutton-Balaban, N. (2009). Virtual meetings in the Middle East: implementing the Contact Hypothesis on the Internet. *The Israeli Journal of Conflict Resolution, 1,* 63–86.

Mezirow, J. (1997). Transformative learning: theory to practice. *New Directions for Adult and Continuing Education, 74,* 5–12.

Miller, N. (2002). Personalization and the promise of Contact Theory. *Journal of Social Issues, 58,* 387–410.

Molleman, E. (2005). Diversity in demographic characteristics, abilities and personality traits: do faultlines affect team functioning? *Group Decision and Negotiation, 14,* 173–193.

Mollov, B. (2006). *Results of Israeli and Palestinian student interactions in CMC: an analysis of attitude changes toward conflicting parties.* Paper presented at the Annual Meeting of the International Communications Association, Dresden, Germany, June 19–23, 2006.

Mortensen, M., & Hinds, P. J. (2001). Conflict and shared identity in geographically distributed teams. *The International Journal of Conflict Management, 12,* 212–238.

Neuberg, S. L., & Cottrell, C. A. (2002). Intergroup emotions: a biocultural approach. In D. M. Mackie & E. R. Smith (Eds.), *From prejudice to intergroup relations: Differentiated reactions to social groups* (pp. 265–283). New York, NY: Psychology Press.

Nolan, R. W. (1999). *Communicating and adapting across cultures.* Living and working in the global village. Westport, CT: Bergin & Garvey.

Otten, S., & Moskowitz, G. B. (2000). Evidence for implicit evaluative in-group bias: affect-based spontaneous trait inference in a minimal group paradigm. *Journal of Experimental Social Psychology, 36,* 77–89.

Paolini, S., Hewstone, M., Rubin, M., & Pay, H. (2004). Increased group dispersion after exposure to one deviant group member: testing Hamburger's model of member-to-group generalization. *Journal of Experimental Social Psychology, 40,* 569–585.

Pate, G. S. (1981). Research on prejudice reduction. *Educational Leadership, 38,* 288–291.

Peña, J., Hancock, J. T., & Merola, N. A. (2009). The priming effects of avatars in virtual settings. *Communication Research, 36,* 838–856.

Peng, W., Lee, M., & Heeter, C. (2010). The effects of a serious game on role-taking and willingness to help. *Journal of Communication, 60,* 723–742.

Pettigrew, T. F. (1971). *Racially separate or together?* New York, NY: McGraw-Hill.

Pettigrew, T. F. (1997). Generalized intergroup contact effects on prejudice. *Personality and Social Psychology Bulletin, 23,* 173–185.

Pettigrew, T. F. (1998). Intergroup contact theory. *Annual Review of Psychology, 49,* 65–85.

Pettigrew, T. F., & Tropp, L. R. (2000). Does intergroup contact reduce prejudice? Recent meta-analytic findings. In S. Oskamp (Ed.), *Reducing prejudice and discrimination* (pp. 93–114). Mahwah, NJ: Erlbaum.

Pettigrew, T. F., & Tropp, L. R. (2006). A meta-analytic test of intergroup contact theory. *Journal of Personality and Social Psychology, 90,* 751–783.

Pettigrew, T. F., & Tropp, L. R. (2008). How does intergroup contact reduce prejudice? Meta-analytic tests of three mediators. *European Journal of Social Psychology, 38,* 922–934.

Plant, E. A., & Devine, P. G. (2003). The antecedents and implications of interracial anxiety. *Personality and Social Psychology Bulletin, 29,* 790–801.

Polzer, J. T., Crisp, C. B., Jarvenpaa, S. L., & Kim, J. W. (2006). Extending the faultline model to geographically dispersed teams: how collocated subgroups can impair group functioning. *Academy of Management Journal, 49,* 679–692.

Postmes, T., Spears, R., & Lea, M. (1998). Breaching or building social boundaries? SIDE-effects in computer-mediated communication. *Communication Research, 25,* 689–715.

Postmes, T., Spears, R., & Lea, M. (2002). Intergroup differentiation in computer-mediated communication: effects of depersonalization. *Group Dynamics: Theory, Research, and Practice, 6,* 3–16.

Power, S. A. (2011). On social psychology and conflict. *Psychology & Society, 4,* 1–6.

Ramsbotham, O., Woodhouse, T., & Miall, H. (2011). *Contemporary Conflict Resolution* (3rd ed.). Cambridge, UK: Polity Press.

Reicher, S. D., Spears, R., & Postmes, T. (1995). A social identity model of deindividuation phenomena. *European Review of Social Psychology, 6,* 161–198.

Rothbart, M., & John, O. P. (1985). Social categorization and behavioral episodes: a cognitive analysis of the effects of intergroup contact. *Journal of Social Issues, 41,* 81–104.

Ruesch, M. (2011). *A peaceful net? Intergroup contact and communicative conflict resolution of the Israel-Palestine conflict on Facebook.* Paper presented at the First Global Conference on Communication and Conflict, Prague, Czech Republic, November 3–5, 2011.

Sassenberg, K., & Boos, M. (2003). Attitude change in computer-mediated communication: effects of anonymity and category norms. *Group Processes & Intergroup Relations, 6,* 405–422.

Sassenberg, K., & Moskowitz, G. B. (2005). Don't stereotype, think different! Overcoming automatic stereotype activation by mindset priming. *Journal of Experimental Social Psychology, 41,* 506–514.

Sawyer, J. E., Houlette, M. A., & Yeagley, E. L. (2006). Decision performance and diversity structure: comparing faultlines in convergent, crosscut, and racially homogeneous groups. *Organizational Behavior and Human Decision Processes, 99,* 1–15.

Schroeder, R. (2006). Being there together and the future of connected presence. *Presence: Teleoperators and Virtual Environments, 15,* 438–454.

Shelton, J. N., & Richeson, J.A. (2005). Intergroup contact and pluralistic ignorance. *Journal of Personality and Social Psychology, 88,* 91–107.

Spears, R., Postmes, T., Lea, M., & Wolbert, A. (2002). When are net effects gross products? The power of influence and the influence of power in computer-mediated communication. *Journal of Social Issues, 58,* 91–107.

Sproull, L., & Kiesler, S. (1986). Reducing social context cues: electronic mail in organizational communications. *Management Science, 32,* 1492–1512.

Staples, D. S., & Zhao, L. (2006). The effects of cultural diversity in virtual teams versus face-to-face teams. *Group Decision and Negotiation, 15,* 389–406.

Stephan, W. G., & Stephan, C. W. (1984). The role of ignorance in intergroup relations. In N. Miller & M. B. Brewer (Eds.), *Groups in contact: The psychology of desegregation* (pp. 229–257). Orlando, FL: Academic Press.

Stephan, W. G., & Stephan, C. W. (1985). Intergroup anxiety. *Journal of Social Issues, 41,* 157–175.

Stephan, W. G., Stephan, C. W., & Gudykunst, W. B. (1999). Anxiety in intercultural relations: a comparison of anxiety/uncertainty management theory and integrated threat theory. *International Journal of Intercultural Relations, 23,* 613–628.

Stock, O., Zancanaro, M., Rocchi, C., Tomasini, D., Koren, C., Eisikovits, Z.,... (Tamar) Weiss, P. L. (2009). The design of a collaborative interface for narration to support reconciliation in a conflict. *AI & Society, 24,* 51–59.

Tajfel, H., & Turner, J. C. (1979). An integrative theory of intergroup conflict. In W. G. Austin & S. Worchel (Eds.), *The social psychology of intergroup relations* (pp. 33–48). Monterey, CA: Brooks/Cole.

Tajfel, H., & Turner, J. C. (1986). The social identity theory of intergroup behavior. In S. Worchel & W. G. Austin (Eds.), *Psychology of intergroup relations* (pp. 7–24). Chicago, IL: Nelson-Hall.

Tausch, N., Tam, T., Hewstone, M., Kenworthy, J. B., & Cairns, E. (2007). Individual-level and group-level mediators of contact effects in Northern Ireland: the moderating role of social identification. *British Journal of Social Psychology*, *46*, 541–556.

Thompson, L., & Nadler, J. (2002). Negotiating via information technology: theory and application. *Journal of Social Issues*, *58*, 109–124.

Tidwell, L. C., & Walther, J. B. (2002). Computer-mediated communication effects on disclosure, impressions, and interpersonal evaluations: getting to know one another a bit at a time. *Human Communication Research*, *28*, 317–348.

Todd, A. R., Bodenhausen, G. V., Richeson, J. A., & Galinsky, A. D. (2011). Perspective taking combats automatic expressions of racial bias. *Journal of Personality and Social Psychology*, *100*, 1027–1042.

Trew, K. (1986). Catholic-Protestant contact in Northern Ireland. In M. Hewstone & R. Brown (Eds.), *Contact and conflict in intergroup encounters* (pp. 93–106). Oxford, UK: Blackwell.

Turner, J. C. (1975). Social comparison and social identity: some prospects for intergroup behavior. *European Journal of Social Psychology*, *5*, 5–34.

Turner, J. C., Hogg, M. A., Oakes, P. J., Reicher, S. D., & Wetherell, M. S. (1987). *Rediscovering the social group: A self-categorization theory*. Oxford, UK: Basil Blackwell.

Turner, R. N., Hewstone, M., & Voci, A. (2007). Reducing explicit and implicit outgroup prejudice via direct and extended contact: the mediating role of self-disclosure and intergroup anxiety. *Journal of Personality and Social Psychology*, *93*, 369–388.

UNESCO (1945). Constitution of the United Nations Educational, Scientific and Cultural Organization. [Online] Retrieved November 22 2011 from http://www.unesco.org/education/information/nfsunesco/pdf/UNESCO_E.PDF

van Knippenberg, D., Dawson, J. J., West, M., & Homan, A. C. (2010). Diversity faultlines, shared objectives, and top management team performance. *Human Relations*, *64*, 307–336.

Voci, A., & Hewstone, M. (2003). Intergroup contact and prejudice toward immigrants in Italy: the mediational role of anxiety and the moderational role of group salience. *Group Processes & Intergroup Relations*, *6*, 37–54.

Walther, J. B. (1992). Interpersonal effects in computer-mediated interaction. a relational perspective. *Communication Research*, *19*, 52–90.

Walther, J. B. (1996). Computer-mediated communication: impersonal, interpersonal, and hyperpersonal interaction. *Communication Research*, *23*, 1–43.

Walther, J. B. (1997). Group and interpersonal effects in international computer-mediated collaboration. *Human Communication Research*, *23*, 324–369.

Walther, J. B. (2009). Computer-mediated communication and virtual groups: applications to interethnic conflict. *Journal of Applied Communication Research*, *37*, 225–238.

Walther, J. B., & Carr, C. T. (2010). Internet interaction and intergroup dynamics. In H. Giles, S. Reid, & J. Harwood (Eds.), *The dynamics of intergroup communication* (pp. 209–220). New York, NY: Peter Lang.

Wilson, W., & Kayatani, M. (1968). Intergroup attitudes and strategies in games between opponents of the same or of a different race. *Journal of Personality and Social Psychology*, *9*, 24–30.

Wilson, J. M., Straus, S. G., & McEvily, B. (2006). All in due time: the development of trust in computer-mediated and face-to-face teams. *Organizational Behavior and Human Decision Processes*, *99*, 16–33.

Worchel, S., Rothgerber, H., Day, E. A., Hart, D., & Butemeyer, J. (1998). Social identity and individual productivity within groups. *British Journal of Social Psychology*, *37*, 389–413.

Word, C. O., Zanna, M. P., & Cooper, J. (1974). The nonverbal mediation of self-fulfilling prophecies in interracial interaction. *Journal of Experimental Social Psychology*, *10*, 109–120.

Worthy, M., Gary, A. L., & Kahn, G. M. (1969). Self-disclosure as an exchange process. *Journal of Personality and Social Psychology*, 13, 59–63.

Yabar, Y., Johnston, L., Miles, L., & Peace, V. (2006). Implicit behavioral mimicry: investigating the impact of group membership. *Journal of Nonverbal Behavior*, 30, 97–113.

Yablon, Y. B. (2007). Feeling close from distance: peace encounters via Internet technology. *New Directions for Youth Development*, 116, 99–107.

Yablon, Y. B., & Katz, Y.J. (2001). Internet-based group relations: a high school peace education project in Israel. *Education Media International*, 38, 175–182.

Yee, N., & Bailenson, J. N. (2006). Walk a mile in digital shoes: the impact of embodied perspective-taking on the reduction of negative stereotyping in immersive virtual environments. In *Proceedings of PRESENCE 2006: The 9th Annual International Workshop on Presence*, Cleveland, OH, August 24–26, 2006.

Yee, N., & Bailenson, J. (2007). The Proteus Effect: the effect of transformed self-representation on behavior. *Human Communication Research*, 33, 271–90.

Yee, N., Bailenson, J. N., & Ducheneaut, N. (2009). The Proteus Effect: implications of transformed digital self-representation on online and offline behavior. *Communication Research*, 36, 285–312.

Zajonc, R. B. (1965). Social facilitation. *Science*, 149, 269–274.

Chapter 13

The Internet as Psychological Laboratory Revisited: Best Practices, Challenges, and Solutions

Edward G. Sargis, Linda J. Skitka,
and William McKeever

Introduction

People increasingly incorporate the Internet into how they live, work, and play. The Internet enables people to connect with family and friends, find news and information, and work more effectively. Scholars have powerful new tools including Google Scholar, societal listservs, web portals for manuscript submissions, and alternative ways to collect data. The goal of this chapter is to review some of the ways social scientists in general and social psychologists in particular use the Internet to collect data, best practices for web-based data collection, and emerging issues in web-based data collection in psychology such as sampling, data quality, and data security.

How Are Social Psychologists Using the Web in their Research?

Before turning to issues of best practices, we first examined the ways in which social psychologists are using the web to collect data. To this end, we reviewed the content of nine journals that published empirical research in social psychology in 2009 and 2010. Of the 1547 articles we reviewed, 173 (11%) reported at least one study that used the Internet to collect data remotely. Of the total 265 studies reported in the 173 articles, 92 (35% of the total studies) used the web to facilitate a lab study, such as to collect pre-measures from participants who also completed part of the study in the lab. The other 173 studies (65% of the total studies published) were completed entirely online (see Table 13.1). This is a substantial increase in the number of published studies in social psychology that used Internet methods compared to 6 or 7 years ago, when the base rate was closer to 1% (Skitka & Sargis, 2005, 2006). The highest publication rate of Internet-based studies was in the field's flagship journal, the *Journal of Personality and Social Psychology*, followed closely by *Personality and Social Psychology Bulletin*. Given the percentage of these papers appearing in the top-tier journals in the field, it appears that Internet-based research has become a mainstream practice in social psychology, and that web-based data collection may even be interpreted as a sign of quality.

Ninety-six percent of the studies in our sample were translational, 4% were novel, and none reported phenomenological research. Translational research entails taking a methodological approach developed offline, such as a questionnaire, and "translating" it into something that can be deployed over the Internet. Novel research goes beyond translational research methods to develop new and creative ways of using the Internet in research, and phenomenological studies

Table 13.1 Target journals that published articles reporting on research conducted on the web, total articles published during 2009–2010, and penetration of web-based research

Journal	Number of articles that reported Internet research 2009–2010	Total number of articles published in 2009–2010	Penetration (% of articles that reported on Internet research)
Asian Journal of Social Psychology	4	61	7%
Basic and Applied Social Psychology[a]	4	38	11%
British Journal of Social Psychology	2	81	2%
European Journal of Social Psychology	13	136	10%
Journal of Applied Social Psychology	20	246	8%
Journal of Experimental Social Psychology	40	384	10%
Journal of Personality and Social Psychology	47	295	16%
Personality and Social Psychology Bulletin	37	258	14%
Social Psychology and Personality Science[b]	6	48	13%
Total	**173**	**1547**	**11%**

[a]At the time of coding, only year 2009 of *Basic and Applied Social Psychology* was available electronically.
[b]At the time of coding, only year 2010 of *Social Psychology and Personality Science* was available.

explore the potentially unique impact of web-based social interaction on people's thoughts, feelings, and behavior (Skitka & Sargis, 2005). The percentage of novel studies in our current sample is similar to what we found in previous analyses—8% in Skitka and Sargis (2005) and 5% in Skitka and Sargis (2006). In our previous reviews, however, nearly half of the papers we found that used the Internet to facilitate data collection were examples of phenomenological research, such as how Internet use relates to well-being and depression. Our current review of social psychological journals found no examples of phenomenological research from 2009 and 2010.

Further investigation suggests that interest in the phenomenology of Internet use has not waned, but scholars are no longer publishing this research in general social psychological journals. Instead, they are opting for more specialized journals that have emerged in recent years (e.g., *Cyberpsychology, Behavior, and Social Networking* (*CSBN*) and *Computers in Human Behavior* (*CHB*)). A quick glance at the table of contents of *CSBN* and *CHB*, for example, indicates that research interest in how the Internet affects people's day-to-day lives is vibrant and ongoing.

In summary, there is considerable growth in the number of scholars who are turning to the web to facilitate data collection. Most researchers are adapting methods commonly used offline for online use, such as modifying paper and pencil questionnaires for online use. Moreover, this research appears to be well received by the scholarly community, and is faring particularly well at the top-tier journals in social psychology. We turn next to the emerging literature on best practices in web-based research, issues associated with probability and non-probability web-based sampling, and issues of data security.

Best Practices

Much of the research on best-practices for web-based data collection is being conducted by public opinion and survey researchers and methodologists, who share social psychologists' increasing enthusiasm for using the web to facilitate data collection (see Couper, 2008; Das, Ester, & Kaczmirek, 2011; see also Gosling & Johnson, 2010). These researchers have identified some of the unique challenges associated with web-based research and a number of best practices for implementation of Internet studies.

One major challenge of turning to web-based research is the loss of a certain amount of control. Relevant issues include whether participants carefully read and understand instructions, the tendency to drop out of the study before finishing due to boredom, various task demands, and the tendency to provide mindless responses. The choices researchers make when designing web-based research can have a significant effect on either reducing or exacerbating these kinds of problems.

Overall Look and Feel of the Study

Experts generally agree that surveys should appear scholarly and professional (e.g., Couper, 2008; Fraley, 2004) and particular attention should be paid to usability (Couper, 2008). There are an infinite number of ways one can customize online measures. There may be a temptation to make one's web page look elaborate or incorporate attractive design features that do little to improve data quality. However, the relative simplicity or complexity of designs does not make much of a difference in data quality. For example, one study varied whether content was presented in a plain style (a simple text-based, black and white survey), whereas another used a graphic style (e.g., it included an organizational logo and varying colors; Walston, Lissitz, & Rudner, 2006), and whether the study was presented as publicly or privately funded. Completion rates were higher for the graphic style when it was government sponsored and displayed a logo for the US Department of Education, but overall simplicity or complexity of design had no major effect. That said, an aesthetically displeasing layout, such as one that uses a mixture of fonts, asymmetrical layouts, and contrasting rather than consonant color schemes, can harm response rates, increase the number of skipped questions, and skew the data toward more negative beliefs and opinions (Mahon-Haft & Dillman, 2010). A scholarly and professional appearance therefore appears to be important to web survey design, but adding graphic bells and whistles does not.

Visual Elements in Web-Based Research

At its core, the Internet is a visual medium and it is easy to use rich images in web-based research. It is often presumed that graphical elements help keep respondents engaged and therefore might prevent drop-out. One should not assume that the potential impact of visual elements on participant responses, however, will be neutral. Participants can interpret visual images as meaningful information for deciding how to respond. For example, participants who saw a picture of a woman jogging reported their own health to be worse than those who saw an image of a woman in a hospital bed (Couper, Conrad, & Tourangeau, 2007). Another study found that people reported higher support for protecting animals when animal pictures accompanied text than when they did not (Shropshire, Hawdon, & Witte, 2009). Although these findings might suggest how to design effective persuasive appeals, they also suggest that choices about including visual information in studies should be made with care. Moreover, the belief that the increased visual appeal of these elements improves response rates and/or decreases dropout rates is not supported by the data (Shropshire, et al., 2009).

Multi-Item Versus Single-Item Pages

By changing a few settings or a few lines of code, researchers can choose to arrange all survey items individually, in particular groupings, or as a single continuous page. Presenting multiple items per page reduces completion times—something that can also reduce dropout rates (Toepoel, Das, & Van Soest, 2009; Vehovar, Manfreda, & Batagelj, 2000), but only if people are not required to scroll down the page to see all the items (Toepoel et al., 2009). Respondents subjectively report a preference for surveys that have only a few items per page, despite increased completion times (Thorndike et al., 2009; Toepoel et al., 2009).

With respect to data quality, multiple items grouped together on a screen tend to result in greater inter-item correlations than when items are presented individually (Couper, Traugott, & Lamais, 2001; Toepoel et al., 2009). However, conclusions based on data collected using single- and multi-item per screen formats tend to be identical (Thorndike et al., 2009). We therefore suggest that researchers present a small number of items per page to eliminate the need for scrolling because of increased usability for participants.

Progress Bars

Many web-based studies include a text or graphics-based progress indicator that lets participants know how much of the survey remains. The guiding assumption is that providing information about progress is likely to increase completion rates. Although some studies support the notion that progress bars enhance completion rates (e.g., Conrad, Couper, Tourangeau, & Peytchev, 2010; Couper et al., 2001), others indicate that progress bars have little or no effect on completion rates (Heerwegh & Loosveldt, 2006; Matzat, Snijders, & van der Hoorst, 2009), and yet others indicate that the presence of progress indicators reduces completion rates under some circumstances (Conrad et al., 2010; Crawford, Couper, & Lamias, 2001).

One reason for the mixed evidence of the usefulness of progress bars is due to how these bars are designed. Progress bars often use surface characteristics of a survey, such as the number of questions completed by a participant relative to the total number of questions, as the reference point for displaying progress. However, these indicators can distort or overestimate how much time is required to finish the study. For example, when a study is programmed to skip certain questions as a function of responses to prior questions, progress bars based on the total number of items are likely to underestimate progress. In addition, some questions take longer to answer than others, which can limit the information value of progress bars. Having a progress bar is associated with higher drop-out rates when participants encounter several open-ended items at the beginning of a survey, largely because participants assume the remainder of the survey will be similarly slowly paced (Crawford et al., 2001). Moreover, feedback of slow progress early in a study is associated with greater attrition than when participants receive slow progress feedback later in the survey. Faster progress feedback early in a study yields perceptions of greater interest and shorter completion times (Conrad et al., 2010). All other things being equal, time-consuming questions such as open-ended responses should therefore be placed at the end rather than beginning of studies, especially if progress feedback will be provided to participants.

Even though most participants prefer to have a progress indicator when given a choice (Heerwegh & Loosveldt, 2006), other research found that when participants had to click a button to check their progress, only 37% of participants bothered to check at all, and the vast proportion of those who did check only did so only once (Conrad et al., 2010). Taken together, progress bars may therefore not be as important for facilitating completion rates as most web researchers assume, and researchers should consider the relative trade-offs of using them in any particular study.

Response Formats in Web-Based Research

There are several response formats one can use in web-based research. Radio buttons, drop-down menus, sliders, and open-ended text boxes are commonly used response options (see Fig. 13.1 for an example of each). Radio button scales and drop-down menus both allow users to select from a number of available options, whereas slider scales ask participants to place their responses on a continuum. When radio buttons and slider scales are used, every choice option is displayed on the screen along with the question. Drop-down menus, however, often hide most or all available response options until users click on a box and/or scroll through a menu.

Radio button scales generally yield higher quality data than either slider scales or drop-down menus (Couper, Tourangeau, Conrad, & Crawford, 2004). Drop-down menus yield more missing data than radio button scales (Healy, 2007) and are vulnerable to primacy and recency effects (Couper et al. 2004; Galesic & Yan, 2011; Healy, 2007). Although problematic for these reasons,

a. Radio button response format.

The internet has transformed the way I do research.

Strongly disagree	Disagree	Neither agree nor disagree	Agree	Strongly agree
◎	◎	◎	◎	◎

b. Dropdown menu response format.

The internet has transformed the way I do research.

c. Slider response format.

The internet has transformed the way I do research.

Strongly disagree ┃━━━━━━━▼━━━━━━━┃ Strongly agree

d. Text-box response format.

Please discuss the ways in which the internet has transformed your research. There is no need to limit your response to the size of the box below:

[Click here to enter text]

Fig. 13.1 Examples of radio button, drop-down menu, slider, and open-ended text boxes response formats.

drop-down menus are nonetheless useful for collecting factual information about participants, for example, their age, education, or country of origin (Couper et al. 2004).

Slider and radio button scales are equally reliable (Cook, Heath, Thompson, & Thompson, 2001; Couper, Tourangeau, Conrad, & Singer, 2006). The use of slider scales in online surveys, however, is associated with higher drop-out rates compared to radio button scales (Couper et al., 2006), perhaps because slider scales place higher cognitive demands on participants (Funke, Reips & Thomas, 2011). Slider scales also have a number of other limitations relative to other scale options, including that respondents' browsers must be configured to run JavaScript (required to program a slider scale), which can make these items take longer to load. One study found that the number of people who exited a study before even declining to participate (i.e., presumably before the survey fully loaded) was 16–18% higher when slider-scales were used, compared to other versions of the same survey, probably because the study took an average of 12 extra seconds to load (Walston et al., 2006).

Although JavaScript has some downsides, most survey software solutions (e.g., Qualtrics) nonetheless rely on Java or other client-side programs to facilitate the collection of detailed Internet paradata (e.g., IP addresses, when participants access a survey, and how long participants take to complete it). JavaScripts can also enable more nuanced paradata, including tracking changes in user responses as they complete a measure and tracking lurkers (i.e., those that look at all of the survey questions without answering). Thus, the potential benefits of incorporating JavaScript into one's study may outweigh the risks of higher drop-out rates.

Response Option Spacing, Labeling, and Alignment

Research on the alignment of items and response options in web-based studies has been facilitated by the identification of heuristics that participants tend to use when completing web-based surveys (Tourangeau, Couper, & Conrad, 2004, 2007; see Toepoel & Dillman, 2011a for an overview). For example, respondents tend to assume that the visual midpoint of a scale is the typical or middle response ("the middle is typical" heuristic). This heuristic is particularly important when deciding where to place nonsubstantive (e.g., *Don't Know*) response options relative to more substantive response options within a scale. For example, when nonsubstantive responses are grouped with more substantive response options (*Slightly, Moderately*), responses are pulled in the direction of the visual midpoint of the scale. When a visual dividing line between substantive and nonsubstantive response options is present, however, the true midpoint of the scale is perceived as equal to the conceptual midpoint (Tourangeau et al., 2004). The "middle is typical" heuristic can skew participant responses when the spacing between response options is uneven. For example, when spaces between response options at the right of the scale are narrower than the left, thus pulling the visual midpoint of the scale toward the left, responses are more likely to be skewed toward the left end of the response scale (Tourangeau et al., 2004). Including a verbal or numeric label for each response option attenuates the effects of spacing (Toepoel & Dillman, 2011b; however, see Schwartz (1996) for how numeric labels can potentially bias results). Therefore, when constructing response scales, ideally all scale options would be evenly spaced, and each option should have its own verbal label (Toepoel & Dillman, 2011a; Tourangeau et al., 2004, 2007). If researchers want to have nonsubstantive response options, they should be visually separated from the scalar responses.

Open-Ended Items

Another commonly used response format is a text box for open-ended questions. One issue to consider with open-ended questions is the amount of space to make visible for user responses.

In HTML (hypertext markup language) programming there are two important parameters one can set for each text box—the size of the box that is displayed, and the maximum number of characters that can be entered into the box. This affords the survey designer the ability to display a small box, but allow for a large amount of text to be entered (or vice versa).

Text box size and written instructions affect the quality of answers to open-ended questions (Smyth, Dillman, Christian, & McBride, 2009). Increasing the size of the text box increases the response quality among those who responded to the survey late in the fielding period, but not early. More importantly, regardless of text box size, participants who received instructions that they should not limit their response to the size of the box gave higher quality responses than those who did not (Smyth et al., 2009).

Text box size also affects the quality of text-based quantitative data. For example, participants asked to think of ten acquaintances and then to indicate how many of them were of various ethnicities in text boxes associated with each ethnic category were to provide answers that sum to ten. Participants asked to do this task were nearly twice as likely to provide an inappropriate response if provided a large rather than small response box (e.g., instead of entering a number as instructed, participants would enter "about three," or "between four and five," Couper, Traugott, & Lamias, 2001). Thus, text boxes should be customized for the size of an appropriate response.

We have found it particularly useful to include as the final item in an online study an open-ended text box with the question "Is there anything you would like to add or would like the researchers to know?" Because it is last, it will not hurt completion rates. Moreover, responses often provide critical insight into problems with the implementation of the study (e.g., unclear questions, formatting problems on one or another browser), and sometimes can be a rich source of information about the topic of study.

Preventing and Detecting Satisficing

Satisficing is the tendency for participants to use minimal cognitive effort to plausibly respond to a survey question (Krosnick, 1991). Rather than give a thoughtful appraisal of choice alternatives, a satisficing participant selects the least effortful response. Examples of satisficing can include failing to discriminate carefully between response categories (e.g., *Somewhat* versus *Very Much*) or choosing answers at random. Satisficing can occur for a number of reasons. Many participants in online studies are primarily motivated to obtain an incentive (for example, see the later discussion of Mechanical Turk (MTurk)). Web participants are also vulnerable to any number of distractions that could interfere with their ability to concentrate or accurately complete measures (e.g., phone calls or other distractions in the immediate environment).

Satisficing is a bigger concern in web-based studies than those conducted using other methods. For example, web studies tend to yield more "*Don't Know*" responses and to have less differentiation in responses than data collected using telephone surveys (Fricker, Galesic, Tourangeau, & Yan, 2005) or face-to-face interviews (Heerwegh & Loosveldt, 2008). In a study with a sample of over 23,000 participants, Johnson (2005) found a 6% rate of satisficing responses (operationalized in this study as the participant selecting the same response category nine or more consecutive times) on a Big Five measure of personality measure, which was much higher than the 0.9% rate found when using pencil-and-paper versions.

There are many potential strategies for detecting possible satisficing. For example, one can examine the amount of time participants spend answering questions, and exclude those who respond too fast to have carefully considered them. Another simple approach is to include several reverse-scored items interspersed throughout a questionnaire because satisficing participants often consistently choose responses only on one end of scales (e.g., Heerwegh & Loosveldt, 2008; Johnson, 2005). Savvy participants, however, may vary their responses throughout a measure without reading their content (see our discussion of professional participants in the section on sampling). Thus, another method to detect satisficing is to include instructional manipulation checks (IMCs; Oppenheimer, Meyvis, & Davidenko, 2009). IMCs are simple instructions embedded in a study that instruct the participant to select a particular response or to ignore a particular question. For example, in a computer-based administration of measures in a lab study, Oppenheimer et al. (2009) presented participants with instructions to click the title at the top of the page rather than select a response. Forty-six percent of the sample failed this IMC. When those participants were excluded from the data set, there was a corresponding increase in statistical power, despite the reduction in sample size (Oppenheimer et al. 2009, study 1). When participants were forced to retry a failed IMC before continuing, the quality of their subsequent responses improved and they became indistinguishable from those who initially passed the IMC (Oppenheimer et al., 2009, study 2).

When feedback is the primary incentive for participants' involvement in a study, they are unlikely to satisfice (Gosling, Vazire, Srivastava, & John, 2004; Johnson, 2005). Moreover, people who choose to participate in a study out of personal interest are less likely to satisfice than those who have agreed to be a member of an online panel or subject pool (Chang & Krosnick, 2009). Although maximizing the interest-value of one's study is one strategy to reduce satisficing, we suggest including IMCs to provide some protection and detection. One possibility is including an IMC at the beginning of a study (e.g., a short reading comprehension test that must be passed to continue to the real study), which would not only detect satisficers, but would probably lead unmotivated participants to drop out early as well.

Populating Your Study

Fifty-five percent of the studies we reviewed for this chapter used college students to populate their studies, even though they collected data remotely on the web. The advantages of online data collection with college student samples are many, including automated data entry, running many participants simultaneously without the need to contend with scheduling hassles and space constraints, and limiting staff time to programming the study. To the extent that the subject pool at a given university is set up to easily allow participants to participate in studies online, or the university is willing to allow researchers to distribute email blasts requesting students' participation in studies, it is not surprising that college student samples are a popular option for populating studies. There are also web site portals that allow researchers from universities without subject pools to have access to college student participants.

Although university subject pools are typically an inexpensive and easy way to populate studies, it is increasingly possible to use community samples. For example, in addition to providing a very user-friendly shell for designing web surveys, Qualtrics also sells access to an opt-in panel of possible participants. Many researchers have also had success posting Craig's List ads and recruiting hundreds of participants in relatively short periods of time, often for no incentive or a small incentive such as a lottery.

Mechanical Turk

Increasingly popular is turning to Amazon's MTurk for participants (e.g., Alter, Oppenheimer, & Zemla, 2010; Erikson & Simpson, 2010). MTurk is a crowdsourcing marketplace that allows users to distribute work to a larger number of potential workers. Work is broken down into one-time tasks (HITs, or human intelligence tasks) that workers are paid to complete. Work might include tasks such as the translation of text into a different language, finding an email address for a business, or completing questionnaires on various topics. Potential workers browse among posted tasks and can complete those for which they qualify. "Requesters" (those requesting work to be done) can use either a set of pre-existing qualifications (e.g., a given country of origin, workers 18 years of age or older, or even how many HITs a worker has submitted in his/her lifetime) or set unique qualifications such as completing a brief screening questionnaire. Tasks are typically simple enough to require only a few minutes to complete, and workers can sort tasks by reward level and length of time required. Rewards for completing HITs can be as low as $0.01, and rarely exceed $1.00. When translated into an hourly wage, workers are estimated to be willing to complete HITs at a return of about $1.40 per hour (Horton & Chilton, 2010). Requesters set up an Amazon account and fund it for the purpose of paying workers, and funds are automatically transferred from the requester to the worker's account when a HIT is completed. Moreover, Amazon.com has numerous pages instructing users how to set up an MTurk account, qualify workers, etc., all of which is quite user-friendly.[1]

There has been considerable interest in describing the demographics of MTurk samples. Early reviews of MTurk samples indicated that about 70–80% were from the United States (US) (Ipeirotis, 2009; Ross et al., 2010). Due to changes in the way Amazon.com is willing to pay non-US workers (they recently added the option to be paid in cash instead of gift cards), there has been a very recent increase in non-US workers on MTurk. For example, Indian workers now make up approximately 34% of MTurk workers (e.g., Eriksson & Simpson, 2010; Paolacci, Chandler, & Ipeirotis, 2010—keep in mind, however, that one can qualify workers based on nationality).

A closer examination of current US workers reveals that they are more often female (65%), slightly younger, more highly educated, and lower in income than the national average. Only a small percentage of US workers claim MTurk as a primary source of income (about 14%), but a majority indicated that earning additional income is a primary motivation for completing tasks on MTurk (61%). That said, many MTurk workers claim they participate in part for entertainment (41%) or for just "killing time" (32%) (Paolacci et al., 2010). Taken together, the demographics of MTurk US workers are similar to other opt-in Internet samples, but taken as a whole, MTurk samples are more diverse than most other opt-in panels due to increased levels of participation of people globally (Buhrmeister, Kwang & Gosling, 2011; Paolacci et al., 2010), which may be an advantage for some researchers.

Data quality on MTurk seems to be comparable to college student subject pools. One study that compared the degree of failure on instructional manipulation checks for college student and MTurk samples found that college students were more likely to provide thoughtless responses (6.47%) than were those on MTurk (4%) (Paolacci et al., 2010), but survey completion rates were higher with college students (99%) than MTurk (92%). Moreover, effect sizes were quite similar in college student and MTurk samples when asked a number of common judgment and decision-making questions (Paolacci et al., 2010).

Problems with Nonprobability Samples on the Web

Access to "opt-in" samples, such as MTurk, is relatively easy and inexpensive, but there are some downsides. Opt-in panel members look in many ways like college students and Internet users in general, but that does not mean that they are representative of the population at large. For example, as of December 2010 it was still the case that 33% of Americans do not use the Internet

---

[1]   At present, there are some challenges for non-US researchers to become requesters. See Buhrmester (2010) for work-arounds and a continuously updated MTurk guide for social scientists.

(Pew Internet and Life Project, 2010a), and the adoption curve has largely plateaued at 73–77% penetration since 2005. Black or Hispanic people are 11–24% less likely to be online than their white peers, and only 46% of American adults age 65 or older and 63% of those with incomes under $30,000 a year use the Internet. Internet use is also highly correlated with education (Pew Internet and Life Project, 2010b). Although many differences between Internet users and nonusers disappear once one accounts for these demographic differences in Internet use, an examination of differences between Internet users and nonusers who completed the 2000, 2002, 2004, and 2006 General Satisfaction Survey (GSS) revealed that Internet users are more liberal on some social issues than nonusers, and were more sociable and optimistic. Moreover, these findings have been remarkably stable over time (Robinson & Steven, 2009). Other comparisons of web-users and nonusers have found that users are higher in trust of others, have broader social networks, and generally believe that people are more fair than do nonusers (Lenhart et al, 2003). Opt-in samples of web-users are also more politically knowledgeable and engaged than are random samples of the population (Chang & Krosnick, 2009).

In addition to problems associated with differences between Internet users and nonusers that could introduce bias into web-based research is the problem of volunteerism. Studies based on self-selected volunteers—especially from large and largely unknown populations—are subject to nonmeasurable biases. Although all studies are prone to multiple sources of error, two known problems with opt-in panels include the inability to calculate estimates of true sampling error (the difference between a sample statistic used to estimate a population parameter and the actual but unknown value of the parameter) and problems with coverage (when all members of the population do not have an equal or known probability of being included in the sample—a serious problem with opt-in studies). When one samples from a known population, these kinds of errors can be legitimately estimated and adjusted for in data analysis, because one can calculate the probability of inclusion in the sample. Although researchers calculate "standard errors" all the time, they are not scientifically or mathematically informative when one does not have a probability sample of the population. Moreover, to the extent one has a biased sample, collecting large samples just multiplies the bias instead of reducing it.

Our goal in raising these issues is not to say nonprobability samples have no value. When the goal of social psychological research is to document whether two variables relate to each other or to test theoretical propositions, it may not be as important to get the strength of the association precisely correct. Learning that the variables relate is sufficient to reject the null hypothesis (Petty & Cacioppo, 1996). However, when the goal is to make claims about effect sizes and the generalizability of a finding in a population, sample quality matters, and there is mounting evidence that opt-in web-based research is not as accurate as research using probability sampling, either on the web or elsewhere (see especially Yeager et al., 2011).

Marketing research can provide some examples of the problems associated with the accuracy of opt-in samples. For example, General Mills conducted the same concept test with two samples drawn from the same opt-in panel, but the two studies yielded completely divergent recommendations about whether the company should launch the product. It ultimately turned out that one sample had much more experience taking web-based surveys, and this factor largely determined why one sample had a less positive impression of the product than the other (for more about this example and others, see Baker, 2008). In short, despite being drawn from the same panel, the conclusions reached by the two studies were quite different largely because the panel was (1) not representative in the first place, and (2) there is no way to randomly sample from opt-in panels. In regard to the second factor, people choose when to participate, and there can be systematic reasons why they choose to participate at any one time rather than another (e.g., it's the end of the month and people may need an influx of cash, or a project like implicit.org may be mentioned in the press and drive some traffic to the site).

A related problem is that there is a greater than chance likelihood that some respondents in opt-in panels are study "professionals." As noted earlier, 14% of those surveyed on MTurk used their participation as a primary source of income. Other research has estimated that 10% of panel participants account for 81% of study responses in the ten largest opt-in web panels, and 1% of participants account for 34% of responses (Langer, 2009). In short, a small number of highly motivated participants are providing the vast majority of responses to studies using opt-in panels. Professionals are also more likely to try to game the system, and to know what characteristics are most likely to lead to pay-off in screening questionnaires, which can introduce a host of yet other problems (Langer, 2009).

Although social psychologists have not become terribly concerned about these issues as yet, others have. For example, *The New York Times* publication standards state that "Self-selected or 'opt-in' samples – including the Internet, e-mail, fax, call-in, street intercept, and non-probability mail-in samples – do not meet The Times's standards, regardless of the number of people who participate" (see http://www.nytimes.com/packages/pdf/politics/pollingstandards.pdf). The Associated Press and *The Washington Post* have similar policies. It might be somewhat embarrassing to admit that many of us in the scientific community have lower standards than the press on what counts as quality data (social psychology is not alone: for a detailed discussion, see Langer, 2009).

Accessing Probability Samples on the Web

There are a number of true probability national panels available for research. The Longitudinal Internet Studies for the Social Sciences (LISS) panel is a true probability sample of households in the Netherlands, with about 5000 households and 8000 total participants. The LISS sample was drawn from national population registers, and potential participants were approached by mail, telephone, or in person with an invitation to participate in scientific research. If potential participants did not have access to the web, they were loaned equipment. In 2010, a special sample of immigrants stratified by region was added to the panel. Funding for maintaining the panel is provided by the Netherlands Organization for Scientific Research, researchers from anywhere in the world can apply for access, and proposals are evaluated through peer review.

Knowledge Networks (KN) is the only company so far to build an Internet-enabled probability sample panel in the US. Panel participants were recruited by telephone using a random-digit-dial (RDD) recruitment methodology. The KN panel now includes about 30,000 households and 43,000 adults. RDD involves generating random numbers associated with a known area code and exchange, and calling people with the request to participate. Because widespread cell phone use is beginning to erode the effectiveness of RDD, KN switched to address-based-sampling several years ago, which bases participant recruitment on mailing recruitment materials to randomly selected residential addresses (see DiSogra, 2010). To ensure that they have a sample that is independent of whether people have prior access to the Internet, KN, like LISS, offers participants a free device to connect to the Internet if needed, and pays participants' Internet service provider charges as part of an incentive to participate. Every household member age 13 and up is given their own KN account, and they are asked to complete one to two studies per month. KN has also recruited a number of nationally representative specialty panels, including Hispanic, teacher, and physician panels.[2]

---

[2] A third representative panel of respondents is available in Germany through Forsa.Omninet. Because (1) very few specifics about its sampling procedures are available, (2) there is little or no evidence of academic

Unlike LISS, KN is a for-profit enterprise and one about equally geared toward conducting commercial and government/academic research. Researchers therefore generally require grant funding to buy access to the KN panel. However, some scholars concerned about data quality in the social sciences wrote a large National Science Foundation grant to facilitate greater research access to true probability samples in the US (see the Time-sharing Experiments in the Social Sciences (TESS) program; see http://www.tessexperiments.org/ for details). The program is open to any faculty member, postdoctoral fellow, or graduate student affiliated with any social science or social science-related department anywhere in the world, with the only requirement being that the study uses an experimental design. Proposals are brief (five pages) and are subject to peer review. TESS has now funded more than 250 studies.

Because LISS and KN are sampling from known populations (the Netherlands and the US, respectively), it is possible to estimate sampling errors and to generate sample weights for the data, which will increase the accuracy of study conclusions. Both panels are much less prone to coverage biases or infiltration by professionals because they do not allow people to opt-in, but instead recruit participation within their full respective national populations (KN estimates that its panel coverage is at 97% of the US population). Another advantage of these panels is that LISS is entirely free for academic use, and there are ways to obtain free access to KN as well. Both panels also maintain a great deal of information about their panelists, so it is possible to recruit representative samples of (for example) specific minority groups, parents of children under the age of 10, or adherents of particular political philosophies, which will be a very attractive feature for many researchers.

Incentives

The vast proportion of social psychological research still relies on college student subject pools for research participants (see Feldman-Barrett, 2005; Henry, 2008; Sears, 1986 for problems associated with social psychology's over-reliance on student samples). The usual incentive for college students to participate has been fulfilling course requirements or earning extra credit. Although firms like KN and LISS have their own incentive policies, researchers using opt-in or other convenience samples need to explore incentives besides course credit, including either pay for service, such as deposits into PayPal accounts, online gift cards, payments to MTurk accounts, or offering "lottery tickets" and the chance of winning a larger incentive. A meta-analysis found that incentives increased the likelihood that a participant would (1) respond to a study by 19% and (2) finish the study measures by 27% (Göritz, 2006).

Incentives can take many forms, something we explored in our review of Internet-based studies in social psychology. Because most samples in our review were composed of college students, the most frequent incentive was course credit (32%). For nonstudent participants, the most common incentives were money or gift certificates (these two incentives were used 25% of the time in our full sample). Researchers have some options for packaging incentives. For example, one option is to give every participant a small incentive, for example, studies using MTurk might offer between 15 and 25 cents for a completion. Another common approach is to offer a chance to win a larger prize upon completion of the study in the form of a lottery (used by 17% of the studies reviewed).

---

use of this panel, and (3) the existence of considerable negative press attention about alleged biases in their political polling (e.g., an alleged tendency to push poll), we decided not to cover this firm in any detail in this chapter.

Lotteries have the advantage that for a limited, prespecified amount of funds, the researcher can collect data from an unlimited number of participants.

Lotteries can increase participation rates in online surveys and lead to fewer incomplete responses than a small token incentive, particularly for one-time studies rather than those using longitudinal panel designs (Bosnjak & Tuten, 2003; Göritz, 2010). Telling participants they will know whether they won a lottery immediately upon completing their participation improves response rates by 6% compared to a condition that offers delayed notification (Tuten, Galesic, & Bosnjak, 2004). Lotteries are therefore effective strategies for incenting participation, and are generally more economical than other approaches.

A nonmonetary incentive that some participants may find appealing is feedback. This was the incentive in 3% of the studies in our sample. One advantage of web-based measurement is the ability to instantaneously compute individualized feedback for participants. Websites like project-implicit.net and outofservice.com have collected data from massive numbers of participants with the incentive of feedback alone. Promises of feedback significantly increase participation rates relative to no feedback controls, and nearly to the same level as a lottery condition with delayed notification of lottery winners. A lottery with immediate notification, however, has a stronger incentive effect than the promise of immediate feedback (Tuten et al., 2004).

Data Security

As important as collecting data that is of the highest quality from research participants is keeping that data secure. Researchers have an obligation to protect sensitive information collected from research participants, in particular, sensitive information that can be linked directly to specific participants. Ideally, data would be collected without any identifiers. Depending upon the nature of one's research; however, it may be necessary to collect certain identifiers. Sometimes this information is collected for practical purposes such as collecting email addresses to allow one to notify winners when a lottery is a participation incentive. Regardless, Institutional Review Boards (IRBs) are increasingly concerned about data security in general, and of identifiable data in particular. Although a full treatment of data security is beyond the scope of this review, we review some basic guidelines.

Secure Data Transfers

Data transfer represents a major vulnerability to data security—that is, any movement of data from one server to another, from a computer to a back-up drive, sending data by email, etc. A motivated hacker can relatively easily access unsecured data during data transfers. One solution is to make sure that information is passed through an encrypted connection using hypertext transfer protocol secure (HTTPS). Normal, unsecured web traffic is transferred, unaltered, using regular hypertext transfer protocol (HTTP). When using HTTPS, the information being sent between the user and the server is encrypted. Anyone intercepting the transmission of data would be unable to read the data. For a HTTPS session to occur, the server must present the user's browser with third-party validated security credentials (e.g., one generated by VeriSign; Westfall & Ma, 2010).

To see whether your host server is HTTPS compliant, simply change the "http" in the web address of the questionnaire or experiment to "https." The data will be encrypted if the page displays normally after this change. (Note: it is also important that any subsequent web addresses that the survey will pass information to also use "https" in their web address). The steps for making a server accept HTTPS connections is beyond the scope of what we can cover here, but there are many instructive resources on the web, and this is well within the skillset of most information technology staff members (presuming your home university does not block their use—some do to protect their own systems; Thiele & Kaczmirek, 2010).

Researchers should also use secure connections such as HTTPS when they download data remotely from a survey host such as SurveyMonkey or Qualtrics. Most survey software shells can be accessed via a secure connection and are themselves password protected. In addition, there are free secure file transfer protocol programs available that will encrypt data transfers from a server to the researcher. If HTTPS is available, use it; if it is not, one should minimally alert potential participants that the data being collected will not be secured during transfer, and could therefore be vulnerable.

Secure Storage

Another potential security vulnerability lies in the storage of data. Once sensitive data leaves a server, it is important that protections are put in place to protect data on local machines. An easy way to secure data storage is file encryption. Although there are commercial products available, there are also many free sources of encryption software. Before shopping around for encryption software, be sure to check with your local IRB about any requirements they may have about data security (e.g., the authors' university requires NIST (National Institute of Standards and Technology)-compliant encryption). Encryption software will make password protected "file containers" that can protect data on any kind of computerized storage device ranging from USB drives to cloud based systems such as Dropbox.

Passwords

Passwords are usually the first line of defense between a would-be attacker and data. Passwords are used to protect accounts for survey software shells, access to self managed servers, and the encryption software just mentioned. It is important that the passwords used in these contexts are "strong" passwords. A strong password is one that is (1) between eight and 14 characters and contains letters, numbers, and nonalphanumeric characters; (2) does not correspond with any other passwords the user has for any other websites or systems; and (3) does not use any common words. One useful strategy is to use a mnemonic: Pick a sentence you are likely to remember, such as "I love to dance the Cha-Cha" and use the first letter of each word to yield: Il2dtCC (we used 2 instead of "t" for "to" because most passwords require at least 1 number). Alternatively, one can use a random password generator (there are many available on-line, e.g., http://www.pctools.com/ guides/password/). Given the increasing need for more complex passwords, many are finding password-management software such as LastPass or KeePass useful. This software is often free or charges a nominal monthly fee (fees usually also enable extra features). It encrypts and stores all your passwords, and some programs automatically plug in your password at appropriate sites. The advantage of these services is that the only password you will need to remember is the one to your password protection program.

The landscape of security threats and solutions is constantly changing. Although data security is important for a number of reasons, IRBs (and especially those with rigorous government oversight due to the number of grants received at a given site) are increasingly requiring that data security plans be included with all new research proposals and renewals. Therefore these protections will no longer be simply desirable, but are likely to be mandated.

Conclusion

The Internet has evolved into an important tool for social psychological research. The Internet's ability to connect vast numbers of people and the richness of information that can be displayed and collected makes it an ideal research tool in many respects. The amount of Internet-based research being published in top-tier social psychological journals has skyrocketed in recent years and will likely continue to grow. As we learn more about the potential challenges of web-based research (e.g., a tendency to drop-out or satisfice and maintaining data security), we are also increasingly learning more about how to meet them. Similar to the growing interest in turning to the web for research is a burgeoning interest in research on best practices of web-based research. We encourage researchers interested in these issues to keep in touch with these developments as much as possible. Fortunately, and perhaps not surprisingly given the topic, a website has emerged as a major clearinghouse for information about best practices for web-based research (http://www.WebSM.org), something we encourage researchers interested in using the web for their research to explore whenever confronted with choices or decisions about designing the strongest study possible.

References

Alter, A. L., Oppenheimer, D. M., & Zemla, J. C. (2010). Missing the trees for the forest: A construal theory account of the illusion of explanatory depth. *Journal of Personality and Social Psychology, 99*, 436–451.

Baker, R. (2008). A web of worries: Online research has been booming but after 12 years of exponential growth, is it losing its luster? *Research World, June*, 8–9.

Bosnjak, M., & Tuten, T. L. (2003). Prepaid and promised incentives in web surveys: An experiment. *Social Science Computer Review, 21*, 208–217.

Buhrmester, M. (2010). Amazon Mechanical Turk guide for social scientists. Retrieved 4 July 2011 from http://homepage.psy.utexas.edu/homepage/students/buhrmester/MTurk%20Guide.htm

Buhrmester, M., Kwang, T., & Gosling, S. D. (2011). Amazon's mechanical turk: A new source of inexpensive, yet high-quality, data? *Perspectives on Psychological Science, 6*, 3–5.

Chang, L., & Krosnick, J. A. (2009). National surveys via RDD telephone interviewing vs. the Internet: Comparing sample representativeness and response quality. *Public Opinion Quarterly, 73*, 641–678.

Conrad, F. G., Couper, M. P., Tourangeau, R., & Peytchev, A. (2010). The impact of progress indicators on task completion. *Interacting with Computers, 22*, 417–427.

Cook, C., Heath, F., Thompson, R. L., & Thompson, B. (2001). Score reliability in web or Internet-based surveys: Unnumbered graphic rating scales versus Likert-type scales. *Educational and Psychological Measurement, 61*, 697–706.

Couper, M. P. (2008). *Designing effective web surveys*. New York, NY: Cambridge University Press.

Couper, M. P., Conrad, F. G., & Tourangeau, R. (2007). Visual context effects in web surveys. *Public Opinion Quarterly, 71*, 623–634.

Couper, M. P., Tourangeau, R., Conrad, F. G., & Crawford, S. D. (2004). What they see is what we get. *Social Science Computer Review, 22*, 111–127.

Couper, M. P., Tourangeau, R., Conrad, F. G., & Singer, E. (2006). Evaluating the effectiveness of visual analog scales: A web experiment. *Social Science Computer Review, 24*, 227–245.

Couper, M. P., Traugott, M. W., & Lamias, M. J. (2001). Web survey design and administration. *Public Opinion Quarterly, 65*, 230–253.

Crawford, S. D., Couper, M. P., & Lamias, M. J. (2001). Web surveys: Perceptions of burden. *Social Science Computer Review, 19*, 146–162.

Das, M., Ester, P., & Kaczmirek, L. (Eds.). (2011). *Social and behavioral research and the Internet: Advances in applied methods and research strategies*. New York, NY: Routledge/Taylor & Francis Group.

DiSogra, C. (2010). Update: Address-based sampling nets success for KnowledgePanel recruitment and sample representation. *Accuracy's Impact on Research: A Knowledge Networks Newsletter, Spring*, 1–2.

Eriksson, K., & Simpson, B. (2010). Emotional reactions to losing explain gender differences in entering a risky lottery. *Judgment and Decision Making, 5*, 159–163.

Feldman-Barrett, L. (2005). How random is that? *APS Observer*. Retrieved June 29, 2011 from http://www. psychologicalscience.org/observer/getArticle.cfm?id=1838.

Fraley, R. C. (2004). *How to conduct behavioral research over the Internet*. New York, NY: Guilford Press.

Fricker, S., Galesic, M., Tourangeau, R., & Yan, T. (2005). An experimental comparison of web and telephone surveys. *The Public Opinion Quarterly, 69*(3), 370–392.

Funke, F., Reips, U. D., & Thomas, R. K. (2011). Sliders for the smart: Type of rating scale on the web interacts with educational level. *Social Science Computer Review, 29*, 221–231.

Galesic, M., & Yan, T. (2011). Use of eye tracking for studying survey response processes. In M. Das, P. Ester, & L. Kaczmirek (Eds.), *Social and behavioral research and the Internet: Advances in applied methods and research strategies* (pp. 349–370). New York, NY: Routledge/Taylor & Francis Group.

Göritz, A. S. (2006). Incentives in web studies: Methodological issues and a review. *International Journal of Internet Science, 1*, 58–70.

Göritz, A. S. (2010). Using lotteries, loyalty points, and other incentives to increase participant response and completion. In S. D. Gosling, & J. A. Johnson (Eds.), *Advanced methods for conducting online behavioral research* (pp. 219–233). Washington, DC: American Psychological Association.

Gosling, S. D., & Johnson, J. A. (Eds.). (2010). *Advanced methods for conducting online behavioral research*. Washington, DC: American Psychological Association.

Gosling, S., Vazire, S., Srivastava, S., & John, O. (2004). Should we trust web-based studies? A comparative analysis of six preconceptions about Internet questionnaires. *American Psychologist, 59*, 93–104.

Healey, B. (2007). Drop downs and scroll mice: The effect of response option format and input mechanism employed on data quality in web surveys. *Social Science Computer Review, 25*, 111–128.

Heerwegh, D., & Loosveldt, G. (2006). An experimental study on the effects of personalization, survey length statements, progress indicators, and survey sponsor logos in web surveys. *Journal of Official Statistics, 22*, 191–210.

Heerwegh, D., & Loosveldt, G. (2008). Face-to-face versus web surveying in a high-Internet-coverage population: Differences in response quality. *Public Opinion Quarterly, 72*, 836–846.

Henry, P. J. (2008). Student sampling as a theoretical problem. *Psychological Inquiry, 19*, 114–125.

Horton, J., & Chilton, L. (2010). The labor economics of paid crowdsourcing. In *Proceedings of the 11th ACM Conference on Electronic Commerce*, USA. Retrieved from http://papers.ssrn.com/sol3/papers.cfm?abstract_id=1596874

Ipeirotis, P. (2009). Turker demographics vs. Internet demographics. Retrieved June 30, 2011 from http://behind-the-enemy-lines.blogspot.com/2009/03/turker-demographics-vs-internet.html

Johnson, J. A. (2005). Ascertaining the validity of individual protocols from web-based personality inventories. *Journal of Research in Personality, 39*, 103–129.

Krosnick, J. A. (1991). Response strategies for coping with the cognitive demands of attitude measures in surveys. *Applied Cognitive Psychology: Special Issue: Cognition and Survey Measurement, 5*, 213–236.

Langer, G. (2009). *Survey reporting standards*. Paper presented at the Survey Quality Conference, Harvard University Program on Survey Research.

Lenhart, A., Horrigan, J., Rainie, L., Allen, K., Boyce, A., Madden, M., & O'Grady, E. (2003). *The ever-shifting Internet population: A new look at Internet access and the digital divide*. Washington, DC: The Pew Internet and American Life Project.

Mahon-Haft, T. A., & Dillman, D. A. (2010). Does visual appeal matter? Effects of web survey aesthetics on survey quality. *Survey Research Methods, 4*, 43–59.

Matzat, U., Snijders, C., & van der Horst, W. (2009). Effects of different types of progress indicators on drop-out rates in web surveys. *Social Psychology, 40*, 43–52.

Oppenheimer, D. M., Meyvis, T., & Davidenko, N. (2009). Instructional manipulation checks: Detecting satisficing to increase statistical power. *Journal of Experimental Social Psychology, 45*, 867–872.

Paolacci, G., Chandler, J., & Ipeirotis, P.G. (2010). Running experiments on Amazon Mechanical Turk. *Judgment and Decision Making, 5*, 411–419.

Petty, R. E., & Cacioppo, J. T. (1996). Addressing disturbing and disturbed consumer behavior: Is it necessary to change the way we conduct behavioral science? *Journal of Marketing Research*, *33*, 1–8.

Pew Internet and Life Project (2010a). Internet adoption, 1995–2010. Retrieved June 30, 2011 from http://www.pewinternet.org/Trend-Data/Internet-Adoption.aspx

Pew Internet and Life Project (2010b). Demographics of Internet users. Retrieved June 30, 2011 from http://www.pewinternet.org/Trend-Data/Whos-Online.aspx

Robinson, J., & Steven, M. (2009). Social attitude differences between Internet users and nonusers. *Information Communication and Society*, *12*, 508–524.

Ross, J., Irani, L., Silberman, M. S., Zaldivar, A., & Tomlinson, B. (2010). Who are the crowdworkers?: Shifting demographics in Mechanical Turk. In *CHI EA '10: Proceedings of the 28th of the international conference extended abstracts on human factors in computing systems* (pp. 2863–2872). New York, NY: ACM.

Schwarz, N. (1996). *Cognition and communication: Judgmental biases, research methods and the logic of conversation.* Hillsdale, NJ: Erlbaum.

Sears, D. O. (1986). College sophomores in the laboratory: Influence of a narrow data base on social psychology's view of human nature. *Journal of Personality and Social Psychology*, *51*, 515–530.

Shropshire, K. O., Hawdon, J. E., & Witte, J. C. (2009). Web survey design: Balancing measurement, response, and topical interest. *Sociological Methods & Research*, *37*, 344–370.

Skitka, L., & Sargis, E. (2005). Social psychological research and the Internet: The promise and peril of a new methodological frontier. In Y. Amichai-Hamburger (Ed.) *The social net: The social psychology of the Internet* (pp. 1–26). Oxford, UK: Oxford University Press.

Skitka, L. J., & Sargis, E. G. (2006). The Internet as psychological laboratory. *Annual Review of Psychology*, *57*, 529–555.

Smyth, J. D., Dillman, D. A., Christian, L. M., & McBride, M. (2009). Open-ended questions in web surveys: Can increasing the size of answer boxes and providing extra verbal instructions improve response quality? *Public Opinion Quarterly*, *73*, 325–337.

Thiele, O., & Kaczmirek, L. (2010). Security and data protection: Collection, storage, and feedback in Internet research. In S. D. Gosling, & J. A. Johnson (Eds.), *Advanced methods for conducting online behavioral research* (pp. 235–253). Washington, DC: American Psychological Association.

Thorndike, F. P., Carlbring, P., Smyth, F. L., Magee, J. C., Gonder-Frederick, L., Ost, L. G., & Ritterband, L. M., (2009). Web-based measurement: Effect of completing single or multiple items per webpage. *Computers in Human Behavior*, *25*, 393–401.

Toepoel, V., Das, M., & Van Soest, A. (2009). Design of web questionnaires: The effects of the number of items per screen. *Field Methods*, *21*, 200–213.

Toepoel, V., & Dillman, D. A. (2011a). How visual design affects the interpretability of survey questions. In M. Das, P. Ester, L. Kaczmirek, M. Das, P. Ester, & L. Kaczmirek (Eds.), *Social and behavioral research and the Internet: Advances in applied methods and research strategies* (pp. 165–190). New York, NY: Routledge/Taylor & Francis Group.

Toepoel, V., & Dillman, D. A. (2011b). Words, numbers, and visual heuristics in web surveys: Is there a hierarchy of importance? *Social Science Computer Review*, *29*, 193–207.

Tourangeau, R., Couper, M. P., & Conrad, F. (2004). Spacing, position, and order: Interpretive heuristics for visual features of survey questions. *Public Opinion Quarterly*, *68*, 368–393.

Tourangeau, R., Couper, M. P., & Conrad, F. (2007). Color, labels, and interpretive heuristics for response scales. *Public Opinion Quarterly*, *71*, 91–112.

Tuten, T. L., Galesic, M., & Bosnjak, M. (2004). Effects of immediate versus delayed notification of prize draw results on response behavior in web surveys: An experiment. *Social Science Computer Review*, *22*, 377–384.

Vehovar, V., Manfreda, K. L., & Batagelj, Z. (2000). Design issues in web surveys. *Proceedings of the Survey Research Methods Section of the American Statistical Association*, 983–988.

Walston, J. T., Lissitz, R. W., & Rudner, L. M. (2006). The influence of web-based questionnaire presentation variations on survey cooperation and perceptions of survey quality. *Journal of Official Statistics, 22,* 271–291.

Westfall, J. E., & Ma, A. (2010). *Locking the virtual file cabinet: A Researcher's guide to Internet data security.* Unpublished Manuscript.

Yeager, D.S., Krosnick, J., Chang, L-C., Javitz, H., Levendusky, M., Simpser, A., & Wang, R. (2011). Comparing the accuracy of RDD telephone surveys and Internet surveys conducted with probability and non-probability samples. *Public Opinion Quarterly, 75,* 709–747.

Author Index

Subject Index